THE PROBLEM
OF SOCIAL RESPONSIBILITY
FROM THE PERSPECTIVE OF
THE MENNONITE CHURCH

J LAWRENCE BURKHOLDER

Institute of Mennonite Studies
3003 Benham Avenue
Elkhart, IN 46517

1989

To Harriet

The Problem of Social Responsibility from the Perspective of the Mennonite Church was a dissertation submitted to the faculty of Princeton Theological Seminary in partial fulfillment of the requirements for the degree of Doctor of Theology, Princeton, New Jersey, 1958.

Published by the Institute of Mennonite Studies, 3003 Benham Ave., Elkhart, IN 46517-1999.

ISBN 0-936273-14-3
Printed in the U.S.A.

PREFACE

This volume was presented to the faculty of Princeton Theological Seminary in 1958 as a doctoral thesis. The degree was granted *summa cum laude.*

The subject of the thesis was chosen for several reasons: first, the concept of "social responsibility" as developed by the World Council of Churches meeting in Amsterdam in 1948 provided a broadly accepted framework by which to examine on a comparative basis the social attitudes of the Mennonite church and of the major Protestant denominations. The second reason is personal. It provided an opportunity to reflect upon ethical and theological problems that I encountered as a young Mennonite relief worker in India and China from 1944-49.

I was particularly interested in the ethical implications of responsibility as they pertained to public administration. On the basis of my experience, initially as a relief worker under church auspices and later as a relief administrator within the public sphere, I was convinced that social responsibility as private charity or prophetic criticism was relatively morally unambiguous. But to accept the responsibilities of public administration carried with it the price of public accountability, loss of personal freedom and the experience of moral ambiguity, partisan pressures and tragic necessity.

At the same time, however, public administration offered strategic advantages of public power and an opportunity to work toward structural changes. Furthermore public approaches to social needs appeared to be the only way to help the masses. Hence the ethical dilemma of social responsibility arises in its most acute but effective form.

I was awakened to the pathos of public responsibility in 1947 in connection with my duties as Secretary of the National Clearing Commission of the United Nations (UNRRA) with offices in Shanghai and Nanking. The task of the commission was to distribute residual supplies (mostly surplus U.S. army and navy) scattered throughout China. The supplies consisted of food, cotton, wool, mobile hospitals, trucks, tractors, river barges and naval landing craft. It would seem simple to give things away. But since the major recipients were the Nationalist government of Chiang Kai-shek and the revolutionary forces of Mao Tse-tung, the commission was caught in the cross fire of power politics and civil war.

What impressed me most was the ambiguity of power. Without power nothing could be accomplished but when power was exercised, invariably some people were helped and others were either deprived or hurt. Most decisions, however well motivated, were preferential. And even though UNRRA supplies were intended for civilian use, they were protected by the military and UNRRA personnel routinely received military escort in dangerous situations. Furthermore the freedom and disinterestedness of agape love acquiesced to the legal rigidities of distributive and punitive justice.

As a Mennonite nurtured on the Schleitheim confession and the "Anabaptist Vision," I was forced to ask what I was doing in the public domain. Did not Jesus respond to the disappointed benefactor with such words as "Man who made me a divider over you" (Lk. 12:14)--an incident cited by Schleitheim for rejection of the magistracy. For after all, is not the "division" of rights, privileges, and property the essence of public responsibility?

Eventually I came to see life dialectically according to which multiple demands required one to choose between equally valid but contradictory obligations. To make simple choices among discrete social alternatives seemed no longer possible. Reality became for me ambiguous and could be described only by the use of paradox. Having been brought up with a two kingdoms theology, polarity itself was no problem. But to discover that reality is itself ambiguous and that separation from the world is illusory in the ultimate sense, provoked me upon return to United States to study Christian ethics. Later I was led to a study of metaphysics as an attempt to understand the structure of the moral situation.

I would not deny that I was disappointed upon finding that my experience of moral ambiguity met virtually no approving, let alone sympathetic responses from Mennonites in the 1950s--except from students. At that time Mennonite scholars were busy articulating a sectarian ethic for the Mennonite community. Social idealism seldom reached beyond church sponsored relief work. Furthermore, justice was given no place within the Mennonite glossary. Non-violent resistance was considered "unbiblical." Hence I was reproved and the typed thesis, having been rejected for publication, turned brown in the dusty shelves of libraries.

In retrospect, those years in China were the most exciting and satisfying of my life. Although I learned from concrete experience that the way of an idealist in the public realm is problematic, the rewards are great when faced honestly and openly with a lively sense of the grace of God.

Now some 30 years later, through the kindness of the Institute of Mennonite Studies the doctoral thesis is published, albeit in limited quantities. The problem of social responsibility remains with us. But the delineation of the problem has undergone revisions since the 1940s and 50s when the sectarian ethics of the Mennonite church were still intact and most major denominations upheld with similar consistency their traditional positions.

I trust that this text, though dated, may yet contribute to the evolution of a mature Mennonite ethic.

J. Lawrence Burkholder
July 1988

TABLE OF CONTENTS

INTRODUCTION..1

1. THE DILEMMA OF SOCIAL RESPONSIBILITY 10

  I. The Great Revival of Social Responsibility 10
    A. Is Social Responsibility the Question?......................................10
    B. The Development of Conviction for Social Responsibility 11

  II. The Meaning and Scope of Responsibility 14
    A. An Ambiguous Term 14
    B. An Attitude of Accountability..14
    C. The Practical Form of Responsibility 16
    D. The Relevance of Political Responsibility...................................17
    E. The Inner Spiritual Attitudes of Responsibility............................18

  III. Social Responsibility--A Crucial Problem of the
    Mennonites..21
    A. The Problem of Social Structure 21
    B. Mennonites and the Problem of Social Involvement.......................22
    C. The Relevance of the "Anabaptist Vision" 23
    D. The Dilemma of Social Responsibility......................................25

  IV. The Problem of Christ and Culture 26
    A. Social Responsibility--A Problem of "Christ and Culture" 26
    B. Points of Tension 27
    C. Mennonitism and the Rejection of Culture 30

  V. Summary..32

2. CHRISTIANITY AS DISCIPLESHIP 38

  I. The Religious Basis of Social Doctrine 38
    A. The Religious Ethic of Luther 39
    B. The Religious Ethic of Calvin 39

  II. *Nachfolge* -- The Central Idea of Anabaptism 39
    A. The Essence of Christianity 39

B. Discipleship as Primitivism..41

III. *Nachfolge* Outside the Anabaptist Tradition 41

IV. Discipleship as Suffering 43
    A. The Historical Occasion..44
    B. The Literature of Martyrdom 46
    C. The Theology of Suffering..47
    D. Comparison with Luther's Concept of Suffering 51

3. CHRISTIANITY AS DISCIPLESHIP (cont'd.)...............................60

    I. Love as Nonresistance 60
    A. Nonresistance--A Central Doctrine 60
    B. An Ultimate Attitude Toward Life 60
    C. Central to Mennonite Ethics...61
    D. Nonresistance and Pacifism 61
    E. The Origin of the Doctrine of Nonresistance 63
    F. Nonresistance and War 65
    G. The Problem of the Magistracy..68

    II. A Missionary World View 76
    A. The Great Commission 76
    B. Implications for the Family 78
    C. The Church vs. Culture..80

    III. Conclusion..82

4. ANABAPTISM AND THE CORPUS CHRISTIANUM 93

    I. The Conception of the Corpus Christianum...............................95
    A. The Organic Ideal of Unity..97
    B. The Rise of the Corpus Christianum 97
    C. The Contribution of St. Thomas Acquinas 99
    D. The Significance of Monasticism...101
    E. The Position of the Reformers 102

    II. The Anabaptist Dissent...103
    A. Voluntarism and the "Free Church".......................................103
    B. Nonconformity to the World..107

    III. The Restitution of the Church...109
    A. The Church as a Fellowship...110
    B. The Disciplined Church...111
    C. The Church as a Gemeinschaft 113

IV. Implications for Society...114

5. THE MENNONITE COMMUNITY...127

I. The Problem of Natural Community...127
   A. Christianity--A Founded Religion..127
   B. Significance of the Family..128
   C. Radical and Conservative Attitudes in the Early Church...................128
   D. Significance of Paul...129

II. The Anabaptist-Mennonite Answer..130
   A. The Mennonite Community--A Religious Community.......................131
   B. The Theoretical Possibility of Unambiguous
       Social Structures...131
   C. The Mennonite Community and Calvin's
       "Holy Community"...132
   D. A Restricted Community...133
   E. An Agrarian Community..133

III. Types of Mennonite Communities...137
   A. The Hutterian Pattern of "Full Community"......................................137
   B. The Closed Community..141
   C. The "Open" Community of American Mennonites.............................146

IV. Conclusion...153

6. MENNONITE SOCIAL SERVICE...160

I. The Rejection of Political Responsibility...160
   A. Mennonites and the Franchise..163
   B. Mennonites and Office-Holding..164
   C. Mennonites and Prophetic Witness to the State...............................167
   D. The Basis of Nonparticipation..173

II. An Alternative Approach to the Problems of Society.............................175
   A. Significance of the Problem of War..176
   B. Voluntary Service--An Integral Aspect of
       Mennonite Life...178
   C. The Guiding Principles of Voluntary Service...................................179

7. THE CHALLENGE OF THE RESPONSIBLE SOCIETY.......................191

I. The Meaning of the Responsible Society...192
   A. The Relation of the Responsible Society
       to Democracy...193
   B. The Relation of the Responsible Society to

Totalitarianism 194

II. The Scope of the Responsible Society in the Light
    of the Modern Problems 195
    A. The Problem of Technical Civilization 195
    B. The Problem of Work 197
    C. Justice and Freedom and the Centralization
       of Power 197

III. Modes of Social Influence 198
     A. Public Pronouncements 199
     B. Social Action Programs 201
     C. Responsibility of the Christian as an Individual 202

IV. The Limitations of the Idea of the Responsible
    Society 204

V. Basic Theological Convictions 209
   A. The Christian Conception of Man 210
   B. The Lordship of Christ 210

VI. The Responsible Society and the Mennonite Church 212
    A. The Framework of Social Ethics 212
    B. The Social Implications of the Lordship of Christ 214

VII. Conclusion 214

CONCLUSION 222

BIBLIOGRAPHY 225

INTRODUCTION

This treatise is an elucidation of a crucial problem in the contemporary life of the Mennonite church in its American environment. It is a problem which lies at the very heart of its existence as a peculiar religious body. It involves issues that have tended to separate the Mennonite church from the general stream of Christianity. These issues concern the essence of Christianity, the nature and task of the church, the relation of the church and the world, and the approach to Christian ethics. This problem is the problem of social responsibility. It may be stated as follows: To what extent is the Christian, as a member of the church, responsible for the corporate life of the world and how should this responsibility be expressed in concrete social action?

Those who are acquainted with the history of social doctrine realize that this is a question with which the entire Christian church is involved. From the beginning of Christian history, the universal church has been faced with the problem of what to do about the world. No once-and-for-all solution has been found. The most obvious solutions have proved equally impossible. On the one hand, the church has tried to enter history by forming an "unambiguous" Christian world culture. On the other hand, the church has attempted to withdraw from the world. Neither of these have worked. Between these two extremes there have been many dialectical Christian social policies. They have attempted to embody both the absolutism of the gospel ethic and the relativism of social structure by expressing the one in the inner realm of the spirit and the other in the external realm of things. There have also been attempts to express the absolutism of Christ non-dialectically by *selective* participation in culture. But whatever the "strategy," a "distance between" the pure spirit of Christ and the structure of society remains. Therefore the concern of Christian social ethics has been (1) to understand *why* the tension between Christianity and social organization exists and (2) to understand *what* should be done about it.

All serious attempts to understand these questions involve genuine theological issues. The tension between Christianity and social structure cannot be explained in sociological categories alone. Genuine social policy is built upon decisions seemingly far removed from the practical matters of social ethics. Often the theological basis for social policy is more implicit than explicit but ideas about the economic relations of the Trinity, the relation of the realm of nature to the realm of grace, the relation of God's love to His justice and the precise meaning of *agape* love are decisive for the practical problems of social ethics. All the so-called social "strategies" of the church reflect general theological orientations.

Although the tension between Christianity and society has always existed, it assumes a critical form in contemporary life. This is due to the fact that we have entered what Richard Kroner calls the "post-Christian period" of secularization. This means that whereas the tension between Christianity and the world was once an internal affair of Christendom, it is now a tension between the Christian ideal and a world which no longer makes a general Christian commitment, a fact most clearly understood by the missionary movement. In most countries of the West, the church has lost its power to control society. The Medieval synthesis of the church and the "secular" order is a thing of the past, both as a formal relationship and as an inward spiritual bond. This raises, of course, a question about the relevance of Medieval and Reformation social doctrines which assume a unified Christian social order. Therefore the successors to the great churches of the Reformation especially face the question of social responsibility in the following form: To what extent and in what way should Christians accept responsibility for a civilization which is avowedly secular?

Another fact of the modern world which adds moral pathos to the problem of social responsibility is the fact of physical power through technological advance, now inseparably tied to social forces. With the advent of atomic weapons, destructive power has reached the point where annihilation of the human race is a possibility. This raises in the breast of every sensitive Christian the dread of social power and involvement. To enter actively and *responsibly* into the struggles of the world may ultimately result in the destruction of humanity--a tragedy which exceeds all previous conceptions. And yet, to remove one's self from the world at the hour of its greatest need to deny the relevance of Christianity for the world seems to encourage an illusory innocence. And so Christians as individuals and the church as a body face, each in its own way, a most serious conflict in which to be fully socially responsible is to be placed in the position of one who administers "absolute" power in the name of Him who was the perfect example of "weakness"--even unto death on the cross.

This treatise, however, is interested primarily in the problem of social responsibility from the perspective of the Mennonite church and not from the perspective of the main stream of Protestantism. This brings forth considerations beyond those of most Protestant bodies. These considerations emerge from the peculiar faith and historical experience of the Mennonites as a small religious minority. Even those who are slightly acquainted with the ethical seriousness of the Mennonites on the one hand and the ambiguity of the social and political realm on the other hand can understand why social responsibility is a special problem to the Mennonites. Some of the peculiar principles of Mennonites which seem to clash with responsibility for the social and political realms are nonresistance, non-swearing of oaths, non-litigation, brotherhood love and mutuality, separation from the world, absolute honesty, objection to compromise and vast accumulation of subtle "in group" attitudes and psychological predilections which are frequently found among self-conscious minority groups. In a general way, the social implications of these ethical principles and spiritual attitudes have been "typed" by Ernst Troeltsch under the term "sect." As a result Mennonites have been known outside Mennonite circles principally by the important distinctions between the "Church," the "Sect," and the "Mystical Group."[1]

The subject of social responsibility has been chosen as a topic for discussion within Mennonitism because it is an urgent contemporary problem. From the standpoint of traditional Mennonitism it may be critical. This is due to the fact that the Mennonite church is caught in a tug-of-war between opposing forces. It is a struggle between the traditional Mennonite "way of life" and social involvement. The logic of Mennonite theology, ethics and history points in the direction of radical rejection of social responsibility for the sake of a "new and separated" people. However, the logic of present day social, economic and educational tendencies among Mennonites points toward greater involvement and responsible participation in the affairs of the world. Sociologists and historians who are familiar with sectarianism know that this problem is bound to appear sometime in the lives of all idealistic, separatistic communities. However, the question is whether American Mennonites, who are now increasingly caught in the "whirl" of American life, will be able to avoid at least some of the adverse experiences of other sects by the knowledge of the problem gained through modern social sciences. Will it be possible for at least one dissenting group of the Reformation to maintain *some* of the peculiar doctrines and practices of the faith in the modern period in the face of the seemingly relentless forces of conformity to the general practice of society? What is, of course, more important than the question of holding on to traditional patterns is the question of how to make what is genuinely Christian in the Mennonite position relevant to the Christian church as a whole and relevant also to the world.

The purpose of this thesis is to contribute in a preliminary way to a better self-understanding of the Mennonite situation with respect to the problem of social responsibility, which the author regards as one of the most crucial problems facing the Mennonites today. This is preliminary to a constructive statement regarding the contribution of Mennonites to the world today. The method which is employed is one which was developed by Max Weber and Ernst Troeltsch and which is rather loosely called sociology of religion (Religions-Soziologie).[2] It is, of course, closely associated with the subject matter of Christian social ethics. Religious sociology is a dispassionate analysis of social phenomena from the standpoint of their theological, historical and social roots. Christian social ethics adds to social analysis a dogmatic element derived from a theological premise. Therefore social ethics attempts to articulate a social policy. This treatise is obviously a blend of the two, but it leans toward sociology of religion in the tradition of Weber and Troeltsch since the body of the thesis is a historical and theological description of the Mennonite situation, out of which may come materials for a new social philosophy.

The procedure is to state in Chapter 1 what is meant by the term social responsibility and to show how social responsibility involves an ethical dilemma. In Chapters 2 and 3 an attempt is made to examine relevant theological and ethical roots of the Mennonite ethic in early Anabaptism, from which the Mennonites are direct descendants. Assuming that the social policy of any Christian group must be seen in the light of its definition of the essence of Christianity, Anabaptism is described in terms of the central conception of "discipleship." Chapter 4 is a discussion of the dissent of the Anabaptists against the fundamental social structure of Christendom, the *corpus christianum*. Thereupon the discussion moves in Chapter 5 to a statement of the main types of social structure which have been promoted historically by Mennonites. This is not intended to be an exhaustive statement but rather a statement which shows the kind of social outreach Mennonites have emphasized in view of their peculiar relation to society. Chapter 7 brings to the discussion the challenge of the ecumenical idea of social responsibility. In the concluding chapter the author states briefly what he considers to be the most formidable sociological, ethical and theological factors which the Mennonite church should consider in constructing an adequate contemporary social policy.

Attention must be given to the place which this treatise occupies in Mennonite studies. Scholarly studies among American Mennonites may be said to be less than forty years of age. Until recent years Mennonites have shown virtually no interest in scholarly research of any kind. This is due to a traditional fear of education, worldliness and change. However, a small number of competent Mennonite scholars have devoted themselves to the understanding of the historical, cultural and theological roots of Mennonitism during the past thirty years. The result has been a revival of interest in Mennonite history, hitherto an obscure chapter in Reformation history. This interest is demonstrated by an exhaustive collection of Mennonite Anabaptist documents totaling 14,000 volumes in the Mennonite Historical Library at Goshen, Indiana. Furthermore, the *Mennonite Quarterly Review*, edited by Harold S. Bender, a historical quarterly published since 1927, has been an important channel of communication between Mennonite and non-Mennonite historians. At the same time the discovery during the past twenty years of numerous Anabaptist documents of the sixteenth and seventeenth centuries such as court records, tracts and writings in the archives and private collections of Europe has laid the basis for a fruitful study of the "left-wing of the Reformation." Evidence of exhaustive historical research in the area of Anabaptism and Mennonitism may be found in the *Mennonite Encyclopedia*.[3]

However, an examination of the writings of Mennonite scholars such as Harold S. Bender, Guy F. Hershberger, Robert Friedmann, Erland Waltner, John C. Wenger and C. Henry Smith indicate that their work has had to do largely with a purely historical understanding of Mennonites and their Anabaptist forefathers. This is understandable in view of the general neglect of scholarly interest in Anabaptism in comparison to the major movements of the Reformation. Furthermore the sheer complexity and obscurity of the movement itself has demanded an unusual acquaintance with widely scattered and diverse sources before general statements about Anabaptism as a whole could be made. This has meant, however, that not much has been done to reconstruct Anabaptist theological and social thought beyond the main lines of emphasis. Furthermore the complete absence of theological discussion within American Mennonitism until the last few decades has meant that many of the questions which a living theological tradition normally asks of its original sources of inspiration have not yet been asked.[4] Therefore it is fair to say that Mennonite theology, both historically and contemporary, is in its rudimentary stages. It may be that Anabaptism will eventually be seen to contain a theology of considerable depth, but it is fair to say that this theology is largely implicit and not as easily accessible to those theologies which have been set forth in systematic form.

The dominant theological concern of Mennonite scholarship in recent years has been the discovery of the "essence of Anabaptism." By essence is meant the central motif which brought it into existence as a separate religious phenomenon, the inner reality of the movement. Mennonites have been asking, what is the center, the controlling idea of Anabaptism?[5] The necessity for discussion on this level arises from the fact that Anabaptism was an extremely dynamic, fluid and diverse movement without a single leader or creative personality, such as Luther and Calvin. Furthermore, after 1527, it was largely a fugitive movement. As such, very little could be accomplished in the realm of theological thought. This explains at least partly why Anabaptism has been characterized in varying and contradictory terms, such as "Spiritualism," "Legalism," "Quietism," "Revolution," "Existentialism," "Biblicism" and "Discipleship."[6] Of course, much of the ambiguity has arisen from the fact that when scholars discuss Anabaptism they frequently have different groups in mind. However, it must be admitted that even the "in group" of Mennonite scholars who have only the direct, undisputed progenitors of the American Mennonites in mind and who agree fundamentally regarding what Anabaptists believed, do not necessarily agree about where the emphasis should be placed. For example, Harold S. Bender claims that the essence of Anabaptism is "discipleship;" Robert S. Friedmann sees Anabaptism as a kind of "existentialism" of which "Gelassenheit" is the central idea; a friendly "outsider" such as Franklin H. Littell concludes that the meaning of Anabaptism is to be found in the "restitution" of the "true church" based upon the New Testament pattern; Roland Bainton emphasizes the radical social ethics of the Anabaptists by calling them the "left-wing of the Reformation" and John C. Wenger emphasizes their Biblicism. Certainly all of these interpretations refer to genuine elements in Anabaptism. This leads to the observation that "Anabaptism was probably too dynamic a movement to be reduced to a simple definition."[7] At any rate, it is clear that Mennonite theology is in its earlier stages, a fact which is disconcerting to one who would like to examine the social thought of a religious group from the standpoint of a thoroughly tested and tried theological tradition but exhilarating to one who enjoys the freedom and dynamics of an individualistic movement.

The social problems of Mennonitism have received more consideration than have theological problems. This is due to the fact that Mennonites are preeminently a practical people and because the doctrine of separation from the world has forced practical sociological problems. The organization of the Mennonite Community Association in 1949 and frequent articles in *The Mennonite Quarterly Review* about Mennonite community life, together with the publication (from 1947 to 1953) of a monthly magazine called *The Mennonite Community* are evidence of a great interest in the sociological dimension.

The main impetus to social thought and action has been the endeavor to carve out a total way of life in accordance with the biblical doctrine of nonresistance. It is fair to say that all Mennonite social thought is avowedly an inference of nonresistance. This is clearly evident in Guy F. Hershberger's *War, Peace and nonresistance,*[8] the volume which has served Mennonites since 1944 as a semi-official statement of the "non-resistant way of life." Mennonite social thought has almost without exception operated on assumptions and within the categories of sectarianism. Furthermore, Mennonite social thought has been limited in scope largely to the problems of the "Mennonite community." The "social ethics" of Mennonites have been confined to the principles and problems of Mennonite community life. No one from within Mennonite circles has as yet examined Mennonite social ethics from the perspective of the total social order by employing the categories of "social realism." This has been done from outside the denomination by John C. Bennett and a few others, but only briefly.[9]

This treatise is intended to inject into Mennonite social ethics the question of social responsibility. It is not intended to force social responsibility upon Mennonitism as an absolute norm or a principle of judgment. It is intended to elucidate the problem which is presently occupying the minds of Mennonites as they become increasingly involved in the total social order. To this author's knowledge nothing has been written specifically by Mennonites about social responsibility in the broader sense in which the term has come to be used. A large number of articles have been written on the relation of the church to the state but these generally reflect a simple dichotomy which political and social affairs of modern times have rendered inadequate and which for that reason need to be replaced by a more genuine and living dichotomy of the church and the total social order.

The reader will find that the author has relied heavily on the observations of Ernst Troeltsch in *The Social Teachings of the Christian Churches* for his interpretations of the general problem of social responsibility and for his understanding of the history of Christian social policy. It should also be acknowledged that the author's own criticisms of Mennonite social attitudes have been influenced somewhat by the social realism of Reinhold Niebuhr. The attempt to state the theological, historical and sociological factors which underlie present social policy of the Mennonites has required a rather broad use of Mennonite literature. Competing elements, such as the theological basis of Mennonite social policy, historical materials, concrete social applications, and underlying ethical principles have made it difficult to limit the work to desired proportions.

It is necessary to make a statement about the particular group of Mennonites under study in this thesis. This is an examination of the social policy of those American Mennonites officially called "The Mennonite Church" but which is one of nineteen branches of Mennonites listed in the *Mennonite Yearbook, 1957*.[10] The group under examination is the largest single branch of the Mennonite church, with a baptized membership of 77,369 in the United States and Canada.[11] The next largest branch of the Mennonite tradition is the General Conference Mennonite Church with a membership of 49,769.[12] Within Mennonite circles the former are usually called "Old Mennonites" when being distinguished from other Mennonite bodies. The (Old) Mennonites came to the United States mainly from Switzerland, South Germany, the Palatinate and the Netherlands in successive migrations beginning in 1683. Traditionally they have had a tendency to settle in rather close knit agricultural communities, of which Bucks County and Lancaster County, Penna., are among the oldest.

The reason this study is limited to a single branch of the Mennonite church is that the social attitudes of Mennonites as a denomination are so diverse that generalization is impossible. Anyone acquainted with the social attitudes of the extremely conservative Amish, when compared with the more liberal General Conference Mennonites, realizes that these groups cannot be treated under the same heading in spite of the fact that they belong to the same general tradition. With respect to the adjustment of Mennonites to the American environment, the (Old) Mennonites represent roughly a median position among Mennonite groups.

It should also be pointed out that this thesis is not concerned with the European Mennonite church. In contrast to American Mennonites the traditional tension between the church and the social and political order has long been lost among European Mennonites. The Dutch Mennonites especially have not only accepted social responsibility in the usual sense of participation in a democracy, but they have produced an unusual number of high ranking political leaders as a matter of pride and satisfaction.

One other matter must be clarified, i.e., the meaning of the terms "Anabaptist" and "Anabaptism." These terms are used here to refer to that segment of the "left-wing" of the Reformation which constitutes the spiritual and linear ancestors of the American Mennonites. This means that of all the multifarious groups of dissenting Christians of the sixteenth century to which the authorities appended the opprobrious appellation "Anabaptist," this thesis is interested in only a select few. When the term Anabaptist is used in this thesis, unless the context clearly indicates the contrary, reference is being made to that group of evangelical Anabaptists which arose in 1525 in Switzerland, under the leadership of Conrad Grebel and Felix Manz, and kindred Brethren in south Germany, Moravia and Holland. The Anabaptists, who incidentally called themselves "Brethren," constituted the conservative, biblical dissenting type which should be differentiated from chiliastic, spiritualist, anti-trinitarian and millenarian groups. The Anabaptists described here are disassociated from those groups whose excesses have caused the term "Anabaptist" to mean, even in scholarly circles, precisely what Luther meant by "Schwärmer," and "fanatics." Fortunately recent studies have clearly indicated that an accurate and fair understanding of Anabaptism is impossible unless discrimination is made between Anabaptist groups. A notable advance was made by Troeltsch who significantly located the center of the Anabaptist movement in Zürich and who saw the Mennonites as the extension of that movement. Important also is the fact that Troeltsch distinguished between the conservative Anabaptists and the radicals of Münster and the Spiritualists. Subsequently, Mennonite scholars such as John Horsch, Harold S. Bender, Robert S. Friedmann and others substantiated this point of view by historical research, with considerable success.

Therefore when Anabaptism is described in this thesis, no reference is being made to the radical, fanatical, millenarian or spiritualistic groups of Christians which sprang up almost everywhere during the Reformation. The Anabaptist groups referred to here are the Swiss Brethren and their spiritual brethren including the Hutterites of Moravia and the Dutch and South German evangelical Anabaptists. Of these, the (Old) Mennonites stem primarily from the Swiss Brethren, even though they were named after a leader of the Dutch Mennonites, Menno Simons (1496-1561).

ABBREVIATIONS

MDGD.....*Man's Disorder and God's Design*, 3 Vols.

MQR..... *The Mennonite Quarterly Review.*

STCC.....Ernst Troeltsch, *The Social Teachings of the Christian Churches*, 2 Vols.

WA ..... *Luther's Works*, Weimar Edition.

Endnotes

1 Ernst Troeltsch, *The Social Teachings of the Christian Churches*, trans. by Olive Wyon, vols. I and II, 3rd. ed., (London: George Allen and Urwin, Ltd., 1931).

2 Max Weber must be given credit for having been the first to conceive of a systematic sociology of religion. This is his greatest contribution. With respect to the relationship between Christianity and society, Weber was especially interested in the significance of economic factors. His friend Troeltsch used fundamentally the same method but extended it to the entire history of the church. In America the stimulus of Weber and Troeltsch can be seen in H. Richard Niebuhr's account of the social sources of denominationalism. For a statement of the "method" of sociology of religion see Joachim Wach, *Sociology of Religion* (Chicago: Univ. of Chicago Press, 1944), pp. 1-17. The significance of Weber in the development of sociology of religion is described by Talcott Parsons in his "Studies in Max Weber's Sociology," *In The Structure of Social Action: A Study in Social Theory with Special Reference to Recent European Writers* (New York: McGraw-Hill Book Co., 1937, Ch. XIV.

3 *The Mennonite Encyclopedia*, eds. Harold S. Bender and C. Henry Smith (Scottdale, Penna.: Mennonite Publishing House. First volume published in 1955. The third volume of a contemplated four-volume encyclopedia was published in 1957).

4 The first Mennonite systematic theology by an American Mennonite was published in 1954. Cf. John C. Wenger, *Introduction to Theology* (Scottdale, Penna.: Herald Press, 1954).

5 Cf. Franklin H. Littell, *The Anabaptist View of the Church* (American Society of Church History, 1952). Especially Chapter II, "The Quest for the Essence of Anabaptism," pp. 19-49.

6 *Ibid.* See also Robert Friedmann, "Conception of an Anabaptist," *Church History*, IX (1940), pp. 341-365.

7 Paul Peachey, "The Modern Recovery of the Anabaptist Vision," *The Recovery of the Anabaptist Vision*, ed. by Guy F. Hershberger (Scottdale, Penna.: Herald Press, 1957), p. 330.

8 Guy F. Hershberger, *War, Peace and Nonresistance* (Scottdale, Penna.: Herald Press, 1944).

9 Cf. John C. Bennett, *Christian Ethics and Social Policy* (New York: Charles Scribner's Sons, 1946), pp. 41-46.

10 *Mennonite Yearbook and Directory, 1957*, ed. by Elrose D. Zook (Scottdale, Penna.: Mennonite Publishing House, 1957), p. 48.

11 *Ibid.*

12 *Ibid.*

CHAPTER 1
THE DILEMMA OF SOCIAL RESPONSIBILITY

I. The Great Revival of Social Responsibility

A. *Is Social Responsibility an Open Question*? The convictions of Protestant theologians today are so strongly and uniformly in favor of social responsibility that it is virtually no longer an open question. This does not indicate a deliberate bias or a closed spirit. Rather, it indicates the tendency of Christian social thought during the past fifty years.[1] That individual Christians and church bodies should maintain an interest in the affairs of the world and should relate themselves *responsibly* to the problems of the economic and political realms has become axiomatic. Nearly all writings on social ethics urge Christian responsibility for the social and political order. The major concern of social ethics today is to arouse an attitude of responsibility among the ministry and especially among the laity which is commensurate to the immensities and complexities of the modern world.[2]

It should be acknowledged, of course, that the actual social influence of the church is far below the ideal set by the theologians. It is no exaggeration to say that the social power of the church has been largely surrendered to the secular forces of the modern world. With the breakdown of Christendom and the advent of great secular, economic and political powers, the church is actually no longer *the* dominant social force in society.[3] The disturbing discrepancy between the numerical size of the church and its influence on society is a common cry. Henry Steel Commager says, "Never before have the churches been materially more powerful and spiritually less effective."[4] Many reasons for social ineffectiveness may be cited--the spirit of accommodation, individualism, latent sectarianism and pietism, perfectionism, misunderstanding of the separation of church and state, exaggerated dualism between the Kingdom of God and the Kingdom of Satan, the conviction that politics is inevitably "dirty," weariness and confusion in the face of modern complexities and social dynamics. Whatever the reason, the church today is a relatively minor factor in the actual formation of modern culture despite its institutional growth and despite what Albert T. Rasmussen calls the "great revival of social responsibility" during the past twenty-five years.[5] The feeling, therefore, that social responsibility is no longer an open question rests more directly upon what theologians say ought to be than upon what is.

B. *The Development of Conviction for Social Responsibility.* Some of the major factors in the development of this conviction must be mentioned.

First in importance is the Social Gospel movement in America through the influence of Walter Rauschenbusch. With revivalistic passion Rauschenbusch awakened the American churches to the social dimension of the Gospel. The purpose of the Social Gospel in America at the beginning of the twentieth century was to "Christianize the social order."[6] The ultimate goal was to bring in the Kingdom of God through the gradual transformation of social structures. In order to make socially explicit the "progressive" tendencies of history, the church embraced the world including the modern city, the capitalistic economy and public education. The tension between the church and the world was relaxed at the beginning of the twentieth century and Christians were taught to make the world the sphere of their Christian responsibility. That certain seeds of Christian responsibility were implicit in the idea of the Kingdom of God in America from the very beginning could be maintained by a study of theocratic assumptions of colonialism,[7] but the Social Gospel movement was the first to bring this to fruition under the conditions of cultural pluralism and with tinges of utopianism. In spite of a great shift in theological orientation in America, the emphasis upon social responsibility of the Social Gospel movement appears to be an essential aspect of American Christianity.

Soon to succeed the Social Gospel movement in America was the movement of Christian social realism under the influence of Reinhold Niebuhr beginning about 1930. Through Niebuhr's influence a revolution occurred in the realm of social thought both within the Christian church and to a certain extent among secular thinkers. Niebuhr rejected certain basic social and theological assumptions of liberalism[8]--its superficial understanding of sin, its naive conception of social dynamics, its equation of the possibilities of personal and social morality, its neglect of class conflict, its identification of Christianity with bourgeois society, its middle class optimism, its pacifism and its implicit perfectionism. He replaced these with assumptions of sin and grace grounded in Reformation theology and with social realism,[9] and in doing so he forestalled a perfectionistic "out," which would have been the logical consequence of liberal presuppositions once the actual social ambiguities were indelibly engraved upon a generation which experienced the great depression and the rise of modern totalitarianism. Niebuhr's main interest was to undergird social passion with an adequate theology and an honest understanding of social dynamics. Therefore Christian ethics adopted new categories--the idea of the morally "ambiguous," "tragic necessity," "compromise," class struggle, force, social complexity, balances of power, the "tolerable peace," the theological significance of secular forces, the inevitability of involvement, and love (*agape*) as an "impossible possibility."[10] For Niebuhr and his followers the Kingdom of God became a norm of judgment rather than a social goal.[11] Politically he tended toward socialism but his doctrine of sin precluded utopian illusions.[12] It is fair to say that American Christian social thought has undergone a thorough revision through the influence of Niebuhr and his students. *But at least one characteristic of liberal social thought has been retained; that is, an equally strong conviction for social action.*

An examination of social thought in Europe reveals similar tendencies toward socially responsible attitudes even though the theological and the political situation has been more diversified than in America. Although many churches in Europe have been traditionally quietistic, a new social awareness has developed in many countries.[13] In England the influence of William Temple, F. H. Oldham and V. A. Demant[14] has brought the Christian conscience to bear especially on the economic problems. Furthermore the great leaders in the revival of Reformation theology on the continent, such as Karl Barth and Emil Brunner, have emphasized the necessity of social witness, even though they have disagreed frequently regarding theological foundations for social action. In spite of Barth's emphasis upon the supernatural character of Christianity, he has held forth clearly in his political writings the necessity of full democratic responsibility.[15] Likewise Brunner makes social responsibility an implication of the Christian understanding of the orders of creation in *Divine Imperative*.[16] Undoubtedly both of these theologians were greatly influenced by the rise of totalitarianism upon Christian soil and the necessity of a social witness against its recurrence. In fact, the great surge of feeling in favor of greater Christian participation in the social and political realms in Europe stems from a re-evaluation of Christian duty in the light of Hitler's Germany.[17] The full impact of this development is reflected in the ecumenical idea of the "Responsible Society."

Another factor which accounts for the growing sense of responsibility is the conception of the democratic way of life. Political history in the West has moved for the past four hundred years in the direction of popular sovereignty. This means that responsibility has been, at least theoretically, distributed among the people. Size and complexity of political institutions have made pure democracy impossible. But representative democracy has characterized the life of great nations, and especially America.[18]

It is frequently pointed out that the relation of Christianity to democracy is highly involved. Democracy has both Hellenistic and Christian roots. The resistance of certain theocratic monarchies to democratic reforms proves that democracy has not made its way easily on Christian soil. However, in most Western democracies today, Christian duty and democratic duty are held closely together and are sometimes unwittingly identified. Although the rights and duties of a democracy may be purely secular, they are thought generally to be in line with Christian duty. Furthermore the idea of separation of church and state has not necessarily meant the Christian abandonment of society.[19] Quite to the contrary it has offered freedom of political criticism which would probably not have been possible otherwise. That Christians should exercise their democratic duty has become axiomatic. The thought of what would happen if all Christians were to abandon political responsibility in a nation which is predominately Christian is enough to undergird Christian duty.[20] Since the texture of modern life involves the great interdependencies of vast economic, educational, welfare and political institutions and since America and Europe have experienced industrial, and now technical revolutions, the abandonment of democratic responsibility appears to be the abandonment of life itself.

Furthermore the necessity of responsibility has been undergirded by modern studies in sociology, psychology and ethics. These have clearly indicated that everyone today is socially and psychologically involved in and dependent upon the total social order. With the coming of the industrial revolution, the "organization revolution," and "other-directedness," social dependency has become increasingly a fact of life. One's life is determined not simply by personal decision but by one's place within a vast network of social determination.[21] This has serious consequences for the freedom of the individual. It has, in fact, resulted in what is sometimes called the "social crisis" of our times. Society is both a threat as well as a support to freedom. At any rate, "involvement" has become a stock word in ethics and it has deep theological and psychological implications regarding corporate guilt and moral responsibility.[22] Especially with the advancement of technological power in addition to industrial might, involvement with and responsibility for the total order introduce problems of baffling proportions. Hence social responsibility has been tied up with social survival. The issue whether one should or should not assume responsibility for the social order takes the form of the question whether one wills or does not will the modern world in all its complexity, it achievements and sin to continue.

If then social responsibility seems so utterly crucial to modern civilization, how can Christian social responsibility be questioned? Should it not remain a closed question? The answer to this lies in the fact that responsibility involves the most momentous and crucial moral and spiritual dilemmas of existence. It has important implications for the nature and work of the church. Tied up with responsibility are implications involving the theory of ethics, the relation of the church and the world, the nature of the Christian calling, the problem of guilt and of war. It is a most torturous and complex question for it brings into focus the tension between Christ and world culture, the relation of love and justice, the conflict between the Kingdom of God and the Kingdom of Satan. Those who regard social responsibility as a closed question should consider the devastating words of Arnold Toynbee in his *Study of History* who, having reviewed the entangling cultural and political alliances of the churches in Europe, concludes that "the effect of the unholy *marriage de convenance* between Religion and Politics was to make Religion itself anathema." Furthermore Toynbee feels that secular indifference to religion today is largely the outcome of the alliance between the church and the modern state and he draws this conclusion: "We are still reacting against a subordination of Religion to Politics which was the crime of our sixteenth century and seventeenth century forbears."[23] It is true that this quotation from Toynbee cannot be used to support a strategy of complete withdrawal from social and political responsibility. It is used merely to reinforce the statement that when the church, conceived either as individual Christians or as corporate bodies, shares responsibility for the state and society as a whole, it is running a risk of losing its integrity as a "new society" which is essentially "not of the world." Social responsibility should therefore be an open question even in the minds of those who by tradition make the corporate life of the world a matter of direct Christian duty.

II. The Meaning and Scope of Responsibility

A. *An Ambiguous Term.* As the term "social responsibility" is used today in numerous writings in the field of social ethics and especially by the ecumenical movement, it is an ambiguous term. The term is seldom used with scientific precision. What it means to be socially responsible in the definite sense has not been stated by any theologian or ecumenical council according to the writer's knowledge. Sometimes it is used with no more precision than a slogan. It is claimed that one must be socially responsible but precisely what it means to be socially responsible is seldom stated.

However, this ambiguity is not altogether due to carelessness. It is a result of the complexity of the social situation in the modern world and of the general problem of how to define Christian duty in a changing social situation. For the same reason that a certain degree of ethical relativism is necessary to cope with moral complexities, it is necessary to define social responsibility in broad terms. A particular set of attitudes and actions which may be socially responsible in one situation may be different from responsibility in a nation offering less freedom. It is conceivable that situations may arise when the greatest contribution to the social and political orders is complete withdrawal and the life of prayer. The form of responsible action should not be too strictly outlined lest it result in a new legalism.[24] Nevertheless, the term can be used with sufficient definiteness to be a usable term and the realm of definite meaning should be stated.

B. *An Attitude of Accountability.* Social responsibility involves, first of all, a general attitude of accountability. The word responsibility means to be accountable or answerable. The German equivalent, *Verantwortung*, brings out the idea of accountability or "answerability" clearly. The verb *verantworten* means to answer or to account for something which has been entrusted to one's control. Sometimes it carries the added meaning of liability and even guilt. S. Paul Shilling has defined social responsibility as follows:

> A 'responsibility' is an instance of accountability for something within one's control.... The word 'responsibility' is synonymous with the ethical term 'duty.' My responsibility is what I ought to think or do as a person among other persons, sharing a common life, and answerable for my conduct to society and to God.[25]

This definition attempts to answer two fundamental questions: (1) for what am I responsible and (2) to whom am I responsible? These questions may be answered by the statement that the Christian is responsible to God and society.

But to say that the Christian is responsible for society may seem to indulge in overgeneralization. Society is an inseparable mass of economics, education, aesthetics, family and political realms all meshed in a vast network of complex relations. How can any single person or church group really assume responsibility for society as a whole?

The truth is, of course, that individual responsibility for the totality of things in the active sense is impossible. The individual can share actively only some of the burdens of the world. For only a few of the problems of the world can one assume complete responsible. Many people feel responsible for political and social situations without any opportunity to turn the feeling into action. This is, incidentally, one of the sources of modern anxiety. Modern communication has made man aware of the total world situation for which he feels he must do something but because of the vastness and complexity of relations, he finds himself helpless. A person may be able to control his private affairs or the affairs of his family and business with reasonable assurance but the average man, as well as the average group intent upon social action, feels bound by existing conditions. Therefore, the constant barrage of exhortations to "do something" sometimes produces objections such as those eloquently expressed by James Agee:

> It is fashionable to feel, and to force upon others, an acute sense of social responsibility.... People have been badgered half out of their minds by the sense of a sort of global responsibility: the relentless daily obligation to stay aware of, hep to, worked-up over, guilty towards, active about, the sufferings of people at a great distance for whom one can do nothing whatever; a sort of playing-at-God (since He is in exile) over every sparrow that falls, with the sense of virtue increasing in ratio to the distance. This enormous and nonsensical burden can be dropped with best intelligence and grace by religious men; in any case by Christians. Believing in the concern, wisdom and mercy of God and in ultimate justice, roughly aware of how much (and how little) attempts at social betterment can bring, rid of illusory responsibilities, Christians can *undertake real and sufficient ones: each to do no less than he as a human being is able*...for the human beings within his sight and reach and touch; and never to presume it other than anti-human to do more. Thus alone, it becomes possible to be quiet, to begin to learn a little bit thoroughly, directly, through the heart, to begin, in fact to be human.[26]

The ardent advocates of social responsibility would readily admit some truth in this protest. No one can be *actively* responsible for all of society's problems. *Social responsibility does, however, imply a general attitude of identification with the world.* The socially responsible person believes that he is a participant in the human struggle for truth and justice as these values are manifested in the social and political realms. He identifies himself with the stream of secular history and feels obligated to the world. The problems of the world are at least in a general way his problems. He addresses himself to them in so far as he is *aware* of them and as far as he is *free* to do something about them. As Karl Barth says, "The citizen is responsible in the whole sphere of his freedom, political and non-political alike."[27] Obligation extends to the limits of that freedom. The question facing the Christian is, to what extent am I free to exert social and political influence?

With respect to the objects of responsibility, viz., God and society, it is important to remember that God is primary. The fact of social responsibility and the forms which responsibility takes must be determined first of all by one's understanding of God's will for his life in Christ. The social attitude and work of the Christian must be grounded first of all not in social, economic or political theory, nor even in the existing order of society, but in the knowledge of God's will. This means that whatever may be said about duties within a democracy, or civic responsibility as a fact of secular life, these must be seen in the light of one's primary duty to God. This may seem so obvious that it need not be mentioned, especially in view of the general teaching in the Bible against idolatry and in view of Christ's admonition to "Render therefore to Caesar the things that are Caesar's, and to God the things that are God's" (Matt. 22:21) and the apostles' decision to "obey God rather than men" (Acts 5:29). However, it cannot be gainsaid that one of the subtle dangers of modern democratic life for Christians is to have their social sense cultivated and their responsibility defined by secular forces alone. No matter what form social responsibility may take, it must be regarded as an attempt to serve in accordance with the will of God. This, of course, underscores the necessity of a theology of politics.

C. *The Practical Form of Responsibility.* It is not the writer's purpose to engage in a complete analysis of social and political freedom and resulting obligations. This would require extensive knowledge of political science and it would become highly involved if full consideration were given to the varying degrees of freedom under existing political conditions. Assuming, however, the freedom which is granted to the average individual in western democracy, a general statement of the kind of social and political action and attitudes which the average Christian citizen should assume if he wishes to be socially responsible may be mentioned briefly.

The socially responsible citizen will at least vote in local and national elections and belong to a political party. The entire democratic system presupposes this right and duty. Without use of the referendum, government would likely fall into the hands of autocratic powers. Of course, the mechanics of voting do not exhaust responsibility. More important than the act of voting is the preparation of the Christian for voting. This preparation includes an intelligent understanding of the issues and personalities involved in elections, party membership,[28] and, if it is to be an expression of Christian faith, as well as citizenship, it must come under the judgment and grace of God.

Furthermore the socially responsible Christian must make a place in his conception of Christian duty for the holding of a political office. Admittedly very few Christians have the opportunity or experience the "call" to executive responsibility in public office. The crucial question is, however, not whether the individual actually holds a political office but whether the political office, as such, is regarded as a Christian vocation. If a Christian declares that he cannot serve as a legislator or politician, as a matter of principle, this is crucial for social responsibility and for his entire approach to social ethics. The socially responsible person will at least hold theoretically to the essential validity of the political office. The importance of this principle is amply demonstrated in the conflict between the sixteenth century Anabaptists and the Reformers regarding the magistry. The Reformers saw that the denial of the magistracy as a Christian "vocation" removed the entire realm of politics from Christianity. It implied not only the breakdown of Christendom, a synthesis of all of life which was then considered more essential to the Christian cause than would be the case today, but it meant also the paganization of one of the most significant realms of life. Therefore the attitude of the Christian toward the political office is the most decisive test for social responsibility as well as for social ethics in general.

There are, of course, many less formal ways in which social responsibility may express itself. Without indulging *ad nauseam* in typical American activistic programs for community betterment and without giving the impression that social and political salvation rests upon the number of mothers who can be convinced that their place is outside the home, social responsibility may be said to include at least an awareness of social and political affairs of the local community and of the larger units of society together with at least some social participation outside the home. Participation in service organizations, relief societies, hospital service, community development societies, fund raising campaigns, parent-teacher's associations, school boards, ladies' aid and hundreds of other organizations and functions which are becoming increasingly a phenomenon of American social pluralism open up opportunities for the expression of Christian concern.

D. *The Relevance of Political Responsibility.* In order to further clarify what is meant by social responsibility it is necessary to indicate the peculiar significance of the political dimension. The term social responsibility is a broad term referring to the relation of the Christian individual and the church to society as a whole. But as stated previously, society may be understood in terms of certain particular realms such as the educational, economic, artistic, social and political. However, there is a certain realm which has always assumed a unique social significance. That is the political realm. The political realm is unique because it is the human authority which is most comprehensive in its reach and most sovereign in its demands. Examined socially, the political authority is the final arbiter of human institutions. The political authority legitimizes all other organizations. It alone has the right to take life. This is not to say that the state is absolute in the Machiavellian sense. It is not morally autonomous. It receives its authority and direction from outside itself. But even if the state may be said to derive its authority theocratically and democratically or by a strange mixture of origins as in the case of the United States, the government remains the supreme executor of social control. Even the church of the modern period appeals to the national constitution for its rights. Furthermore it is the political order which maintains peace and order or, at least, is responsible for peace and order even though the actual conditions of public tranquility may reside more directly in the moral sense of the people.

Furthermore the importance of the political realm for the life of man is increased in the modern period because of the expansion of government into areas once considered outside the direct perspective of the state. With the coming of the welfare state and the general tendency toward socialism, the political and the social realms have merged into a vast bureaucratic inter-dependency in which the political becomes increasingly synonymous with cor-porate life itself. This means that politics and human destiny are tied together to an extent not generally conceived by political thinkers of former generations. That the modern state presents a problem to individual freedom is the com-mon cry of those who fear the "omnicompetent" state.[29] Nevertheless it means that to be really socially responsible, to assume *the* responsibility for society, one must relate himself especially to the political realm. In his analysis of the thought of the Frontier Fellowship, a fellowship of the students of Reinhold Niebuhr, the relevance of the political dimension became increasingly clear to the generation which began to view ethical problems from the perspective of social realism in the 1930's. Paul Lehmann, a member of this fellowship says:

> What is going on in a changing world is pre-eminently a matter of politics. For politics, in the broad sense, have to do with the foun-dations, structures, and ends of human community. What happens in the world has human relevance insofar as it makes human com-munity possible or problematical. The dynamics of change in the world are compounded of natural processes and social forms and, sooner or later, make political analysis and political responsibility imperative if life is to be worth living.[30]

Social responsibility is really political responsibility broadly conceived. At least one cannot claim to be socially responsible in the sense in which the term is used in this thesis unless he is politically minded. In the broadest sense of the term, social responsibility is equivalent to responsibility for the total cultural order but this responsibility must be approached not by latching on to any facet of culture. One has become socially responsible when he has seen his relation to society in terms of his relation to the political order. In this respect political responsibility is the test of social realism.[31]

E. *The Inner Spiritual Attitudes of Responsibility.* In order to understand the meaning and scope of social responsibility it is necessary to speak not only of certain social activities but of some of the inner attitudes and spiritual con-sequences of responsibility. Responsibility is a unique kind of relationship. *Responsibility is decision making involvement for which one is held accountable.* The very essence of responsibility is, in fact, decision making. To be in a posi-tion of responsibility is to be in a position in which one has both the power and the duty to take courses of action in which there are bound to be consequences for which he is held accountable.[32] Responsibility many be seen as character-istic of the work of the executive, the ship captain, the airplane pilot, the surgeon and the mother. The responsible person is bound to decide and stay with his decision. He cannot *capriciously* abandon his position or "office." He is morally committed to stay in his station[33] unless he is forcibly displaced or convinced that to remain would be disastrous for all concerned. Responsibility is by nature grave. It is grave because it ordinarily involves the destiny of other people. Therefore responsibility produces anxiety and failure results in guilt. Many people can stand only a minimum of responsibility.

Probably Max Weber has worked through the spiritual and ethical implications of responsibility more thoroughly than any other theologian. With Weber, *Verantwortung* was introduced into the language of modern ethics with decisive results. He claimed that there are really two kinds of ethics. These are the ethics of sentiment (*Gesinnungsethik*) and the ethics of responsibility (*Verantwortungsethik*).[34] The former is an ethic based upon pure goodness alone, precisely the Sermon on the Mount, in which the consequences are completely excluded as a criterion for action. The consequences of the act make no essential difference. The act is validated by its intrinsic qualities rather than by pragmatic values. This kind of conduct is "perfect" when considered in isolation but from the standpoint of the stream of culture it may be "irresponsible." In fact, it is irresponsible for the simple reason that the horizontal dimension is completely overlooked. The latter, on the other hand, is an ethic based upon the fact that a person must be responsible for all predictable consequences. The responsible agent is bound by the situation. He must stay by his "station"--come what will. He must make decisions not on the basis of pure principle, but on the basis of practical possibilities. He must compromise, use organizational power and possibly even physical power. He experiences the irrational but the no less genuine experience of one who has forfeited the innocence of personal morality for the guilt of corporate morality. With Weber, the tension between the *Gesinnungsethik* and the *Verantwortungsethik*, both of which are found within his Lutheran background, assumed major proportions in his *Gesammelte Politische Schriften*. J. P. Mayer says in this connection: "Weber's moral honesty almost reaches the point of self-destruction."[35] For in politics the moral ambiguity of responsibility reaches its tragic depths. Weber was not able to reconcile the God of love who was revealed on the cross with the God who makes politics a "calling." Weber was caught in the eternal conflict between the claims of love and justice. "The genius or demon of politics," he writes, "lives with the God of love and also with the God of the church in an inner tension which at any time may break out into an unsolvable conflict."[36]

The tragic aspect of responsibility is also seen by Brunner in his *Divine Imperative*. Brunner relates the conflict between goodness and "necessity" to original sin. He says:

> The contrast between that which God wills and what we do ourselves, in our 'official' capacity, remains culpable and terrible.... We never see the real meaning of 'original sin,' we never perceive the depth and the universality of evil, or what evil really means in the depths common to us all, until we are *obliged* to do something which,

in itself, is evil; that is, we do not see this clearly until we are obliged to do something in our official capacity--for the sake of order, and therefore for the sake of love--which apart from our 'offices,' would be absolutely wrong.[37]

Although the conflict between what God ultimately wills and what one is obliged to do has always been recognized in one way or another, it is only in modern times that its full significance is recognized. For whereas this tension was once the price of nobility and soldiery, modern democracy extends the conflict to any citizen who reflects upon it. Corporate responsibility has replace monarchical and aristocratic responsibility since the days of Luther and so the problem of moral ambiguity has been extended to the entire population. Hence one of the great modern problems is the problem of corporate guilt. Social responsibility is the obligation of the individual Christian and the empirical church to share the guilt, as well as the praise of social and political policies.[38]

One other consideration regarding the meaning and scope of social responsibility is the sense in which this is shared both by the church as a body and the Christian as an individual. Certainly the church defined as the body of believers and the individual Christians who compose it express their responsibility differently. The church, for example, is less likely to take an active role in politics than is the individual. The church as an organization under the conditions of democracy usually hesitates to take a stand on political issues unless there is a rather clearly defined moral or religious question involved. Usually the church does not associate itself with a particular political party, though this has on rare occasions happened. But the Christian, on the other hand, expresses his individual liberty by party affiliation and membership in competitive associations without violating principle. *In this thesis social responsibility ordinarily refers to the attitude and action of individual Christians.* However, it is possible to speak of socially responsible churches if no more than to refer to those denominations which make a place in the teaching of the church for responsible action by their individual members, whether they are kings, nobles or magistrates of Reformation times, or presidents and statesmen of more recent times. Another mark of the socially responsible church is its occasional official pronouncements on public affairs.[39] The study of the social teachings of the Christian churches by Troeltsch permits one to make a broad distinction between those churches which take a general position of responsibility and those which do not. The distinction is made on the basis of the church's ultimate goal for the total social order. *A church may be said to be socially responsible if it seeks to produce a Christian culture including the political order, without necessarily stipulating how this is to be accomplished. On the other hand, a church which declines the task of Christianizing the total social order but prefers to concentrate on the church as a separate body, and therefore refuses to enter into the problems of society as a whole, may be said to reject social responsibility.* This is one way of stating the essential difference between the *church* and the *sect* according to Ernst Troeltsch. His distinction between the church and the sect is imperfect since some of the groups which Troeltsch lists as sects have historically gone far in the direction of a Christian society, though under the conditions of the "free church."[40] Nevertheless it may be said that in general the *church* attempts to dominate society whereas the *sect* seeks to separate itself from society for the sake of purity.

III. Social Responsibility--A Crucial Problem of the Mennonites

A. *The Problem of Social Structure.* As a result of the industrial revolution with its powerful impact upon all aspects of culture, the Christian church is facing momentous, though not new, problems. The church has always struggled with the contradiction between the pure gospel of love and the administration of justice, between the ideal of poverty and the "vocation" of accumulated wealth, between the weakness of the cross and the power of sword, between the principles of service and the principles of authority, between preoccupation with things of the Kingdom of God and the distractions of cultural involvement. But his basic problem of Christian ethics is intensified even more today by the nature of the social structure. This structure emerged with the industrial revolution and with the rise of the "world city." It was Weber and Troeltsch who first saw what modern capitalistic industrial civilization, with its vast political as well as economic institutions, means for Christian ethics.[41] It involves the shift from a relatively simple and personal agrarian and artisan culture to the culture of vast impersonal power and organization. Troeltsch knew that the modern world presented "an entirely new state of civilization."[42] This new civilization is summed up by power, bureaucracy, impersonality, materialism and politics. Troeltsch knew that this is not the ethos in which the Gospel lives most naturally for the "ethos of the Gospel is a combination of infinite sublimity and childlike intimacy,"[43] of brother love, mercy, nonresistance, the absence of tension and harshness, and self-sacrifice. Troeltsch even went so far as to say that "this is an ideal which requires a new world if it is to be fully realized."[44] He felt that the very structure of modern life is opposed to the pure religious ideal. The ethics of the Gospel are not enough to support life amid the struggles of a capitalistic culture, a culture interpreted by the categories of Marx. Neither Lutheranism nor ascetic Protestantism could meet the new situation. Nor was Troeltsch able to suggest an approach to ethics adequate to the situation. His wistful closing words are moving because of their childlike simplicity:

> Nowhere does there exist an absolute Christian ethic which only awaits discovery; all that we can do is to learn to control the world-situation in its successive phases.... There is no absolute ethical transformation of material nature or of human nature; all that does exist is a constant wrestling with the problems which they raise.[45]

In his epoch making volume on *Moral Man and Immoral Society*, Niebuhr presented this dilemma by showing that corporate morality tends to be less moral than personal morality, that with numbers and complexity, relations become political and politics is intrinsically less moral than primary relations.[46] Hence the ethical problem has been, how can *agape* love be related to social structure? The significance of the Christian social philosophies of recent years in America, beginning with Niebuhr and continued by John C. Bennett and others, is that while accepting the contradiction between the pure love of the Gospel and the structure of the modern world, they show how love which is "the law of life" may be relevant to social organization, even though it cannot be said to be a direct social possibility.

B. *Mennonites and the Problem of Social Involvement.* A study of Mennonite life indicates that the problem faced by Weber, Troeltsch and Niebuhr is now facing the Mennonites as well. Until recent times, the Mennonite church has not been forced to face the problem of love and structure. This has been the case because of their agrarian withdrawal from the main stream of culture. Traditionally Mennonites have been a farming people.[47] They have formed stable communities by the application of industry and virtue under the conditions of agricultural simplicity. They have cultivated a strong program of mutual aid, of church discipline and of independence. However, the modern capitalistic spirit originating in the great urban centers is now invading the rural areas of America causing an "agricultural revolution." This revolution is turning simple agrarianism into a highly organized way of life in accordance with the spirit of capitalism. With it the traditional "Mennonite way of life," which was once thought to provide the best conditions for the "simple life" of purity and love, is being replaced by the habits and conceptual framework of the petty bourgeois. Furthermore Mennonites are showing a marked tendency to enter into business and manufacturing.[48] The *Mennonite Community* monthly magazine which was published from 1947 to 1953 attempted to meet the challenge of capitalistic bureaucratic culture, by diffusing Mennonite life with brotherhood community concepts, but with no marked success. For all practical purposes, Mennonites have adopted the practices and the business structure of the world. Hence on this level they too are faced with the essential conflict between pure love and capitalistic culture.

The breakdown of Mennonite rural solidarity is also due to an awakening of Mennonites to the needs of the world. They have begun to mingle with the world in foreign missions, world relief service and education.[49] Mennonite historians lay great stress upon the "Great Awakening"[50] in the Mennonite church during the latter part of the nineteenth century. This spiritual awakening broke the arid complacency which characterized American Mennonitism for three hundred years and introduced ideas of missions and education. Since then Mennonites have launched a vigorous missionary program and Mennonite young people are serving as relief workers in the troubled spots of the world. Consequently Mennonites have become increasingly conscious of the problems and the ways of the world. This has meant that traditional isolationism and social separatism have been suddenly qualified by a world outlook. Still more significant is the fact that higher education is beginning to make its impact upon Mennonite thought. With the introductions of the liberal disciplines such as science, the arts and history in Mennonite colleges, contact is made with the world on a level which makes social responsibility seem reasonable indeed. Hence Mennonites are now found in nearly all professions and many of them are considerably integrated in world culture.

What this means is that the Mennonites are finding that they are involved in world culture and the question is whether the Mennonite interpretation of Christianity will support the tendency toward responsibility for the institutions of the world. The "strategy of withdrawal"[51] which has been traditional with Mennonites and which in fact constitutes one of the classic Christian approaches to culture is being dissipated by both the movement of world culture upon the Mennonites from without and the tendency of the Mennonites to move into the world from within. Traditionally, Mennonites solved the problem of involvement by cultural and geographical isolation. They have fled to almost all parts of the world to escape the world. The dominant concern of Mennonitism for over three hundred years has been "separation from the world" (*Absonderung*). Their overwhelming fear has been the loss of their "peculiar principles." With instinctive regularity Mennonites have "solved" the problem of worldliness by "fleeing." But his method is no longer feasible for three reasons: (1) Mennonites do not know where to flee.[52] Traditonally Mennonites have migrated from the centers of civilization to primitivism. But opportunity for primitivistic isolationism is fast disappearing from the face of the globe. (2) They are becoming in recent years so much involved in the culture of America that the Abramhamic search for "a city which has foundations, whose builder and maker is God" has become to many a "remote" idea. (3) Isolation for the sake of protecting the tradition is increasingly viewed as a violation of the spirit of the Great Commission and the Lordship of Christ and as a mere concession to ethnic ties.[53]

It is clear therefore that the social forces resident in Mennonitism point to an accelerated rate of cultural accommodation. What does this mean for social responsibility? It undoubtedly means on the one hand that with the loss of the typical social and psychological conditions of sectarianism, Mennonites may as a matter of course accept social responsibility. Responsibility may result as an inevitable concomitant of involvement. Along with involvement in business, the professions, higher education, social welfare and world missions, Mennonites may simply accept the world as the logical consequence.

C. *The Relevance of the "Anabaptist Vision."* As over against the social force towards greater social participation and conformity, there is, however, in the contemporary Mennonite situation another important factor which tends to pull, at least theoretically, in another direction. That is the recent discovery of and commitment to the historical and theological roots of the Mennonites. This study began about thirty years ago with the work of Mennonite historians such as John Horsch and Harold Bender.[54] After several hundred years of religious quietism and extreme conservatism, the American Mennonites have been awakened to their historical heritage in Anabaptism. This has resulted in a general interest in Anabaptism beyond Mennonite circles as well, a significant development in view of the fact that Anabaptism has been an obscure and highly complicated, and now highly controversial, movement of the Reformation. This has led the Mennonite church to examine her faith and practices in the light of her historical origins. *Anabaptism has therefore emerged as a kind of norm by which the Mennonite church judges her life and mission.* The term which is used in Mennonite circles for the Anabaptist interpretation of Christianity is the "Anabaptist Vision."[55]

Although not all Mennonite scholars agree exactly as to what the Anabaptist Vision includes, it is quite clear that Anabaptism was a radical sectarianism based upon New Testament realism. It was an attempt to restore to Christendom the faith and life of the early church. This vision included synoptic discipleship, absolute nonresistance, the perfectionism of the Sermon on the Mount, non-swearing of oaths, simplicity of life, the lay ministry, a tendency toward charismatic leadership, the universal call to lay missionary activity, the ban, rejection of "worldliness" in all its forms including the magistracy, war, participation in government, and a general attitude of separation from the world. Probably the most thorough and logical Anabaptists were the Hutterites who grouped all these ideas within a unique structural pattern of life, namely Christian communism. As described in Chapter IV, the Anabaptists actually challenged the basic Medieval and Reformation premise of Christian civilization with the idea of the true disciplined church of committed believers.

What this actually means for social responsibility is, in broad outline, clear. It means decline of responsibility for the world. One wishes for a word less loaded with reproach than "social irresponsibility," for to speak of peace-loving, nonresistant, harmless, suffering Anabaptists as socially irresponsible is inadequate. The Anabaptists were certainly not socially irresponsible in the sense which the term is ordinarily used. They wanted to carry forth in a literal way the Kingdom-centered Christianity of the Synoptics. However, this simply brings out the *irony* of the Gospel of love in relation to social institutions in general. For the structure of society as we know it, i.e., society which is ordered by the principles of *justitia civilis*, operates on a radically different level from the principles of the higher righteousness of the Kingdom. Therefore when a body of Christians such as the Anabaptists insist upon the higher righteousness as a consistent pattern of life, they may become not only a neutral quantity, but even a threat to society. This is one of the main reasons that the early Anabaptists were persecuted so severely.

What would happen to the Mennonite Church if it were to return to the Anabaptist vision? Undoubtedly it would revolutionize the church. It would completely reverse the present tendency of the Mennonite Church toward the pattern of the typical American denomination. It would revive the sectarian spirit of radical discontinuity with the world and with other Christian bodies. It would emphasize the necessity of a third kind of Christianity which is basically distinct from Catholicism and Protestantism. *With respect to social responsibility, Mennonites would categorically refuse to attach their energies and their ambitions to the purposes of a great world culture and civilization.* Mennonites would concentrate upon the church, the perfecting of the saints, the preaching of the word, personal charity, the experience of brotherhood and true community (koinonia), and the establishment of a radically new order in accordance with the Spirit. The kingdom of God would be placed "first." The church would despair of the world with its emphasis upon materialism, technology, luxury and balances of power. It would revive the Johannine rejection of the world! "Do not love the world or the things in the world. If anyone loves the world, the love of the Father is not in him.... And the world passes away, and the lust of it; but he who does the will of God abides forever" (I John 2:15;17). It would revive the Petrine conception of the people of God as a peculiar people. "But you are a chosen race, a royal priesthood, a holy nation, God's own people, that you may declare the wonderful deeds of him who called you out of darkness into his marvelous light. Once you were no people but now you are God's own people; once you had not received mercy but now you have received mercy" (I Peter 2:9-10). It would restate the fundamental Mennonite principle that the church of the New Testament is normative for all times, notwithstanding the replacement of Roman autocracy with modern democratic and socialistic forms of government. It would also have radical implications for education, especially for the liberal arts, since they are not easily correlated with the outlook and concern of Christianity.[56]

D. *The Dilemma of Social Responsibility.* The question of social responsibility comes to Mennonites in the form of a dilemma. To some Mennonites it is a more genuine dilemma than to others, depending upon the value placed upon the social responsibility. To those who see no value in social responsibility, the dilemma is simply the proverbial struggle of the sect for existence in an evil culture. Social responsibility is regarded entirely from the standpoint of the danger of compromise. However, to those who see positive value in responsible participation in the affairs of the world--notwithstanding the moral ambiguities of involvement--the dilemma comes as one of conflicting duties. Love itself demands responsible participation in society for it is in the social realm that the Christian meets the neighbor. To avoid responsibility is the same as "passing by on the other side" unless it can be proved that the neighbor can be helped more effectively by some other way than through the legitimate channels of social action. Thus the contemporary Mennonite who is committed on the one hand to the high ethic of Christ and who is on the other hand aware of opportunities to meet human need through participation in the struggle for social justice is caught in a genuine dilemma.

Probably the most significant factor in the dilemma of social responsibility is the redefinition of the neighbor in the light of the modern conception of social dynamics.

Whereas the neighbor has been conceived traditionally in terms of personal, face-to-face relationships, it is clear to all who have studied sociology and economics that, in addition, the neighbor must be conceived impersonally as a member of a class or a group. In the modern period the neighbor consists not only of the man next door or the farmer in the adjoining land but he consists of the Negro as a class, or the laborer, or the Japanese manufacturer whose livelihood is dependent upon American tariff policy. The neighbor is any group of men who appear to be in need. Furthermore if the corporate neighbor is to be the recipient of Christian love, the way to help him (sometimes the only way) is to engage in the struggle for justice through the use of social and political power. To do this means compromise but to restrict the scope of love to personal relations because of the inherent ambiguities of social struggle is virtually the same as destroying one's personality, once the vision of world need has been seen in its social dimension.

IV. The Problem of Christ and Culture

A. *Social Responsibility--A Problem of "Christ and Culture."* When the deeper implications of social responsibility are considered, it becomes clear that the problem is ultimately one of Christianity and culture. If responsibility is conceived with reference to the full range of opportunities and responsibilities for social power and influence, it is evident that social responsibility is the same as cultural responsibility or responsibility for the "world."[57] This is another way of saying that social convictions regarding particular problems and policies generally reflect a total attitude toward culture. One could illustrate this fact by comparing the ethical attitudes of Tertullian regarding marriage, law, wealth and war with the ethical attitudes of St. Thomas Aquinas regarding similar subjects. They differ in particulars primarily because their attitudes toward the entire human enterprise, as it is expressed in culture, is fundamentally different. Tertullian adopted an essentially sectarian attitude toward civilization whereas St. Thomas adopted a Catholic view in which unity and universality dominated his thought. Therefore the problem of social responsibility cannot be treated on the level of attitudes toward particular aspects of social and political life. Ultimately it resolves itself into the question of what to do about civilization as a whole. Should the church seek to separate itself from the world for the sake of purity and righteousness or should the church enter responsibly into the world for the purpose of establishing a comprehensive Christian civilization? Should the church concentrate its energies upon its own internal operations or should it seek to express itself indirectly in the "secular" structures of the world? Should the church limit its attention to the problem of the "people of God" or should the church put its shoulder under the problems, the sufferings, the struggles, the failures and the sin of the world? Should the church insist on its own perfection or should it accept evil as a necessary accompaniment of the responsible attitude toward society?

The question of the relation of Christianity and culture has become an increasingly important question to the churches in the modern period. The question has been defined and the major positions of the Christian church have been presented by Richard Niebuhr in *Christ and Culture*. A more philosophical and less historical treatment has been prepared by Richard Kroner in *Culture and Faith*.[58] Niebuhr points out that the Christ and culture problem is an "enduring problem."[59] The history of Christianity reveals diverse views both in theory and practice. "The debate is as confused as it is many sided."[60] It began with the days of Jesus Christ's humanity, though the "people of God" in the Old

Testament were faced with a problem of much the same nature in their relation to the heathen. The same problem emerges in the minds and hearts of individuals as well. The problem is twofold. It is a vocational problem and a moral problem. Vocationally it is a question of the extent to which a disciple who is totally committed to Christ and His Kingdom may devote himself to the purposes and program of world culture. Morally it is a question of how to relate the extraordinary ethic of Christ and the kingdom to the ethics of civil society in which the Christian is involved. The problem appears to anyone who compares Christ and His ethic, His orientation in the Will of God and the Kingdom of God with the purposes and possibilities of civilization. Niebuhr notes that "not only pagans who have rejected Christ but believers who have accepted him find it difficult to combine his claims with those of their societies."[61] Culture appears to be distraction from the things of the Kingdom of God as well as a downward pull from the lofty ethical ideals of Christ. Culture comes to the sensitive Christian as a threat. Even though the Christian resorts to all kinds of casuistry, he still finds himself continuously beset by the conflict between the absolute demands of Christ and the relativities of culture to which he seems at times to be absolutely bound. Most "solutions" to this problem emphasize one element of the Gospel at the expense of another-- hence the problem remains.

B. *Points of Tension.* Specifically what are the reasons for the tension between Christ and culture? It will be possible only to give them a brief summary treatment here.

(1) In view of the fact that Christ's ethic and His basic orientation in the Kingdom of God completely neglects the claims of world culture, His followers, who must necessarily live in sinful culture, are left in a condition of extreme tension. According to the Synoptic account, Christ was not interested directly in the claims of culture and He made no effort to relate Himself nor His ethic responsibly to the existing cultural situation. Specifically, He did not direct His life and mission to the practical problems of the nation. By contrast, the Jewish leaders were interested in the total culture for the purpose of establishing a holy nation. The responsible leaders of the Jews sought to bring all elements of the national community into a cultural synthesis. Not only personal piety but social morality and national religion were dedicated to the goal of a total community committed totally to God. This required the practical oversight and the exercise of ecclesiastical and political authority. It required a highly complicated legal casuistry. It required education and nurture and a comprehensive approach to society which included all the facts of national life. It called for strategic decisions, necessary compromise and an ethic calculated to work within the limitations of an imperfect society.

However, Jesus was essentially indifferent to the immediate problems of the Jewish nation. *He was interested in the Kingdom of God which was different from existing religious and social institutions.*[62] Without going into the question of precisely how Jesus conceived the Kingdom of God in relation to history, it is safe to say that He did not expect the Kingdom to grow directly out of Judaism. The Kingdom of God was conceived as a *new* order. Therefore preparation for the Kingdom took forms which were not intended to further the immediate, practical interests of organized religion among the Jews. Without denying the preparatory significance of Jewish history and institutions for the Kingdom, Christ did not consider responsible participation in the cultural problems of His day the way to prepare for the coming of the Kingdom.

Jesus recognized one supreme allegiance which was so demanding that all other allegiances were reduced to negligible proportions. For Christ the one consuming reality, to which He called His disciples, was the new order which, whatever form it would take, would conform to the perfect will of God.

It is claimed by the contemporary Jewish scholar, Joseph Klausner, that Jesus' "irresponsible" attitude toward the total situation of the Jews was the main source of conflict between Him and the *responsible* leaders of Judaism. Jesus is supposed to have even imperiled Jewish civilization by His indifference toward the cultural interests of the Jews. Klausner says:

> Judaism is not only religion and it is not only ethics: it is the sum-total of all the needs of the nation, placed on a religious basis. It is a national world-outlook with an ethico-religious basis.... Judaism is a national life, a life which the national religion and human ethical principles...embrace without engulfing. Jesus came and thrust aside all the requirements of the national life; it is not that he set them apart and the relegated to their separate sphere in the life of the nation: he ignored them completely; in their stead he set up nothing but an ethic-religious system bound up with his conception of the Godhead.[63]

Jesus' rejection of Zealotry is another indication of His attitude toward Jewish national aspirations.[64] Furthermore His ethic of turning the other cheek and going the second mile completely overlooks the comprehensive needs of the cultural situation. Even the prudential defenses of personal life, as well as resistance of the Romans, seem to be totally outside Jesus' program for Himself and His disciples.

(2) Furthermore, not only was Jesus indifferent to the socio-political order of His day, but His absolute ethic transcends any conceivable cultural system. Jesus called for an "extraordinary" ethic. It was calculated to "exceed" the righteousness of even the Scribes and the Pharisees (Matt. 5:20). In other words, Jesus' ethic was higher than even the highest ethical possibility of the Jewish religio-political community and any other community for that matter. The extraordinary quality of Jesus' ethic arises from its sole source in the will of God (Matt. 5:48). It is calculated to meet only one requirement, i.e., perfection based upon the concept of a perfect God. For this reason, Jesus' ethic is unprudential and nonpragmatic. It does not attempt to meet the practical demands of social existence. Jesus does not consider what goes into *ordinary* civil life--the balancing of private and public egos, the establishment and maintenance of law, the administration of punitive and distributive justice, the arbi-

tration of interests, the preservation of the values of the family and tradition, the accumulation of wealth, and the maintenance of public institutions.

Consider the extraordinary requirements of Christ's ethic. It requires the abandonment of physical and institutional power, of arbitration between contending egos (Luke 10:13-14), of anxiety for the physical basis for life (Matt. 6:25), of revenge (Matt. 5:38-42), of the oath (Matt. 5:33-37), of compromise and of concern for existence (Matt. 10:28). Jesus calls for an absolute commitment to the goodness of God which takes the form of indiscriminate forgiveness (Matt. 18:21-22), of nonpreferential love (Matt. 5:43-48), of simple trust in God for the necessities of life (Matt. 6:19ff), of love for enemies and of the way of the cross (Mark 8:34-36). This is a purely religious ethic which, judged from any other standard, appears to be foolish.

Both the content and the practical implications of the ethical saying of Jesus are, of course, controversial. However, it seems abundantly clear in the light of modern New Testament studies that the ethic of Jesus cannot be considered the basis for an ethic of culture *in the ordinary sense*. The assumption of the Social Gospel that the Sermon on the Mount represents a social and political possibility seems naive to this generation. The assumption that the Sermon on the Mount can become the basis for national policy seems entirely beside the point. Reinhold Niebuhr quoted Karl Barth as saying that this ethic "is not applicable to the problems of contemporary society nor yet to any conceivable society."[65] In similar language Alfred North Whitehead said: "As society is now constituted a literal allegiance to the moral precepts scattered throughout the Gospels would mean sudden death."[66] Of course, Reinhold Niebuhr is the one who most effectively emphasized the impossible character of Jesus' ethic for society as a whole. His position regarding the impossibility of Jesus' ethic both for the individual and the political order is presented as follows:

> The ethic of Jesus does not deal at all with the immediate moral problem of every human life--the problem of arranging some kind of armistice between various contending factions and forces. It has nothing to say about the relativities of politics and economics, nor of the necessary balances of power which exist and must exist in even the most intimate social relationships. The absolutism and perfectionism of Jesus' ethic sets itself uncompromisingly not only against the natural self-regarding impulses, but against the necessary prudent defenses of the self, required because of the egoism of others. It does not establish a connection with the horizontal points of a political or social ethic or with the diagonals which a prudential individual ethic draws between the moral ideal and the facts of a given situation. It has only a vertical dimension between the loving will of God and the will of man.[67]

Certainly Niebuhr should be interpreted at this point. He is not saying that the ethic of Jesus is a *metaphysical* impossibility dictated by the material nature of the world. Nor is he saying that the complexity of social affairs is the final reason why Christ's ethic is impossible. Nor is it a problem of structure as such, though the structure which sinful men construct exaggerates individual egoism. He is saying that society *as it is organized* in accordance with sinful human nature cannot embody the absolute ethic of love as a "simple possibility." There is a direct contradiction, for example, between the forgiving love of Christ and the self-assertion, the aggression,[68] as well as the legal correction bound to business life and police court action, even though these are generally regarded as normal. Niebuhr is making the observation that people simply are not good enough to live entirely by the law of love. The fault is ultimately in the human will. But Jesus' ethic makes no concessions to the defective will!

The tension between Christ and culture does not only appear when His ethic is held over against the larger formations of society. The tension created by His ethic applies to personal conduct as well. It touches certain basic personal desires and ambitions which are just as important. Reference may be made to Jesus' attitude toward marriage and wealth. Although Jesus' attitude toward marriage is not one of ascetic denial based on a dismal metaphysical view of flesh and matter, it is clear that Jesus saw the natural ties of the family and the binding tendencies of family loyalties and preferences as a danger to the universality of the Kingdom (Mark 3:31-35). Jesus realized that the most powerful foes of the Kingdom are not necessarily those generally considered absolutely bad. They are all those interests and loyalties which, though good in themselves, draw men away from the ultimate concern of life. Furthermore, anxiety about material security is discouraged. In His discourse on security Jesus calls for simple trust in the benevolence of God. He notes that the Gentiles seek after food, drink and clothing (Matt. 5:32) and that their rulers "lord it over them."

It is clear therefore that when the Gospel of the Kingdom is held over against the purposes and goals of civilization they are in a relation of tension, and sometimes clearly in conflict. Over against the virtues and vices which build nations and empires, Christ's teachings result in a "transvaluation of value." No great civilization has ever been built upon the Beatitudes. Civilizations are directed toward material wealth, power, technology and reason. The virtues of civilization are not calculated to emulate the "poor," the "meek," the "merciful," the "pure in heart" and "nonresistant peacemakers." To be sure these qualities may be injected into the ethics of the "wise men after the flesh," the "mighty" and the "noble," as temporary and supplementary emollients to the classical virtues of power. But they are seldom, if ever, the driving forces of civilization.[69] Even the Middle Ages came under the judgment of Christ's "impossible" ethic.[70]

C. *Mennonitism and the Rejection of Culture.* As a result of the conflict between Christ and the world, the Mennonite position throughout its history has been confessionally, and to a large extent in actual practice, one of cultural rejection. According to Richard Niebuhr's analysis, the Mennonites represent the sectarian "Christ against Culture" position "since they not only renounce all participation in politics and refuse to be drawn into military service, but follow their distinctive customs and regulations in economics and education."[71] This is a fair statement of the Mennonite position since it represents in a general way the actual practice of Mennonites throughout history and it is certainly in accordance with Mennonite principles of separation from the world.

But even though it can be said that, in a general way, Mennonites are against culture, present day Mennonites are beginning to ask questions which are not exactly typical of sectarianism. These questions are emerging through the practical experience of living in a great modern democracy and from the theoretical stimulus of the "Christ and Culture" problem as it is currently discussed by theologians outside Mennonite circles. Paul Peachy says: "In practice great uncertainty regarding the Christian's relation to the general culture obtains among Mennonites today."[72]

Some of the major questions facing the Mennonites today are as follows: Is there an intrinsic conflict between Christ and culture? Until the present time Mennonites, who have spent most of their history evading the main stream of culture, have answered ironically in the negative. Culture is in itself not evil. It can be redeemed if it comes under the complete domination of Christ and His church. However, as the world is now organized *much* of culture is evil. To the Mennonites, therefore, this means that Christians must separate themselves from the evil in culture. This they claim to be a possibility. In fact, the entire approach of Mennonitism assumes the possibility of the unambiguous embodiment of an ethical ideal. Hence the Mennonite approach remains undialectic.[73]

But the most difficult question facing the Mennonites is whether they should then try to build up a truly "Christian culture" of their own. Should they try to inject Christian principles into as much of life as possible and bring upon the face of the earth as *comprehensive an order* as can be based upon absolutistic Christian principles. At this point the Mennonites are uncertain. It can be shown that they have built up more or less independent social orders from time to time, but these have been largely accidental rather than intentional. Furthermore, the question as to what a truly Christian order would involve has seldom been considered except by the Hutterites, and to a certain extent, by Guy F. Hershberger with his "Mennonite Community" idea.[74] In addition, a desire of some Mennonites to find positive ways of witnessing to the state and community along lines of social and international policy raises the question of the ultimate relation of the church to the larger order. Shall the Mennonite church take unto itself the great problems of international relations and seek to exercise a prophetic voice? If so, shall it seek to impose upon the political scene its absolutistic demands of Christ or should the Mennonite church speak with a "wisdom" which is tempered by a realistic analysis of political facts? These are unanswered questions and it is evident that they are all questions arising from the fundamental problem of how a church which subscribes to the radical ethic of Christ is to face the problems of corporate life in this world.

V. Summary

The dilemma of social responsibility is the dilemma of "ethical Christianity." It is the dilemma of those who conceive of Christ not only as Saviour but as Lord and who accept the teaching of Christ as normative for all His followers under all circumstances. For when the radical commands are taken seriously and when they are turned into general principles for life, tensions immediately emerge between the pure ethic and the life of the participant in an evil society. This is due to the fact that the normal processes of business, law and government depend upon principles which are lower than the ethic of the Sermon on the Mount. A clash inevitably follows from the fact that Christ's ethic does not take into consideration the structure of society as it has come to be described by *justitia civilis*. Christ's ethic is an extraordinary ethic based upon the principles of the perfection of God.

The clash between Christ's ethic and the facts of social existence are simply inescapable. However, the problem assumes critical proportions in the case of the disciple who not only realizes that his personal life is involved in a network of social relations based on principles lower than the highest, but that he may be called to participate *responsibly* in the total social order. In other words, he is not only in the social order but bound to it and responsible for it. This means also that he is not only confronted with his own personal weakness, but he is confronted also with the ambiguity of the total social order. Furthermore, if he assumes the position of responsibility, he is tied to the ethical limitations not only of himself but of mankind in general.

In the modern world the dilemma of social and political responsibility is presented in its most extreme form by the administration of military weapons which are virtually capable of destroying the world. Today responsibility in power politics makes at least the threat to use ultimate weapons a necessity. Therefore the disciple who is in the position of responsibility cannot avoid the deepest experience of moral conflict. But to pull out from all those realms of life in which there is a clash, great or small, would likely mean the abandonment of life. So the dilemma of the Mennonites and all ethically oriented Christians.

Endnotes

1 Cf. John C. Bennett, *The Christian as Citizen* (New York: Assoc. Press, 1955), pp. 14ff.

2 John C. Bennett, *Christian Realism* (New York: Charles Scribner's Sons, 1942), pp 74ff. Even Fundamentalists are being aroused to social action. Cf. Carl F. H. Henry, *The Uneasy Conscience of Modern Fundamentalism* (Grand Rapids, Mich.: William B. Eerdmans, 1947).

3 The significance of the "breakdown of Christendom" for the church is considered at length by J. H. Oldham, *The Church and its Function in Society* (New York: Willett Clark and Co., 1937), pp. 60ff. Lesslie Newbigin refers to the dissolution of the mediaeval synthesis which Reformation theologies take for granted as the "reason why the doctrine of the church is in the center of our thinking." Lesslie Newbigin, *The Household of Faith* (New York: Friendship Press, 1953), pp. 1-4.

4 Henry Steel Commager, *The American Mind* (New Haven: Yale University Press, 1950), p. 167.

5 Albert T. Rasmussen, *Christian Social Ethics* (Englewood Cliffs, New Jersey, 1956), p. 83.

6 Cf. Walter Rauschenbusch, *Christianizing the Social Order* (New York: Macmillan Co., 1917).

7 Cf. H. Richard Niebuhr, *The Kingdom of God in America* (New York: Willett, Clark and Co., 1937), pp.45-46.

8 Cf. Reinhold Niebuhr, *Reflections on the End of an Era* (New York: Charles Scribner's Sons, 1934).

9 Cf. Hans Hofmann, *The Theology of Reinhold Niebuhr*, trans. Louise Pettibone Smith (New York: Charles Scribner's Son's, 1956), pp. 89ff.

10 Reinhold Niebuhr, *An Interpretation of Christian Ethics* (New York: Harper and Brothers, 1935), pp. 103f.

11 *Ibid.*, p. 31.

12 Cf. Arthur Schlesinger, Jr., "Reinhold Niebuhr's Role in American Political Thought and Life," *Reinhold Niebuhr, His Social and Political Thought*, ed. by Charles W. Kegley and Robert W. Bretall (New York: Macmillan Co., 1956), pp. 125-150.

13 Cf. John C. Bennett, *Christian Ethics and Social Policy* (New York: Charles Scribner's Sons, 1946), pp. 52-53.

14 Cf. D. A. Demant, *Religion and the Decline of Capitalism* (New York: Charles Scribner's Sons, 1952).

15 Cf. Karl Barth, "The Christian Community in the Midst of Political Change," *Against the Stream* (London: SCM Press, 1954), pp. 53-124.

16 Emil Brunner, *The Divine Imperative*, trans. by Olive Wyon (Philadelphia: Westminster Press, 1947), p. 223.

17 In so far as the emphasis upon social responsibility is theological, it should be seen as a reaction mainly to pietistic influences in Europe and sectarian influences in America.

18 In his description of democracy in America Alexis de Tocqueville said, "It is difficult to say what place is taken up in the life of an inhabitant of the United States by his concern for politics. To take a hand in the regulation of society and to discuss it is his biggest concern, and, so to speak, the only pleasure an American knows...." Alexis de Tocqueville, *Democracy in America*, cited by David Riesman, *The Lonely Crowd* (New Haven: Yale Univ. Press. 1950), p. 177.

19 Winthrop C. Hudson, *The Great Tradition of the American Churches* (New York: Harper and Brothers, 1953), p. 60.

20 The fear that abandonment of the political office could only result in the triumph of the wicked was an observation of Plato. "He who refuses to rule is liable to be ruled by one who is worse than himself." *Republic* (Jowett), p. 25.

21 The loss of true individuality and human freedom in modern society is a current concern among sociologists and psychologists. Cf. Erich Fromm, *The Sane Society* (New York: Rinehart and Co., 1955); David Riesman, *The Lonely Crowd* (New Haven: Yale Univ. Press, 1950), Part II.

22 This is a major emphasis of Edward LeRoy Long in *Conscience and Compromise* (Philadelphia: Westminster Press, 1954).

23 Arnold J. Toynbee, *A Study of History*, vol. V, 5th ed. (London: Oxford University Press, 1951), pp. 670-671).

24 Speaking to this point Dietrich Bonhoeffer speaks about duty as defined by the "concrete place": "The attempt to define that which is the good once and for all has, in the nature of the case, always ended in failure. Either the proposition was asserted in such general and formal terms that it retained no significance as regards its contents, or else one tried to include in it and elaborate the whole immense range of conceivable contents, and thus to say in advance what would be good in every conceivable case; this led to a casuistic system so unmanageable that it could satisfy the demands neither of general validity nor of concreteness." Dietrich Bonhoeffer, *Ethics*, ed. by Eberhard Bethge, trans. by H. H. Smith (London: SCM Press, 1955), p. 23.

25 S. Paul Shilling, "The Christian Bases of Rights, Freedoms and Responsibilities," *The Church and Social Responsibility*, ed. by J. Richard Spann (New York: Abingdon-Cokesbury Press, 1953). p. 12.

26 James Agee, *Partisan Review* (Feb., 1950), pp. 108-109. Cited by Marquis Childs and Douglass Cater, *Ethics in a Business Society* (New York: Harper and Brothers, 1954), p. 153.

27 Karl Barth, *op. cit.*, p. 37.

28 The tendency of many Christians to engage in "non-political politics" is scored by William Miller. Miller deplores especially the failure of Christians to engage in politics within the party. "They overestimate voting and underestimate political parties: they think that simply by casting a ballot every two years for the cleanest-shaven candidate they will be politcally effective. They therefore fail to act through the party, word, caucus, convention, or influence channels which control policy and personal choice." William Miller, "A Theologically Based View of Protestant Politics," *Religion in Life*, vol. XXI (Winter, 1952), p. 57.

29 The modern state has been described as a collective stomach assimilating all the peculiar qualities of groups into a common man. John C. Bennett sees the extension of the powers of the state as an occasion for social responsibility: "This seems to be the age of the state and it would be a mistake to deny that the state must increase its functions in many directions. It alone has the power, and it alone is in a sufficient central position to do necessary planning in a complicated technological society. But the more extensive the work of the state becomes, the more important it is to encourage associations within the large community which are independent of the state. The church is the association which has proved over and over again to be so tough that the state cannot absorb it. It becomes for that reason a protection of human freedom, since it is the voice of criticism that continues to sound when most other voices have been silenced." *Christian Ethics and Social Policy*, p. 91.

30 Paul L. Lehmann, "The Foundation and Pattern of Christian Behaviour," *Christian Faith and Social Action*, ed. by John A. Hutchison (New York: Charles Scribner's Sons, 1953), p. 94.

31 Reinhold Niebuhr says, "The test of the realism of a moral or religious world view is its attitude toward politics because in that attitude it reveals its understanding of the persistence and inertia of collective egoism against the aspirations and demands of the spirit." *Reflections on the End of an Era* (New York: Charles Scribner's Sons, 1934), p. 209.

32 Albert T. Rasmussen, *op. cit.*, p. 153.

33 Emil Brunner, *op. cit.*, pp. 223ff.

34 Max Weber, Politik als Beruf," *Gesammelte Politische Schriften* (München: Drei Masken Verlag, 1921), p. 441.

35 J. P. Mayer, *Max Weber and German Politics* (London: Faber and Faber, 1943), p. 90.

36 Max Weber, *Gesammelte Politischen Schriften*, p. 447.

37 Brunner, *op.cit.*, p. 227.

38 Cf. Bonhoeffer, *op. cit.*, pp. 209-215.

39 See Chapter VII, below.

40 Ernst Troeltsch, *STCC*, Vol. I, pp. 691ff.

41 Cf. Max Weber, "Die protestantisch Ethik und der Geist des Kapitalismus," *Religions-Spziologie*, I (Tubingen: J.C.B. Mohr, 1920), pp. 55ff.

42 *STCC*, Vol. II, p. 1001.

43 *Ibid.*, p.999.

44 *Ibid.*

45 *Ibid.*, p. 1013.

46 Niebuhr states his thesis in these words: "The thesis to be elaborated in these pages is that a sharp distinction must be drawn between the moral and social behaviour of individuals and social groups, national, racial, and economic; and that this distinction justifies and necessitates political policies which a purely individualistic ethic must always find embarrasing." *Moral Man and Immoral Society* (New York: Charles Scribner's Sons, 1931), p. xi.

47 See Chapter V, below.

48 Cf. *The Directory of Mennonite Employers*, compiled by The Mennonite Research Foundation, Goshen, Indiana, March, 1956.

49 See Chapter VI, below.

50 John C. Wenger, *Glimpses of Mennonite HIstory and Doctrine* (Scottdale, Penna.: Herald Press, 1947), pp. 188f.

51 The term "strategy of withdrawl" has been popularized by John C. Bennett as one of the four classical Christian social strategies. It is not without significance that although many sects in the history of the Catholic and Protestant churches could be used to exemplify this approach to the social order, the Mennonites were chosen as the most consistent exemplar. *Christian Ethics and Social Policy*, pp. 41-46.

52 At a regional conference on economic problems sponsored by the Economic and Social Relations Committee at Souderton, Penna. (near Philadelphia) April, 1956, it was disclosed that only 20% of this once solid farming Mennonite community are now farmers. Consideration of the sociological influence of "suburbia" upon this community led this conference to consider three possibilities: (1) for the Mennonites to move to other parts of United States or Canada where thy can preserve their peculiar way of life in rural simplicity. (2) Remain in the Philadelphia area and attempt to remain loyal to the basic principles of Mennonitism even within urban conditions--admittedly a difficult road. (3) Enter actively and aggressively into the total social situation and seek to penetrate all social structures with Christian principles as much as possible.

53 Cf. Paul Peachy, "Early Anabaptists and Urbanism," *Proceedings of the Tenth Conference*

on Mennonite and Cultural Problems, Chicago, 1955, pp. 75-83. Peachey claims in this article that withdrawal is not a necessary implication of Anabaptism. It is a characteristic of "ethnic" Christianity. This is his thesis: "If the genius of Anabaptism is the creation and perpetuation of the distinctly religious community, and is thus involved in social heterogeniety, then the urban environment provides a more congenial setting for a vital Anabaptism than does the rural. The fact that Mennonites today are a rural people and can barely gain a foothold in the city indicates that ethnic forces have taken precedence over the religious as the dynamic of community." p. 82.

54 An extended treatment of the significance of Anabaptist studies in recent years and the exceptional contribution of Harold S. Bender is contained in a volume presented to Bender as a sixtieth anniversary tribute. Especially significant is the survey of Anabaptist historiography by Guy F. Hershberger in Chapter I and the statement of the unique work of Bender in Chapter II by Ernst H. Correll. *The Recovery of the Anabaptist Vision*, ed. by Guy F. Hershberger, pp. 1-28.

55 The "Anabaptist Vision" is the title given Harold S. Bender's presidential address before the American Society of Church History, December, 1943. *Church History*, XIII (March, 1944), pp. 3-24. This is accepted by many within the Mennonite church as a statement of the ideal which the modern Mennonite church should strive to recover.

56 Kermit Eby, a minister of the Chruch of the Brethren and Professor of Sociology at the University of Chicago, has urged Brethren educators to educate for sectarianism. He says, "If I were a Brethren educator, I would be avowedly sectarian. Otherwise why be a Brethren educator at all? I am convinced that deep in our heritage there are paricularistic values which are of transcendent importance." Kermit Eby, "Education for Sectarians," *Gospel Messenger*, Vol. 104 (April 23, 1955).

57 The word "culture" as it is used in the modern English speaking world needs to be defined. It is an extremely ambiguous word. "Culture" is used mainly in two ways. It sometimes refers to the artistic realm, i.e., to "activity in which the intellectual element is not a mere means to an end." Brunner, *op. cit.*, p. 483. However it is used in this thesis in a more comprehensive way. The write accepts the definition of Richard Niebuhr as follows: "What we have in view when we deal with Christ and culture is that total process of human activity and that total result of such activity to which now 'culture,' now the name 'civilization,' is applied in common speech. Culture is the 'artificial, secondary environment' which man superimposes on the natural. It comprises language, habits, ideas, beliefs, customs, social organization, inherited artifacts, technical processes, and values. Writers frequently had in mind when they spoke of 'the world,' which is represented in many forms but to which Christians like other men are inevitably subject, is what we mean when speak of culture." *Christ and Culture* (New York: Harper and Brothers, 1951), p. 32.

58 Richard Kroner, *Culture and Faith* (Chicago: University of Chicago Press, 1951).

59 Richard Niebuhr, *Christ and Culture*, Ch. I.

60 *Ibid.*, p. 1.

61 *Ibid.*, p. 10.

62 Cf. John Bright, *The Kingdom of God* (New York: Abingdom Press, 1953), Chapter VII.

63 Joseph Klausner, *Jesus of Nazareth* (London: George Allen and Unwin, Ltd., 1925, p. 390.

64 Cf. Oscar Cullmann, *The State in the New Testament* (New York: Charles Scribner's Sons, 1956), p. 24.

65 Cited by Reinhold Niebuhr, *An Interpretation of Christian Ethics*, p. 51.

66 Alfred North Whitehead, *Adventures of Ideas* (New York: Macmillan Company, 1933),

p. 18.

67 Reinhold Niebuhr, *An Interpretation of Christian Ethics*, p. 39.

68 *Ibid.*, p.41.

69 Cf. Reinhold Niebuhr's sermon entitled, "Transvaluation of Values," *Beyond Tragedy* (London: Nisbet and Company, 1938), pp. 197-213.

70 Richard Kroner sees the tension between Christ and culture arising out of the inheritance of a Greek civilization by Christians. "What else could arise under these circumstances than the most intense renewals of the tension between culture and faith." *op. cit., p. 258.*

71 Richard Niebuhr, *Christ and Culture*, p. 56.

72 Paul Peachy, "The Modern Recovery of the Anabaptis Vision,"*The Recovery of the Anabaptist Vision, op. cit.,* p. 334.

73 Cf. Paul Miniger, "Culture for Service," *MQR*, XXIX (January, 1955), p. 9. Ironically the Mennonites, whose peculiar emphasis in history has been separaton from the world are far more confident of finding a rational and ethically consistent solution to the problem of faith and culture than those who have entered the cultural domain and have been forced to find "paradoxical solutions." For example, Richard Kroner says, "Faith consummates culture, it integrates man and provides him with the means whereby he can overcome secular self-contradiciton. The antinomies of experience are thus solved not intellectually, but spiritually. However, this 'solution' paradoxically generates new tension, the tension between faith and the entire enterprise of culture. Because faith transencds the whole cultural horizon and surpasses the very meaning and fucntion of faith triumph over all cultural realsm by consummating them, but it makes civilization, as such, questionable." Kroner, *op. cit.*, p. 239.

74 Guy F. Hershberger, *War, Peace and Nonresistance*, rev. ed., Chapter IV.

CHAPTER 2
CHRISTIANITY AS DISCIPLESHIP

I. The Religious Basis of Social Doctrine

In the light of the tendency of certain scholars of the modern period to attribute social doctrine to secular origins,[1] Ernst Troeltsch made a significant contribution in *The Social Teachings of the Christian Churches* by his emphasis upon the role of the "fundamental religious idea." By the fundamental religious idea, Troeltsch meant the pure religious essence of the Gospel.[2] Troeltsch taught that the Gospel as a religious reality lies causally behind Christian social doctrine. It is a mistake to interpret the social doctrines of the churches simply by an empirical examination of economic, social and political affairs, or to assume that social reality gives rise to a religious element through reflex action. To the contrary, social teachings of the Christian churches arise out of theological understandings.

This does not deny the powerful influence of historical forces. A Christian social ethic is the adjustment of the Gospel to the general stream of culture. One of Troeltsch's major observations was the role of the "relative natural law," a means by which Christianity lives in the world of both nature and grace. A compromising attitude toward the relativities of social life was not only acknowledged by Troeltsch but emphasized as well. Nevertheless, he insisted that the starting point is the Gospel and therefore various social doctrines reflect various elements of the Gospel. When adjustments to social, economic and political realities are made, it is the peculiar understanding of the Gospel by the church which determines the extent and the nature of the adjustment and its justification. Therefore, when for example, Troeltsch began his discussion of the social teachings of the Reformation, he said: "For us the main point of interest is the result of the new religious idea of the Reformation. This...is our problem: in what did this change of Christian thought consist? What were the religious ideas, and what were their social results?"[3] Speaking specifically of Luther he stated that "Luther's religious ideas were not due to the reflex action of social, or even of economic, changes; they were based essentially and independently upon the religious idea, which alone gave rise to the social, economic and political consequences.... Only very indirectly can we here discern certain traces of the influence of social, economic and political causes."[4]

A study of the social ethics of the period of the Reformation reveals three major ethical systems based upon three interpretations of the Gospel, corresponding to the major traditions of the Reformation, namely Lutheranism, Calvinism and Anabaptism. Certainly the differences between Lutheranism and Calvinism are minor compared with the differences between the major reforming groups and the Anabaptists. But differences there are and they are due largely to the theological emphasis rather than to the social differences between Wittenberg, Geneva and Zürich.

A. *The Religious Ethic of Luther.* The social ethic of Luther was essentially an extension of Christianity interpreted anew in the light of his understanding of the relation of grace to law. Christianity for Luther was the experience of forgiveness through justification by faith. It was a revival of Pauline theology. Luther's social thought was intended to show how a "justified" man could be related to the permanent orders (*Ordnungen*) of the world. Admittedly Luther's ethic is a matter of dispute between those who go so far as to say that he had no ethic and those who attribute to him an ethic of "active love."[5] But whether his ethic is characterized by his doctrine of the "realms," or by the difference between personal and corporate morality, or by compromise, or by anti-perfectionistic emphasis upon the receding ideal or by his acceptance of the "Church Type" of politico-ecclesiastical organization, it should be remembered that all these aspects of his social ethics are made possible by a basic interpretation of Christianity as the experience of forgiveness. *It is grace which makes, for example, "compromise" possible.* It is the experience of forgiveness in the sight of God which makes it possible to participate in the guilt of "dual citizenship." It is the conception of the love of God in the experience of salvation which enables a man to love his neighbor. Therefore, since the foundation and pattern of his social ethics rest upon a religious base and particularly upon the doctrine of justification through faith, Luther's ethics may be called "justification ethics."

B. *The Religious Ethic of Calvin.* Calvin, on the other hand, thought of Christianity primarily as response to the sovereign grace of a Holy and Just God who wills obedience to his law in Christ. The central social conception of Calvin, namely the Holy Community, is a direct result of his idea of a Transcendent Will who has ordained a divine society to exhibit the moral qualities of His nature, namely active love and justice within a *dynamic* order.[6] Seldom in history has a more strenuous attempt been made to realize a comprehensive social ideal than in Geneva under Calvin's influence. It surpasses in cleanness of conception and rigor of administration any corresponding attempt to organize a Christian society during the Middle Ages. The Old Testament idea of theocracy which Calvin translated into the idea of Christocracy through the Lordship of Christ was the logical social expression of Calvin's fundamental conception of the nature of Christianity as obedience to the gracious sovereign Will of God.

II. *"Nachfolge"* -- The Central Idea of Anabaptism

A. *The Essence of Christianity.* We turn now to the central idea of

Anabaptist social thought. This writer accepts the view of Harold S. Bender which was articulated in an article entitled "The Anabaptist Vision" in which Bender states that: "First and fundamental in the Anabaptist vision was the concept of the essence of Christianity as discipleship." By discipleship he means "a way of life of the individual and society so that it may be fashioned after the teachings and example of Christ."[7] It is a life of regeneration, moral transformation, holiness and love in accordance with the New Testament ideal.[8] It is a return to the radical simplicity, the uncompromising purity and the culture of defying absolutism of Christ and His message of the Kingdom of God. It exalts the cross as a principle of life and fellowship among martyrs. It makes no provision for the structures of organized society. It defies the world as the Kingdom of God judges the world. Its direction and its spirit are eschatological and its hope is centered entirely in the order of redemption.

The term which the Anabaptists used for discipleship was *Nachfolge Christi*. This term is found repeatedly in Anabaptist documents. The "Schleitheim Confession," which was adopted in 1527 just two years after the beginnings of Anabaptism, expresses the motif of Nachfolge in simple terms as follows: "Christ teaches and commands us to learn of Him, for He is meek and lowly in heart and so shall we find rest unto our souls.... Thus shall we do as He did, and follow Him, and so shall we not walk in darkness. For He himself says, He who wishes to come after me, let him deny himself and take up his cross and follow me."[9] Anabaptists were interested as a matter of first importance in "participation" in the life of Christ. Every ethical question was answered by a precedent, a command or a principle derived from Christ. The simple statement, "Thus shall we do as He did," contains the fundamental ethical methodology of the Anabaptists. Christ is not only Saviour but He is also the Revealer of the divine will and most of all He is Lord. His Lordship implies absolute obedience to His commandments, especially those contained in the Sermon on the Mount.

To claim that Christianity is discipleship may appear to the modern reader to result in a mere tautology. Discipleship has become an ambiguous term. It clearly implies a basic loyalty to Christ, a spiritually motivated life but it does not necessarily imply a definite pattern of life. Do not the diverse and contradictory forms of life which have been approved by the Christian church prove that discipleship no longer designates a peculiar quality of life? The Popes, James I, Luther, St. Simeon Stylites, Menno Simons, countless crusaders, martyrs and even soldiers and inquisitors have been designated disciples. When used in this way, however, "discipleship" is meaningless. It simply reflects traditional bias. The Anabaptists, however, were intent on putting meaning into this term. They were not unlike Kierkegaard who pointed out that "when all are Christians, Christianity *eo ipso* does not exist.... If we are all Christians, the concept is annulled."[10] For Kierkegaard genuine Christianity is *determinate* and in this respect his *Attack Upon "Christendom"* bore striking similarities to the "dissent of the Anabaptists." Discipleship must take precise forms. Not anyone who says Lord, Lord is a disciple, but the one who *does* the will of God. Therefore to say that Christianity is discipleship is to speak of a

particular kind of life based upon absolute commitment, not to Christ as a figure to be worshiped, or to be believed or to be rescued by, but to be *obeyed*. In
this sense, the statement that Christianity is discipleship is not a tautology.

B. *Discipleship as Primitivism*. Anabaptism was a return to primitive
Christianity. It reached behind sixteen hundred years of history in search for
"pure" Christianity.[11]   Anabaptism rejected the Middle Ages and even
bypassed Paul and certain later writings of the New Testament in search for a
starting point. Anabaptism begins with the Synoptics and interprets the
Epistles in light of synoptic primitivism. This is one of the major differences
between Lutheranism and Anabaptism. Lutheran returned to Paul and interpreted Christ and the Kingdom of God from the standpoint of Paul's theology
of Grace. *This means that the problem of the problem of the Christian life is fundamentally different in Lutheranism, and to a lesser extent in Calvinism, than in
Anabaptism.* The problem of Lutheranism is the salvation of the soul. It is in
many respects more subtle, abstract and internal than the problem of the
Anabaptist. *The problem of Anabaptism is how to be obedient to the commands
of Christ and the "law of love."* Anabaptism thinks in terms supplied by Christ's
earthly ministry and the response of the disciples.

III. *Nachfolge* Outside the Anabaptist Tradition

Nachfolge Christi is really a variant on a theme of piety and literalism
which has characterized the lives of many of the great saints. The "imitation of
Christ" as a Christian pattern has appeared among the mystics and the
monastics and frequently reappears in times of moral and spiritual decay as a
kind of judgment upon the church as a whole. It is an aspect of Catholic piety.
Monasticism is the institution which is designed to make this kind of piety possible in the world. The most outstanding example of one who took Christ
literally was St. Francis. He was especially conscious of Christ's demands of
poverty. "Few, if any, after Jesus himself have exemplified such total renunciation as did Francis of Assisi. The poverty which this humble man adopted was
as close to an approximation to that of Christ as he could discover and apply."[12]
Another great approximation of Christ was Thomas a' Kempis, who has done
more to uphold the idea of imitation than any other saint. The opening
sentence of his famous devotional book exhibits the basic concept of *Nachfolge*.
"He who follows Me, walks not in darkness,"says the Lord. By these words of
Christ we are advised to imitate His life and habits, if we wish to be truly
enlightened and free from all blindness of heart."[13]

The imitation of Christ of Thomas a' Kempis is, however, of a different
quality from the imitation upheld by the Anabaptists. The former concentrates
more on the cultivation of inward piety, the beauty and tenderness of the soul
which is dedicated to spiritual things. It is mystical in nature and it leads to the
withdrawn life of the monastery where contemplation and renunciation are
encouraged. Harold Bender has criticized Thomas a' Kempis' idea of discipleship from the point of view of the Anabaptists. He prefers the more
aggressive, external, and socially critical, as well as socially creative, character

of Anabaptism. Bender says:

> Basically this is mysticism mixed with asceticism. The social dimension is almost entirely lacking, and criticism of the total social and cultural order with a view to the establishment of a full Christian order in the brotherhood and church of the living Christ in the midst of the present world is missing. This type of 'following' Christ does not meet the fullness and richness of the New Testament concept, and is not at all the Anabaptist idea. Thomas a' Kempis and all those many who follow in his train evade the conflict with the world, avoid the constructive labor of establishing the true church, and thus escape the real cross-bearing experience of true discipleship. There is more kinship between Thomas and the later Pietists than the Anabaptists.[14]

What Bender is referring to is the monastic quality of Thomas a' Kempis' imitation of Christ. This is imitation within the walls of an order so dedicated and so recognized by the world that conflict with the world is really avoided. Anabaptists, on the other hand, defied the world; they were basically opposed to the world order and aggressively struggled against the main cultural currents.

Another type of discipleship is that of the Spiritualists of the Reformation--men such as Schwenckfeld and Sebastian Franck.[15] To these men Christianity was primarily the enjoyment of mystical piety. They sought to follow Christ but they found him through inward experience and commitment and not so much in external forms or in concrete ethical decision.

The social implications of this kind of Christianity so impressed Troeltsch that he regarded it as a major "Type" to be contrasted with both the Church and the Sect.[16] The Spiritualists arose in protest against the characteristic failures of both the "Church Type" and the "Sect Type." It attempted to off-set the externalism, the structural rigidity, traditionalism and mass mediocrity of the Church by the formation of spiritual fellowship groups within the "invisible church." These groups became intimate circles for personal inward sharing in freedom. Organizational structure and authoritarianism were replaced by the indeterminacy of the Holy Spirit. They attempted to off-set the divisive ethical strictness of the Sect by a less rigid interpretation of the Sermon on the Mount and by less emphasis upon the external realization of Christ's commands. Furthermore evangelical spiritualism avoided discipline and for the most part the Spiritualists attempted to avoid an open break with the Church.[17]

Recent scholarship has clearly revealed a cleavage between the Anabaptists and the Spiritualists concerning the meaning of discipleship,[18] notwithstanding subsequent interaction between these two movements. Robert Friedmann has traced this relationship in his authoritative book entitled *Mennonite Piety Through the Centuries*.[19] The main point of the original tension, however, was the extent to which discipleship implies an ethically committed and socially critical ecclesiastical body. The sect is by nature nonconformed and this nonconformity goes beyond the inner life of the individual. It involves a new social order with a cultural emphasis of its own which is always in conflict with the general stream of life. The Spiritualists had a "strong sense...of deep opposition to the world, a hatred of the carnal and selfish worldly temper; in this respect it was much closer to the ascetic ideal than were the churches. As a movement, however, it lacked the element of asceticism, the legalistic spirit and the practice or regular discipline.... This form of spirituality is remote...from that of the Anabaptists and the Mennonites."[20]

The difference between Spiritualism and Anabaptism is demonstrated most forcibly by the polemical writings between Schwenckfeld and Pilgrim Marpeck, the greatest Anabaptist theologian. To Marpeck and his colleagues the "Stillstand," as they called the Spiritualists, looked like deliberate cowardice in the face of the sufferings of those who took the Biblical covenant and ordinances seriously. According to Marpeck:

> Schwenckfeld errt nur das innerlich und denVerklerten herlichen unleidenden Christum im hymel und nit den leydenden auf erden, ja nur das wort von seiner glori und herligkeit und nit von seinem kreuz und trüebsol, wie ers also haubt vor der verklerung und hymelfart hot trogen und noch heut seinem unverklerten leib zu tragen gebürt.[21]

The Anabaptists, though conscious of the primacy of the Holy Spirit, were convinced that the spiritual and the material, the inner and the outer, the essence and the form of religion cannot be separated.[22]

We come now to a discussion of the particular elements of the Anabaptist conception of discipleship which are especially relevant for our study of the Mennonite attitude toward social and political responsibility. They are as follows: (1) Discipleship as suffering and insecurity; (2) Discipleship as the exercise of love and nonresistance; (3) Discipleship and the "Great Commission;" (4) Discipleship and culture.

IV. Discipleship as Suffering

The most obvious fact to the student of Anabaptist history is the fact of suffering. The blood of the martyrs appears on almost every page of Anabaptist writings. Suffering is both a part of their history and an integral part of their theology. Christianity and persecution go hand in hand. Those who avoid suffering are looked upon with suspicion as cowards who shrink from the cross. Christianity is interpreted as "heroic suffering." Suffering is the place of the ultimate struggle between powers of good and evil. Suffering for Christ's sake advances the Kingdom of God. Conrad Grebel, founder of the Swiss Anabaptist movement, said:

> Rechte glaubige Christen sind schaff mitten under den wölffen, schaff der schlachtung, müssend in angst und nott, trübsal, verfol-

gung, liden und sterben getoufft warden. Und ob du darumb liden müsstest, weist wol, das es nit anderss mag sein. Christus muss noch mer liden in seinen glideren.[23]

Before enlarging on the Anabaptist theology of suffering, we must establish the fact of their suffering and the extent of their suffering.

A. *The Historical Occasion*. The occasion of their suffering was the persecution of religious minorities by Catholic, Lutheran and Reformed parties before the days of religious toleration, during the 16th and 17th centuries. Anabaptism was a capital crime. Anabaptists were persecuted with a severity which may have surpassed the persecution of the early Christians in Rome. The manner of persecution included banishment, confiscation of property, the denial of citizenship, imprisonment and death by fire, water and sword. Torture by methods normally associated with the Inquisition became the lot of thousands of Anabaptists. In spite of the fact that Luther and Zwingli condemned Romish intolerance during the earlier part of their reformatory labors, their enthusiasm for freedom of conscience was soon turned into bitter hatred for dissenters when they faced the practical implication of tolerance for the principle of the unity of the church and the state.

The reason for the severity of persecution of dissenters by Christian authorities resides in the Mediaeval and Reformation conception of Christian civilization.[24] When the total order including the church and the state is organically united, religious dissent is a threat to the foundation of the entire religio-social order. Religious dissent is virtually unthinkable in view of the ideal of the *corpus christianum* which ties together social, political and religious affairs into an organic unity. At the time of the Reformation the structure of religio-political unity was being shifted from a Catholic to a Protestant basis. The shift was not one of basic principle however since the idea of the unity of Christian civilization which informed the Middle Ages was retained by the Reformers.[25] Persecution of religious minorities was not due to the absence of liberal democratic ideas as such. Nor was it the result of political ineptitude which lacked the characteristic art of modern democratic states of balancing the interests of the individual and society or to hold in dynamic constructive tension the essentials of any great socio-political system, namely freedom and order. The problem lay in the fundamental theory of the *corpus christianum*, the theory of the unity of Christian civilization which can be retained beyond a certain point only by the use of force.

The first noted Anabaptist victim of persecution was Felix Manz. The persecution of Manz was typical of a long list whose records of torture and death are contained in various Anabaptist chronicles. Here is C. Henry Smith's account of the death of Manz, an event which gave the signal to all Anabaptists that they stand in the line of the martyrs:

> On January 5, 1527, with hands tied to his knees so as to prevent any possible escape from the water, accompanied by a Reformed clergyman who tried to the last to secure a recantation, the unhappy

man was rowed to the town hall in Zurich down the Limmat, his mother and brother following along the banks shouting words of encouragement. Just where the Limmat broadens into beautiful Lake Zurich, reflecting the blue sky above and the deep green hills along the shore, just about where the upper bridge now spans the stream, Manz uttering his last prayer, "Father into thy hands I commit my soul," was tossed overboard and disappeared beneath the waves, the first of a long line of martyrs who preferred to die rather than give up their faith. On the same day George Blaurock as an alien, "stripped to the waist" was whipped out of town.[26]

Among the early leaders of the evangelical brothers who were killed were George Blaurock, Hans Lüdi, Hans Brötti, Leonhard Schiemer, Jerome Köls, Jacob Hutter, Wolfgang Brandhuber and Thomas Herman.[27]

Convinced that the struggle with Catholicism was "but child's play" compared with the struggle with Anabaptism, Zwingli approved a policy of dreadful severity which was adopted not only in Switzerland, South Germany, and Thuringia but in all the Austrian lands as well as in the Low Countries. The period of most intense suffering was from 1527-1560. In 1529 a decree was issued by the Diet of Spires passing sentence of death upon all Anabaptists, detailing that every Anabaptist and rebaptized person of either sex should be put to death by fire, sword or some other way. This decree was reinvoked and intensified. In 1551 the Diet of Augsburg issued a decree requiring the judges and jurors who had scruples against putting Anabaptists to death to be deprived of their positions and punished.

The intensity of persecution indicates the strength of the Anabaptist movement and the extent to which Anabaptism had invaded the ranks of the common people. In 1531 Bullinger wrote that "the people were running after them as though they were the living saints"[28] and Sebastian Franck wrote in the same year, "The Anabaptists spread so rapidly that their teaching soon covered the land as it were. They soon gained a large following, and baptized thousands, drawing to themselves many sincere souls who had a zeal for God.... They increased so rapidly that the world feared an uprising then though I have learned that this fear had no justification whatsoever."[29] Eventually the ordinary processes of detection and correction proved inadequate to cope with the spread of Anabaptism and so courts and trials were abandoned in many instances. Armed executioners and mounted soldiers were sent out into the land to track down Anabaptists in the villages and mountains with order to "kill them on the spot" singly or *en masse* without trial. In the Providence of Swabia, in South Germany, four hundred mounted soldiers were, in 1528, sent against the Anabaptists with orders to kill them at sight. This proved too small a number and so the army was increased to eight hundred and later one thousand.[30] The Mennonite historian, John Horsch, reports that in various provinces an imperial provost marshal by the name of Berthold Aichele, with his assistants, put many Anabaptists to death. On Christmas day, 1531, he drove seventeen men and women into a farm house near Aalen in Wurttemberg and burned the building together with the inmates. Three hundred and fifty Anabaptists were executed in the Palatinate before the year 1530. The Count of Alzey, in that province, after having put many to death, was heard to exclaim: "What shall I do? The more I kill the greater becomes the number."[31]

It cannot be denied that the Anabaptists had a vision and an enthusiasm which was contagious and their moral rectitude frequently put their persecutors to shame. The masses were impressed by a genuineness of religious concern and by their courageous disregard for safety. Seldom has Christianity produced such valiant willingness to die for the truth. When Michael Hassel died in prison at Hohenwittling in Wurttemberg, the warden is reported to have said: "If this man did not get to heaven, I shall despair of the courage even to knock at Heaven's gate."[32] In Zwingli's last book against the Anabaptists, written in 1527, he wrote, "If you investigate their life and conduct, it seems at first contact irreproachable, pious, unassuming, attractive, yea, above this world. Even those who are inclined to be critical will say that their lives were excellent."[33]

Persecution took place first in Switzerland and South Germany but eventually it spread to the Low Countries. It is estimated that Dutch martyrs numbered 1500. Menno Simons wrote appreciatively, however, about a few tolerant princes and magistrates. The following quotation from Menno Simons reveals both the pathos of suffering and the consolation of occasional kindness:

> If the merciful Lord did not, in His great love, temper the hearts of the magistrates, but if they should proceed according to partisan instigation and blood-preaching of the earned ones, no pious person could endure. But as it is, some are found who, notwithstanding the railing and the writing of the learned ones, suffer and bear with the miserable, and for a time show them mercy, a thing for which we will ever give praise to God, the most High, and express our gratitude to such kind and fair governors.[34]

The first country to offer religious toleration to the Mennonites was Holland. The last martyr was burned to death in Friesland in 1574.[35] When William of Orange came to power, Mennonites were given considerable freedom and were soon recognized as an asset to the civil community. But in South Germany, Switzerland and Moravia, Anabaptism as a vital living force was exhausted. It was consigned to the outlying districts, a scattering of fugitive congregations, with its vision and enthusiasm crushed. "The descendants of the seven or eight hundred exiles who crossed into the Palatinate between 1671 and 1711, only a part of whom came to Pennsylvania, now (1945) number over a hundred thousand, while the descendants of those who remained in Switzerland and were saved for the Mennonite faith count up hardly more than fifteen hundred."[36]

B. *A Literature of Martyrdom.* This fiery ordeal which nearly exterminated the Anabaptists has left a vast literature of martyrdom found in

such works as (1) *The Complete Writings of Menno Simons* (2) *Martyr's Mirror*
(3) *Die Älteste Chronik der Hutterischen Brüder* (4) *Ausbund* and (5) *Lieder der
Hutterischen Brüder*. The most outstanding of these is *Martyr's Mirror* by
Theileman J. van Braght. The complete title of this significant and beloved
Mennonite volume is *The Bloody Theater or Martyr's Mirror of the Defenseless
Christians Who Baptized Only Upon Confession of Faith, and Who Suffered and
Died for the Testimony of Jesus, Their Savior, From the Time of Christ to the
Year A.D. 1660.*[37] This is a collection of thousands of martyr stories from the
beginning of Christian history to the time of its compilation in 1669. It
represents the work of a prominent Dutch Mennonite who died at the age of
thirty-nine in 1664. The book is divided chronologically; stories of martyrs are
grouped by centuries.

The stories begin with the beheading of John the Baptist and continue
with illustrated accounts of the stoning of Stephen, the beheading of James, the
burning of Barnabas, Mark dragged to the stake and the beheading of Paul.
All these and many others are illustrated in stark realism which leaves nothing
for the imagination. Detailed court records, accounts of disputations, personal
letters sent from prisons are included. No attempt is made to cover the cruelty
of the oppressors nor the paradoxical docility of defenseless Christians who
would not hurt anyone but who would not compromise an inch for the sake of
peace. Sometimes the accounts are colored by a miraculous or romantic tinge.
There is the case of Leonard Keyser whose body could not be burned and so
he had to be cut into pieces and thrown into the river. Imaginations of martyrs
were vivid. Each instance of "heroic suffering" was considered an eschatological event. Each slain sheep witnessed to the "truth" and each execution
brought the Kingdom nearer. Despite certain melodramatic tendencies, the
Martyr's Mirror is a valuable source for the theology of suffering. The fact that
the Mennonite church devoted itself to the collection and illustration of stories
of horror indicates more than a morbid psychology. It indicates a profound
believe in a theology of the two Kingdoms, the *Civitas Dei* and the *Civitas
Diaboli* of St.Augustine, though with an eschatological rigor which went
beyond Augustine.

Mention should also be made of the *Hutterian Chronicle*.[38] The Hutterites were more history-minded than other groups of Anabaptists. In the
house of the *Vorsteher* historical records were kept with diligence. Speeches,
confessions, correspondence and especially their sufferings were recorded.
The *Great Chronicle*, as it is usually called, is noted also for its hymns. These
hymns are valuable for their accounts and interpretation of suffering.

The *Ausbund*[39] is the oldest hymnbook of the Swiss Brethren and is still
used by the Amish in America. A large section is devoted to martyr hymns.
Hymns were written by such early martyrs, around 1527, as Felix Manz,
Michael Sattler, Hans Hut. Other martyr hymns were written by later martyrs
such as Leonard Schiemer, Hans Schlaffer, George Blaurock and Hans
Leuphold. These hymns reveal the soul of Anabaptism. They were written "at
the foot of the cross."

C. *The Theology of Suffering*. We come now to a consideration of the theology of suffering and temporal insecurity. In an article by Ethelbert Stauffer entitled "Täufertum und Martyrertheologie" appearing in *Zeitschrift für Kirchengeschichte*[40] we find an analysis of Anabaptist suffering as martyr theology. Stauffer shows that the Anabaptists regarded themselves as participants in a long line of martyrs beginning with the Maccabees during the second century B.C. This line of martyrs includes the saints of God who have successfully withstood the devil and his agents as the cosmic struggle between the forces of good and evil is continued in the body and the soul of God's children. This line goes back to the beginning of history. Abel was the first to advance in the direction of the Kingdom. All people before and after Christ who suffered for the "truth" were united to Christ. "Von Anfang sind die Heiligen all umb Christi willen gestorbin hie."[41] The root idea of the Theology of Martyrdom has been summarized by Stauffer as follows:

> Es ist der uralte Widerstreit zwischen göttlicher und dämonischer Ordnung, der in der Verfolgung des Gottesvolks jetzt seine letzte Schärfe erreicht. Darum sind die Heiligen, die in der Arena zu Tode gefoltert werden, die Agonisten Gottes, die letztlich mit dem Satan selber ringen. Wo aber dieser Kampf durchgehalten wird bis aufs Blut, da wird der Tod zum Sieg. Der Märtyrer, der sein unschuldiges Leben dahingegeben hat, wird zum Sühnopfer fur die Sünden seines Volkes und zum Wegbereiter einer neuen Zeit. Zugleich aber ist der Tod der Heiligen das drohende Zeugnis gegen die Verfolger, über sich hinausweisend in die Zukunft. Sobald der letzte Märtyrer gefallen und die Zahl der Blutzeugen voll ist, wird der Tag der Vergeltung hereinbrechen, den Märtyrern ein Tag der Herrlichkeit, den Verfolgern ein Tag der Schrecken. Sie werden sehen, in wem sie gestochen haben, und die so lang verborgene macht Gottes nun am eigenen Leibe erfahren. So kommt im Martyrium der Heiligen der kosmische Kampf zwischen Gott und Widergott zugleich zum entscheidenden Ausbruch und zum entscheidenden Sieg. Das Martyrium ist verstanden in seiner ätiologischen und teleologischen Notwendigkeit.[42]

The Cross of Christ is the supreme instance of the theology of martyrdom. This is not to say that the Anabaptists regarded Jesus as a martyr. All the martyrs stand beneath the cross. Jesus is not a model but rather an archetype whose victory over Satan on Calvary guaranteed the ultimate victory of the Kingdom and gave martyrdom a theological significance. Thus the Anabaptists saw in Christ's death a cosmic significance which would be complete only when suffering had run its course in the saints. Baptism for the Anabaptists was a baptism unto death in accordance with Jesus' interpretation of baptism. "I have a baptism to be baptized with..." (Luke 12:50). Jesus offered the disciples a baptism of blood. The cross was a dreadful reality to be endured before glory. Sometimes Jesus spoke of his death as a "cup." He asked His disciples, "Are you able to drink the cup...?" (Matt. 20:22). According to Mark's Gospel, Jesus taught the disciples that He must "suffer many things...and be killed." This was followed with the charge to take up the cross as a condition of discipleship. "If any man would come after me, let him deny himself and take up his cross and follow me" (Mark 8:31-35). Clearly the call to follow and to bear the cross are one and the same. Just as Jesus *must* bear the cross, so *must* his disciples. Dietrich Bonhoeffer, commenting on this passage in a manner reminiscent of the Anabaptists, wrote:

> Jesus must therefore make it clear beyond all doubt that the "must" of suffering applies to His disciples no less than to Himself. Just as Christ is Christ only in virtue of his suffering and rejection, so the disciple is a disciple only in so far as he shares His Lord's suffering and rejection and crucifixion. Discipleship means adherence to the person of Jesus, and therefore submission to the Law of Christ. In other words, it means the cross.[43]

Furthermore, the Gospel of John reports Christ as saying that the grain of wheat must die if it will bring forth fruit (John 12:24). The Book of Hebrews exalts the *via dolorosa* as the way of true believers throughout history in a style not unlike that of the histories of martyrs, such as *The Martyr's Mirror*. And Paul declares that he has "suffered the loss of all things" so that he "may know him and the power of his resurrection, and may share his sufferings, become like him in his death" (Phil. 3:10).

It is clear that suffering is an essential part of the experience of discipleship as described in the New Testament and this is the basis for the theology of martyrdom. This theology remained alive in the early church. Ethelbert Stauffer says that the martyr theology remained alive as long as the church remained a martyr church. However, when persecution was replaced by the Constantinian accord between the church and the state, this theology became a matter of history.[44] It is true that it remained an undercurrent of Catholic piety but it emerged primarily among heretical groups. It became the theology of the sects. Luther was taken up with the moods and ideas of martyrdom during the early days of his work as a reformer. In 1523, upon hearing of two young Augustinian monks who were burned at the stake in Brussels, he exclaimed, "Ich vermeint, ich sollte ja der erste sein, der um dieses heiligen Evangeliums wegen sollte gemartert werden; aber ich bin des nit würdig gewesen!"[45] Luther composed a martyr hymn under the impact of this event, "Eyne hubsch Lyed von zweyen Marteren Christi zu Brussel von den Sophisten zu Loven verbrant."[46] Thus, in the early days of the Reformation, Luther was taken up with the idea that God's almighty power was expressed essentially in the deeds of the martyrs. This view, however, changed when he established a state church in accordance with Constantinian principles inherited from the Middle Ages. Then he distinguished between "true" martyrdom and "false" martyrdom. The martyrs in Protestant countries were "falsche Merterer...Rottengeister, Widerteuffer, und der gleichen." The change in Luther can be accounted for by factors other than the state church. Luther's basic conception of Christianity as the experience of forgiveness through justification by faith resulted in a conception of inner suffering (*Anfechtungen*) which depreciated the traditional *imitatio Christi* interpretation. More will be said about Luther's conception of suffering later in this chapter.

Suffering for the Anabaptists was the inevitable price of discipleship. Menno Simons said that:

> It can never be otherwise...than that all who wish to obey and follow Jesus Christ...must first deny themselves wholeheartedly and then sacrifice all that they have. They must take upon themselves the heavy cross of all poverty, distress, disdain, sorrow, sadness, and must so follow the rejected, the outcast, the bleeding and crucified Christ.... Yes any man who is not ready for this hated and scorned life of the cross and sorrow, and who does not hate father and mother, son and daughter, husband and wife, houses and lands, money and goods, and his life moreover, cannot be the Lord's disciple.[47]

The Christian lives under the cross just as Christ lived under the cross before he died. The theological point of view is that the cross of Christ is the supreme revelation of God as love. This revelation of the nature of God, however, is not to become the subject of speculation for the *Schriftgelehrten*. This cannot be understood by theological thought. It is, rather, to be understood by experience in the life of the believer. One can know Christ only when he is in the way with Christ and supremely when he dies with Christ. The Anabaptists were critical of state churches for they had accepted the cross as an object of faith but not as a principle of discipleship.

Furthermore, the Anabaptists associated martyrdom with the revelation of "truth." Truth is revealed when men and women suffer for Christ's sake. The characteristic expression for God's revelation is not the *Word* as in Lutheranism but "truth." What the Anabaptists held before the world was what they regarded as the truth and, strangely enough, the highest expression of the truth was precisely the apparent defeat of truth in martyrdom.

> Die weil das Wort die Wahrheit war,
> So machts die Welt nit leiden.[48]

Although they believed that suffering love would eventually be translated into triumphant love and that truth would prevail over evil, in this age truth is revealed only in weakness and defeat.

A cosmic conception of suffering appears in certain hymns. One is reminded of Paul's passage in Romans 8:22 where mention is made of the groaning creation waiting for the revealing of the sons of God. Anabaptists frequently came to the conclusion that the principle of pain has infected the entire universe including the created order. All creation is caught in the throes of anguish.

> All Creatur bezeugen das
> Was lebt in Wasser, Luft und Gras
> Durch Leiden mus es enden.[49]

The Christian is confident that suffering will finally end but it cannot end until the Devil has been defeated by the heroic patience of the Godly.[50]

> Wer dann in Gottes Man nit will,
> Der mus zuletzt in Teufels Ziel
> Mit schwer 'm Gewissen enden.[51]

One of the deepest motives in the theology of martyrdom is the problem of theodicy. "Why this suffering?" was a question deep in the hearts of these people. The Anabaptists were personally involved in the deepest problem of theology and philosophy with their own lives. Their lives bore witness to a profound seriousness which was grounded in an "existential" awareness of the limits of finitude and the depth of sin. They were impressed by the shortness of life, the principle of pain and death. Instruments of torture occupied their minds. The "cruel sword" and the "horrible tongs" stood for the fact that the devil is still in this world. They lived in apocalyptic awareness of the issues of life and history.

D. *Comparison with Luther's Concept of Suffering.* In recent years the works of Luther have had a profound influence upon theological thought. One of the elements of Lutheran theology which is emphasized is *theologia crucis*. We must briefly compare Luther's conception of Christian suffering with the Anabaptist conception of suffering.

It must be stated that Luther did not mean by *theologia crucis* what the Anabaptists meant by "taking up the cross." The difference is revealed by the fact that when Luther spoke of *conformitas Christi* he did not mean the same as *imitatio Christi.* Conformity did not mean willful duplication of the life and passion of Christ. Conformity to Christ was dreadful resignation to the Holy Spirit as the condition of the sinner before a Perfect and Almighty God. The cross was that humiliation which must be suffered before healing can take place.

The suffering of the cross was, for Luther, inner conflict. It was the feeling of guilt or the feeling that one was forced into a narrow pass from which there was no escape. Of Luther's inner experience Roland Bainton writes:

> Luther's tremor was augmented by the recognition of unworthiness. "I am dust and ashes and full of sin!" Creatureliness and imperfection alike oppressed him. Toward God he was at once attracted and repelled. Only in harmony with the Ultimate could he find peace. But how could a pygmy stand before divine Majesty; how could a transgressor confront divine holiness? Before God the high and God the holy, Luther was stupefied.... The word he used

was Anfechtung.... It may be a trial sent by God to test man, or an assault of the devil to destroy man. It is all the doubt, turmoil, pang, tremor, panic, despair, desolation, and desperation which invade the spirit of man.[52]

Regin Prenter says, "What Luther has to say about inner conflict is...closely connected with the very heart of his whole conception of Christianity."[53] He quotes Luther as saying, "Wenn ich noch eine Weile leben sollt, wollt ich ein Buch von Anfechtungen schreiben, ohne welche kann kein Mensch weder die Schrift verstehen noch Gottesfurcht und Leibe erkennen, ja, er kann nicht wissen, was Geist ist."[54] Prenter points out that Luther neither regarded inner conflict as a psychological abnormality nor a sign of a diseased state of mind. It is the way God accomplishes his purposes of revealing to man his true state as a sinner. In this respect inner conflict is inevitable.

Numerous parallels between the Anabaptist interpretation of suffering could be drawn. Both see the utter necessity of suffering but the former thinks of suffering primarily as physical pain, loss of life, loss of possessions, the denial of life's natural and social securities, the loss of social approval, while the latter thinks of suffering primarily in terms of guilt, humiliation, the resignation of one's independence and one's egoistic pride to the sovereignty of God's grace. The former is grounded most directly in the Gospels and the latter most directly in Paul. The former interprets the Christian life as active volitional fulfillment of God's will whereas the latter interprets the Christian life essentially as resignation. From the former, Luther feared Pharisaical pride, "the problem of monastic piety." From the latter, the Anabaptists feared moral indifference and what Bonhoeffer has called "cheap grace." Both Anabaptist-Mennonite and Lutheran traditions give ample ground for both fears. It cannot be denied that Anabaptism soon developed into a rigid legalism or a hypermoralism, eventually threatening the evangelical doctrine of salvation by grace. With respect to Lutheranism one needs only to accept a fraction of Kierkegaard's criticism of the Danish state church to realize what can happen to a church which falls into the illusion of identifying "ordinary Christianity" with discipleship.

The Anabaptist view of suffering should also be compared briefly with Kierkegaard's conception. Here we are again involved in comparing the Anabaptist conception of Christianity as discipleship with the Lutheran conception of Christianity as guilt and forgiveness. For Kierkegaard, suffering was a central category.[55] But what did he mean by suffering? Certainly Kierkegaard did not mean by suffering the ordinary misfortunes which may come to any man regardless of who he is or what he believes. Bearing the cross is quite different from suffering a physical illness. "Essential suffering" is not even suffering for Christ in the sense of deliberate sacrifice or submission to martyrdom. Despite all that Kierkegaard had to say about the state church and the careless living which existed under that system (it would be wrong to say that Kierkegaard was a crypto-Anabaptist calling for a free church system) and despite the fact that no one else since the Anabaptists has so urgently and persistently directed the eyes of Christendom to the lofty ideals of Christ as Kierkegaard, it is abundantly clear that Kierkegaard did not define suffering in the ultimate sense as martyrdom or any kind of loss of property or reputation. In fact, Kierkegaard, though pointing up the tension which exists between genuine discipleship and ordinary life within "Christendom" was the first to deny martyrdom as in any sense corresponding to a Christian ideal. Kierkegaard insisted that a man does not have the right to let himself be killed since this is to make a murderer of the other man. Jesus is the exception, of course, because he was the unique Son of God who died for the sins of others. The Christian martyr, in other words, needs to be forgiven for not having found a more amicable solution to the problem than can be provided by his death. Martyrdom is something which must be thrust upon the Christian, somehow beyond his control. It should be in the hands of God alone. The kind of life a Christian lives so far as external relationships is concerned is largely a matter of Providence, or as Luther would define the Christian life, in terms of the "station." In the last analysis, Kierkegaard is socially and ecclesiastically a good Lutheran.

"Essential suffering," as Martin J. Heinecken points out in his volume, *The Moment Before God*, consists in the Christian's "inability to give outward expression...to his infinite resignation, i.e., the detachment of his heart from worldly loves."[56] Essential suffering is the experience of humiliation which the Christian experiences when he contemplates the infinite gulf between what he knows to be God's perfect will in Christ and his inability to realize this in real life. It is the tension between the inner spiritual awareness of God's demands and what is implied by naming the name of Christ. Suffering is the inability to prove to the world that one is a Christian. Suffering is the knowledge that one cannot get rid of sin even by giving his body to be burned. Therefore this suffering is quite independent of a man's earthly lot. Good fortune may actually provide the occasion for a more intense awareness of the contradiction between the ideal and the performance than misfortune. This may have been the case of Kierkegaard's father who attributed his business success to divine punishment for cursing God in a moment of despair. This is the kind of suffering in which all sensitive Christians participate. Kierkegaard, despite all that he had to say about the Christian life in his *Attack Upon "Christendom,"* despite his insistence that "Grace...must never be used to suppress or diminish the requirement; for in that case Grace must turn Christianity upside down,"[57] claimed that the Christian should for all practical purposes accept his "vocation" in the typical Lutheran sense, whether this meant poverty or wealth, pain or pleasure, marriage or celibacy. For the Anabaptists this kind of "dialectical" thought would have been considered double talk. Internal suffering without outward implications was regarded by men such as Pilgram Marpeck as cowardice. The Anabaptists would have encouraged Kierkegaard, in view of the fact that he saw that the life and piety of the State Church is not Christianity, to advocate a genuine reform with logical external implications. But this is advice which comes from the other wing of the Reformation where quite a different conception of Christianity informed the matters of *practical* conduct.

This is no place to make a final judgment regarding the merits of one conception of suffering as compared with the other. Kierkegaard's conception of suffering is profound and subtle. It is a view which fits the circumstances of Christian civilization, i.e., it is the view which is calculated to make responsible participation in a total Christian order possible despite its ambiguity, though it needs to be remembered that Kierkegaard did not regard himself a Christian; he was becoming a Christian.

One can only wonder what form the conversation would have taken if Kierkegaard could have visited Anna of Rotterdam, an imprisoned Anabaptist mother as she prepared a letter for her son, Isaiah, on the 24th of January, 1539 before she died the martyr's death. For, in this encounter two kinds of "existentialism," representing the deepest and the best in two great Christian traditions, would have come face to face--the unlearned, simple but strong martyr faith of Anna, and the learned, dialectical, despairing faith of Kierkegaard. Here are excerpts from Anna's "pathetic" letter in which the theology of martyrdom is heard with apocalyptic overtones:

> My son, hear the instruction of your mother; open your ears to hear the instruction of my mouth. Behold I go today the way of the prophets, apostles and martyrs, and drink of the cup of which they all have drunk. I go, I say, the way which Christ Jesus...Himself went...and who drank of this cup, even as he said, "I have a cup to drink of, and a baptism to be baptized with; and am I straightened until it be accomplished!" Having passed through, He calls His sheep, and His sheep hear His voice, and follow Him withersoever He goes.
>
> This way was trodden by the dead under the alter, who cry saying: Lord, Almighty, God, when wilt thou avenge the blood that has been shed? White robes were given unto them, and it was said to them; Wait yet a little season, until the number of your brethren that are yet to be killed for the testimony of Jesus, be filled.
>
> But where you hear of a poor, simple, cast-off little flock (Luke 12:32), which is despised and rejected by the world, join them; for where you hear of the cross, there is Christ."[58]

What would Kierkegaard have advised Anna? Would he have advised her of her responsibility as a mother of Isaiah? Would he have advised her to go home and fill her vocation? Would he have detected in her a subtle sense of personal accomplishment called pride? Would he have persuaded her that she has really not faced the full implications of the Christian ethic even by giving her body to be burned? If she would really understand the infinity of God's demands, she might know that she cannot hope, even by her martyrdom, to fulfill God's law. Would he have told her of the uniqueness of the incarnate Christ and that only Christ is really expected to live by His ethic? On the other hand, might he not have refused to give her counsel? For, in the last analysis, practical Christian conduct according to Kierkegaard is a matter of personal responsibility and decision. The practical side of his Christian ethics is not *determinate* in nature and cannot be stated in the form of principles. A decision is made by an individual in the moment before God and not in conformity to a law. Possibly the major difference between Anna and Kierkegaard is that the former claimed to *be* a Christian and the latter claimed to be *becoming* a Christian. Was Kierkegaard who, except for his mysterious reluctance to marry, lived the life of the gentleman by enjoying fine cigars, excellent wine, the theater, the Deer Park, and elegant parties, though inwardly ill at ease, the Christian in disguise?[59]

Endnotes

[1] Cf. Karl Kautsky, *Die Vorläufer des neueren Sozialismus* (Stuttgart: J. H. W. Dietz, 1895). Also Eduard Bernstein, *Sozialismus und Demokratie in der grossen englischen Revolution* (Stuttgart: J. H. W. Dietz, 1922). Kautsky and Bernstein were interested particularly in the supposed connection between Christianity and socialistic and communistic movements. They are among the most radical and utopian interpreters of Christian social developments. H. Richard Niebuhr attempted to show the connection between social movements and denominationalism but from a far more moderate point of view. Cf. Niebuhr, *The Social Sources of Denominationalism* (New York: H. Holt and Co., 1929).

[2] *The Social Teachings of the Christian Churches*, Vol. I, p. 51.

[3] *Ibid.*, II, p. 465.

[4] *Ibid.*, pp. 465-466.

[5] A summary of the diverse interpretations of Luther's ethic is to be found in George Wolfgang Forell, *Faith Active in Love* (New York: American Press, 1954), pp. 16-43.

[6] Cf. Troeltsch, *STCC*, II, pp. 588ff. Also Max Weber, "Die protestantischen Ethik und der Geist des Kapitalismu," *Gesammelte Aufsätze zur Religionssoziologie*, I, pp. 100ff.

[7] Harold S. Bender, "The Anabaptist Vision," *Church History* XIII (March, 1944), p. 14.

[8] This is the view of Johannes Kühn. Kühn claims that *Nachfolge* is the central idea of Anabaptism. "Diese Zentralidee war konkret religiös. Es war Jesu Gebot, in seiner Nachfolge ein heiliges Gemeinschaftsleben zu führen." Johannes Kühn, *Toleranz und Offenbarung* (Leipzig: F. Meiner, 1923), p. 224.

[9] "The Schleitheim Confession," trans. by J. C. Wenger, Art. 6. John C. Wenger, *The Doctrines of the Mennonites* (Scottdale, Penna.: Mennonite Publishing House, 1950), p. 72.

[10] Søren Kierkegaard, Attack Upon "Christendom," trans. Walter Lowrie (Princeton, New Jersey: Princeton Univ. Press, 1946), p. 166.

[11] Undoubtedly the Humanistic search for origins, both sacred and secular, in which Erasmus and Zwingli participated, explains in part this tendency in Anabaptism. Especially since Conrad Grebel, Zwingli's convert, was a humanist for eight years and since the return to a Golden Age of literature, art, politics and religion was a common concern among intellectuals of the 16th century, it can be understood why the Anabaptists would be attracted by the vision of primitive purity and simplicity. The relationship of Anabaptism to Humanism is discussed at length by Robert S. Kreider in "Anabaptism and Humanism," *MQR*, XXVI (April, 1952), pp. 123-141. Kreider indicates that the extent to which Humanism may be regarded as an influence upon the rise of Anabaptism is a matter of dispute. Certainly some were touched by the fresh winds of Humanism more than others. Leonhard von Muralt in his *Konrad Grebel als Student in Paris* (Zürich, 1936), p. 133, claims that Grebel's position is unthinkable apart from the Humanistic influences which flowed into his mind through Zwingli. In his discussion about the ideological sources of Grebel's theology, however, Harold S. Bender is more inclined to attribute Grebel's theology to his personal study of the Bible. Cf. Harold S. Bender, *Conrad Grebel* (Goshen College, Goshen, Ind.: Mennonite Historical Society, 1950), pp. 197-203. Kreider concludes however, by saying: "I am inclined to believe that humanist influences continued to operate in subtle and perhaps profound ways in Grebel, the Evangelical and the Biblicist. There are overtones of the humanist in his desire to bring to rebirth the form and the spirit of the primitive church and to do this on the basis of the conscientious study of the New Testament record. It

does not seem necessary to minimize...Grebel's relationship to humanism in order to establish the fact that he was the leader of a uniquely new and creative historical movement." "Anabaptism and Humanism," *MQR*, XXVI (April, 1952), pp. 129-130.

[12] Ray C. Petry, *Francis of Assisi* (Durham, N. Carolina: Duke U. Press, 1941), p. 3.

[13] Thomas a' Kempis, *The Imitation of Christ*, trans. Aloysius Croft and Harry F. Bolton (Milwaukee: Bruce Publishing Co., 1940), Bk. I, ch. I, p. 1.

[14] "The Anabaptist Theology of Discipleship," *MQR*, XXIV (Jan. 1950), p. 30. This criticism of the piety of Thomas a' Kempis is made notwithstanding the fact that eventually Anabaptism has led historically to its own type of "withdrawal."

[15] The excellent introduction on *Spiritual and Anabaptist Writers* by George H. Williams and Angel M. Mergal makes clear the basic difference between the "Evangelical Anabaptists" to whom "the Gospel became a new law" and the Spiritualists to whom the "Spirit was central in their life and thought," pp. 30ff.

[16] Troeltsch, *op. cit.*, II, pp. 729ff.

[17] G. W. Williams and Angel Mergal, *op. cit.*, p. 35.

[18] One of the outstanding achievements of Troeltsch is his distinction between the Anabaptists and the spiritualists. At this point he breaks new ground. He says, "Anabaptists and Spiritual reformers ('Täufer und Spiritualisten') has become a stock phrase, as if in essentials both were the same. This is, however, an entirely erroneous idea. For these two movements are like separate streams, which only mingle their waters now and again, but which historically vary greatly both in their sources and in their development." *Ibid.*, pp. 729-730.

[19] Robert Friedmann, *Mennonite Piety Through the Centuries* (Goshen, Indiana: Menn. Hist. Soc., 1949), Chapter X.

[20] Troeltsch, *STCC* II, p. 752.

[21] *Quellen und Forschungen Zur Geschichte der oberdeutschen Taufgesinnten im 16, Jahrhundert*, ed. J. Loserth (Wien und Leipzig: Carl Fromme, 1929), Rede ;74, p. 160.

[22] It was the conviction of Troeltsch that the "Third Type," i.e., the Mystical and Spiritual groups possessed within them the seeds of the future. He was convinced that the "Third Type" would predominate in the modern period. With the breakdown of the *corpus christianum* ideal of the unity of Christian civilization and with the separation of Church and State in secular modernity, together with the inability of the Sect to maintain itself in the world, the future belonged to that type which would give up the task of applying the Gospel directly and determinedly to the structures of society and would in no way project itself into the world as an official institution concerned with the ordering of the world along predetermined lines. Rather this group of highly educated individuals, held together as a voluntary association, concerns itself about the "spirit of Christianity" and this group lives personally in the spirit of the Gospel. It indirectly shapes attitudes and cultivates a spiritual ethos but it is "unable to formulate for itself the unwritten social program which the Gospel contains nor to apply it clearly to the conditions which oppose it." Troeltsch, *op. cit.*, I, p. 381.

[23] Conrad Grebel, "Epistle 97;" "Epistle 100," *Thomas Müntzers Briefwechsel*, ed. H. Böhmer and P. Kirn (Leipzig, 1931), cited by Harold S. Bender, *Conrad Grebel*, p. 276.

[24] Roland Bainton points out that persecution by Protestants began with Zwingli and not Luther. In view of Zwingli's appreciation of the Rennaissance to which he was introduced by Erasmus, his intolerant attitudes may seem contradictory. Nevertheless it must be remembered that "the form of dissent which arose in Zurich was not so much directed against dogmas as agianst the very nature of the Church and its relation to civil society." *The Travail of Religious*

Liberty (Philadelphia: Westminster Press, 1951), p. 60.

[25] Cf. R. Sohm, *Kirchenrecht*, I (Leipzig: Duncker and Humbolt, 1892), pp. 548f.

[26] C. Henry Smith, *The Story of the Mennonite*, p. 20.

[27] John Horsch, *Mennonites in Europe* (Scottdale, Penna.: Mennonite Publishing House, 1950), p. 300.

[28] Cited by Bender, "The Anabaptist Vision," *MQR*, XVII (April, 1944), p. 15.

[29] Cited by *ibid.*, p. 5.

[30] Horsch, *op. cit.*, p. 301.

[31] *Ibid.*

[32] *Ibid.*, p. 304.

[33] S. M. Jackson, *Selected Works of Huldreich Zwingli* (Philadelphia: 1901), p. 127. Cited by Bender, *op. cit.*, p. 15.

[34] "Reply to Gellius Faber," *The Complete Writings of Menno Simons*, trans. Leonard Verduin and ed. John C. Wenger (Scottdale, Penna.: Herald Press, 1956), p. 779.

[35] Horsch, *op. cit.*, p. 310.

[36] Smith, *op. cit.*, pp. 161-162.

[37] Trans. Joseph H. Sohm (Scottdale, Penna.: Mennonite Publishing House, 1950). For a discussion of the theology of the *Martyr's Mirror* see A. Orley Swartzendruber, "The Piety and Theology of the Anabaptist Martyrs in van Braght's *Martyr's Mirror*," *MQR* XXXVIII (Jan., 1954), pp. 5-26.

[38] *Die Älteste Chronik der Hutterischen Brüder*, ed. A. J. F. Zieglschmid (Ithica, New York: Cauyga Press, Inc., 1943).

[39] *Ausbund* (Lancaster, Penna.: Lancaster Press, Inc., 1941). The subtitle of this hymnbook is as follows: *Wie sie in dem Gefängnis zu passau in dem Schloss von anderen rectgläubigen Christen hin und der gedichtet worden.*

[40] LII (1933), pp. 545-598.

[41] *Leider der Hutterischen Brüder*, p. 670. Cited by Stauffer, *op. cit.*, p. 563.

[42] Stauffer, *op. cit.*, pp. 545-546.

[43] *The Cost of Discipleship*, trans. by R. H. Fuller (New York: Macmillan Co., 1949), p. 71.

[44] Stauffer, *op. cit.*, p. 549.

[45] Luther, *WA*, XII, p. 74, cited by Stauffer, *op. cit.*, p. 551.

[46] Luther, *WA* XXXV, p. 411, cited by Stauffer, *ibid.*

[47] Menno Simons, "The Cross of the Saints," *Complete Works*, p. 583.

[48] *Leider der Hutterischen Brüder*, p. 214. Dietrich Bonhoeffer stands in the tradition of martyr theology with his statement that: "Suffering has to be endured so that it may pass away. Either the world must bear the whole burden and collapse beneath it, or it must fall on Christ to be overcome in him. He therefore suffers vicariously for the world. His is the only suffering with redemptive efficacy. But the church knows that the world is still seeking for someone to bear its sufferings, and so, as it follows Christ, suffering becomes the church's lot too. As it follows Him beneath the cross, the Church stands before God as the representative of the world." Bonhoeffer, *op. cit.*, p. 76.

[49] *Leider d. Hut.*, p. 47.

[50] The cosmic importance of suffering as reflected in the hymns of the Anabaptists is emphasized by Stauffer. "Der Leidcharakter der Kreatürlichkeit ist Schicksal." *Op. cit.*, p. 575.

[51] *Leider d. Hut.*, p. 47.

[52] Roland H. Bainton, *Here I Stand* (New York: Abingdon-Cokesbury Press, 1950), p. 42.

[53] Regin Prenter, *Spiritus Creator*, trans. John M. Jensen (Philadelphia: Muhlenberg Press, 1953), pp. 13-14.

[54] *WA*, "Tischreden," IV, 4777. Cited by *ibid.*, p. 14.

[55] Cf. Søren Kierkegaard, *Concluding Unscientific Postscript*, trans. by David F. Swenson and ed. by Walter Lowrie (Princeton, N.J.: Princeton Univ. Press, 1941), p. 382ff.

[56] Martin J. Heinecken, *The Moment Before God* (Philadelphia: Muhlenberg Press, 1956), p. 291.

[57] "What do I want?" *Attack Upon "Christendom,"*, p. 38.

[58] van Braght, *Martyr's Mirror*, p. 453.

[59] Cf. Martin J. Heinecken, "Kierkegaard as a Christian," *The Journal of Religion*, Vol. XXVII (January, 1957), pp. 20-30.

CHAPTER 3
CHRISTIANITY AS DISCIPLESHIP (cont'd.)

I. Love as Nonresistance

We come now to a discussion of the second major element of discipleship according to the sixteenth century Anabaptists, namely, the exercise of love as nonresistance. This unique practice has characterized the movement from its inception in 1525. In line with this emphasis, the Mennonite church has been known as one of the historic peace churches along with the Quakers and the Church of the Brethren. It distinguishes the Anabaptists and the Mennonites from the main stream of Protestantism which, except for certain individuals and certain passing phases of its history, has not been pacifist.[1]

A. *Nonresistance--A Central Doctrine.* It is impossible to overestimate the importance of the doctrine of nonresistance for either the Anabaptists or their Mennonite descendants. It is not a peripheral idea lying outside the Gospel itself. It is not a fortuitous emphasis depending upon the nature of the historical situation. Nonresistance has been considered an essential implication of the Christian faith and it is so comprehensive in its range of influence that not a single social or political attitude is left unaffected. Nonresistance issues directly from a conception of God as love and from a conception of Divine redemption as centered in a sacrificial act. It is closely connected with a theory of the propagation of the Gospel according to which all methods of force are rejected and it coincides with the essence of the Christian community as a Brotherhood living in eschatological tension. It is a major factor in the idea of the "free church."

B. *An Ultimate Attitude Toward Life.* Furthermore, nonresistance involves an ultimate attitude toward life. To be nonresistant really means to accept in principle the insecurity of the cross. It implies the loss of all things for Christ including one's own historical existence, if need be. Nonresistance qualified all life's pleasures and ambitions by a final resignation. It implies the complete renunciation of defense whether for one's self, for one's children or for one's possessions. This is a kind of complete submission to God and the neighbor which the Anabaptists called *Gelassenheit.* In the last analysis, nonresistance when personally accepted, not as a law but as inward commitment to Christ, means the transcendence of the will to exist and the consequent victory over the anxiety and pride of life. It involves a quality of faith in God which enables the Christian to absorb evil and even to lose everything for the sake of

Christ. For the nonresistant Christian, the guards of life are down. He is open to his neighbor's enmity as well as his kindness. Since nonresistance is essentially sacrificial love, it represents Christian ethics at its highest level.[2] Nonresistance gives Mennonitism its absolute quality.

C. *Central to Mennonite Ethics*. The place of nonresistance in Anabaptist ethics is one of centrality. This has remained true to the present day among the Mennonites. All social problems are judged by whether they exhibit the principle of nonresistance. For this reason Guy F. Hershberger's *War, Peace and Nonresistance*[3] serves the Mennonite church today virtually as a textbook on social ethics. In presenting the idea of nonresistance with its theological roots and in working out its implications for life, Hershberger was compelled to present the essentials of a community ethic. It is not uncommon to find Mennonite writings on the subjects of nonresistance and industrial conflict, nonresistance and community living, nonresistance and missions or nonresistance and the oath.[4] *Nonresistance is the form and expression of love which has become almost synonymous with love itself for Anabaptists and Mennonites.* The assumption is that if one really accepts nonresistance as an inward spiritual conviction, he will, by God's grace, have made the final resignation of life apart from which no real Christian ethical life of love is possible. It is assumed that if Brethren can submit to the cross as a matter of spiritual orientation, the basic condition for an ethic of love will have been reached.

The narrowing of the concept of love to nonresistance as general tendency among the Anabaptists and their Mennonite descendants is intended to combat the ambiguous use of the term "love." By nonresistance the Anabaptists meant to demonstrate the absolute quality of sacrificial love in contrast to the various psychological and organizational relationships of "egoistic" mutuality which, though moral in the conventional civil sense, may not involve the pinnacle of love of the New Testament. They discerned the difference between unrighteousness and complete uncalculated submission to God and to the neighbor in the spirit of Calvary. They knew in their way the difference between complete disinterestedness and balances of power, no matter how much those balances may be clothed with traditional sanctities.[5] The Anabaptists sought to duplicate the love of God. This quality was exhibited on Calvary as non-resistant sacrificial love.

D. *Nonresistance and Pacifism*. It should be stated at the outset that the term nonresistance is preferred above pacifism for the purpose of stating the Anabaptist view. Pacifism designates to the modern mind a general attitude toward war as an instrument of national policy. It is a term which came into common use during the period between World War I and World War II. At that time many individuals as well as denominational bodies renounced war as inconsistent with Christian ethics.[6] The renunciation of war by the churches was generally accompanied by an optimistic view of human nature and a neat correlation between sacrificial and triumphant love. With the Anabaptists, however, nonresistance was a comprehensive Christian ethical attitude which was directed more to the life of the church as an independent body than to the state. Nonresistance was not regarded as a way to a warless world. It was conceived as a personal approach to the problem of evil. In so far as it represents a relationship between collective entities, the only entity which was thought of as a nonresistant possibility was the church. Just as the New Testament advocates nonresistance as a way with personal enemies, so the Anabaptists thought of nonresistance as a matter of personal relations. The problem of international conflict was considered only in so far as their own individual nonresistant attitudes were involved, even though they deplored the weary round of conflict between kings and princes as evidence of collective sin. The crucial question to the Anabaptists was whether they as individual Christians were ready to live the life which is implied by the Sermon on the Mount. Would they be willing to covenant with God not to resist evil regardless of the agent or the form of evil? Would they turn the other cheek to the oppressor, to the thief or to the foreign enemy? Would they find the grace to suffer any loss in the spirit of the cross and to submit to unjust suffering? To the Anabaptists, nonresistance stood for complete repudiation of all means of retaliation and for commitment to love the enemy. Such commandments as follows were accepted in dead earnest and they were given concrete application. "Repay no man evil for evil.... Live peaceably with all. Beloved never avenge yourselves, but leave it to the wrath of God.... No, if your enemy hungers, feed him; if he is thirsty, give him drink.... Do not overcome evil by evil, but overcome evil with good" (Rom. 12:17-21). Thus nonresistance has quite different roots, different premises and different goals from what is generally known as pacifism.

Nonresistance came to the Anabaptists as a test of genuine Christianity. The central problem of the Anabaptist was obedience to the absolute demands of nonresistance. Am I willing to become "defenseless for the sake of the Gospel?" was the supreme question to the Anabaptists. The true disciple was the one who had become meek, gentle and submissive to the cruelty of the world. Oddly, the figure of the "soldier" was used to describe the life of the disciple. But this figure was used in such a way as to heighten the pathos. The Anabaptist soldier was a "suffering soldier" of the cross. Anabaptists said, "We must let ourselves be despised, persecuted, killed.... A genuine soldier of the cross must have true resignation, and must mortify his own life."[7] This attitude of true resignation was represented by the word *Gelassenheit*. This term is sometimes translated "yieldedness." It signifies an inner conquest of the will to power and existence. It is what it means to "lose one's life" for Christ. Robert Friedmann has made extensive reference to the Anabaptist attitude of *Gelassenheit* and he defines it as:

> "yieldedness," signifying an inner surrender and conquest of one's self. "Wir Müssen in Christus still halten" is a phrase which is met time and again in Anabaptist tracts. It does not mean resignation and quietism (so well known from mystical tracts) but is part and parcel of Anabaptist activity. Gelassenheit is the first step to true brotherhood, the overcoming of selfishness.[8]

The concept of *Gelassenheit* comes through in the famous letter of Michael

Sattler to the church at Horb as he awaited execution in May 1527. Sattler wrote, "In this peril I completely surrendered myself unto the will of the Lord, and...prepared myself even to death for His testimony...(yet) I deemed it necessary to stir you up to follow after us in this divine warfare."[9]

E. *The Origin of the Doctrine of Nonresistance.* The main source of Anabaptist convictions for nonresistance was their independent study of the Scriptures.[10] As early as 1522 Andreas Castelberger was investigated for his teaching about war in his "Bible school." The report of the investigation states:

> Andreas said much about war; how the divine teaching is so strong against it and how it is sin; and he expressed the idea that the soldier who had plenty at home in his fatherly inheritance and goods and yet went to war, and received money and pay to kill innocent persons and to take their possessions from people who had never done him any harm, such a soldier was before Almighty God, and according to the Gospel teaching, a murderer and not better than one who would murder and steal on account of his poverty, regardless of the fact that this might not be so according to human laws and might not be accounted so bad.[11]

Basically the same position was represented by Conrad Grebel. In his notable letter to Thomas Müntzer in 1524 this was clearly enunciated--a letter which incidentally clears Grebel from any responsibility for such extremes as occurred under Müntzer's leadership. Grebel stated:

> Moreover, the Gospel and its adherents are not to be protected by the sword, nor are they thus to protect themselves.... Neither do they use worldly sword of war, since all killing ceases with them...if thou are willing to defend war,...then I admonish thee by the common salvation of us all that thou wilt cease therefrom....[12]

It should be pointed out also that the Anabaptist doctrine of nonresistance cannot be attributed to persecution. Nonresistance was declared an implication of the Gospel before persecution set it. Even while Castelberg and Grebel were yet favored students of Zwingli, they came to pacifist conclusions through the independent study of the Bible. Felix Manz, after studying the New Testament stated categorically that no Christian smites with the sword nor resists evil. Furthermore the first Anabaptist Confession, namely the Schleitheim Confession, is the most dogmatic and absolute statement of nonresistance of this period.[13]

The fact that the Anabaptists based their nonresistance upon a literal understanding of the New Testament does not mean that they were legalistic, if by legalistic we mean that they refused to look beyond the command of Scripture to its place within the Gospel of grace. Clearly the gospel of redemption is first in the minds of the Anabaptists. Their starting point is the activity of God which was culminated in the historical event of the cross. What moved the Anabaptists was the divine humiliation by which God stooped to become human and "being found in human form he humbled himself and became obedient unto death, even the death on the cross" (Phil. 2:8). The Sermon on the Mount and, for that matter, the ethical prescriptions of the New Testament were regarded as extensions of the love which was poured out on the cross for the sins of humanity. "Christian nonresistance is rooted in the heart of the Gospel."[14] Nonresistance is applied *agape*. This means that the life of non-resistance is not simply obedience to a command. It is the response of the disciple who owes his salvation to Christ. It is the life of faith and gratitude. It is freedom to love, having been loved by Christ.

This is clearly the intention of an anonymous Anabaptist tract entitled *Two Kinds of Obedience*. The two kinds of obedience which are compared are "filial" obedience and "servile" obedience.

> Obedience is of two kinds, servile and filial. The filial has its source in the love of the Father, even though no other reward should follow, yea even if the Father should wish to damn His child; the servile has its source in a love of reward or of oneself. The filial ever does as much as possible, apart from any command; the servile does as little as possible, yea nothing except by command. The filial is never able to do enough for Him; but he who renders servile obedience thinks he is constantly doing too much for Him. The filial rejoices in the chastisement of the Father although he may not have transgressed in anything; the servile wishes to be without chastisement although he may do nothing right.... The servile looks to the external and to the prescribed command of his Lord; the filial is concerned about the inner witness and the Spirit.[15]

The point of Anabaptism is that the experience of grace does result in an attitude of obedience. How can one but obey Christ who has been saved by him? The Christian life, including the practice of nonresistance, is the fruit of redemption. Redemption is the root and nonresistance is the fruit.

Therefore much of the criticism which has been directed against the pacifism of the Social Gospel does not apply to Anabaptism. An example is the statement of John A. Hutchison: "Theologically it (pacifism of Social Gospel) was often based upon the very questionable assumption that the Christian religion is simply a matter of following Jesus or practicing the way of love."[16] Anabaptism, to the contrary, grounded its pacifism in the evangelical Gospel. The active life of following Jesus and practicing the way of love were simply the inseparable results of reconciliation to God. Obedience, therefore, became a highly personal religious experience. It was not a cold calculating exercise of casuistry. It was a personal concrete response to the call of Christ to take up the cross. Obedience was not a response to a law or code but a response to a person who is alive and who spoke the same message to sixteenth century disciples as he spoke to the twelve. "If any man would come after me, let him deny himself and take up his cross and follow me. For whoever would save his life will lose it; and whoever loses his life for my sake and the gospel's will save it" (Mark 8:34-35).

It is certainly true that the Anabaptists were literalists, by which we mean that they interpreted the Scripture for what it seemed to say and they accepted the commandments of Christ and the Apostles as valid for them as well. Whether this approach to the Christian life violates the spirit of evangelical Christianity depends largely upon the spirit of the individual. Anabaptists believed that if the Spirit of Christ is alive in the Christian, then he can receive the commandments of Christ as indicative of a way of life for which he longs. If, on the other hand, the Spirit of Christ is absent, conformity to the teaching of Christ becomes another form of legal righteousness.

It must be admitted that Anabaptist literalism did in fact petrify into a rigid moralism before many years. As the original enthusiasm waned and as the severity of persecution all but destroyed the spiritual integrity of the movement, the genuine spiritual imitation of Christ turned out to be imitation by rote. Legalism, moralism and quietism soon became all too characteristic of this movement.[17] Whether any movement which rests upon the *imitatio Christi* approach to discipleship can escape this danger over a period of several generations is a moot question. Nevertheless, it can hardly be said that the Anabaptists of the first generation were legalists, unless we are ready to say that any group which takes Christ's sayings seriously and which deliberately tries to live according to the law of love is legalistic.

F. *Nonresistance and War.* Thus far an attempt has been made to show that the doctrine of nonresistance represented a basic attitude toward life rather than simply an attitude toward war. Nevertheless, the Anabaptists were conscious of the fact that participation in war is impossible for those who have adopted the ideal of nonresistance. This position was the cause for great tension and misunderstanding between the Anabaptists and the Reformers, even though very few Anabaptists were required to participate in military action. Universal military conscription was not a general pattern until the time of Napoleon. Tension arose because the authorities thought that they saw in the Anabaptist position the potential dissolution of the state. Nonresistance signaled the dismemberment of the church, the undermining of civil authority and the dissolution of Christian civilization.

These fears can be understood by citing an extreme case. This is the case of Michael Sattler, a close friend of Butzer. Sattler was an outstanding leader of the Swiss Anabaptists, as indicated by the fact that he was most likely the author of the Schleitheim Confession of 1527. One of the accusations against Michael Sattler was that he had stated that if the Turks invaded the country no resistance should be offered.[18] Furthermore he is supposed to have said that if war could be justified by the principles of morality, he would prefer to fight against the Christians rather than against the Turks.[19] This charge deeply incensed the court. For years the Turks had been threatening Christian civilization. King Ferdinand had taken emergency measures to arouse the German states to resist with armies and money. The "cruel Turks" had impressed the popular mind by their ruthlessness. They were infidels who were in common cause with the devil. In 1529 they were encamped before Vienna and continued to threaten Western Europe for many years. In the face of this threat to Western culture and Christian civilization, the position of Sattler appeared to be blasphemous and subversive. Sattler was not charged for alliance with the Turks, but his position was considered just as disastrous.

Sattler did not deny the charge. He added to the tension of situation by reaffirming his position that if the Turks should come they should not be resisted since the commandment "Thou shalt not kill" has been given. The only weapon that Christians can use is the weapon of prayer and submission to God's providence. He also admitted that he had said that if war was right, he would prefer to march against supposed Christians who persecute, capture and kill the Children of God. The Turk, after all, knows nothing about Christ. He makes no profession; he is "a Turk according to the flesh." "But you who would be Christians, and who make your boast of Christ, persecute pious witnesses of Christ, and are Turks according to the Spirit,"[20] said Sattler.

This instance reveals the dilemma of Christianity and social responsibility. Sattler was utterly irresponsible from the standpoint of the normal interests of the state. He took no thought whatsoever about what would happen to the state if a sizable number of Christians adopted his view. All horizontal considerations were disregarded. What nonresistance would mean for the total social situation was not a matter of consideration. Sattler was interested only in doing the divine will as revealed in Christ. He was oriented toward the perfect law of God and he felt no responsibility toward the relativities of social and political order except those which could be correlated nondialectically to the will of God. Sattler did not intend social chaos. He was desirous of nothing but peace. However, he was not able to countenance the total social order in such a way as to permit him to lay aside the perfection of God's law as an immediate possibility long enough to deal "responsibly" with the Turks.

The irony of Sattler and the State is the irony of Christianity and political reality. Sattler's enemies could not deny that from the standpoint of personal faith and individual piety he represented Christian attitudes and a Christian way. Butzer called him "a dear friend of God" and a "martyr for Christ." The authorities could not deny that prayer for the Turk is a far more Christian weapon than the sword. They knew also that his complete confidence in God as the Supreme Protector bore an undeniable Christian character. Since Christianity is centered in the divine humiliation of the cross, defenselessness before the Turk would seem to be logically in line with God's way of dealing with evil. For this reason the Anabaptist posed a problem for their socially responsible contemporaries. *It is the problem of the disruptive possibilities of the ethical absolute when projected within the relativities of power structures.* It is the problem of the irreconcilability of pure sacrificial love and egoism. It is the contradiction between *agape* and sinful social structures which is felt so keenly by the historic peace churches. The church is committed to the law of love as the law of God. This law is the law of ultimate reality. The Church knows that the world will be disordered until it conforms to the law of love. Nevertheless, it cannot tolerate the law of love without qualification because the structures of society are ordered along other lines. They are ordered to resist evil, to oppress lawlessness, to demand civil obedience and to require varying degrees of conformity to the sinful collective ego. In this respect the "Christian State" is no different from the pagan state.

The radical position of the Anabaptists baffled the authorities of the sixteenth century. The Anabaptists presented in concrete form the tension between Christianity and the state. What should those who are responsible for the security and the order of society do with people who combine the absolute ethic of Christian love with an aggressive radical spirit? How shall the authorities handle those whose only desire is to witness for Christ, to love the enemy, to live absolutely honestly and openly and yet who for this very reason neglect civil responsibilities, historical continuities and who even upon occasion defy duly appointed officials[21] and utter criticisms of the social and ecclesiastical powers which imply revolutionary change? Ironically, the authorities feared the Anabaptists despite their sheep-like nonresistance because their call for true discipleship and a true church implied a totally different social and political order in which the unity of civilization would of necessity be replaced by some kind of pluralism--an almost unthinkable idea for the day in which they lived. What Anabaptists wanted was the end of the *corpus christianum* ideal of Christian civilization which was the basic structural idea of the church since the days of Constantine.

Dealing with Anabaptists singly was no severe problem for the Swiss and German authorities. What they feared, however, was a general social revolution of a kind for which Münster seemed to stand. What disturbed them most was the possibility of a popular uprising against the state in the name of utopian idealism.[22] However, the Anabaptists refused to take advantage of the possibilities of popular uprising. "It would have been possible upon occasion for the leaders of the Brethren who were preaching to great crowds illegally during the early period of the movement to rouse the people, probably successfully due to their great numbers, to revolutionary action against the civil officials who tried to interfere with and break up the meetings. No such actions occurred, however. The Anabaptists rather permitted themselves to be imprisoned than to lead civil uprisings."[23] Nevertheless, the Anabaptists were a social threat even though they had no social program.[24] Their ideas had a popular appeal and furthermore they were zealous in communicating these ideas through "unofficial" channels and by officially unapproved methods. They used nothing more forceful than the testimony of their words and lives but these ironically possessed more explosive power than armies in many instances and against these it was far more difficult to obtain a Christian case.

Robert Kreider reports that "the Swiss governments resourcefully employed a wide range of methods in their efforts to suppress the Anabaptists."[25] First, they used the techniques of persuasion, debate, public disputation, polemical tracts and pastoral counseling. However, these were unable to stop the advance of the movement. Second, they tried the techniques of legal restriction. These included the banning of all unauthorized meetings and unauthorized preaching. Compulsory infant baptism and attendance at regular church services were added. Public confessions were enforced and Anabaptist writings were censored. These, however, likewise failed to stem the progress of the Anabaptists. Finally, the authorities resorted to physical coercion and economic privation. Children of Anabaptists were declared illegitimate and not legal heirs. Banishment was a most common practice. The fact that the government yielded gradually to methods of torture indicates the pathos of the problem. Why would even such mild mannered Christians such as Haller, Capito and Oecolampadius submit to the awful "logic of persecution?"

The answer seems to lie in the fact that these men felt responsible for the maintenance of the social order which at that time was indissolubly united with the church. Nonresistance as a religious attitude could not be separated from severe social consequences, because of the conditions of the Mediaeval synthesis of Christianity and the entire cultural process. Religious freedom, separation of church and state, the "gathered church" and minority rights were principles not yet regarded as desirable possibilities. But it should be admitted that even the freedoms of modern pluralistic society do not solve the basic dilemma of radical Christianity and the world. For even modern democratic states are not in a position to tolerate nonresistance except in the case of small quietistic sects such as the Mennonites. If a major portion of the population of a state which carries responsibility for the balances of power in the international situations were to become nonresistant, the real issue would be revealed.

The recent experience of the modern state with the pacifism of religious liberalism is hardly a case in point since this brand of pacifism was shot through with a strong prudential appeal which was, incidentally, easily dissipated when the logic of Reinhold Niebuhr and the exigencies of German National Socialism seemed to show that prudence lay with military resistance. The coming and going of liberal pacifism resulted from the fact that this movement never had strong Biblical roots. It was essentially a dream of a warless world, a hope which resulted largely from the idea of progress as the gradual social realization of the Kingdom of God. Anabaptism, on the other hand, was singularly Biblical in its approach to nonresistance. It neither had the time nor the inclination to work out the political implications of its doctrine. It had no comprehensive social ethic to replace the ethic of Christian civilization in its various Mediaeval and Reformation forms. It was simply an appeal to New Testament Christianity, and the New Testament was not known to grant concessions to prudential morality.

G. *The Problem of the Magistracy.* A problem of nonresistance which had greater practical consequence for the Anabaptists than military service was the problem of the magistracy. This problem was faced directly not because Anabaptists aspired to political office but because of the meaning of the general position for Christian civilization. The importance of this question cannot be overestimated for our study since the problem of social responsibility first appeared to the Anabaptist-Mennonite tradition in this area. Their handling of this question cast the die for at least four hundred years of Mennonite history so far as the main attitudes of the Mennonites toward political participation is concerned. From the standpoint of the Reformers and the civil authorities this was likewise important since it indicated their general attitude toward public institutions.

Although there is evidence of a slight difference in emphasis among various groups of Anabaptists, it may be said that the Anabaptists as a whole rejected the office of the magistrate as a Christian vocation and the basis for this rejection was the claim that the magistracy ultimately rests upon the use of the "sword." Virtually all Anabaptists saw the problem at first sight. Since nonresistance forbids the use of coercion, the magistracy, though necessary in sinful society and though clothed with the dignities and the sanctities of law, cannot be discharged by those who have renounced force.

We choose to discuss the attitude of the Schleitheim Confession toward the magistracy because this document represents a notable historical precedent for the (Old) Mennonites and it presents the general question of social responsibility in its most extreme form.[26] The controlling idea in the Schleitheim Confession regarding the magistracy is contained in the statement that "The sword is ordained of God outside the perfection of Christ."[27] This statement makes both positive and negative assertions. *In the first place, it acknowledges that the sword, by which is meant government with its civil and military establishments, is grounded in God's plan for this world.* It is ordained.[28] The Anabaptists were not Anarchists. Numerous statements of the Anabaptists at court trials indicate that they honored and feared government, basing their respect on Romans 13 and 1 Peter 2:13. These passages, particularly the latter, are repeated over and over in support of the rather paradoxical ideal that the King should be honored and his authority should be obeyed (unless the will of the authorities violated conscience) while at the same time, the Christian should not desire the position of authority.[29] "Be subject for the Lord's sake to every human institution, whether it be to the emperor as supreme, or to governors as sent by him to punish those who do right.... Honor all men. Love the brotherhood. Fear God. Honor the Emperor" (1 Peter 2:13-17). It is therefore wrong to accuse the Anabaptists of doing away with government. Government is ordained of God as a permanent institution, i.e., as long as sin remains in the world. It is true that the Anabaptists seldom thought of government in the more positive theological categories such as the orders of creation. As Biblicists they were not aware of, or at least showed very little dependence upon the theological and philosophical thought which had developed in connection with the relation of the realm of creation to the realm of redemption and all that this problem means for the doctrine of the Trinity, for the Logos Christology and for the complex relation of justice and love. Nor did they show any considered knowledge of the tradition of *lex naturae* which, according to Troeltsch, played such a profound role in bringing the realms of nature and grace together for purposes of social doctrine.[30] Nevertheless, the Anabaptists were aware of the traditional role of government: "It (the sword) punishes and puts to death the wicked, and guards and protects the good. In the Law the sword was ordained for the punishment of the wicked and for their death, and the same (sword) is (now) ordained to be used by the worldly magistrates."[31]

It may be noted that the function of the government according to the Schleitheim Confession is negative. This, however, is to be expected because of the day in which it was written. Luther regarded government in virtually the same manner. Both traditions derive their conceptions largely from Romans 13. It should be remembered that the conception of government as a positive force for good and as the creator of values rather than protector of values is to a large extent a modern conception. At any rate, the Anabaptists were not sentimentalists who denied the place of a forcefully maintained order in society. They were not generally opposed to the death penalty, as this confession clearly indicates. The state has the right and the duty under God to take life. In other words, the Anabaptists can hardly be associated with, for example, the anarchism of Tolstoy.[32] Tolstoy took a strictly monistic attitude toward ethics by his literal interpretation of the Sermon on the Mount and his uncompromising insistence that its principles should 'be embodied universally.' This would of course result in the removal of government and all agencies of force and public control. Tolstoy's ideas rested finally upon a German idealistic philosophical foundation rather than upon evangelical Biblicism. The Anabaptists recognized, to the contrary, the legitimacy of the "sword."

In the second place, it should be noted that the sword is ordained outside the perfection of Christ.[33] This is a crucial point for our understanding of Anabaptist thinking about the magistracy. Here the dualism of Anabaptism is brought to bear in full force. It is a dualism which begins with the fundamental antagonism between God and Satan and which finds historical expression in the Kingdom of God and the Kingdom of Satan. These Kingdoms are in relentless conflict and will continue until Christ is victorious in the end. Anabaptism, by declaring that "the sword is outside the perfection of Christ" places government within the domain of the devil since government rests ultimately upon the use of force. This is paradoxical since government is ordained by God and providentially ordered. Nevertheless, government belongs to the "world." It arose because of sin. It is God's way of holding sin in check and yet these processes of control are sinful since they cannot correspond to the law of love. Even though the administration is just, the use of the sword is "devilish."

One can, of course, attribute the dark attitude of the Anabaptists toward the state partly to persecution. They had an almost morbid dread of the forceful instruments of the state. They called them "the unchristian, devilish weapons of force--such as the sword, armor."[34] Their suffering at the hands of these weapons simply made them all the more susceptible to the basic idea that the state is really devilish in character despite its divine ordination.

Careful reading of the Schleitheim confession indicates that it is clearly an answer to an opposing view of the magistracy. Apparently the magistracy was presented by some as a way of expressing love. In Article 6 the problem is stated in these words. "Now it will be asked by many...whether a Christian mayor should employ the sword against the wicked for the defense and protection of the good, or for the sake of love." This would appear to have placed the magistracy in its very best light. It is an argument which has taken many forms in the development of Christian social philosophy but which seems here to suggest that it may be better to have Christian magistrates than nonchristian ones. The magistracy is a way of expressing love through the administration of justice. It is the strongest argument for the Christian statesman. Apparently the opposition acknowledged the tension which rends the heart of any sensitive magistrate as he judges and orders punishment but they claimed that love can nevertheless temper the administration of justice with redemptive concern for the criminal. It is dangerous at this point to try to reconstruct the argument for the "liberal" party for fear of reading into the argument more than may have been there. It is instructive, however, to note that the argument of the opposition took the very highest form. Its appeal was that of love and it would seem to say that love at times requires "strange" instruments of compulsion to accomplish its redemptive purposes. This is what Luther called the "strange" work of love.[35] It represents a reluctance to divorce Christ completely from political institutions or to draw an arbitrary distinction between the order of creation and the order of redemption in the empirical realms. Most likely the opposition held out for a more generous attitude toward the relativities of social and political structure in the name of love itself.

The position of this Confession is, however, one of uncompromising absolutism by direct and literal appeal to the historical Christ. In typical Anabaptist fashion, the teaching and example of Jesus is brought forth as complete and final revelation of God's absolute will. The first reply to the liberal opposition recalls the incident of the woman taken in adultery (John 8:1-11). On this occasion Jesus refused to punish the woman in accordance with the law. Rather He admonished her "in mercy and forgiveness and warning, to sin no more."[36] What this means is that the Swiss Anabaptists were committed to the absolute ideal of forgiving love which constitutes the essence of the ethic of Christ. The Anabaptists knew that this approach to evil could not become the principle upon which the magistrates operate and so the only alternative for a Christian was to give up the magistracy. The *imitatio Christi* approach is demonstrated here again by the statement that, "Such an attitude (Jesus's treatment of the woman taken in adultery) we also ought to take completely."[37]

The uncompromising position of the Anabaptists is carried even one step further when the problem moves from the use of force by the magistracy to the "passing of judgment" upon disputes. Reference is made to that aspect of magisterial duty which deals with the administration of "distributive" justice. This is not the case of punitive justice using coercive means. It is simply the just arbitration of contending interests. These interests may be those of individuals or families or business enterprises. This is not a problem of violence but a problem of egoism in its social and psychological forms. The question is, may the Christian permit himself to be in a position of determining what is just in the case of contending egos?

The answer of the Schleitheim Confession is as follows: "Christ did not wish to decide or pass judgment between brother and brother in the case of the inheritance, but refused to do so. Therefore we should do likewise."[38] This is a clear reference to the incident recorded in Luke 12:13-15 in which Jesus refused the role of mediator in a dispute. *He refused to serve as one who would pronounce justice as an authoritative teacher of the law.* Jesus' reluctance to enter into the relativities of competitive struggle, his total obliviousness to the "natural self-regarding impulses" which were held in competition, his transcendence over the give and take of ordinary life and his other-worldly orientation were accepted as the ideal for the Christian. One may question whether the Anabaptists were fully aware of where this ethic would take them if Jesus' attitude toward contending egos would be accepted as a normative principle. *It would virtually call for a complete withdrawal from life in society since the very structure of society presupposes the stuff of egoistic passion, the balancing of powers and the exclusive right to property.*

This confession finally takes up the question of whether one should submit to magisterial duty if he is chosen. Presumably some of the Anabaptists felt duty bound to serve in this capacity because they had received an appointment. Again the answer comes directly and singularly from the life of Christ.

> They wished to make Christ king, but he fled and did not view it as the arrangement of his Father. Thus shall we do as he did, and follow Him, and so shall we not walk in darkness. For He Himself says, He who wishes to come after me, let him deny himself and take up his cross and follow me. Also, He Himself forbids the force of the sword saying, "The worldly princes lord it over them, etc., but not so shall it be with you."[39]

From this it is evident that the Anabaptists accepted the nonpolitical character of Christ's life and mission as a precedent for His followers. They interpreted Christ's mission to be a deliberate rejection of power for the accomplishment of his purposes. Jesus associated the political approach to the world's problems with the Gentiles (Luke 22:25). The Gentiles lord it over others. This is the nature of the political structure. But Jesus called upon his disciples to adopt a completely different role, namely the role of the servant. This truly amounted to a "transvaluation of values." Political structure and Christian "servitude" were held over against each other as opposites.

The rejection of the magistracy meant the denial of politics as a Christian vocation. Not only did the Schleitheim Confession place the political reference to magistrates as "worldly." The rejection of the magistracy meant the rejection of that entire realm of life which we call political.

The extent to which this contradicted the thinking of the Reformers is clearly evident. Luther "solved" this problem in terms of his reinterpretation of the Christian calling. Luther accepted the "office"of judge, soldier, hangman as a legitimate Christian vocation in line with his acceptance of all the permanent structures of society as "given" by God. When Luther closed the doors of the monasteries, he opened the world for the vocational interpretation of work. Consecrated fulfillment of duties in ordinary life assumed Christian significance. It was no longer necessary to join a cloister to serve God genuinely. God deals with men essentially through the orders of creation (Ordnungen).

The political office is not the least of these. To those in authority he said, "Are you a prince, a lord spiritual or secular? Who has more to do than you, in order that you subjects may do right, peace is reserved, and no one suffers wrong?"[40] Furthermore, Luther was not inhibited by the brutality which the "office" sometimes entailed.

> Should you see that there is a lack of hangman, beadles, judges, lords, or princes, and find that you are qualified,you should offer your service and seek the place, that necessary government may by no means be despised and become inefficient or perish.[41]

His position was that the Christian calling is determined by the nature of social existence. The duties of the magistrate, soldiers and hangmen are necessary functions in divine society. These may be defined in terms of natural law. The duty of the Christian is to live in them as Christians and serve the neighbor in them.

The basic difference between the Anabaptists and Luther was that Luther looked to the permanent orders of creation as the clue to the Christian vocation whereas the Anabaptists looked to the life of the historical Jesus alone. Thus when Luther left the cloister he was really abandoning the *imitatio Christ* approach to the problem of the Christian vocation. This has been stated very well by Alexander Miller.

> What Luther in fact suggests is that if the earthly example of Christ is made the prime significance of His Person then the logic of the matter is the cloister, or at least celibacy and the teaching ministry. But if it be recognized that the work which Jesus as the Christ did was a *unique* work, a work which only he could do and for which he chose the conditions, then it becomes possible to believe that the common man's best service of Christ is not the mechanical following of his earthly example in celibacy and the renunciation of the normal work of citizenship, but the acceptance and faithful performance of the work Christ lays on us in home and state and particular vocation.[42]

In this connection Luther said:

> You ask, Why did not Christ and the disciples bear the sword? Why did He not also take a wife, or become a cobbler or a tailor? If an occupation or office is not good because Christ Himself did not occupy it, what would become of all occupations and offices, with the exception of the ministry which alone He exercised? Christ fulfilled His own office and vocation, but thereby did not reject any other. It was not meant that He should bear the sword, for He was to bear only that office by which His kingdom is governed and which properly serves His kingdom. Now it does not concern His kingdom

that He should be a married man, a cobbler, a tailor, a farmer, a prince, a hangman or a beadle, neither is the sword or secular law of any concern, but only God's Word and Spirit, by which His people are *inwardly governed*.[43]

Calvin agreed with Luther that the magistracy is a legitimate Christian vocation. This is to put it mildly. A significant portion of the *Institutes of the Christian Religion*, Bk. IV, Ch. XX. is devoted to the defense of the magistracy. This defense is made in line with a comprehensive treatment on the nature of civil laws and the Christian attitude toward the state. His entire treatment of this subject is closely integrated with his theological thought since the state has functions directly connected with religion, and law and religion have a common source and a common end which is God. *Concerning the merits of the magistracy, Calvin held that this office is not only legitimate but the most sacred and honorable in human life*. After enumerating the "honorable titles" ascribed to judges and lords in the Bible, such as "gods," "ministers of God," "holy men" and "vice-regents of God," he concludes: "Wherefore no doubt ought now to be entertained by any persons that civil magistracy is a calling not only holy and legitimate, but far the most sacred and honorable in human life."[44]

This most exalted conception of the magistracy, though supported by many scriptural references, arises at the same time from his general appreciation of civil polity as such and the way in which this is tied to his conception of God. Calvin, both as theologian and lawyer, had a keen appreciation for the political order, for it provides the basis for life in community within which righteousness and service exist. He placed civil order on the same level of necessity as the natural order. Calvin wrote: "The exercise of civil polity...is equally as necessary to mankind as bread and water, light and air, and far more excellent. For it not only tends to secure the accommodations arising from all these things, that men may breathe, eat, drink, and be sustained in life.... It comprehends all these things while it causes them to live together."[45] But over and above Calvin's astute awareness of the important role of the political dimension in human affairs, with which political philosophers beginning with Plato would generally agree, lies the idea of Christian theocracy or the total community dedicated to God and governed by God's servants. Calvin retained the magistracy for Christendom because he thought in terms of Christian universalism in line with the Mediaeval idea of *corpus christianum*. To Calvin the rejection of the magistracy really meant the rejection of the idea of Christian society.

A further difference between Calvin and the Anabaptists lies in the general attitude toward earthly existence. The Anabaptists attempted to carry out the logic of their "heavenly citizenship" and their "earthly pilgrimage" as well as their spiritual orientation to mean that they need not, in fact ought not, become intimately tied up with the affairs of this world, and especially those affairs which clearly deviate from the law of love. Their membership in the eternal Kingdom of God led them to believe that they dare not divide their loyalties as magistrates must. To the Anabaptists it was a problem of either/or. In line with this view the following statement appears in the Schleitheim confession:

> The government magistracy is according to the flesh, and the Christians' is according to the Spirit; their houses and their dwelling remain in this world, but the Christians' are in heaven; their citizenship is in this world, but the Christians' citizenship is in heaven; the weapons of their conflict are war and carnal and against the flesh only, but the Christians' weapons are spiritual, against the fortification of the devil.[46]

Calvin shared the view that the Christian's citizenship is in heaven and life in this world is but a journey of short duration. He appreciated the difference between the eternal and the temporal and he longed for the blessedness to come. Nevertheless, Calvin felt that this journey needs to be sustained by political supports. Citizenship in heaven and responsible citizenship on earth are not related to each other as contraries. He held that human nature is so weak that true religion cannot exist apart from those "aids" of civil polity which Geneva was designed to give. Hence he called for active participation in politics as long as we are on the earth.

> This civil government is designed, as long as we live in this world, to cherish and support the external worship of God, to preserve the true doctrine of religion, to defend the constitution of the church, to regulate our lives in a manner requisite for the society of men, to form our manners to civil justice, to promote our concord with each other, and to establish general peace and tranquility; all which I con-fess to be superfluous, if the Kingdom of God, as it now exists in us, extinguishes the present life. But if it is the will of God, that while we are aspiring towards our true country, we be pilgrims on the earth, and if such aids are necessary to our pilgrimage, they who take them from man deprive him of his nature. They plead that there should be so much perfection in the church of God, that its order would suffice to supply the place of all laws; but they foolishly imagine a perfection which can never be found in any community of men.[47]

Thus there would seem to be no way of reconciling the views of the Reformers and the Anabaptists regarding the magistracy, even though some of the objections to the magistracy have been removed by history as, for example, the separation of church and state and freedom of religion. The problem still remains since politics and military work cannot be correlated to nonresistance. *As long as a group of Christians hold to the absolute ethic of Christ as a direct or "simple possibility" of life, no "responsible" relation to the state is possible.* The operations of the state and the operations of true love and brotherhood are basically different. Pure nonresistance is at variance with any political structure, ancient or modern, autocratic or democratic.

II. A Missionary World View

    A. *The Great Commission.* We come now to a consideration of the third element of the Anabaptist concept of discipleship, namely fulfillment of the "Great Commission." This consideration deals with the basic questions: What is the central duty of the disciple? What form does his life take? What is the disciple's essential calling? Into which channels do his energy and time go?

    We have already stated that the Reformers answered this question in terms of the reinterpretation of the mediaeval conception of the calling. A Christian's duty is defined by the permanent structures of earthly existence. Luther was confident that God wills the Christian to stay in the "place" where he happens to be, whether this means to be a saddler or a lawyer. There he finds his neighbor whom he is to serve in love. The Christian calling is to do the work of the world well. This is intended to bestow on all areas of life a divine benediction. No useful occupation is to be excluded. Only nonproductive or definitely harmful occupations as robbery are unfit as Christian callings. Furthermore, Luther emphasized responsibility within the family as a Christian calling. He was of the opinion that no higher calling exists than that of mother or father. "Luther subdivides the divinely instituted secular realm into a multitude of 'offices,' 'callings,' and 'ranks.' The three main groups of orders within the secular realm are the family (or society, 'family' being used in a wider sense than at the present time), the government, and the empirical church. Luther said: Three kinds of callings are ordained by God; in them one can live with God and a clear conscience. The first is the family (*Hausstand*), the second is the political and the third the church or the ministry; and he added, 'after the pattern of the three persons in the Trinity.'"[48]

    Calvin was essentially in accord with Luther in regard to the calling. He went beyond Luther, however, by paying more attention to the social consequences of the calling. With Calvin it was an important thing to *choose* the most significant calling. The positive use of talents for the "transformation" of the world into a truly "holy" community gave to the concept of the calling a dynamic quality which is missing in Luther. Weber, of course, emphasized this in his interpretation of Calvinism as a formative factor in the capitalistic spirit.[49]

    With this background we now turn to the Anabaptists. *Did they have a conception of the calling or a comprehensive idea which took its place? The answer lies in their conception of the relevance of the "Great Commission" for the Christian life.* In line with their conception of Christianity as discipleship, they took special notice of the final words of the risen Lord to his disciples:

> All authority in heaven and on earth has been given to me. Go therefore and make disciples of all nations, baptizing them in the name of the Father and of the Son and of the Holy spirit, teaching them to observe all that I have commanded you; and lo, I am with

you always, to the close of the age (Matt. 28:18-20).

These words came to the Anabaptists as if Christ had spoken to them personally. The Great Commission, the essential task of the entire church, constituted the Christian calling. The major task of the Christian is to fulfill the Great Commission. This brought to the Anabaptist a conception of the world as a vast mission field and the church essentially as an evangelistic fellowship. The real work of the Christian is that of missionary or evangelist. He is to be "on the way" heralding the news of the ascension of Christ, His Lordship and His grace.

For the Anabaptists the Christian task is the same as that of the Apostles. Anabaptists of the sixteenth century were convinced that they must begin where the Apostles left off. Franklin H. Littell has pointed out that the very order of the words of the Matthew 28 passage was important. He cites the following Anabaptist proclamation:

> Firstly, Christ said, go forth into the whole world, preach the Gospel to every creature. Secondly, he said, whoever believes, thirdly--and is baptized, the same shall be saved. This order must be maintained if a true Christianity is to be prepared and though the whole world rage against it. Where it isn't maintained there is no true church of God....[50]

It is impossible to overestimate the significance of this conception of the calling. It would not have had such radical implication if it had been understood to apply to a select group of Christians as, for example, the monks during the Middle Ages. However the Anabaptists interpreted the Great Commission to be applicable to *all* who were baptized. It applied to all Christians at all times. Therefore to become an Anabaptist was not unlike the experience of the call of Levi at the seat of custom (Mark 2:14) or Peter by the Sea of Galilee. *A moment's reflection reveals that this conception of the calling carried within it a revolutionary social potential which, if accepted by the laity, would change the structure of society from one of statistic entrenchment within the orders of creation into a dynamic, fluid, loose order of witnessing itinerants.* Franklin Littell, who has brought to light this aspect of Anabaptism, says:

> By traditional exegesis the words (the Great Commission) were directed only toward His immediate audience, the Apostles, whose travels to the far corners of the earth had been long a part of the Christian legend. There had been from time to time vocational groups in the Great Church which strove to fulfill the Master's world view, notably the Franciscans. *But the Anabaptists were among the first groups to make the Commission binding upon all church members.* In their organization, the promise to go where sent was part of the ceremony of admission to the "True Church." They "went freely under the cross" where the representatives of the state churches

dared not go, and for the Gospel's sake were made pilgrims and
martyrs throughout the known world.[51]

It has also been pointed out that since the responsibility for the expansion of
the faith was moved from the princes to the members of the church themselves, the Anabaptists may be considered the "forerunners" of the modern
missionary movement.

This meant that the ordinary man received a commission involving a
world view to which he was vitally related. It was a view of Christ and his
Lordship resulting from the Ascension. It meant that "the earth is the Lord's
(Christ's) and the fullness thereof." This gave the evangelical *Täufer* an incen-
tive to go to all parts of the world to make His Lordship known and effective in
terms of evangelical conversations and the establishment of true worshiping
communities. The preface to His commission with its claim to all authority
(Matt. 28:18) in heaven and earth enabled the Anabaptist as His disciple to
confront kings and princes with the confidence of the ambassador of a Superior
Power.

The right to preach by authority received directly from Christ rather than
through the officials of the state church was a major problem to the
Reformers. The Reformers attacked this practice from the standpoint of the
unity of the church, the validity of the office of preaching and from the standpoint of civil peace and security. The orderly ordination of the ministry
seemed to be threatened by these "hedge" preachers. For the Reformers the
calling was associated with the official procedures. With respect to the validity
of a calling direct from Christ, they said "God sent only the Apostles into the
world...."[52] The very structure of the church seemed to be threatened by
"unlearned" men who took upon themselves the right to preach Christ; hence
the severe persecution.

To conduct missionary work among the parishes of the state-church also
implied that Christendom was not Christian after all. It challenged the
assumption that the multitudes were truly converted. It reflected upon the
effectiveness of compulsory religion and the identification of the "territory"
with the church.

B. *Implications for the Family.* According to the Anabaptist conception
of discipleship, the Christian must be ready to heed the call to preach Christ at
any time--leaving the family, the job and the community behind. One of the
terms which the Anabaptists used to describe this life of the pilgrim was "living
loose." By this they meant a definite break with culture. The normal demands
of family, community responsibility, occupation and national allegiance were
qualified by the superior demands of Christ. One faithful missionary wrote of
his condition:

> I am cut loose from all the world, from wife, from father, and
> mother and sister according to the flesh, and from all men; but this
> is right; Christ was also cut loose from all men and from his dis-
> ciples; it is enough that I be as he was....[53]

Thousands of Anabaptists traveled widely throughout Europe preaching in towns and villages. Mobility became a prime factor of discipleship. Anabaptist literature is replete with letters from members of this movement who were "on the way." Robert Friedmann has listed about four hundred epistles and similar writings, written by about eighty Hutterian Brethren. "Of these writers about half (that is forty) were martyrs, having been executed by fire and sword. Most of them were ministers of the word (*Diener des Wortes*) or missionaries "(*Sendboten*)."[54]

The word "go" grasped their minds and it posed a threat to every social and cultural establishment. It appeared to place a qualification on all cultural attachments and all those permanent structures which make civil life possible. It called for "heroic Christianity." The symbol of the knight of faith was revived, though without arms.

The one institution which seemed to be threatened most was the family. The Anabaptists accepted the family as a sacred institution. However, they were soon to realize the meaning of Jesus' warning about the demands of this natural institution. They remembered his words about hating father and mother, brother and sister. They also realized something of the economic aspects of the problem. Undoubtedly there was a tension between the dangerous life of the evangelical *Täufer* as he spent his days apart from the loved ones, often in prison, and the family as the basic institution of society. Here faith and culture clashed.

The conflict between discipleship and the family is witnessed to in many letters between husbands and wives. One of Menno Simon's finest letters is addressed to the wife of the Dutch Anabaptist elder, Leonard Bouwens. She feared for his life and wished to have him released from his responsibilities with the church. Menno replied reminding her of her duty to place her faith in the Father.

> Yes, dear sister, be of good cheer and comfort.... The necessities of life will be provided for us. If you are solicitous of your husband's natural life, then remember and believe that our life is measured by spans, that life and death are in the hands of the Lord, that not a hair falls from our heads without the will of the Father.[55]

The meaning of the radical demands of discipleship for the family is one of the major problems of this kind of heroic Christianity. The Catholic Church sought to solve this problem through the celibacy of the clergy and the institution of monasticism. While a larger proportion of the Christian population entered into marriage and all those institutions which are organized for the support of marriage and the family, a small number of the Christian population accepted the radical ethic of discipleship and embodied it in ascetic discipline. Luther, as previously stated, destroyed the mediaeval system of the double standard by a reinterpretation of the Christian calling according to which he accepted the ordinary work of the permanent orders of creation. Nevertheless, the Lutheran tradition was never able to free itself from the tension which is presented by the radical demands of Christ. This has come forth with unusual clarity in Kierkegaard through his criticism of Christendom. Kierkegaard clearly saw the tension between discipleship and marriage. He was critical of the State Church for having lost sight of the tension. It is an interesting coincidence that obscure Anabaptists and the Danish thinker came to use the same expression to describe the relation of the Christian to this area of culture, namely, "living loose." Here is one of Kierkegaard's profound statements in which the concept of "looseness" appears:

> To become a Christian in the New Testament sense is such a radical change that, humanly speaking, one must say that it is the heaviest trial to a family that one of its members becomes a Christian. For in such a Christian the God-relationship becomes so predominate that he is not "lost" in the ordinary sense of the word; no, in a far deeper sense than dying he is lost to everything that is called family. It is of this Christ constantly speaks, both with reference to himself when he says that to be his disciple is to be his mother, brother, sister, that in no other sense has he a mother, a brother, a sister; and also when he speaks continually about the collision of hating father and mother, one's own child, etc. To become a Christian in the New Testament sense is to loosen (in the sense in which the dentist speaks of loosening the tooth from the gums), to loosen the individual out of the cohesion to which he clings with the passion of immediacy, and which clings to him with the same passion.[56]

C. *The Church vs. Culture.* In the final analysis, the Anabaptist understanding of the calling as missionary service is part of the all-consuming preoccupation with the affairs of the church rather than with culture at large. To the Anabaptists, accepting Christ and becoming an active and responsible member of an expanding church constituted the calling. All cultural attachments and goals were radically subordinated to these. It is certainly true that Anabaptists came to regard marriage and work as a calling. However, the "proper calling" was to submit one's life to the active work of the fellowship. Furthermore, one's job or profession could be called Christian only in the sense that it contributed to the work of the church. Anabaptists chose their professions accordingly. Pilgram Marpeck[57] is an outstanding example of this theology of work. Marpeck was a gifted engineer who, having been forced to flee the Tyrol, settled with his family in Strasburg in 1528. There he made an outstanding contribution to the city through his supervision of the construction of aqueducts. He was also a craftsman. Through his planning, the city received its lumber from the Black Forest by river. For a century, logs which were floated down the tributaries of the Rhine to Strasburg were called "pilgrims," having been named after Marpeck. His connection with Anabaptism was "winked at" by the Strasburg authorities for a while because of his professional contribution. Eventually, however, Marpeck was forced to leave Strasburg, primarily because of his attitudes toward "schwören and wehren." From this time (1532) until his death in 1556, he moved from place to place in South Germany and the Tyrol. Here and there he received engineering jobs. For awhile he was Ulm on the Danube river in Württemberg, where he established a number of congregations. When forced to leave one place he would simply go to another and "earn his bread there" without feeling that he was being deprived of his Christian calling. For his real calling was the work of the church and his "secular" work was of relatively little concern even though his competency ultimately led him to the position of *Stadtverkmeister* of Augsburg. His outstanding accomplishment in engineering was really a sideline so far as he was concerned. His real interest and his real purpose in life consisted in his witnessing for Christ and his writing for the church. With the Anabaptists, work was given Christian significance, but its significance was derived mainly from its indirect support to the church as the way by which a disciple earns his bread. In contradistinction to Luther, they did not start with God's will in society. They began with the church. They did not permit the calling to be determined by the structures of creation. They subordinated these structures to the superior requirements of witnessing discipleship.

If the interpretation of Alan Richardson in *The Biblical Doctrine of Work* is correct, it is fair to say that the Anabaptist conception of the calling is really another instance of their return to the New Testament. Richardson points out that:

> the New Testament does not refer to "vocation" in the modern sense of a secular "profession" or "avocation." In the New Testament "vocation" (*klesis*, "calling") means God's call to repentance and faith and to a life of fellowship and service in the church.... The Bible knows no instance of a man's being called to an earthly profession or trade by God. St. Paul, for example, is called by God to be an apostle; he is not called to be a tent-maker. It is hardly too much to say that the Bible is uninterested in the various professionals and occupations in which men engage for the sake of earning a livelihood, provided that they are honest....
>
> This does not mean that Christians ought therefore to be entirely unconcerned about questions of secular employment.... They have Christian value, however, only in so far as they can be made a means to the end of the Gospel.[58]

The tension between the missionary call to "go" and the call of cultural responsibility to "stay" was never completely resolved by the Anabaptists. Not everyone was able to be on the move. The inevitable demands for security kept some at home. Others went out to preach.

Possibly the most effective practical solution to the problem of the conflict between the interests of Gospel itinerancy and the interests of natural stability was that of the Hutterites. The communistic communities which developed in Moravia under the able leadership of Peter Ridemann, author of the basic document of Hutterianism entitled *Rechenschaft*[59] (1540), were really bases of missionary enterprises. The principle of complete community (*Gemeinschaft*) with its severe discipline was calculated to implement the Great Commission. The Hutterite community with its tight organization was not in its early days an introverted cell with no sense of world responsibility. It was part of a world vision. It was a concentration of spiritual and material strength expressly intended to be disseminated throughout the world for the purpose of the formation of new Christian communities. It was a matter of general practice for Hutterites to be sent out two by two into the world to preach the Gospel while others remained behind for reasons of support. One of the purposes of the Hutterite communities in Moravia was to prepare havens of rest for persecuted Anabaptists of all kinds. Franklin Littell says, "The Hutterian Brethren developed one of the most perfect missionary organizations of the time, and strongly under-wrote the work of the Tyrol, South Germany, and even in the Netherlands, with personnel and place of refuge. The original Anabaptist impulse survived most vigorously in those congregations which were most missionary."[60] In the Hutterite community, as long as the members were tolerated by the authorities, the natural requirements of life including food, shelter, work and community were amply supplied while at the same time the entire life in community was dedicated to the world. This was perhaps the most successful attempt to bring the permanent natural requirements of culture into harmony with the fundamental missionary impulse of discipleship in Anabaptist history.

We come now to the concluding summary section of our discussion of the Anabaptist concept of discipleship, namely its general implication *for culture, with particular reference to that central reality in world culture, namely the political realm.*

III. Conclusion

Our conclusion is that the Anabaptist interpretation of Christianity, viz., discipleship is at best in a constant state of tension with culture. When the (1) methods and (2) goals of discipleship and culture are compared, the inescapable conclusion is that they tend to pull in opposite directions. If by discipleship we mean a type of Christianity based upon the life and teachings of Christ and if by culture we mean human institutions organized according to the basic principles of social and political structure, then we are bound to conclude that an undialectical relationship between the two is impossible. They clash at the very center of their natures. What are some of these points of tension?

A. *The tension between the unqualified vertical lines of duty to God in discipleship and the horizontal lines of duty within world culture.* The disciple is oriented toward the perfect will of God as revealed in Christ. Therefore no historical demand may justify compromise. However, world culture not only permits but requires compromise. The disciple is a perfectionist. He is not necessarily a perfectionist in the sense that he claims to have achieved perfection. He is a perfectionist in the sense that Christ was a perfectionist, i.e., he knows no authority, he knows no law, he knows no institution which may lay on him a hold prior to the absolute will of God as revealed by Christ.[61] No horizontal sense of prudential responsibility for the family, for the economic order, or for the religio-political order may make the disciple into anyone but one who imitates God alone. The immediate situation with its demands for compromise, with its bid for adjustments, with its eye to consequences and with its inexorable involvements in the stream of relativities is completely disregarded. The position of Jesus and his way of discipleship is grounded in cultural obliviousness. Jesus' ethic is the perfect fruit of prophetic religion. It does not appeal to any socio-political result for its justification. It does not speak directly to any complex social situation. It is interested only in personal fulfillment of the revealed law of love. Jesus did not derive his ethic from an analysis of the cultural situation. He did not countenance and therefore did not speak to the immediate problems of Jewish socio-political life. He simply called for a group of followers whose lives are oriented in the Kingdom of God.

On the other hand, the genius of culture is to qualify conduct based upon the perfect will of God by requirements relative to the immediate socio-political situation. Culture resists the absolute. It cannot easily accommodate the pure Gospel of love. This is not to say that culture is completely intolerant of love. Culture is normally a strange and complex combination of egoistic and altruistic principles. It combines a reduced form of love with various subtle and obvious forms of aggressive egoism. Culture as we have experienced it does not tolerate pure love or pure egoism. Therefore neither the egoistic anarchy described by Hobbes as the condition of "each against all" nor the altruistic utopianism described by Marx, when each will give according to his ability and receive according to his need, are cultural possibilities. At best culture represents a balance of egoistic and altruistic impulses. Therefore the disciple who is dedicated to the pure ideal of love and the perfect laws of the Kingdom as described in the Sermon on the Mount cannot accept responsibility for a total culture.

B. *The conflict between heedlessness of self-sacrifice in discipleship and the prudential self-regarding principles of culture.* As we have seen, Christianity, as presented in the New Testament and Christianity and as interpreted by the Anabaptists, accepted the cross as a matter of personal commitment. The ministry of suffering was interpreted as an extension of the perfect work of Christ. God is revealed most ambiguously in his sacrifice, the expression of pure *agape*. This means that the disciple renounces historical securities when these in any way clash with the securities of others. The disciple therefore renounces all those social and political defenses which are intended to guarantee his security. He refuses to compete in the rivalries of history except those of a purely spiritual kind which may be advanced by spiritual means. For as Reinhold Niebuhr says:

> It is impossible to symbolize the divine goodness in history in any other way than by complete powerlessness, or rather by a consistent

refusal to use power in the rivalries of history. For there is no self in history or society, no matter how impartial its perspective upon the completions of life, which can rise to the position of a disinterested participation in those rivalries and competitions. It can symbolize love only by a refusal to participate in the rivalries. Any participation in them means the assertion of one ego against another.[62]

Culture, on the other hand, is mindful first of all of the very opposite of sacrifice, namely survival. Survival, of course, ranges from the sheer will to exist to the maintenance of the finer religious and aesthetic values. Nevertheless, the will to provide the means of existence through prudent accumulation of goods and institutionally entrenched traditions and mechanisms of social and political power is the most basic drive of culture. Therefore if the disciple attaches himself to the aims and ideals of a culture, he is bound to abandon his ethic of pure sacrificial love and exchange it for an ethic of resistance.[63]

The clash between discipleship and culture is most evident in the realm of political structures. The realities of politics betray more vividly than personal relationships the difficulties of the historical realization of the ideal relationship of love. The essence of politics is the conquest of anarchy by the coercion of human interests into some kind of order, offering human beings at the same time at least a minimum of mutual support. The end of political action is justice. In this respect politics is both necessary and right. But it is a reign of justice which is guaranteed not by love mutuality but mainly by egoistic mutuality. It is, in other words, a forced mutuality by which government as a third party constantly surveys, proscribes and enforces an armistice between sometimes contending and sometimes co-operating powers. This is not to say that the goals of politics and love are absolutely antithetical. The social expression of love is always *dynamic* justice. The Kingdom of God will be characterized by the principle of justice. Nevertheless the methods and the presuppositions of justice in the political realm are quite different from those of the Kingdom. In politics justice is coerced and in the Kingdom justice is achieved by free uncalculating consent. Hence Emil Brunner goes to the extreme by placing love and justice at opposite poles. Brunner says:

> Justice is a totally different thing (than love). When we are just, and deal justly, we render the other what is his due. Justice makes no free gift; it give precisely what is *due* to the other, no more and no less. Its basis is strictly realistic, sober and rational...for it loves the unworthy. This love is only to be comprehended by him for whom the "foolishness of the cross" is no folly, but who recognizes in it "the power of God."[64]

In view of the inevitable conflict between discipleship love and social and political structures it is understandable why the Anabaptists felt that following Christ meant rejection of direct participation in the political realm. No government can be absolutely loving, forgiving and completely sacrificial.

C. *The conflict between the other worldly orientation of discipleship and the this worldly orientation of cultural involvement.* In our discussion of Anabaptism and the Great Commission it was indicated that the notion of "looseness" was used by the Anabaptists to define their relation to culture. All cultural ties were subordinated and if needs be sacrificed for the sake of the spreading of the good news. The enemy of discipleship is the process of settling in one place in cultural entrenchment with all that this means for the development of political organization and economic wealth. This follows a line of Biblical thought which sees culture as at least a threat to true faith and godliness if not a fatal error. All through her history, Israel was tempted to add to the simplicity of nomadic life the rudiments of advanced culture and in so doing to exchange her faith in the transcendent God of prophetic religion for the imminence of acculturated, institutionalized cultic practice. Coming from a desert background, Israel resisted the culture of the Fertile Crescent. Echoes of this feeling are even found in the traditions preserved in Genesis 2:11 (J). The story of the Tower of Babel reflects a nomadic protest against the proud culture of the Fertile Crescent.[65] Furthermore, "the first city was built by a murderer, Cain, who was incensed by the fact that his agricultural offering of the 'fruit of the ground' was not as acceptable to Yahweh as his brother's nomadic gift of the firstlings of the flock" (Gen. 4:1-17).[66] Noah was the first to plant a vineyard and he became a spectacle of nakedness and drunkenness. Abraham was a nomadic tent-dweller who left the walled city of Haran with the securities of advanced culture. "By faith he sojourned in the land of promise, as in a foreign land, living in tents.... For he looked forward to the city which has foundations, whose maker and builder is God" (Heb. 11:10). In true eschatological expectation, Abraham looked forward to a city but it was not a city of worldly culture. It was the city of God. It may be remembered also that when Jacob agreed to settle in Egypt, he sought guarantees that he could settle his family in the undeveloped "land of Goshen" (Gen. 46:34) where he could retain the simplicity of his faith and way of life at the edge of Egyptian culture. The struggle between the faith of the Israelites and the Canaanites is likewise a familiar story. The Canaanitish threat was essentially the threat of the imminence of culture. Deity and culture were so intimately related in the fertility cults that they were inseparable. Furthermore, the simple charismatic rule of the judges was eventually overthrown by demands for central political organization in the Kingdom. The reluctance of God to grant Israel a king can be explained partly by the dangers of the worship of culture and the attempt to obtain premature securities outside of God. "And the Lord said to Samuel, 'hearken to the voice of the people in all that they say to you; for they have not rejected you, but they have rejected me from being king over them.'" (1 Samuel 8:7). Even well into the period of the Kingdom the reaction against culture persisted through those who looked to the wilderness journey as the outstanding period of religious immediacy. This is the position of the Rechabites, a primitivistic sect of Israel who may be compared to the American Amish by their cultural reductionism (Jer. 35). The dangers of cultural affluence for genuine religious faith was a constant theme of the prophets, particularly Isaiah and Micah. In Isaiah Chapter 2 the prophet chastises the "house of Jacob" for being "full" of the things of the nations round about. They are full of diviners, full of silver and gold; the land is "filled" with horses, chariots and they "strike hands with foreigners." Certainly the Rechabite answer and the prophetic answer to the problem is not the same. The Rechabites were the thorough-going cultural reductionists. Nevertheless the prophets knew that with high culture hearts are weaned away from God.

Jesus stands in the tradition of prophetic religion. The center of his teaching is the Kingdom of God (Mark 2).[67] Much literature has appeared in recent years concerning the problem of the relation of His ethics to His eschatology.[68] This much is clear. Jesus was not dedicated to the continuity of the institutional, political and cultural life of the Jews. Nor did he intend to replace Jewish national life with another earthly system. His Gospel concerned the coming reign of God over all the earth. In the meantime, he called his followers to sell their possessions and give to the poor (Luke 12:33), to have simple faith which transcends anxiety (Matt. 6:27), to renounce certain filial responsibilities (Matt. 8:21), to take up the cross and to become a servant. None of these practices and their underlying spiritual attitudes support culture. When expressed in their absoluteness they are against culture since they strike at the permanent structures of civilization. They are otherworldly (John 18:36). By that we mean they belong to the Kingdom of God and not the Kingdom of men.

The revival of the ethic and the Kingdom orientation of Jesus by the Anabaptists made it impossible for them to become involved responsibly in the total cultural scene of the sixteenth century. It is true that Christian eschatology and social responsibility are not necessarily contradictory. Ray C. Petry has clearly shown in his *Christian Eschatology and Social Thought* that:

> Christian social thought has been largely barren aside from the inner vitality of eschatology.... In the first fifteen hundred years of Christian history, at least, eschatology provided the basic motivation and nucleating matter for Christian social thinking.[69]

Nevertheless, eschatology can become the basis for a total social order only when it is grafted into non-eschatological ways of thinking. This is the point which Troeltsch makes over and over. It is true that the Middle Ages possessed a strong eschatological emphasis. But we know also that secular philosophy played a major role in the thinking of the Middle Ages. Not only the eschatology of the Kingdom of God but also Plato's hierarchy of being and the natural theology of St. Thomas were combined into a sometimes confusing combination of historical and ontological ideas. The genius of the Anabaptists, however, was their pure Biblicism, their total preoccupation with the idea of the Kingdom of God and therefore their complete neglect of the great problems of cultural life in this world.

One of the major differences between the Reformers and the Anabaptists is the fact that whereas the Reformer's attitudes were determined by considerations of the total ecclesiastical-political situation, presented by Christendom, the Anabaptists never thought "responsibly" in terms of entire historical processes. The Anabaptists had their citizenship in heaven; they were pilgrims and strangers; they had no abiding city; like Abraham they went out "not knowing whither they went;" they shunned riches and learning; they practiced separation from the world; they drew distinctions between the Kingdom of God and the Kingdom of the world, not only theoretically but with concrete reference to existing institutions. Such disciples do not take upon themselves the direct responsibility for the world of culture. They look for a radically new order of life called the Kingdom of God and they do not feel responsible for a smooth transition from one to the other.

Endnotes

[1] The fact that the Christian church as a whole has not been pacifist and the reasons why are discussed by Reinhold Niebuhr in his essay, "Why the Christian Church is Not Pacifist," *Christianity and Power Politics* (New York: Charles Scribner's Sons, 1940), pp. 1-32. Paul Ramsey also deals with the question as to why the Christian church gave up its doctrine of nonresistance by the time of Augustine. He notes that St. Ambrose (340-396 A.D.) and St. Augustine (345-430 A.D.) "were the first to give fully elaborated theoretical defense of Christian participation in armed conflict." Ramsey points out that although they formulated the theory of the *justum bellum*, they held to nonresistance in case of personal conflict. They developed a doctrine of "vocational resistance" in conformity with social responsibility. Cf. Paul Ramsey, *Basic Christian Ethics* (New York: Charles Scribner's Sons, 1951), pp. 171ff.

[2] Reinhold Niebuhr speaks to this point as follows: "The ethics of nonresistance as taught on the Sermon on the Mount are in perfectly consistent relation with the love symbolized in the Cross.... The final majesty, the ultimate freedom, and the perfect disinterestedness of the divine love can have a counterpart in history only in a life which ends tragically, because it refuses to partipate in the claims and counterclaims of historical existence." *The Nature and Destiny of Man*, II (London: Nisbet and Co., 1943), p. 75.

[3] *Op. cit.*

[4] The broad implications of nonresistance are stated by Guy F. Hershberger as follows: "The Christian doctrine of nonresistance is a comprehensive doctrine in two respects. First, the divine love on which it is based is an integral part of the Gospel itself, not a mere appendage to be attached or detached as convenience may require. Second, this basic divine love has many facets, reaching out into every corner of the Christian's life so that whether one is dealing with economic problems, with industrial relations, with the race question, or with neighborhood, community, and family relations, one is continually confronted with the necessity of applying the principle of love and nonresistance. In other words, it is an ethical principle which is much more far-reaching than the mere question of participation or nonparticipation in military service." "Nonresistance: Its Foundation and Outreach," *MQR*, XXIV (April, 1950), p. 156.

[5] The differences have been carefully articulated by modern theologians such as Anders Nygren in *Agape and Eros*, trans. Philip S. Watson (London: S.P.C.K., 1953) and by Reinhold Niebuhr in *The Nature and Destiny of Man*, II. Nygren's great work has the virtue of making the contrast between the complete disinterested love of the New Testament (agape) and love (eros) of classical thought. *Eros* is always tainted with the elements of egoism. Reinhold Niebuhr has shown that the love of Jesus as described in the Sermon on the Mount is sacrificial love and this must be distinguished from what he calls egoistic mutuality. While sacrificial love may culminate in altruistic mutual love, the former does not wait upon the latter. "The cross symbolizes the perfection of 'agape' which transcends all particular norms of justice and mutuality in history." *Ibid.*, p. 77.

[6] It should be remembered, of course, that pacifism has had a long history among individuals and small groups, especially in America. In 1815 Noah Worcester, a New England clergyman founded the Massachusetts Peace Society. William Ellery Channing was a pacifist who was convinced that "the tendencies of civilization are decidedly toward peace." *Discourses on War* (Boston: Gin and Co., 1903), p. 48. Pacifism, however, received its most ardent support as an aspect of the social gospel, the leading exponent of which was Walter Rauschenbusch. Pacifism

was conceived as an implication of the Kingdom of God. The Kingdom of God was expected with the gradual Christianization of the social order. In 1929 the Presbyterian General Assembly renounced "war as an instrument of national policy." W. W. Van Kirk, *Religion Renounces War* (Chicago: Willett, Clark and Co, 1934), p. 10. Other denominations passed similar resolutions. Van Kirk said in 1934, "The churches are speaking their mind on the cause and cure of war." *Ibid.*, p. 91. In 1933 the Federal Council of Churches urged the continuation of negotiations for disarmament and the abolition of certain kinds of weapons. Furthermore, large numbers of individuals renounced personal participation in war. The theology behind much of the pacifist movement, except for the historic peace churches, was that of the social gospel and was summed up by Rauschenbusch as follows: "Jesus...lived in the hope of a great transformation of the national, social, and religious life about him.... The Kingdom of God is...not a matter of saving human atoms, but of saving the social organism. It is not a matter of getting individuals to heaven, but of transforming the life on earth into the harmony of heaven." Walter Rauschenbusch, *Christianity and the Social Crisis* (New York: 1912), pp. 64-65.

[7] Robert Friedmann, "Concerning the True Soldier of Christ," *MQR*, V (April, 1933), p. 91.

[8] Robert Friedmann, "Anabaptism and Protestantism," *MQR*, XXIV (January, 1950), p. 22.

[9] *Martyr's Mirror*, p. 419.

[10] That the Anabaptist idea of peace was influenced by humanism cannot be denied. However, humanism contributed only to a minor extent in the formation of the Anabaptist position. Cf. Harold S. Bender, "Pacifism of the Sixteenth Century Anabaptists," *Church History* XXIV (June, 1955), pp. 119-120.

[11] Emil Egli, *Aktensammlung zur Geschichte der Züricher Reformation 1519-1533* (Zürich: 1878). Cited by Harold S. Bender, *Conrad Grebel*, p. 200.

[12] Walter Rauschenbusch, "The Zürich Anabaptists and Thomas Müntzer," *American Journal of Theology* (1905), pp. 95, 98.

[13] Art. 6. John C. Wenger, *Doctrines of the Mennonites* (Scottdale, Penna.: Mennonite Publishing House, 1950), pp. 72-73.

[14] Don E. Smucker, "The Theological Basis for Chirstian Pacifism," *MQR*, XXVII (July, 1953), p. 117.

[15] *Two Kinds of Obedience. An Anabaptist Tract on Christian Freedom*, trans. and ed. John C. Wenger, *MQR*, XXI (January, 1947), pp. 18-22.

[16] *Christian Faith and Social Action*, p. 12.

[17] Cf. George H. Williams and Angel M. Mergal, eds. *Spiritual and Anabaptist Writers*, p. 31.

[18] *Martyr's Mirror*, p. 416.

[19] Williams and Mergal, "The Trial and Martyrdom of Michael Sattler," *Spiritual and Anabaptist Writers*, p. 141.

[20] *Martyr's Mirror*, p. 417; Gustave Bossert, "Michael Sattler's Trial and Martyrdom in 1527," *MQR* XXV (January, 1951), pp. 201-218.

[21] Reference is made to the conduct of George Blaurock who attempted to replace the regular preacher, Niklaus Billeter, upon his own authority. Fritz Blanke describes this incident as follows: "Zwischen den beiden entspinnt sich im Angesicht der Gemeinde eine erregete Unterredung. Blaurock fragt—eine rhetorische Frage—den Pfarrer, was er tun wolle. Billeter, als guter Zwingliianer, antwortet: 'Ich will das Gotteswort predigen.' Blaurock entgegnet: 'Nicht du bist, sondern ich bin gesandt zu predigen.'" Fritz Blanke, *Brüder in Christo. Die Geschichte der ältesten Taufergemeinde* (Zollikon, 1525) (Zürich: Zwingli-Verlag, 1955), p. 33.

[22] This fear lies behind much of Calvin's political thought contained in *Institutes of the Christian Religion*, Bk. IV, Ch. XX.

[23] Gordon D. Kaufman, "Some Theological Emphases of the Early Swiss Anabaptists," *MQR,XXV* (April, 1951), pp. 82-83.

[24] The revolutionary implications of even the nonresistant, cross-bearing Anabaptists is presented in a recent study by Lowell H. Zuck, "Anabaptism: Abortive Counter-Revolt Within the Reformation," *Church History*, XXVI (September, 1957), pp.211-226.

[25] "Anabaptists and the State," *The Recovery of the Anabaptist Vision*, Guy F. Hershberger, ed., p. 183.

[26] Behind the Schleitheim Confession lies an unknown opposition party. Cf. Beatrice Jenny, *Das Schleitheimer Täuferbekenntnis 1927* (Thaynagen: Karl Augustin, 1951), pp. 33ff. John C. Wenger, translator of this confession, says that Michael Sattler, most likely the chief editor, "seems...to be setting up a defense against the doctrines of 'false brethren' with antinomian tendencies." *Doctrines of the Mennonites*, p. 69. Knowing who these antinomian brethren were would help our understanding of the Seven Articles. According to the recent scholarship of Jan J. Kiwiet, the Schleitheim Confession arose out of a disagreement between the Swiss Anabaptists under the leadership of Sattler and the south German Anabaptists under the leadership of Hans Denk. Jan J. Kiwiet, *Hans Denk and His Teaching*, B.D. Thesis, February, 1954, Baptist Theological Seminary, Rüschlikon-Zurich, pp. 104-105. The former were more inclined toward New Testament literalism and a more rigorous application of the ethic of Christ than the latter. The Swiss Anabaptists arose in the Zwinglian Reformation in which the appeal to Scriptures in a rather legalistic fashion was a general characteristic, whereas the South German Anabaptists arose under the influence of Luther in which the inward appeal of the Word was a dominant characteristic. These two types of Anabaptism, it is thought, faced each other before the movement was two years old. The Schleitheim Confession reflects this difference. This is not to suggest that the South German Anabaptists accepted the magistracy wholeheartedly. They were aware of the tension between pacifism as the coercive arm of justice but they were less arbitrary in their definitions and more likely to go along with limited participation in government. It was in reality an unsettled question among the South German Anabaptists of which Hans Denk was the leader.

[27] Art. 6.

[28] On the basis of a thorough examination of Anabaptist literature, Hans J. Hillerbrand shows that the divine origin of the office of the magistracy is an integral aspect of the Anabaptist view. *Die Politische Ethik des oberdeutschen Täufertums...des 16. Jahrhunderts*, Doctoral Thesis, 1957, Erlangen, p. 48.

[29] Schleitheim Confession, Art. 6.

[30] *STCC*, I, pp. 343ff.

[31] The Schleitheim Confession, Art. 6.

[32] Cf. Leo Tolstoy, *The Law of Love and the Law of Violence*, trans. by Mark K. Tolstoy (New York: Rudolph Field, 1948); *My Confession, My Religion* (New York: T. Y.Crowell and Co., 1899), Ch. II; *the Kingdom of God is Within You*, trans. by Leo Wiener (Boston: Dona Estes and Co., 1905), Ch. X.

[33] The Schleitheim Confession, Art. 6.

[34] Schleitheim Confession, Art. 4.

[35] Cf. Paul Tillich, *Love, Power and Justice* (London: Oxford University Press, 1954). In dealing with the problem as to how the compulsory element of power may be united with love,

Tillich refers to Luther's concept of "strange love." "Nobody felt the weight of this question more than Luther, who had to combine his highly spiritual ethics of love with his highly realistic politics of absolutistic power. Luther answered with the statement that compulsion is the strange work of love." p. 49.

[36] Art. 6.

[37] *Ibid.*

[38] *Ibid.*

[39] *Ibid.*

[40] *Weimarer Ausgabe*, 10, I, 308, 6ff. (Kirchenpostille, 1922). Cited by George Wolfgang Forell, *Faith Active in Love* (New York: American Press), p. 125.

[41] "Secular Authority," *Works*, Philadelphia Edition, III, p. 241.

[42] Alexander Miller, "Towards a Doctrine of Vocation," *Christian Faith and Social Action*, ed. John A. Hutchison, p. 121.

[43] "Secular Authority," *Works*, Philadelphia Edition, II, p. 246. Cited by *ibid.*, p. 122.

[44] John Calvin, *The Institutes of the Christian Religion*, trans. John Allen, II (Philadelphia: Presbyterian Board of Christian Education, 1936), Bk. IV, Ch. XX, para. 4, p. 775.

[45] *Ibid.*, par. 3, pp. 772-773.

[46] Schleitheim Confesion, Art. 6.

[47] *Op. cit.*, par. 2, p. 772.

[48] Forell, *op. cit.*, pp. 122-123.

[49] For a thorough discussion of the Calvinistic conception of the calling as compared with the Lutheran view, cf. Max Weber, "Die Protestantische Ethik und der Geist des Kapitalismus," *op. cit.*, pp. 99ff.

[50] Lydia Müller, ed., *Glaubensqeugnisse oberdeutscher Taufgesinnten* (Leipzig: M. Heinsuis Nachf., 1938), XX; *Quellen und Forschungen zur Reformationsgeschichte*, p. 15. Cited by Littell, *The Anabaptist View of the Church*, p. 95.

[51] Littell, *ibid.*, pp. 95-96.

[52] Cited by *ibid.*, p. 97.

[53] Josef Beck, ed. *Die Geschichte-Bücher der Wiedertäufer in Osterreich-Ungarn* (Wien: Carl Gerold's Sohn, 1883); XLIII Fontes Rerum Austraiacarum (Hist. Comm. Kaiserl. Akad. der Wiss. in Wien), 2te Abth. Cited by *ibid.*, p. 99.

[54] Robert Friedmann, "The Epistles of the Hutterian Brethren, "*MQR*, XX (July, 1946), p. 153.

[55] Menno Simons, "Sincere Appeal to Leonard Bouwen's Wife, *The Complete Writings of Menno Simons*, p. 1039.

[56] Kierkegaard, *Attack Upon "Christendom,"* *op. cit.*, p. 221.

[57] Cf. John C. Wenger, "The Theology of Pilgram Marpeck," *MQR*, XII (October, 1938), pp. 205-256. *Ibid.*, "Life and Work of Pilgram Marpeck," *MQR*, XII (July, 1938), pp. 137-166. For a study of Marpeck's theology see Jan J. Kiwiet, *Pilgram Marpeck*, Doctoral Dissertation, Zurich, April, 1955.

[58] Alan Richardson, *The Biblical Doctrine of Work*, (London: SCM Press, Ltd., 1952), pp. 35, 37.

[59] Peter Ridemann, *Rechenschaft unserer Religion, Lehre und Glaubens* (Berne: Hutterischen Brüder Gemeine, 1902).

[60] Littell, *op. cit.*, p. 106.

[61] This is precisely the point of D. Bonhoeffer in his *The Cost of Discipleship*.

[62] *The Nature and Destiny of Man*, II, p. 75.

[63] The necessary transition from a Christian ethic of nonresistance to a Christian ethic of resistance as one assumed responsibility for the life of the world is most clearly presented by Paul Ramsey, *Basic Christian Ethics* (New York: Charles Scribner's Sons, 1951), Ch. V. After describing Christ's ethic as one of complete disinterested love for God and the neighbor, including nonresistance, he goes on to show why this absolute ethic is impossible in actual life. It is impossible because of the implications of the *vocation* as a calling to participate responsibly in society. Ramsey believes that as soon as one considers his place in a socially responsible context as parent or citizen, "vocational resistance" is necessary both as an expression of love to the neighbor and the self. "A Christian does whatever love requires, and the possibility cannot be ruled out that on occasion defending himself may be a duty he owes to others." p. 176.

[64] Emil Brunner, *Justice and the Social Order* (New York: Harper and Brothers, 1945), p. 127.

[65] Bernhard W. Anderson, *Understanding the Old Testament* (Englewood Cliffs, New Jersey, 1957), p. 93.

[66] *Ibid.*

[67] Cf. John Bright, *op. cit.*, pp. 187-214.

[68] Cf. especially Amos N. Wilder, *Eschatology and Christian Ethics* (New York: Harper and Brothers, 1950).

[69] Ray C. Petry, *Christian Eschatology and Christian Thought* (New York: Abingdon Press, 1956), p. 16.

CHAPTER 4
ANABAPTISM AND THE CORPUS CHRISTIANUM

In chapters 2 and 3 an attempt was made to describe discipleship as the central idea of Anabaptism. For Anabaptism, discipleship is the "essence" of Christianity. Its importance for social policy therefore is comparable to "Grace" in Lutheranism and to the "Divine Law" in Calvinism. Discipleship is defined as the concrete response of the Christian to the claims of Christ. In this response the total life of the Christian is surrendered in a way which brings the inner disposition and the outward act together. Therefore, in Anabaptism, faith and ethics lie extremely close together. They are distinguishable but inseparable.

Furthermore, discipleship stands for life patterned after the example and teachings of Christ. The historical Christ is accepted as a pattern for *all* Christians at *all* times. The uniqueness of discipleship for Christian ethics in general and for social responsibility in particular lies in the fact that no appeal from philosophy or history is permitted to qualify the terms of obedience to Christ. None of the traditional counter-claims to simple and direct obedience are recognized. The strenuous commands of Christ are held to be historically obligatory and possible. No attempt is made to shift their meaning from one of literal fulfillment to spiritual intention. No qualifying consideration is given to historical circumstances, to social consequences, to multilateral responsibilities, to the comprehensive needs of society, to the vocational calling or to the fact of one's own weakness and sin. All alien sources of moral guidance which in any way tend to lower the level of Christian duty from the substance and the form of Christ's commands are either ignored or deliberately rejected. By alien sources the author refers to moral criteria outside Christ's teaching which the church has from time to time combined with the pure ethic of love in order to translate the Christian ethic into forms which are relevant to the problems of civilization. Examples are the "relative natural law" (Catholicism), the "orders of creation" (Lutheranism), the Old Testament theocratic ideal (Calvinism), philosophical idealism (modern religious liberalism) and the "responsible society" (World Council of Churches at Amsterdam in 1948 and at Evanston in 1954). Anabaptism stands for extreme simplicity in thought and obedience. It is the simplicity of pure love which knows nothing of the complexity and confusion of compromise. It knows nothing of the complicated relationships between the absolute and relative laws of nature of Catholic social theory, nor about the tensions of Lutheran dualistic ethics, nor can it understand Calvin's retention of the laws and institutions of the Old Covenant as a basis for life under the New Covenant. In the last analysis, Anabaptism stands for the earliest and most simple approach to Christian duty, namely, that which issues directly from the life and teaching of the historical Jesus as the Incarnate Lord.[1]

In describing the way of discipleship it was pointed out that discipleship implies suffering in relation to the world. It involves an inner attitude of complete resignation (*Gelassenheit*) to God and to the brother in Christ. Furthermore discipleship means the complete rejection of force. It upholds nonresistance and separation from all coercive structures such as the law court and the military establishment. On the positive side, however, discipleship is interpreted to mean an active lay missionary program of global proportions. The world is a vast mission field, Christendom notwithstanding.

The problem which is considered in this chapter is the problem of the implications of discipleship for the total social structure. Does discipleship imply a positive social ethic? If so, what kind of comprehensive relationship between Christianity and society does the Anabaptist concept of discipleship imply? What does discipleship mean for the broader tasks and purposes of the world. These questions have already been touched in the discussion of discipleship--especially in dealing with nonresistance, the magistracy and the missionary motive. However, they were considered largely from the standpoint of the individual disciple. We wish now to consider the relationship between the Anabaptist conception of the *church* and the total social order.

This problem is approached by a comparison of the two fundamental social theories of the church in its relation to the world since the Middle Ages, namely the *corpus christianum* and the *corpus christi*. The former is the theory of the main body of Christendom, both Catholic and Protestant, of Medieval and Reformation times and the latter is the theory of numerous dissenting groups from the early church to the Anabaptists. This comparison is relevant for the modern period. Its relevance for the modern church lies in the fact that despite the changes which have been wrought through the separation of church and state and the less formal but no less effective influences of the Enlightenment and of Secularism, two general ecclesiastical attitudes toward the social order remain today in line with these fundamental concepts. First is the attitude of social responsibility, i.e., the attitude of the main body of churches which try to dominate the moral and social life of the total community, irrespective of their legal standing with the state. This attitude was cultivated by the *corpus christianum* of the Middle Ages and continued virtually unbroken into the Reformation. Second is the rejection of social responsibility by sects such as the Mennonite Church, together with their fellowship, desiring neither to dominate society nor to be controlled by society, beyond evangelistic witness and individual moral influence. This is the *corpus christi* approach. We cannot understand present social strategies of the churches apart from the place they are given within either of these basic positions.[2] Certainly these positions are broad. Within the *corpus christianum* approach we include the numerous small sects of the Middle Ages and Reformation which separated themselves from the usual life of Christendom and sought to restore the "true" church in its separation from the world according to the pattern of the early church.

It should be stated also that to compare the *corpus christianum* with the *corpus christi* is the same as to compare the "Church" and the "Sect" as defined by Troeltsch in his great sociological study of the churches.[3] Although the typology of Troeltsch has been subjected to considerable study and criticism, especially by those who are aware of the processes of hybridization in the churches of the modern period, this typology continues to serve as a useful basis for our understanding of the really crucial differences in social policy among the churches.[4] Troeltsche's division of the churches into the "Church," "Sect," and "Mystical" groups is especially valuable for our study since the two types in question are represented in their purest form by the Mediaeval and Reformation traditions on the one hand and the sixteenth century Anabaptists on the other hand.

The procedure in this chapter is to define the sociological and theological meaning of *corpus christianum* and then to present the essence of the Anabaptist "sectarian" dissent and its meaning for social structure.

I. The Conception of the *Corpus Christianum*

It is by no means easy to define the *corpus christianum* without resorting to oversimplification or distortion. The *corpus christianum* is a comprehensive view of the church and society containing many of the inescapable obscurities of mediaeval Christianity. It contains the universal tendencies toward unity which are characteristic of mediaeval theological, social and political thought, while at the same time fathers within this unity differences and complexities on every level which challenge the unity and which sometimes threaten to break loose on an independent course. To do justice to both the tendencies toward unity as well as toward plurality and to see them in proper relationship to each other is the problem of anyone who approaches mediaeval Christianity.

Visser 't Hooft has defined the *corpus christianum* as follows:

> The expression Corpus Christianum needs definition. In this study we will use it to indicate the overlapping of Church and world, so that either Church and State, or Church and Nation, are considered as co-terminous realities which have distinct tasks, but which cannot be separated from each other. The relation between the elements within the Corpus may be conceived very differently (Ecclesiocracy, Caesaropapism, Symphony or Collaboration), but in every case that relation is one between a Church which considers the State or Society as a Christian State or Society, and the Sate or Society which recognized that Church as the true Church. The Church is publicly acknowledged by the authorized representatives of the secular world, and the world is looked upon by the church as a baptized and a christianized world. That situation is not the one of the New Testament church. Nor is it our own situation. But since it

has lasted for many centuries and has left an indelible impression on the whole of Church history, it is of the highest importance that we should consider its meaning and its relevance for our own situation today.[5]

The most inescapable meaning of the *corpus christianum* is wholeness or universality. It aims at a single integrated community-state and church. This Christian universality seeks to bring every aspect of individual and corporate existence under the domination of the spiritual realm which is secured historically by the objective institutional Church. Even the most rudimentary processes of life within the natural world as well as the most advanced activities of culture are brought under the all-embracing benediction and judgment of the Christian ethos. The Lordship of Christ is ideally extended beyond the walls of the Church as an institution to include the entire life of the world. The *corpus christianum* as an ideal knows nothing outside itself. It is a totalitarian mode of existence in which every individual and every institution receive their place in ordered society by being *organically* related to the whole. Even though some realms of life resist the domestication of pure "Grace," provision is made within the body of divine society for the "natural," without loss of individuality and without the loss of the final unity. This is an ideal of an all-embracing ecclesiastical civilization.

The limits of the church are hard to determine in the *corpus christianum*. If the church is conceived simply as an objective institution for the dispensation of grace,[6] the lines of the church may be fairly clearly drawn. The church is then easily distinguished from such social institutions as economic and political institutions. Sometimes the church is presented in this way. But when the mediaeval mind comes under the influence of the ideal of the *corpus christianum*, the church and the world are considered one. The meaning of the *corpus christianum* is that the church has taken the world into itself. There are times when *corpus christi* and *genus humanum* are identical. Thomas Aquinas makes this identification as follows: "*Genus humanum consideratur quasi unam corpus, quod vocatur mysticum, cujus caput est ipse Christus et quantum ad animas et quantum ad corpora.*"[7]

This means that the world is in a dependent relation to the church. The church is in a position to guide the whole course of the world. Any major course of action which assumes an autonomous relation to the church violates the essential meaning of the *corpus christianum*. Therefore the church must take within itself the problems of the world. This the mediaeval church tried to do through a theological system which related all things to God in a hierarchy of "being" and through an objective institution of grace which alone possessed the keys to eternal destiny. In fulfilling its comprehensive mission the church really appeared twice, first an empirical institution intimately tied up with the affairs of the world only through this objective institution. This was, of course, the issue between the church and the anti-papists.

The conception of wholeness which lay behind Christendom and *republica christiana* was grounded in the unity of God as the ultimate Being.[8] Oneness in religio-social reality was the logical result of the oneness of God. The world in its totality was conceived as a mirror of God's essential unity. Of course provision was made for the "part" in accordance with the nature of the created world. The genius of mediaeval thought, as it applies to social, political and religious affairs, is its ability to make provision within the unity derived from God for the differences which inevitably appear within the world. But it should be remembered that in mediaeval thought the whole comes before the part and the part receives its proper function through the whole.[9]

A. *The Organic Ideal of Unity.* The figure of speech which was used most frequently to represent the social thought of the Middle Ages was the "body." The ideal of the *corpus Christianum* was an ideal of parts interrelated not unlike interrelation of parts within the "organism." Otto Gierke asserts that "under the influence of Biblical allegories and the models set by Greek and Roman writers, the comparison of Mankind at large and every smaller group to an animate body was universally adopted and pressed.... According to the allegory that was found in the profound words of the Apostle--an allegory which dominated all spheres of thought--Mankind constituted a Mystical Body, whereof the Head was Christ."[10]

St. Thomas defines the body as "a multitude ordained to one end, with distinct acts and duties."[11] Most significant is the end toward which the parts are unified. True Christian society is society organized to serve Christ as the Head. Furthermore the analogy of the body supported two ideas which were dominant in Aquinas' social thought. The first is *Natural Law* and the second is *Life*. The idea of Christ, the Head, pouring vitality into the body as an ordered structure lay behind his general theory of "organic" society. F. W. Dillistone, commenting on the organic ideals of the Middle Ages, says:

> Aquinas believed with all his heart that he was living in an ordered universe and that the secrets of its order would yield themselves to the patient enquiry of the human reason. These secrets were the 'laws' of its structure and it was his aim to set them forth accurately and systematically. The result was a hierarchical system which included the whole universe and within which every individual part could find its proper place.[12]

B. *The Rise of the Corpus Christianum.* One must pause to ask how it is possible that the church could have developed into a world embracing institution in light of its separation from the world during the first three hundred years of its history. It is generally accepted that the early church had no intention of dominating the world. It regarded itself as the body of the elect who were separated from the passing world. The concept of the church as "an elect race, a royal priesthood, a holy nation, God's own people" (I Peter 2:9-10), a patient suffering minority whose only hope of world dominion belongs to the *eschaton* is not easily translated into a concept of the church as the controlling power of civilization. The shift in attitude toward culture by the early church as it developed into the church of the Middle Ages represents the most significant reversal in the history of the Christian church. This change from pre-Constantinian retirement from the pagan world to the aggressive Christianization of the world by preaching as well as political and military coercion is a change which is still not fully clear to the historians. Troeltsch takes the position that the *corpus christianum* is not a part of the original Gospel, though he would not reject it for that reason. Such ideas as the "organic" unity of civilization are in fact "alien" to the Gospel." Troeltsch says:

> After all, it is not simple to build up a civilization and a society upon the supernatural values of the love of God and the brethren. The self-denial and renunciation of the world which are connected with the former, and the renunciation of the claim on justice and force which are connected with the latter, are not principles of civilization, but radical and universal religious and ethical ideas, which are only absorbed with difficulty into the aims of the secular structure, and into the protective measures which the struggle for existence has produced.[13]

After a detailed account of the development of the Christianization of culture during the Middle Ages, he concludes that "it was thus at first actually due to pure coincidence that the social, economic, and political conditions of mediaeval life made a comparatively thorough and direct Christianization of civilization possible."[14] He is certain that "the hierarchical theocratic unity of civilization....could not have been directly deduced from the religious thought of the church as such."[15] Christian civilization came about as a result of the course of events of church history of the West.

In other words, the *corpus christianum* is more directly a result of the practical experience of Christianity in adjusting to the world over the period of a thousand years than a result of the Gospel. The *corpus christianum* is a theological idea but only indirectly so. It is the theology of the advanced stages of mission expansion. If the early church had remained a small minority in a pagan empire, its outlook on the world would likely have remained one of separateness. However, the very success of its evangelistic and moral influence changed its status before the world and, as the Christian community became broader in its social and economic base, it was forced to reckon responsibly with civilization. A denial of human institutions was no longer possible especially after it was looked upon as the only really creative and unifying force left in society.

Eventually a complete theology of Christian civilization emerged with this new status. The first great theologian of Christian civilization was Augustine. His *Civitas Dei* contained within it elements of dualistic apposition. Nevertheless, he was aware of the interpretation of the two cities in history, an acknowledgment which the theologians of synthesis have since used to reinforce their view. What is more important is the fact that Augustine culminates a line of thinking described brilliantly by Charles Norris Cochrane in his study of the encounter of Christian and classical culture according to which Classicism was supposed to have been found deficient as an ultimate explanation (arche') of history and was gradually replaced by a Christian interpretation of events provided by the conception of the Trinity.[16] This Christian movement was begun by Athanasius and Ambrose and climaxed by Augustine. This meant that Christianity possessed a principle of integration which was to replace integration based upon antiquity. Christ came to be looked upon as the logos and bound up with him was the whole realm of providence and the universal outlook upon human institutions which this perspective implies. This is not to say that Augustine abandoned his critical attitude toward the world. But at least he cannot be considered a secessionist of the type presented by Tertullian. Rather, Caesar and all other authorities of the world order had to submit to Christian principles. "For Christ, as he points out did not say, 'my kingdom is not of *The* world, but my kingdom is not of *This* world.' His meaning is best conveyed in the prayer, 'Thy Kingdom come.'"[17]

Another significant change which had a great influence upon the *corpus christianum* was that wrought by Augustine's ascribing to the church the characteristics of the Kingdom of God. In the New Testament the emphasis was upon the Kingdom coming with the advent of Christ upon the clouds (Matt. 24:30). A distinction was made between the Church and the Kingdom of God though this distinction is not absolute. In Augustine, however, the heavenly city which is "to come" is actually present, at least potentially.

> The original distinction between *Ekklesia* and *Basileia tou theou* is forgotten and replaced by Augustine's view that *Ecclesia et nunc est regnum Christi, regnumque coelorum.* Similarly the hope that 'every tongue should confess that Jesus Christ is Lord' is transformed in the theory that already, though in *potentia* and not *de facto*, all men belong to the Church. And the Church thus becomes an all-embracing institution based upon divine prerogatives rather than the community of those who belong to Christ. It is by ascribing to the Church the characteristics of the Kingdom of God and even of identifying the ordinance of the Church (as does Bonifacius VIII in his Bull *Unam Sanctam*) that it becomes possible to see Church and world united in one great comprehensive and unified system.[18]

C. *The Contribution of St. Thomas Aquinas.* The greatest exponent of the *corpus christianum* was St. Thomas Aquinas. This is not to say that Aquinas was the originator of the idea. Aquinas simply articulated in a systematic and comprehensive fashion the fundamental assumptions upon which the mediaeval system had been functioning for many years. The contribution of Aquinas lay in his ability to reconcile, unify and systematize the complex and often contradictory tendencies of the Middle Ages. No theologian in the history of the church has endeavored so earnestly to synthesize Christianity and culture. He developed a complete system of thought which accepted full responsibility for the institutions of culture. H. Richard Niebuhr has claimed that, "Partly because the full weight of the

Roman Catholic Church has been thrown into the scales in his favor, but largely because of the intellectual and practical adequacy of his system, his way of solving the problem of culture and Christ has become the standard way for hosts of Christians."[19] Aquinas brought to the problem of Christianity and the world both the absolutistic demands of Christ and the relative requirements of marriage, law, economics, and war. Aquinas was a monk who took the vows of poverty, celibacy and obedience. "But he is a monk in the church which has become the guardian of culture, the fosterer of learning, the judge of nations, the protector of the family, the governor of social religion. This great mediaeval organization, symbolized in the person of Thomas, itself represents the achievement of a remarkable practical synthesis."[20]

The question arises, however, how it was possible for a monk whose heart was oriented toward the spiritual life of the cloister and whose ethical sensitivity grasped the meaning of Christian love to make a place in his thinking and in his affections for the world. The answer lies in his feeling of duty to bring everything into a unity in obedience to God and to discover the inner laws of nature as a working basis apart from which no true reconciliation of the various elements of culture is possible. Aquinas brought the tradition of *lex naturae* to its finest expression. He did not hesitate to take into his system of thought the natural discoveries of Aristotle and his crowning achievement was the relation of his doctrine of nature with its strong empirical character to his doctrine of super-nature without confusing the two. His reliance upon natural law is clearly seen in his doctrine of man. Man is not simply a pilgrim pursuing his way through a wilderness of sin to the eternal city. Nor is he meant to be cloistered within an ecclesiastical order waiting for the resurrection of the body in order to be free. Man's life in this world is of importance because he is by nature (as Aristotle has said) *animal politicum et sociale* and therefore his life in society must be understood and regulated by the natural law. The state must be organized so that it can support the nature of man.[21] This means that it must conform to natural law. *It was really the acceptance of the idea of natural law which made it possible for the mediaeval church to accept the world.* This has been criticized, of course, as a concession to pagan thought. Some have claimed that Thomas, in reality, never resolved the intrinsic conflicts of his system of thought. Troeltsch says, "Although this structure (Thomas' ethic) may appear very comprehensive, and although it is a great advance on the doctrines of the Early Church, to a great extent the inconsistencies of the Early Church have still been retained. They are...maintained at a deeper level."[22]

Troeltsch is, of course, referring to the fact that the problem of duality which has plagued the church throughout its entire history remains in Aquinas' system. The early church attempted to deal with the problem of the conflict between the gospel and social and political structures by a policy of removal. The early church looked upon government and order as essential to the normal state of society in this world but the church's eschatological outlook and ethical idealism imposed an inevitable division between the church and the world no matter how much that line shifted from time to time. The very meaning of *corpus christianum* is that the duality of the church and the world is absorbed within a higher unity, namely Christendom. However even though it is absorbed, it is not fully digested, for the duality is not removed. Hence the famous words of Stephen of Tournai:

> In eadem civitate sub eodem rege duo populi sunt, et secundum duos populos duae vitae, secundum duas vitas duo principatus, secundum duos principatas duples jurisdictionis ordo procedit. Civitas ecclesia; civitatis rex Christus; duo populi duo in ecclesia ordines, clericorum et laicorum; duae vitae, spiritualis et kernels; duo principatus, sacerdotium et regnum; duplex durisdictio, divinum jus et humanum. Redde singula singulis et convenient universa.[23]

The real question is whether it is possible to "give each its due." The early church was convinced that the purposes of the one are so demanding that it could receive its due only by denying the other and this is likewise the view of the sects.

D. *The Significance of Monasticism.* Closely associated with the acceptance of the law of nature which was consummated in Aquinas was the institution of monasticism. This is the way in which the *corpus christianum* attempted to do justice to the high ethic of Christ while accepting the world at the same time. It follows the line of dualistic ethics by dividing the population. The ascetic continued the tradition of Christ and His ethic of love, discipleship and self-denial while the vast majority wrestled with the problems of the world. The church did not accept monasticism without difficulties. Frequently an ascetic movement began by individual initiative in protest to the worldliness of the church.[24] Sometimes it resembled a revival movement not unlike the Methodist revival movement and the holiness and fellowship movements of the modern period. However, the genius of the *corpus christianum* was its ability to absorb these within the church by a frank acknowledgment of duality--a duality, however, which was not one of supreme embarrassment but one of mutual advantage.[25] The advantage was that the duality constituted a kind of division of labor by which the higher and lower levels of life supported one another. Actually the monastic movement became the "keeper of culture" despite its removal from culture and the world reciprocated by offering an economic and political base apart from which monasticism could not exist. According to the Catholic synthesis, the two orders of life, held in "complementary antithesis," supported the fullness and richness of culture.

Certainly the magnificent structure of Thomistic social thought is an outstanding achievement of the human spirit. How much this actually characterized the mediaeval situation is a matter of the dealings of the Pope and the Emperor. The struggles between the ecclesiastical and the political "arms" for superiority, the absolutizing of the relative findings of natural law,[26] the bestowing of premature blessings upon a static feudal system, the use of coercion in the service of Christian freedom and the interminable conflicts between Christian princes have caused many to regard the mediaeval ideal of unity with cynicism. However, the mediaeval pattern remains the ideal of the Catholic

Church, despite an occasional confession that the circumstances of life have changed so drastically that no more duplication of the Middle Ages is possible. "Catholicism always desires a renewal, at least in its main features, of the general political and social situation upon which it had erected its structure in the Middle Ages, and this is why it maintains, down to the present day, the philosophical and theological method of its architectonic logic."[27]

E. *The Position of the Reformers.* Before turning to the Anabaptist approach to the world order, it is necessary to state briefly the position of the Reformers. The rise of Anabaptism occurred mainly in Protestant countries and so it may be said that the Anabaptist dissent was mainly directed against the principles of Christendom as expressed in Protestant lands. It is unnecessary for our purposes to described the positions of the Reformers in detail. The point which needs to be stated is that the Reformers were committed to the *corpus christianum* ideal and their entire social and political outlook was dependent upon this fact. No matter how the ideal of ecclesiastical civilization was supported theologically, it was retained by both Calvin and Luther. "Lutheranism was based entirely upon the idea of an ecclesiastical civilization, forcibly dominated by a religious ideal,"[28] and the same may be said of Calvinism. Luther's social thought was basically mediaeval even though it employed less philosophical ideas than the social thought of Aquinas. The important fact is that the ideal of the wholeness of Christian civilization was retained.[29]

The position of the Reformers may be judged by their attitude toward religious dissent. Religious dissent lay outside the view of the Reformers. Even when Christendom was broken into small units the principle of forced conformity was retained. The best that the heretic could expect was deportation to a country which might happen to accept his view officially. The Peace of Augsburg was calculated to retain the *corpus christianum* ideal of uniformity by its recognition of some of the German principalities as Roman and others as Lutheran; *cuius regio eius religio.* Most certainly Luther was conscious of the imperfections of the mass church which the territorial church system fostered but he was so much a part of the order which had obtained for a thousand years that no other was seriously considered. Luther was aware of the tension between the Christian ethic in its purity and the necessities of political order but as he grew older and more of the weight of the total Christian cause rested upon him, he sought to bring the church and the state into an increasingly close relationship. The Prince became the defender of the faith and the protector of the church.

Calvin also retained the ideal of Christian civilization. He carried this ideal much further than Luther in matters of social discipline and religious uniformity. The idea of the "Holy Community" of Geneva is the idea of *corpus christianum* implemented far more perfectly than was possible in less rigorously ordered principalities. Calvin's Geneva, as an ecclesiastical civil commonwealth, exhibited great confidence in the possibilities of a uniform religious order.[30] This is due to the fact that many of the tensions between the ideal and the real, between the ethic of the Sermon on the Mount and the ethic of law and coercion, as well as the conflict between personal and collective ethics never seemed to divide the heart and the mind of Calvin. The dichotomy between the Absolute Law of nature and the relative law of sinful institutions does not cause within him the hesitation which Lutheranism always has had to overcome before throwing itself into the work of the secular realm. His idea of Christian society as a "Holy community" in which all of life is governed by the will of God, even embodying some of the strict moral principles of sectarianism in a universal scale, carried the ideal of Christian civilization to its consummation.

II. The Anabaptist Dissent

The discussion turns now to a consideration of Anabaptism as a movement of dissent. This dissent involved a complete rejection of the fundamental socio-religious order which had dominated Christianity for over a thousand years and which had come to be accepted by nearly everyone as axiomatic. It involved the rejection of the *corpus christianum* as a historical ideal, together with its implications for the nature and composition of the church and the relation of the church to society. On the positive side it implied a new conception of the church and radical reconstruction of the relation between church and society in accordance with this concept.

At the outset it should be said that although the fundamental ideas of Anabaptist dissent are clear, it is impossible to know the full implications of this dissent for society for the following reasons: (1) Anabaptism never became a historical fact in the sense of a movement free to express its intrinsic dynamics. As a matter of historical record, Anabaptism was crushed by the authorities before it could consolidate even its fugitive gains. The logic of Anabaptism was not carried out in history because it was not tolerated. The full implications of Anabaptism for society therefore cannot be known by the study of historical records. A certain sense of the theological imagination must suffice where history fails. (2) Anabaptism neither had the opportunity nor the inclination to construct a complete system of thought including a full sociopolitical theory. Anabaptism had no *Summa Theologica* nor anything which corresponded to Calvin's *Institutes of the Christian Religion*. Anabaptism was capable of prophetic insight, fundamental criticism of Christendom and radical nonconformity in some respects ahead of its day.[31] However, its pure Biblicism and its practical tendencies prevented Anabaptists from presenting their doctrines as theological systems. (3) The Anabaptist doctrine of separation from the world carried with it a bias toward worldly institutions with the result that the ultimate meaning of Anabaptism for social and ethical institutions was never fully considered by the Anabaptists themselves. In other words, the Anabaptists seldom considered what would happen to society if their interpretation of Christianity were accepted generally. Indeed their interpretation of Christianity as suffering discipleship seemed to make such a thought heretical.

A. *Voluntarism and the "Free Church."* What was the Anabaptist dissent?

The Anabaptist dissent was a sweeping rejection of all those religio-political ideas which supported the system of the mass church (Volkskirche). *Specifically the Anabaptists stood for a doctrine of religious freedom, separation of church and state and voluntarism which if carried to its logical conclusion would lead to the "free church."* Religious voluntarism is the first element of the Anabaptist dissent. The Anabaptists accused Christendom of substituting principles of birth and political power for principles of individual decision and religious freedom. The territorial church (*Landeskirche*) which rose during the early Middle Ages and which developed into the Church of the Empire (*Reichskirche*) under the able leadership of Charlemagne during the 8th and 9th centuries unified religious and political affairs to the extent that the causes of religion and the purposes of politics were merged into a single objective of total Christian culture. This merger, however, resulted in the transfer of the political principles of compulsion into the domain of religion. Hence baptism became a compulsory act of obedience both to the church and to the state. Baptism and citizenship were conferred simultaneously and, just as citizenship was not a free option in an organized state, so baptism followed the same logic of necessity.[32] Under this system unbelief had neither religious nor political status. It was, in fact, politically eradicated. Men were free to believe but not free to disbelieve. *Hence the very nature of Christianity as a free response to Christ was violated.* Anabaptists held that the freedom to deny Christ is just as essential to the Gospel as the freedom to accept Christ. They held that real decision is personal decision and this is not possible unless the alternatives of acceptance and rejection are live options.

What Anabaptism called for was the reign of religious toleration which for their day was virtually unthinkable. It should be remembered, of course, that the Anabaptists did not advocate religious freedom from the standpoint of human rights or liberal political theory. The emphasis of modern humanistic utilitarianism, and secular movements which have made such a great contribution to the cause of religious freedom is quite distinct from the emphasis of the Anabaptists. The Anabaptists were interested in freedom of religion simply because the Gospel required it.[33] They realized that freedom underlies the moral order, that God placed freedom at the center of personality and that man's eternal destiny rests upon free choice. Over against the sovereignty of God which was emphasized by the Reformers, the Anabaptists were the champions of the freedom of the will. They realized that this freedom has its limits in the social realm lest it lead to anarchy. They did not advocate complete abandonment of force by civil society as did Tolstoy. *Nevertheless, they held that at least one area of life should be kept outside the control of government, namely religious faith.*

The championing of religious freedom brought the Anabaptists into conflict both with the Reformers and the Catholic parties. The Reformation made no direct contribution to the cause of religious toleration even though one may trace a certain emphasis upon individual liberty to Luther and may attribute the right to defy the king who "seduces the faithful from obedience to God" to Calvin's famous "exception" clause in his *Institutes*.[34] It is the conviction of R.

H. Bainton that the cause of religious liberty was hindered rather than helped by the Reformation.[35] Religious liberty hinged on the basic question facing the Reformation parties, namely, how is the Christian cause to be perpetuated? May it submit to the free movement of the Spirit in men's hearts with the consequent possible loss of universal assent and the loss of institutional and political security or must it be perpetuated by the structures of the political power as well? Shall the church look to government for protection even at the price of spiritual autonomy? These questions were uppermost in the minds of Zwingli and his colleagues during the early days of the Swiss Reformation. The difference between Zwingli on the one hand and Conrad Grebel and Felix Manz on the other hand is that the former feared that the separation of the church and the state would lead to the downfall of the church and undermine the authority of the state, whereas the latter were ready to run the risk for the sake of a "true church." The issue found its first direct expression at the second Zürich Disputation in October, 1523 when Grebel and Simon Stumpf openly opposed Zwingli's decision to submit to the Zürich City Council the matter of the reformation of the Zürich Church. This is the first open break leading to the founding of Anabaptism. Harold S. Bender says:

> In 1523-25, at Zürich, are the crossroads from which two roads lead down through history. The road of the free church of committed Christians separated from the state, with full religious liberty; and the road of the state church, territorially fixed, depending on state support, and forcibly suppressing all divergences, the road of intolerance and persecution.[36]

The Anabaptists desired the freedom to preach the Gospel and to let the success of the Gospel depend upon the power of the Gospel. Over and over again they repudiated the sword as an instrument of the Word.[37] According to the court records Felix Manz confessed having recommended that people of other faiths should be left undisturbed.[38] In his petition to the Zürich Council in December 1524, Manz pled that no force should be used against those who refused infant baptism. He pleaded that the Word may be permitted to make its own way, "for if it be allowed to speak for itself freely and singly, no one will be able to withstand it...if only freedom be given and the truth be treated with trust."[39] The same approach was taken by Conrad Grebel in his letter to Thomas Muntzer September 4, 1524, as follows:

> Go forward with the word and establish a Christian church with the help of Christ and His rule, as we find it instituted in Matthew 18 and applied in the epistles. Use determination and common prayer and decision according to faith and life, without command or compulsion; then God will help these and the little flock to all sincerity....
> Moreover, the gospel and its adherents are not to be protected by the sword, nor are they thus to protect themselves.... True Christian believers are sheep among wolves...and must reach the

fatherland of eternal rest not by killing their bodily enemies, but by mortifying their spiritual enemies. Neither do they use worldly sword or war, since all killing has ceased with them.[40]

This bid for independence from state control and the consequent freedom of religious faith and expression was really the beginning of the "free church" movement which has become a part of the religious heritage of the West. It is not necessary for our purposes to trace the history of the "free church" movement nor is it necessary to list the many contributing factors to this religio-political arrangement. It is an essential aspect of the "Great Tradition of the American Churches"[41] and the tendency among the European churches during the past fifty years has been in the direction of the separation of the church from the state. Little did the Anabaptist congregation in Zollikon, "*der ältesten Täufergemeinde*," in Switzerland realize that their practice of coming together for Bible study and fellowship constituted the beginning of the "free church" movement in Reformation times. Fritz Blanke has studied the short life of this congregation before it was destroyed by the authorities in 1527. He describes step by step the pressures laid upon Jacob Hottinger and his followers and pays tribute to them with these words:

> Diese aus urchristlichem und urreformatorischem Quellgrund geborenen Begehren Jakob Hottingers waren der Angelpunkt und das Herzstück der ganzen Täuferbewegung. Und das Dorf Zollikon am Zürichsee war die Stätte, wo innerhalb der protestantischen Geschichte zuerst versucht wurde, eine staatsfreie und auf freiwilliger Mitgliedschaft beruhende christliche Gemeinschaft zu verwirklichen. Ein derartiges Experiment musste im ersten Anlauf misslingen, und der einzige 'Fehler,' den man den Männern und Frauen von Zollikon vorwerfen könnte, wäre dieser, das sie zu früh, bevor die Zeit dafür reif war, zu ihrem Werke antraten. Aber in Wirklichkeit war das keine Schuld, sondern eine Grosstat. Es braucht immer wieder Menschen, die, unbeirrt durch den Zeitgeist, nach neuen Zielen aufbrechn und einem neuen Morgan zuwandern. Die Zolliker 'Bruder in Christo' waren ein solcher Vortrupp. Ihr Wagnis ist night vergeblich gewesen. Dankbar neigen wir uns heute vor ihnen."[42]

The implications of the free church for the *corpus christianum* are momentous. It destroys the official, formal ground from under this kind of socio-political order. It is true that the free church system does not necessarily mean the repudiation of the general ideal of Christian community and the penetration of all of the structures of corporate life with the Christian spirit. It does mean, however, that the church will make its social contribution on an entirely different basis. It will not leaven the loaf and salt the earth as a politically privileged order which receives official sanction, financial aid and even coercive assistance from the state. Rather it will operate as a voluntary organization, making its way in the social fabric as best it can on the basis of its spiritual power and public appeal. The free church, in other words, destroys the political guarantees of success. The church is thrown back upon its own resources. The penetration of social life with the Christian spirit becomes within the free church context a precarious enterprise. It requires a dynamic and flexible approach to society since social change is no longer the result of a uniform policy of an officially controlled ecclesiastical civilization but the result of a number of more or less independent culture producing agents.[43] *In other words, the free church system implies social pluralism and this runs diametrically opposed to the monistic tendencies of the corpus christianum.*

B. *Nonconformity to the World.* Another element of the Anabaptist dissent was a general attitude of nonconformity to the world. This attitude stemmed from the dualistic outlook of the New Testament which interpreted history as a struggle between the two Kingdoms--a struggle which cannot be limited to purely spiritual matters but which included social matters as well. Such Scriptures as Romans 12:2, "Do not be conformed to this world but be transformed by the renewal of your mind" and I John 2:15; 17, "Love not the world or the things in the world.... And the world passes away, and the lust of it; but he who does the will of God abides forever," meant that the basic structure of society is sinful and must be avoided. The Anabaptists were convinced that "Christendom" was worldly and therefore the attitude of the Christian must be one of nonconformity. *Probably this point is stressed more than any other in Anabaptist writings.* On virtually every page of Anabaptist literature the sinful character of society is decried. The evil of the world impressed them on all sides. Force, war, luxury, drunkenness and strife were evidences of the fact that society as a whole is unregenerate. This is a constant theme of Menno Simons. The recent scholarship of Fritz Blanke has reminded us that the emphasis of the early Swiss Anabaptists was repentance.[44] In this respect early Anabaptism may be regarded as a kind of revival movement in which people were convicted of sins and received forgiveness and renewal through Christ.

The fundamental dualism of the New Testament has, of course, never been completely lost by the church even when the main emphasis of the church is focused on the unity of Christian civilization. This dualism was expressed by the monastic vs. world dichotomy of the Middle Ages. However, few Christian groups have been so uncompromisingly rigid in their separation of humanity into two classes and few have been so intent upon translating the dualistic polarity of the two kingdoms into the stuff of historical reality. This dualism is expressed socially in Anabaptism. Whereas Catholicism, Lutheranism and to a much lesser degree Calvinism were able to contain duality within the large unity of life, whether by a graded system of morality or a dialectical approach to ethics, Anabaptists accepted only the logic of separation. To use a modern term, the Anabaptists insisted upon an "unambiguous" approach to the world and this meant various techniques of removal from the world.

The most rigid and uncompromising statement of the duality between the church and the world is found in the Schleitheim Confession. Without hesitation the authors distinguish two humanities and their separate ways and destinies.

> We are agreed on separation.... For truly all creatures are in but two classes, good and bad, believing and unbelieving, darkness and light, the world and those (who have come) out of the world, God's temple and idols, Christ and Belial; and none can have part with the other.[45]

Things from which the Christian must separate himself are listed by the Schleitheim Confession such as "church services" under the auspices of the state, civic affairs, commitments made in unbelief and drinking houses. One of the frequent criticisms of Menno Simons was that of pomp and show and fancy dress. Menno wrote:

> They say that they believe, and yet alas, there are no limits nor bounds to their accursed haughtiness, foolish pride and pomp; they parade in silks, velvet, costly clothes, gold rings, chains, silver belts, pins and buttons.... Notwithstanding all this they still desire to be called the Christian Church.[46]

The oath was also a major point of separation. Sometimes the Swiss government demanded the entire population to take oaths in order to sift out the Anabaptists.[47] But the Anabaptists refused to take oath because of their consciousness of the limits of finite life (Matt. 5:36-37). One should not promise under oath since the conditions of finite existence make an absolute commitment impossible. "So you see it is for this reason that all swearing is forbidden: we cannot fulfill that which we promise when we swear, for we cannot change (even) the very least thing on us.... God swore an oath to Abraham so that he might show that his council is immutable.... But we can do nothing...therefore we should not swear at all (nichts schweren)."[48]

    The practice of separation from the world ironically placed the Anabaptists in a relation to Christendom very much like that of the relation of the early church to the pagan empire. Both the empire and the territorial churches sought to establish an ecclesiastical culture in which all parts function as a harmonious whole. All the processes of economics, law, art, the family and war were intended to reinforce the total fabric. Under such conditions nonconformity became subversive, especially when the nonconformity was directed not against the failures of men within the system but against the system itself. It is difficult for modern man who has become quite accustomed to individual freedoms within a secular, pluralistic order to realize the seriousness of the threat of the nonconformist. Menno Simons' convictions against the wearing of silk and velvet and the carrying of a sword may appear to some to be a matter of private judgment. However, Menno was striking at the customs and assumptions of nobility which were a part of the system and which had received Christian blessing. To criticize the habits of nobility on the basis of Christian principle was to call the entire institution of privilege into question. Likewise the denial of the oath proved to be a far greater threat to civilization than may appear at first sight. The oath was the method of finalizing responsibilities and commitments in a theocratic society. The oath was used by witnesses in court, in connection with property titles and many other public transactions in which the authority of the state was involved. It was the sign of responsibility under God. Therefore to refuse to take the oath seemed to imply an attitude of contempt toward the "divine right" by which the state operates in the world. To the state authorities this spelled chaos. It meant that the foundations of the Christian state were challenged. In the secular state the oath is of less vital importance since it no longer carries theological significance in actuality.[49]

Furthermore, the Anabaptist emphasis upon nonconformity to the world struck at the heart of the *corpus christianum* ideal since there is really no place in the *corpus christianum* for the "world" in the sense of the devil's domain. The *corpus christianum* makes a place for the realm of the relative natural law, the realm of justice and punishment, for marriage and for positive law. These are not the ideal but they still conform to the created order. But no social place is given theoretically to the unambiguously evil. The result is that the church of the *corpus christianum* as the all-embracing historical reality absorbed the inevitable evil of men into itself and became corrupt. The Anabaptists, on the other hand, claimed that a frank and honest reckoning with evil requires a place for evil and that place is outside the church. There will always be two Kingdoms, two humanities, two societies and two destinies. Any system which depreciates duality for the sake of the premature universality of the Kingdom has mistaken history for eschatology.

Furthermore, the assumption that all people within the *corpus christianum* should be treated as potential Christians was rejected by the Anabaptists. It was claimed that some people will never be Christians. The assumption that all are *potential* Christians leads too easily to the notion that all *are* Christians who submit in a perfunctory way to the ordinances of the church.

III. The Restitution of the Church

As we have seen the Anabaptists dissented from the Mediaeval synthesis and essentials of the Gospel such as religious freedom, voluntarism, the free church, separation of the church and state, the necessity of personal decision. But the Anabaptists were not merely negative. They sought to make a positive contribution to the Christian cause. What positive alternative did they propose? *The proposal of the Anabaptists was the "Restitution" of the pre-Constantianian church.*[50] "The Anabaptists were the 'Left Wing' who gathered and discipled a 'true Church' (*Rechte Kirche*) upon an apostolic pattern.... If we inquire about the goals of these Anabaptist groups we are driven at first not forwards but backwards. Their object was not to introduce something new but to restore something old."[51] Their desire was to return to the purity of the Gospel and the genuine qualities of the early church before the processes of accommodation to culture had begun. Littell claims that during the early period of Anabaptism, before the movement had achieved institutional and ideological discipline, the one hope which bound diverse groups of the 'Left

Wing' together was the hope of restoring the early church to a position of triumph.[52]

The religious primitivism of the "Left Wing" carried with it some of the characteristics of primitivism as a philosophical and literary motif. In classical antiquity the Stoics and the Cynics believed in a Golden Age and Jews and Christians have believed in an ideal world before the "fall." The primitive world has been pictured by classical and Christian scholars as a time of perfect peace and satisfaction before such historical ambiguities as law, property, slavery, commerce and war came into existence. This line of thinking is anti-cultural since it associates the ideal with pre-institutional periods. Undoubtedly the early Anabaptists shared the romanticism of primitivism.

The extent, however, to which the Anabaptists were influenced by classical or humanistic primitivism is hard to determine. Suffice to say they were conscious of living in a critical period of history when a new order was to be expected. Others, as well, even Luther, shared the view that the end of the present period was near at hand.[53] In this mood of eschatological expectancy, Anabaptists were of the conviction that the purpose of God for their age was the creation of a "true Church" according to the pattern of the New Testament and they believed that they were divinely appointed to serve God in this restoration.

The assumption which lay behind this eschatology is that the great church of Christendom was a "fallen church."[54] *The fall of man was accepted by all Reformation groups but the Anabaptists believed in a second fall, namely the fall of the church.* The idea of recovery, renewal and restoration presupposes that the original pattern which corresponds to God's will has been lost. Thus the Anabaptist hope of restoration rested upon a definite philosophy of history.

A. *The Church as a Fellowship.* What did the restoration include? *It included a church as a brotherhood committed both to Christ and to one another.* Over against the institutional mass church of the Catholic and Reformation bodies which were dedicated to the ideal of grace stood the Anabaptists as small Bible study fellowship groups who shared a common search for Christ amid the intimacy of personal communion and "charismatic" leadership. Anabaptists sought to go behind the accumulation of institutional organization and hierarchical power structures of Christendom to the freedom and immediacy of spiritual fellowship. Their concept of the church was drawn directly from such New Testament passages as Romans 12, I Corinthians 12 and Ephesians 4. In such a church participation in fellowship and responsible sharing was the privilege of the entire brotherhood. This fellowship was considered the Body of Christ. All members constituted a unity which functioned according to the will of the Head. This was not a mere collection of individuals but a body united by the Spirit of Christ. From this body Christ would raise up leaders. But these leaders would come directly from the group and they would be immediately responsible to the group. The traditional lines between clergy and laity were deliberately renounced.

It is significant that the Anabaptists seldom referred to their communion as a "church" or *"Kirche."* They insisted upon the term "fellowship" or

Gemeinde for their own brotherhood while referring to the mass churches by the use of *Kirche*.[55] *Gemeinde* was the term used by the German Bible when referring to the fellowship as a Body of Christ. To the Anabaptists the church as a *Gemeinde* was a body of believers who shared a common life. The extent to which this sharing was carried varied from time to time. Certain groups such as the Hutterites carried the principles of brotherhood so far as to insist upon a return to the primitive communism of the early church in Acts 2. The Hutterites made the principle of brotherhood the commanding principle of life even though it called for a completely different structuring of life than was characteristic of the world.[56] Others did not carry the principle quite that far though it was common practice among the Anabaptists to require a baptismal vow that if the fellowship was in need of help the entire worldly goods of the applicant would be made available to the fellowship. *To the Anabaptists the one supreme reality of life was the local fellowship which was "gathered" around Christ.* All of life including business, marriage, property and citizenship was brought under the discipline of the group. *Anabaptism stood for the radical rejection of individualism as a philosophy of life.*

In this wing of Protestantism, emphasis was laid upon intimate personal fellowship, simplicity of organization,[57] the encouragement of primary relationships and the elimination of indirect power relationships. They stood for freedom of the spirit, charismatic leadership, mutual aid, the sharing of sufferings and the severing of all binding relationships which threaten the primacy of the church. *This kind of New Testament primitivism clashed with the entire institutional development of the church since the third and fourth centuries.* To the Anabaptists the reality of the church was not an institution but a "gathering" of believers around Christ in fellowship. Their conception of the church is stated most succinctly in Christ's promise that "where two or three are gathered together in my name, there am I in the midst of them" (Matt. 18:20).[58] The church is not an organization, nor a hierarchy, nor is it simply where the Word is preached and the sacraments properly administered. *The church exists where people fellowship together in the Spirit of Christ.* In other words, Anabaptists located the church where there is genuine *koinonia*, by which is meant the sharing of all things in the spirit of Christian brotherhood. When we realize therefore that the Anabaptists were calling for an abandonment of the entire ecclesiastical institutionalism of Christendom which had been the cultural base for a thousand years, we can understand why a few "innocent" Bible study fellowship groups such as those of the Anabaptists would appear ominous for world order.

B. *The Discipled Church.* The restoration also included discipline within the conditions of fellowship. The idea of discipline was not new to the 16th century. The practice of penance and the powers of excommunication together with the coercive arm of the state had for centuries imposed a discipline on the general population. The Anabaptists, however, made discipline a responsibility of the brotherhood. They relocated discipline and altered the processes. Discipline was intended to maintain the purity of belief and morals in a manner which was presupposed by I Cor. 5. The exercise of discipline was intended to

be continuous mutual encouragement to spiritual growth. It was not intended
to express itself simply in excommunication. It was the corporate application
of the principle of criticism without which growth and unity were considered
impossible. The church constituted a "disciplinary body." Its purpose was
restorative and not punitive. It was intended to build up the weak, to heal
wounds of misunderstanding and strife, to open new channels for grace and the
exercise of love.

The administration of discipline was based upon one of the most important passages of the New Testament for the Anabaptists: Matt. 18:15-17.

> If your brother sins against you, go and tell him his fault, between
> you and him alone. If he listens to you, you have gained your
> brother. But if he does not listen, take one or two others along with
> you that every word may be confirmed by the evidence of the two or
> three witnesses. If he refuses to listen to them, tell it to the church;
> and if he refuses to listen even to the church, let him be to you as a
> Gentile and a tax collector.

This passage served as a dynamic formula which became a part of community
life virtually as important as any other aspect of common life. For, in a tightly
knit primary group in which much that is ordinarily left to private discretion
becomes a matter of fellowship concern, the problem of human relations
becomes acute. Hence discipline must be continuous, dynamic, remedial
process of reconciliation. The Anabaptists felt that, contrary to the opinion of
some of their enemies, when discipline breaks down, true brotherhood breaks
down also. Brotherhood is guaranteed only when the processes of reconciliation are kept alive.

The extreme form of discipline for the Anabaptists was the ban (*Bann*).
This they accepted as the Scriptural alternative to the coercive policies of the
state against heresy and immorality. Again and again this ban was acknowledged as the one kind of force that Christians may apply. The administration
of the ban through "spiritual" government was the Christian parallel to
government force.[59] Hence the *Seven Articles* of Schleitheim, the *Five Articles*
of the Hutterian Brethren and the *Eighteen Articles* of Dortrecht devoted at
least one article each on this subject. Discipline through the ban was conceived
as the concentration of spiritual force against an unrepentant offender, looking
to his restoration. It was to be administered in the spirit of Matthew 5:24
according to which it is better to leave the gift at the altar and first be reconciled to the brother than to reverse the procedure. The Matthew 5 passage was
interpreted to mean that congregational reconciliation of all differences must
be realized before the breaking of bread.

The history of the practice of discipline among the Anabaptists and their
Mennonite children is one of the sad stories of this tradition. Although it was
intended to contribute to unity it became virtually a continuous source of division. The problem of the standard of conduct upon which discipline would be
exercised was a constant source of trouble. Different interpretations of the

meaning of the Christian ethic broke the movement into "conservative" and "liberal" groups. This applies particularly to the Dutch Mennonite church under the leadership of Menno Simons.[60] Furthermore, as the church gradually increased the authority of the elder (Hirt), the congregational basis for discipline was replaced by authoritarian leadership. Thus the "spiritual" government of the church took on increasingly the character of government by power.[61] Thus discipline tended to become legalistic, impersonal, hard and defensive.

C. *The Church as a Gemeinschaft.* In addition to concepts of brotherhood and discipline the "restored" church included the idea of community (Gemeinschaft). Throughout the entire Anabaptist movement the individualism of ordinary life which the legal and economic order presupposed was a subject of concern. The Anabaptists asked, "What does brotherhood imply for sharing of the goods of life? Does the 'communion of the saints' invade the realm of property rights, the acquisition of material goods, and the general advancement of private interests?" The Anabaptists observed such radical commands as the one to "Sell your possessions and to give alms" (Luke 12:33) and the case of the "evangelical widow" who gave all she had (Mark 12:42-44). They were conscious of the grasping tendencies of life and the way in which these tendencies lead to slavery. Littell points out that in the early years of the movement the romantic peasant refrain was heard among the Anabaptists as follows: "The animals in the wood and the birds in the air are free."[62]

The real impulse, however, toward *Gemeinschaft* came through the communistic practice of the Jerusalem church described in Acts 4:32. For some Anabaptists the Jerusalem experiment with love communism constituted the absolute ideal in Christian brotherhood. This appeared to be a completely different structure than the structure of the world. It was a structure in which selfishness was ruled out as an essential principle. Not all the Anabaptists adopted a communistic pattern. The Hutterians were the only group which carried the principle of Gemeinschaft to what would appear to be its logical conclusion. However, all Anabaptists had a deep feeling of responsibility for the brother as touching the necessities of life. Especially during persecution, mutual aid became a practical necessity. As they faced death together, the things which are valued by the world took on a different color. The difference between mine and thine was melted by a common pathos. As wanderers and pilgrims on earth, they would share what they had on the basis of need. The Dutch Anabaptists were especially called upon to share with the refugee Swiss Anabaptists.

However, the Anabaptists did not uphold *Gemeinschaft* as a universal ideal. It was not preached as a revolutionary principle for society. *Gemeinschaft* was upheld only as a possibility for the disciplined churches. It was generally understood that this way of life was too demanding for the masses. It was the special calling of those who had caught the vision of life "under the cross." In the writings of men such as Peter Ridemann, the great leader of the Hutterians, and Menno Simons, *Gemeinschaft*, whether in the sense of full community or in the sense of partial community (community of consumption), is treated with reserve in view of the natural reluctance of the human heart to submit to it. The conclusion of the Third of the Five Articles of the Hutterian Brethren is as follows:

> Die Gemeinschaft wär nit schwär
> Wan Nur Der Aigen Nutz Nit War.

John Horsch has pointed out that success in *Gemeinschaft* rests directly upon the depth of religious experience which lies behind it. As soon as religious vitality begins to wane, community of goods becomes an unbearable burden. Twice in the history of the Hutterites, the community of goods was abandoned during periods of religious decline only to be taken up again when religious vitality returned.[63]

IV. Implications for Society

So far in this chapter, an attempt has been made to define the *corpus christianum* as the general approach of the great Caltholic and Protestant churches in Christendom. This was followed by a statement of the main lines of the Anabaptist dissent against the *corpus christianum* and a statement of the vision of the "restoration" of the primitive church. The question of the general effect of Anabaptism on Christian civilization needs yet to be explored. What does the restored church imply for the total social order? To what extent does the Anabaptist vision include a vision of a restored world? Does this view of the church contain a social ethic, implicitly or explicitly?

In the first place, the Anabaptist vision of the restored church implies an exclusive interest in the work of the church as the responsibility of every Christian with consequent withdrawal from political responsibility. Anabaptists stood for the conviction that a Christian's thoughts and energies should be devoted exclusively to the church as the hope of the world. The thing which really matters in the world is the perfecting of the saints "that the church might be presented before him in splendor, without spot or wrinkle or any such thing, that she might be holy and without blemish" (Eph. 5:27). This is the work for which Christ became incarnate and this is the clue to history. Anabaptists saw a line of history from Abraham to Christ and from Christ through his church which they called the "people of God" and this line was held over against the world as its opposite.[64] Destiny lay in one line and not the other and therefore the Christian must apply his interest and energies accordingly.

To the Anabaptists the goal of history was a glorious body of saints who would form a new society corresponding to the new age which was begun with Christ. The work of the Christian is to strive for this truly redeemed society. Before this ideal everything else must take second place. The really important thing to Anabaptists is membership in the body of Christ--not in a remote theological sense that can be understood only by the theologian but in the extremely practical sense of concrete daily commitment of time and energy and suffering for the *Gemeinde*. To the Anabaptist the only thing which *really* matters is the Christian fellowship in which he is a participant. To this he promises complete loyalty. Though he respects the political order in the spirit of I Peter 2, his sense of responsibility lies with the *Gemeinde*.

But the question arises as to whether even his attitude of exclusive attachment to the church would not ultimately force a responsible attitude toward the social and political order when the perspective is lifted from the immediate congregation to the church as a universal phenomenon. It is difficult to answer this question since the Anabaptists never really worked out the implications of their own view by asking what the ultimate religio-political implications would be *if* their movement was a success. Although they were settled on certain basic attitudes, they never faced the implications of their view of the church for the world as a whole. *This is to say that they never really faced the implications of Christianity for culture.* As has been stated they regarded the world as a vast mission field and they entered it with the limited perspective of the missionary who is on the road. The missionary does not know what the final outcome of his mission will be. He does not reflect; he simply acts on the basis of certain "things most surely believed" in a way not unlike that of the early church which did not formulate social policy for the universal church. The only group among the Anabaptists which had a real awareness of the implications of its social doctrine for the world order was the Hutterites. For the Hutterites love communism was a sociological principle which was capable of solving the world's problem of conflict and greed. If only men would lay down their defenses and completely submit to the brother in unlimited sharing, then wars would cease. However, the Hutterites never expected the world to adopt their way. They knew that it was too demanding. It was the possibility of a small number of the world's population. Hence questions as to what would happen *if* the world would accept the system were never made the subject of speculation. *The Anabaptists of the conservative Biblical wing believed that there would always be a world consisting of the domain of evil.* For this reason the social ideals of the Anabaptists were not social utopias like those of liberal social idealism of Marxianism. Anabaptist social ethics are ethics of the separated Christian fellowship. It presupposes the continued reign of evil in the world.

Exclusive concern for the church naturally involved withdrawal from the permanent structures of the world so far as immediate responsibility is concerned. Anabaptists renounced the world because it did not contain the seeds of destiny. The political realm and all the coercive orders belonged to the passing age. Anabaptists live "in" the world but not "of" it. They did not deny that they benefited from the political order but they refused to make the legitimate goals of the world, to say nothing of the folly of the world, their own. Even the improvement of the social order through social and political enlightenment, admittedly an objective which approximates more nearly modern social idealism than sixteenth century thought, was of minor importance. This has led Harold S. Bender to say

This concept of the church leads the Christian to withdraw his major energies from active participation in the general program of

world betterment and attempted reconstruction of the entire non-
Christian world order and focus them on the building of the
Christian community. His hope for the world is the church and the
creation of a Christian social order within the fellowship of the
church brotherhood. Extension of this Christian order by the conversion of individuals and their transfer out of the world into the
church will be his method of working at saving the world; it is the
method Christ and the apostles used; it is the method of the
Anabaptists fathers.[65]

Anabaptism attempted to restore the same relation between the church
and the world which existed during the first century. The early church had no
inclination to join hands with the ruling powers. The early church did not
attempt to solve the social problems of the world. G. Ernest Wright says, "In
the New Testament it is clear that we have much more material dealing with
the responsibility of the community of Christ to its Lord *before* the world than
we have of an active responsibility for the salvation of the world."[66] Its sense of
responsibility was expressed through witness to the Lordship of Christ but it
did not attempt to gain control of the political realms in order to make the
broadest possible impact. Social responsibility was dropped with the abandonment of the theocratic ideal. Theocracy, as an attempt to establish the Kingdom by complete control of the environment, was a far cry from the thinking of
the early church. The early church was not a nation and its thinking bore none
of the characteristics of nation responsibility. "The Church did not consider
itself to be an active instrument of judgment."[67] Both its strong commitment to
the ethics of Christ and the actual situation of a small religious minority within
a vast empire dedicated to pagan gods prevented the church from taking an
active part in the problems and the goals of the nation. Thus it is a mistake to
read back into the thinking and practice of the early church the conception of
the *corpus christianum*. Oscar Cullmann has considered the problem of church
and society in this book, *Christ and Time*, with particular reference to the relation of the universal Lordship of Christ over the church and over the world.
He says:

> The use of the term 'corpus christianum'...finds no support in the
> New Testament.... Christ...is head of the Church and likewise head
> of all visible and invisible beings, but...his body...is represented only
> by the church....[68]

*In the second place, the Anabaptist attitude toward society means that
government and responsibility for the world order fall into the hands of non-
Christian men.*[69] No place is made for Christian statesmen, Christian soldiers
and Christian men of affairs. The consequence is, therefore, the pagan or the
secular state. To those who think in terms of the *corpus christianum* that is, of
course, the awful consequence of a host of errors--perfectionism, Biblicism,
lack of historical realism, legalism, a lack of social awareness and appreciation

for civil affairs. Did the Anabaptists ever consider what a state run by pagans might mean for the peace and harmony of society? Did they realize what it might mean to turn over the world to the devil? Could Christianity itself survive if it received no protection from the Christian state or at least from a state in which Christian men were in power?

Questions of this kind, however, cause no great disturbance to the Anabaptist mind for his view rested entirely upon Biblical authority. Furthermore he suffered so much at the hands of the state that the difference between the Christian and the "pagan" state did not impress him. The Anabaptist was convinced that if government were left to God in his Providence and if the church were left to the leadership of Christ its Head, then the church would be free to be itself and it would by truly "salt" and "light" to the world.[70] The Anabaptists did not fear anarchy because of their belief in God's providential work and because they shared the convictions expressed in I Peter 2 that the exemplary conduct of true Christians would touch the hearts of the "Gentiles" for good. "Maintain good conduct among the Gentiles, so that in case they speak evil against you as wrong doers, they may see your good deeds and glorify God on the day of visitation" (I Peter 2:2).

This view, of course, moves in exactly the opposite direction from the *corpus christianum*. Whereas the *corpus christianum* seeks an organic unity of all things in order to present "all things" to Christ, Anabaptism seeks to drive a wedge between the Christian community and the unregenerate world. One seeks unity and the other duality. One seeks wholeness and the other seeks purity. One exalts universality while the other exalts particularity. One seeks the inner connection between all things; the other seeks to show the difference between things. One expressed the priestly accommodation to the culture and the use of culture for religious ends; the other expressed the prophetic criticism against culture and the dangers of culture for faith. One adjusts to the complexities of history; the other tries to reduce all things to simplicity. One emphasizes the subtle positive influences of Christian nurture apart from conscious commitment; the other is suspicious of Christian nurture lest it replace conscious decision. Thus the *corpus christianum* approach to culture and the *corpus christi* approach bring into opposition manifold differences reflecting deep divergencies of theological opinion.

Endnotes

1 Concentration upon the historic Christ as the norm for Christian ethics has meant that the Anabaptists and their Mennonite descendants have avoided many of the problems of theological ethics which immediately come to the fore when Christ is considered not merely in his earthly manifestation but as the Second Person of the Trinity or as the Logos. When Christ is conceived as the agent of creation or as the sustainer of thrones and dominions or as the One in whom "all things hold together" (Col. 1:15:20), then the problem arises as to how He is ultimately reconciled to nature and history. Seen from the perspective of His relation to the Trinity, Christ must be related theologically to "all things." Therefore the problem arises as to how this is possible in view of the fact that nature and history do not support the freedom and absoluteness of love. It forces the problem of how Christ can be reconciled to structures of human community which seem to be grounded in the nature of existence but which exhibit principles lower than the love of Christ. The Anabaptists failed to see this problem since they immediately relegated anything lower than Christ either to the devil or to Providence—without indicating how Providence and Christ can be separated. Two modern theologians have wrestled with the ultimate unity which lies behind the apparent contradiction between nature and grace, love and justice or Christ and the World. One of these is Nels F. S. Ferre' who by making a distinction between the "Spirit of God" and the "Holy Spirit" seeks to acknowledge the divine workings on two levels in history. Nevertheless he insists that both originate in the pure "agape" of Christ. Ferre' says: "The Spirit of God is God's nature and activity on all levels below Agape, whether instruction, judgment or forgiveness. The Holy Spirit is God's nature and activity on the level of Agape. The distinction is definitely functional, not metaphysical in nature. God's nature is here understood operationally. God is ever the same in Himself.... The Spirit of God and the Holy Spirit are the same Spirit. But God is not undifferentiated being. He operates differently in different media and cirucmstances according to the way he is understood and accepted. He has different *hypostases*, as the Greeks called them.... The Spirit of God is the pedagogical face and hands of the Holy Spirit. Upon the validity of this analysis hangs a great deal of the adequacy of our social analysis." *Christianity and Society* (New York: Harper and Brothers, 1950), pp. 88-89. Another modern theologian who seeks to reconcile the ethical contradiction is Paul Tillich. Tillich seeks unity in "ontology of being." Cf. *Love, Power and Justice*, pp. 11ff.

2 Speaking to this point Troeltsch says: "The vital difference between the Middle Ages and the period of the Primitive Church was this: The Church of the mediaeval period did know this ideal (of 'uniform Christian civilization of the *corpus Christianum'*), both in practice, and, still more, in theory, and as an ideal, with some adjustments to modern requirements, its theory is still operative today in all the social teaching of contemporary Catholicism. This ideal of a Christian unity of civilization, however, was also carried forward into early Protestantism, which to a large extent maintained it by the same methods with which the mediaeval period had learned to establish it and carry it into practice. *Even in modern Protestantism, which is so entirely different, this ideal is still retained as a natural fundamental theory which only needs to be placed upon a new basis*" (italics mine). *STCC*, I, pp. 201-202.

3 *Ibid.*, I-II.

4 For a critical analysis of the methodology of Troeltsch see Benton Johnson, "A Critical Appraisal of the Church-Sect Typology," *American Sociological Review*, XX (Feb., 1957), pp. 88-92. Johnson correctly points out that "although the typology was posed as an ideal type, thereby

consisting in a set of general structual features all of which need not be manifested in every case, the low state of development of ideal-type methodology has meant that for practical purposes each of the two concepts refers to a loosely integrated listing of empirical characteristics," p. 88. Trouble develops when this typology is applied to the successors of Calvinism, particularly the churches of America. The American churches for the most part exhibit characteristics of both the church and the sect. For this reason Leopold von Wiese and Howard Becker have recommended that the term "denomination" should be used for those American "free churches" which possess certain Church characteristics. Credit goes to H. Richard Niebuhr for his effort to adapt Troeltsch's typology to the American scene. Cf. H. Richard Niebuhr, *The Social Sources of Denominationalism*, pp. 117-124. Liston Pope also carried on Niebuhr's methodology by his study entitled, *Millhands and Preachers* (New Haven: Yale University Press, 1942). Pope demonstrated by this historical study the tendency of the Sect to become a Church lest it become extinct.

An evaluation of Troeltsch's method may be found in Roland H. Bainton, "Ernst Troeltsch-Thiry Years Later," *Theology Today*, Hugh T. Kerr, ed., Vol. VIII, Apr. 21, 1951, pp. 70-96, STCC as a "pioneer endeavor of abiding significance." Among Troeltsch's critics is George W. Forell, *op. cit.* Forell attempts to soften the dualistic character of Luther's ethics by less emphasis upon the dichotomy of the love ethic of personal relations and official ethic defined by natural law. Nevertheless, the broad outline of Troeltsch remains valid today.

5 W. A. Visser't Hooft, *Memorandum on the Ethical Reality and Functions of the Church*, Mimeographed, (Geneva: Study Dept., W.C.C., 1940), p. 8.

Before discussing the meaning of the *corpus christianum* it is necessary to speak of the origin of the term and its usage by modern scholarship. Despite the fact that the expression *corpus christianum* refers primarily to the Mediaeval doctrine of the relation of the church and the state, it is conceded that the expression is modern. According to Joseph Bohatec whose work on *Calvins Lehre von Staat und Kirche* (Breslau: M. H. Marcus, 1937) reveals Calvin's dependence upon organic thought of the Middle Ages, "Die Ausdrücke 'corpus christianum" als Bezeichnungen des zugleich gestlichen und weltlichen Organismus kommen tatsächlich in den mittelalterlichen Quellen nicht vor.", p. 583. *Bohatec is confident, however, that the general idea which is represented by the term corpus christianum existed during the Middle Ages even though its character and source may be debated.* The idea of the *corpus chrisianum* has made its greatest impact on modern scholarship through the exhaustive studies of Otto Gierke. Cf. Gierke, *Das deutche Genossenschaftsrecht*, III (4 Vols. Berlin: Weidmonneche Buchhandlung). Commenting on Gierke's basic idea of the organic unity of the Middle Ages, Bohatec says, "Die mittelatterliche Welt- und lebensanschauung beruht auf dem Prinzip der organischen Einheit, d. h. Einheit in der Vielheit." *Ibid.*, p. 581.

Discussion about the conception of the *corpus christianum* during the modern period has been instigated, however, not primarily by problems directly associated with the Middle Ages but by problems of the Reformation. The *corpus christianum* has emerged as an answer to questions regarding the *bacground* of the social and political thought of the Reformation. What was the ground upon which the Reformers based their ideas about the relation of the church and the state? During the past fifty years a number of outstanding scholars have agreed that the general (allgemein) principle and the basic presupposition (*Voraussetzung*) of the Reformers was the idea of a universal Christian society or *Christendom* conceived in organic terms. Hence Troeltsch speaks of the "Selbstverstándlichkeit der Idee des *corpus christianum*." *Soziallehren*, I, p. 485.

One of the outstanding advocates of the basic idea of the *corpus christianum* is Rudolph

Sohm. In his *Kirchenrecht* Sohm seeks a comprehensive frame of reference (Zusammenhang) by which Luther's conception of the relation of the church and the state can be understood. Sohm delcares that this frame of reference is one which Luther inherited from the Middle Ages, namely *Christendom*. The church and the state cannot be understood as two distinct *organizations* but as two authorities, the one worldy and the other spiritual, united by *Christendom* as they were united in the Middle Ages. "In der Christenheit sind zwei Schwerter (zwei Regimente) von Gott gesetzt: das geistliche und das weltliche. Beide haben die Aufgabe, die *Christenheit* zu regieren, aber mit verschiedener Gewalt, das eine mit der geistlichen das andere mit der weltlichen Gewalt. Das Wesen dieser beiden *Schwerter* und damit ihr gegenseitiges Gewaltverhältnis gilt es zu bestimmen. *Dat hat Luther getan.* Seine...Lehre von der Trennung der zwei Regimente stellt lediglich *die reformierte* Lehre des Mittelalters von den zwei Schertern dar. Sie stellt klar die Frage nicht...nach dem Verhältnis zweier Organisationen (Staat und Kirche), sondern lediglich die Frage nach dem Verhältnis zweier *Gewalted* (der geistlichen und der weltlichen), welche demselben einen grossen Organismus der Christenheit angehören." *Kirchenrecht*, I, p. 548f. This is basically the position of Karl Rieker. Rieker applied the organic conception of Mediaeval society to the Reformation as a whole. He employed the term "institution" in the manner of Gierke to represent the state and the church not as organizations but as members of a universal body called *Christendom*. Rieker also employed the comprehensive term of "christliche Gesellschaft." Karl Rieker, *Rechtliche Stellung der evangelischen Kirche Deutschlands in ihrer geschichtlichen Entwicklung bis zur Gegenwart* (Leipzig: Hirschgeld, 1893), pp. 32, 53, 65. He speaks of the "Einheit des weltlichen und des religiösen Lebens.", p. 65. He also employed Luther's terminology of "der Idee des *einen* christlichen Körpers." p. 97. This led to "der Idee des einen *corpus christianum.*" p.97. This expression rested partly also upon the saying of Luther, "Christus hat nit zwey noch zweyerley art corper, einen weltlich, den andern geistlich. Ein haupt is und einen corper hat er." *W. A.* ed., VI, p. 408.

It was Troeltsch, however, who gave Rieker's view its broadest application. According to Troeltsch the *corpus christianum* is the "final assumption" upon which the social philosophy of Lutheranism is based." *STCC*, II, p. 523. With respect to the relation of this conception to Calvinism, Troeltsch holds that "it (*corpus christianum*) possesses a comprehensive sociological fundamental theory, developed by the very same methods used by Catholicism and Lutheranism to achieve the same end." *Ibid.*, p. 617.

The idea of the *corpus christianum* as a comprehensive social philosophy of the Middle Ages is severely criticized, however, by Karl Holl. Holl opposes the views of Gierke, Sohm, Meineke and Rieker. Holl recals that the term *corpus christianum* is of modern origin. He claims it is a catchword (*stichwort*). Holl says, "kommt der Ausdruck *societas christiana* weder im Mittelalter noch auch auch bei Luther überhaoupt vor--ich meine, es müsste einleuchten, dass er im Sinn von christlicher Gesellschaft vor dem 17. Jahrhundert überhaupt unmöglich ist--. und der selten anzutreffende Ausdruck *corpus christianum* - 'der christliche Körper' bedeutet nie das, was die heutigen hineinlegen, den 'zugleich geistlichen und weltlichen Organismus,' sondern immer, und vor allem beiLuther immer, so viel wie corpus mysticum, d. h. einfach *Kirche.*" *Gesammelte Aufsätze zur Kirchengeschichte* (Tübingen: J.C.B. Mohr, 1923), I, pp. 340ff. With respect to the controversy between Holl and the formidable line of scholars such as Gierke, Rieker, Meineke, Sohm and Troeltsch it would appear that the evidence supplied by Gierke's investigation of the sources of the Middle Ages is enough in itself to establish the fact that social and political philosophy of the Middle Ages was organic in character and that it was universal, all embracing and led in the erection of oneness and wholeness. The body of Christ was conceived in broader terms than the church--it included society as well. This author is inclined to agree with Alfred Farner whose study of Zwingli's view of the relation of the church and the state convinced him that Zwingli was deeply indebted to the general assumption of the Middle Ages of the unity of Christian civilization. Farner says "Es wurde gezeigt, wie der Begriff Christenheit die allgemeine Grudlage der mittelalterlichen vom anschagungen Verháltnis von Kirche und Staat bildet. Durch die ausführlichen Belege in den Ausführungen Gierkes und Sohms erwist sich die Kritik Holl für die mittelalterlichen Anschaungen als unhaltbar. Es handelt sick wede 'um die Konstruction eines modernen Rechtshistorikers' noch um eine 'harmlos vorgenommene Unterschiebung." Es hat sick gezeigt, dass die Ausführungen Sohms völlig zu Recht bestehen, d.h. das der mittelalterliche Geist erfüllt war von der Idee der *einen* Christenheit." Alfred Farner, *Die Lehre von Kircheund Staat bei Zwingli* (Tübingen: J.C.B. Mohr, 1930), p. 78ff.

6 Cf. Troeltsch, *STCC, op. cit.*, I, p. 338.

7 Thomas Aquinas, *Summa Theologica*, III, 2.8, a. 1 and 2, ed. Inst. of Mediaeval Studies of Ottawa, 4 vols. (Ottawa: College Dominicain d' Ottawa, 1941).

8 According to Gierke, "denn Gott als das Schleithin einheitliche ein ist vor und über aller Vielheit der Welt, is Quelle und Ziel alles besonderen Seins," *Genossenschaftsrecht*, III, p. 515.

9 Otto Gierke presents the idea of wholeness on mediaeval theory in relation to the metaphysical presuppositions of the age in this outstanding statement: "Political Thought when it is genuinely mediaeval starts from the Whole, but ascribes an intrinsic value to every Partial Whole down to and including the Individual.... Its peculiar characteristic is that it sees the Universe as one articulated Whole and every Being--whether a Joint-Being (Community) or a Single-Being--as both a Part and a Whole: a Part determined by the final cause of the Universe, and a Whole with a final cause of its own.

"This is the origin of those theocratic and spiritualistic traits which are manifested by the Mediaeval Doctrine of Society. On the one side, every ordering of a human community must appear as a component part of that ordering of the world which exists because God exists, and every earthly group must appear as an organic member of that *Civitas Dei*, that God-State, which comprehends the heavens and the earth....

"But as there must of necessity be connexion between the various groups, and as all of them must be connected with the divinely ordered Universe, we come to the further notion of a divinely instituted Harmony which pervades the Universal Whole and every part thereof. To every Being is assigned its place in that Whole and to every link between Beings corresponds a divine decree. But since the world is One Organism, animated by One Spirit, fashioned by One Ordinance, the self-same principles that appear in the structure of the World will appear once more in the structure in its every Part. Therefore every particular Being, in so far as it is a Whole, is a diminished copy of the World; it is a "Microcosmus' or "Minor Mundus' in which the "Macrocosmus" is mirrored. In the fullest measure this is true of every human individual; but it holds good also of every human community and of human society in general. Thus the Theory of Human Society must accept the divinely created organization of the universe as a prototype of the first principles which govern the construction of human communities." Otto Gierke, *Political Theories of the Middle Age*, trans. by F. W. Maitland (Cambridge: Cambridge University Press, 1900), pp. 7-8.

10 *Ibid.*, p. 22.

11 *S. Th.*, III, Q8, a.4. One of the major problems which Aquinas had to face was the relation of unbelievers to the universal body of Christ, i.e., "Whether Christ is the Head of all men." Aquinas attempted to answer this problem by regarding all men as potential believers. Only "on

their departure from this world" do those who are not predestined "wholly cease to be members of Christ." *S. Th.,* III, Q8, a.3.

12 F. W. Dillistone, *The Structure of the Divine Society* (Philadelphia: Westminster Press, 1951), p. 106.

13 Troeltsch, *STCC*, I, p. 202. Troeltsch agrees, however, that the *corpus christianum* represented at least one aspect of the original Gospel, namely the idea of universality.

14 *Ibid.*, p. 256.

15 *Ibid.*, p. 214.

16 Charles Norris Cochrane, *Christianity and Classical Culture* (New York: Oxford University Press, 1944).

17 *Retract.* 1.3.2., quoted by Cochrane, *op. cit.*, p. 510. He interprets Augustine to mean that the structures of the world are to be "transformed" and not to be rejected. Appeal is sometimes made to Augustine as a proponent of the positive approach to culture which was most consistently developed by Calvin.

18 Visser 't Hooft, *Memorandum*, p. 11.

19 H. Richard Niebuhr, *Christ and Culture*, pp. 128-129.

20 *Ibid.*, p. 129.

21 This is not to suggest that Aquinas is interested in the adjustment of society to the nature of man so that man may live abundantly on earth as the end. Social harmony in accordance with *lex naturae* always leads to the further thought that the natural is preparation for the super-natural. This is clearly seen in Aquinas' political writingss in which princes are reminded of their responsibility before the Lord to make life, as preparation for heavenly happiness, a possibility. The king must rule as a kind of tutelage of the Lord. Thomas says, "Since the end of life which we live well at present is heavenly happiness.... The way of true happinesss and the obstructions on the way are revealed in the divine law, the teaching of which is the duty of priests.... The King, having learned the divine law, ought to study especially how the multitude subject to him may live well." *De reg. prin.,* I, 15, quoted by Ray C. Petry, *op. cit.,* p. 280. The contribution of Thomas for the *corpus christianum* is his ability to hold the Eternal Object and the temporal condition in constructive relation.

22 Troeltsch, *op. cit.,* pp. 269-270.

23 *Summa des Stephanum Tornacensis über des Decretum Graticoni* (Giessen, 1891), "Introduction," pp. 1-2; cited by R. W. and A. J. Carlyle, *A History of Mediaeval Political Theory,* II, 3rd ed. (London: William Blackwood and Sons, Ltd., 1936), p. 198.

24 Cf. Waldo Beach and H. Richard Niebuhr, *Christian Ethics* (New York: Ronald Press, 1955), pp. 140ff.

25 Cf. John C. Bennett, *Christian Ethics and Social Policy*, p. 32.

26 Reinhold Niebuhr has been a constant critic of Catholic tendencies to confuse the positive law of a given historical situation with the absolute law of nature. Niebuhr says, "There are...always historically contingent elements in the situation which natural-law theories tend falsely to incorporate into the general norm; and there are new emergents in the human situation which natural-law theories tend to discount because their conception of an immutable human nature can not make room for them." *Faith and History* (New York: Charles Scribner's Sons, 1951), pp. 180-181.

27 Troeltsch, *op. cit.,* p. 279.

28 *Ibid.*, II, p. 515.

29 Thus Sohm, Rieker, Troeltsch.

30 Troeltsch, *STCC*, II, pp. 580ff.

31 Cf. William Hordern, *Christianity, Communism and History* (New York: Abingdon Press, 1954). Hordern feels that the sects have been crushed by the modern church. He is convinced that the sects have "part of the Christian answer to Communism." p. 21.

32 One of the major reasons why the Reformers opposed re-baptism was a politcal implication. Since baptism and citizenship were so closely associated, the rejection of infant baptism constituted civil disobedience. It appeared to defy civil authority and the religious foundation of the state. To the Reformers, Anabaptism therefore looked like a bid for anarchy.

33 The relation of Anabaptism to the history of religious freedom will not be discussed here. The extent to which Anabaptism contributed to the cause of religious freedom is not clear. Certainly Anabaptism made no great contribution if its contribution may be judged by direct results. Possibly this is why M. Searle Bates fails even to name the Anabaptists in his *Religious Liberty, an Inquiry* (1945). Nevertheless it cannot be denied that the Anabaptists virtually stood alone for the principles of religious freedom, voluntarism and separation of church and state during the Reformation. Furthermore it is certain that these principles were introduced into England by Anabaptists and eventually these contributed to the cause of Independency. In England it attached itself even to the Calvinistic movement. Speaking of the origin of ideas of religious liberty which found their way into the English tradition and later into North America, Troeltsch says: "The parent of the 'rights of man' was therefore not actual church Protestantism, but Sectarianism and Spiritualism which it noted and drove forth into the New World. And this can surprise no one who understands the inner structure of orthodox Protestant, and Baptist and Spiritualist thought.... Independency was itself most strongly interpenetrated with Baptist influences, which arising from the remnants of the earlier English Anabaptists, from Holland...and from the American refugees, reacted on England. Not less strongly did the mystical Spiritualism exercise an influence tending to disintegrate ecclesiastical systems and to strengthen the demand for liberty of conscience. *It was now at last the turn of the step-children of the Reformation to have their great hour in the history of the world.*" (italics mine) *Protestantism and Progress*, trans. W. Montgomery (London: G. P. Putnam's Sons, 1912), pp. 122-124.

34 Bk. IV, Ch. 20, par. 32.

35 R. H. Bainton says, "the Reformation at the outset brought no gain for religious liberty. Rather the reverse, for Protestantism arrested Secularist tendencies and made religion again the preeminent concern of men for another century and a half. The spirit of persecution was thereby aroused." "The Struggle for Religious Liberty," *Church History*, X (1941), p. 96.

36 Harold S. Bender, "The Anabaptists and Religious Liberty of the 16th Century," *Archiv für Reformationsgeschichte*, Johrg. 44 (1953), pp. 38-39.

37 Menno Simons wrote to Gellius Faber regarding the religious use of the Sword: "Say good reader, where in all the days of your life did you read in the Apostolic Scriptures that Christ or the apostles have invoked the authority of the magistracy against those who would not hear their doctrine or obey their words? Yes, reader, I know for certain that wherever the magistracy is to execute the ban by the sword, there the true knowledge, Spirit, Word, and Church of Christ are not.

"The Kingdom of the Spirit must be protected and defended by the Sword of the Spirit, and not by the sword of the World. This, in the light of the doctrine and example of Christ and His apostles is too plain to be denied.

"I would say further, if the magistracy rightly understood Christ and His Kingdom, they would in my opinion rather choose death than to meddle with their worldly power and sword in spiritual matters which are reversed not to the judgment of man but to the judgment of the Great and Almighty God alone. But they are taught...that they may proscribe, imprison, torture, and slay those who are not obedient to their doctrine as may also be seen in many different cities and countries." "Reply to Gellius Faber," *Complete Works*, pp, 726. 779.

38 Bender, "The Anabaptists and Religious Liberty of the 16th Century," *op. cit.*, p. 38.

39 *Ibid.*, p. 38.

40 Walter Rauschenbusch, "The Zurich Anabaptists and Thomas Müntzer," *American Journal of Theology*, IX (January, 1905), p. 92.

41 H. K. Rowe has written: "Voluntarism is so obvious a principle, as it is exhibited in American churches, that its significance is overlooked, but it is one of the revolutionary principles adopted by modern ecclesiastical organization." *History of Religion in United States* (New York: Macmillan Co., 1924), p. 54.

42 Fritz Blanke, *op. cit.*, p. 82.

43 An excellent discussion of the implication of the separation of church and state for the social outreach of the church is found in Winthrop Hudson, *The Great Tradition of the American Churches* (New York: Harper and Brothers, 1953).

44 *Op. cit.*, pp. 70ff.

45 Art. 4.

46 *Complete Works*, p. 377.

47 Horsch, *Mennonites in Europe*, p. 368.

48 "Schleitheim Confession," Art. 7.

49 Another area of nonconformity was their refusal to participate in the activities of the guilds. No much is known about this area of conflict, however. We do not know for sure whether the Anabaptists avoided the guilds for the same reason that Mennonites avoid the industrial unions today, namely, because of the coercive principle involved or whether the use of the oath by the guild was the objectionable feature.

50 The interpretation of the Anabaptist conception of the church as sectarian restoration or "restitution" (*restitutia*) is the view of Troeltsch, *STCC*, I, p. 334; of Harold S. Bender, *Conrad Grebel*, p. 210; and of Franklin Littell, *The Anabaptist View of the Church*, pp. 50-93.

51 Littell, *ibid.*, p. 50.

52 The hope of restoring the early church to a position of power "is the threat which ties together *Spiritualisten* and *Täufer*, Swiss Brethren and Polish Brethren, Schwenckfeldians and Hutterians, Mennonites and the followers of Sebastian Franck and Adam Pastor." *Ibid.*, p. 50.

53 Forrell, *op. cit.*, p. 158.

54 Anabaptism cannot be understood unless the idea of the fallen church is presupposed. The fall of the Church constituted for them a turning point in history. The essence of the fall was, however, a matter of disagreement. For the Hutterian wing of Anabaptism the fall began with the abandonment of full community described in Acts 2. Peter Ridemann taught in his *Rechenschaft* that everything was in the beginning created common; he assumed that the communism of the Early Church was a return to Edenic perfection. *Rachenschaft unserer Religion, Lehr und Glaubens, von den Brüdern, so man die Hutterischen nennt, ausgangen...1565* (Ashton Keynes, Wilts., England; Cottswold-Bruderhof, 1938), pp. 92f. In general the fall was associated with the church and the state following the Constantinian coalition in 321 A.D. Christianity as a state religion was considered fallen religion. For the Anabaptists this was amply demonstrated by the fact that the Church accepted the sword.

Opinions among Christians differ in their evaluation of the Constantinian merger of church and state. Some see it as the logical result of the universalistic outlook of Christianity. Cochrane regards it as the "turning point of European history" and "the Triumph of the Cross." *Op. cit.*, p. 177. But a Dutch scholar such as G. J. Heering, speaks of the Constantinian accord with policies of war as the "Fall of Christianity." Heering says: "Emperor Constantine...was converted to Christianity (in 312), and when he exalted this faith into the State religion (in 324), Christianity began to turn toward the State for support, and become reconciled to war and the soldier's calling.... This radical change in the Christian faith, in regard to so vital a matter as war, we cannot regard as other than a disastrous fall, as a fall into a condition of sin. We believe that history justifies our view. Henceforth from this fall into sin we must needs deal with a Christianity degenerate in this respect, a Christianity which is more and more compelled to parade its degeneracy." *The Fall of Christianity*, trans. J. W. Thompson (London: George Allen and Unwin, Ltd., 1928), pp. 54-55; 57. Modern Mennonite scholarship takes a similar position. Paul Peachey connects the Constantinian compromise with the "Decline of the West." Following Constantine "Christianity was no longer primarily the redemptive intervention of God, but a new means to cultural and political ends, subservient to the caprice of the ruling class." Paul Peachey, "Toward an Understanding of the Decline of the West," *Concern* I (June, 1954), p. 19.

55 Harold S. Bender, "The Mennonite Conception of the Church," *MQR*, XIX (April, 1945), pp. 93-94.

56 The Hutterian practice of love communism is discussed at greater length in Chapter V.

57 The tension between the free operations of the Spirit and the complexity of officialdom, between the personal ethic of agape and the impersonal ethic of justice, between the primary group relationship and the indirect group relationship was recognized by the Anabaptists although they never worked out the logic into a theory such as *Moral Man and Immoral Society*. Anabaptists deliberately tried to keep life on as personal a basis as possible and consequently they have always sought simplicity of organization in all phases of life. It would appear that what the Anabaptists stood for can be defeated not only by sin but also by complexity. The Anabaptist way of life in the church as well as in the community thrives best among simple conditions.

58 Cf. Erland Waltner, "The Church in the Bible," *Proceedings of the Study Conference on the Believer's Church* (Newton, Kansas: General Conference Mennonite Church, 1955), p. 66).

59 Cf. "Schleitheim Confession," Art. 2.

60 Cf. Menno Simons, "A Clear Account of Excommunication," *Complete Works*, pp. 457-485; also Christian Neff, *Die Taufgesinnten-Gemeinden* (Karlsruhe: Heinrich Schneider, 1931), pp. 309ff.

61 H. Richard Niebuhr has shown how spiritual movements which begin as operations of the spirit nearly always develop into institutions of power. "Institutions can never conserve without betraying the movements from which they proceed." *The Kingdom of God in America* (Chicago: Willett, Clark and Co., 1937), Ch. V. p. 168.

62 *Op. cit.*, p. 84.

63 John Horsch, *The Hutterian Brethren, 1528-1931* (Goshen, Indiana: Mennonite Historical Society, 1931), p. xvi.

64 Cf. Van Bragt, *Martyr's Mirror*, p. 21.

65 "The Mennonite Conception of the Church," *Op. cit.*, p. 99.

66 *The Biblical Doctrine of Man in Society* (London: SCM Press, Ltd., 1954), p. 129.

67 *Ibid.*, p. 128.

68 Oscar Cullman, *Christ and Time*, trans. by Floyd V. Filson (Philadelphia: Westminster Press, 1950), p. 187.

69 Sometimes the Mennonites have expressed faith in God's goodness and wisdom by raising up the "good heathen" to rule instead of Christians. Cf. John Howard Yoder, "The Anabaptist Dissent," *Concern*, I. p. 53.

70 Taken as a whole, however, Anabaptism was not completely unified regarding the state.

The position of Menno Simons regarding the status of rulers before God, for example, is far less rigid than the position of the Swiss Brethren. The dichotomy between the church and the state is less clearly drawn. He advises rulers of their responsibility before God and their heavenly sword with these words: "Fear the Lord, your God, with all your powers; judge in all wisdom with fear and trembling; help the oppressed; grieve not the distressed; promote the just cause of the widows and orphans; protect the good; punish the evil in a Christian manner; discharge the duties of your offices properly; seek the kingdom and country that will endure forever; and reflect that you, however highly esteemed, upon earth are only pilgrims and sojourners in a strange land...seek his honor and praise in all your thoughts, words, and actions and you shall reign in eternity." *Works* (Elkhart, Indiana: John F. Funk and Brother, 1897), p. 87. In view of the fact that Menno Simons believed in nonresistance it is difficult to see how he could take such a cordial view toward magistrates. It is more than an interesting coincidence that the Dutch church has long ago given up its peace position and has joined in political affairs. Descendants of the Swiss Mennonites have taken a more radical line of rejection of political responsibility.

CHAPTER 5
THE MENNONITE COMMUNITY

I. The Problem of Natural Community

A. *Christianity -- A "Founded Religion."* Joachim Wach describes Christianity as one of the "founded religions."[1] By a "founded religion" he means a religion whose origin is independent of a natural base. It rests upon the religious experience of a "founder." Christianity is different from all "natural" religions since it is not coterminous with a family, a tribe, a race, a nation, or any other natural or cultural grouping. A founded religion has nothing to do with the total aspirations and sentiments of a natural community. In contrast to family or national cults which integrate diverse elements of culture and which seek to express the sentiments and aspirations of the group, Christianity is "founded" independently of any such natural association. In fact, Christianity is not only independent of the natural or cultural unit but cuts across the lines of natural cohesion.

The fundamental principle of social organization of Christianity as of other founded religions is the "circle of disciples."[2] This is a circle of followers who have responded to the call of the Master and who experience a growing sense of solidarity because of their intense loyalty. The basis of their cohesion is not "natural." On the basis of a comparative study of the founded religions, Wach says, "The first disciples in each circle have differed widely from one another in character and in social, cultural, and intellectual background.... The group which the man of God attracts about him may appear as a loosely connected association or as a closely knit unit, bound together by a common religious experience whose nature is revealed and interpreted by the founder."[3] Membership in this group may require a complete break with ordinary pursuits of life and a radical change in social and religious attitudes and affiliations. The ties of family and kinship and the normal relations to the economic and political community are severed or at least subordinated for a time. Wach points out that Jesus' statement that those who "do the will of God" are truly his brothers, sisters and mothers and not his blood relations (Mark 3:31ff.; Matt. 12:47ff.; Luke 8:18ff.) is paralleled elsewhere, as for example, by Buddha's statement: "For some persons even father and mother are no hindrances."[4]

The "circle of disciples" continues as the religio-social organization in all simplicity as long as the Master lives. But "the immediate crisis which marks the birth of a new epoch in the development of the infant religion and causes its structural transformation is the death of the founder."[5] With his passing the solidarity of the circle is threatened. His authority, his guidance and his inspiration are gone. At this point, "primary discipleship" is translated into "secondary discipleship." The Master is gone and so a shift is made from immediate personal relations to an emphasis upon "the new message, the new attitude, the new spirit, and the new tradition which have been left behind with the passing of the founder."[6] The Master becomes an object of worship. His significance is told to the nations. All those who believe in Him and witness to Him become a "brotherhood."

But this *brotherhood* is immediately faced with the problem of natural community. It may retain the loose relationship to the world for a while. The family, occupation, national loyalties and class distinctions may be sacrificed for the sake of the missionary call.[7] But eventually the brotherhood must come to terms with the life of the world. The fact that disciples are men and not angels requires an adjustment to the conditions of natural material existence. Life cannot be sustained for any length of time upon the road. The disciples must settle down. The first generation of pilgrims and strangers may dwell in "tents" and may have no abiding place and may even transcend anxieties about worldly affairs. "Those who have wives (may) live as though they had none, and those who mourn as though they were not mourning, and those who rejoice as though they were not rejoicing, and those who buy as though they had not goods, and those who deal with the world as though they had no dealing with it" (I Cor. 7:29-31). But to any group which continues to exist for any length of time, regardless of its cultural indifference, there comes a time when the permanent structures of natural existence must be given their place.

B. *Significance of the Family.* The first and most significant single adjustment to the world is the acceptance of the institution of the family. The crucial point about marriage is not that it admits the erotic principle into life but that the family ties the disciple to the total social order with more force and comprehension than any other institution. If the family is accepted, then all those institutions which serve the family and which make the family secure must be accepted. The family requires the institutions of property, labor, inheritance, law, education and the state. This is why the mediaeval system of asceticism placed obedience and poverty in the context of chastity. St. Francis may be "comforted by the lack of all things"[8] but the needs of the family cannot be satisfied except by the combined resources of a social order. This applies particularly to the conditions of urban life where natural simplicities are complicated by the abstract systems of justice and impersonal relationships.

C. *Radical and Conservative Attitudes in the Early Church.* The Early Church faced the problem of natural community shortly after the death of Christ. The question which they faced was: What kind of community organization should the Christian brotherhood seek? Does Christianity imply a unique social system of its own which is separated from the world and which is true to its inner impulses of love or does Christianity accept the social structures of the world? Should the brotherhood attempt to bring *all* of life under the control of the spirit so that natural community perfectly complements spiritual community and so that the experience of "koinonia," which is felt in the breaking of bread and the fellowship of the Spirit, may be perfectly supported by the rest of life? Should everyday relationships involving family, economics, property and law be required to submit to the perfection of the Spirit of *agape* or is it possible to limit the expression of true brotherhood and absolute *agape* to the experience of occasional fellowship while the Christian accepts the social structure established by Roman society for purposes of daily living? To what extent should the Christian brotherhood form its own community life?

The Early Church provided no uniform answer to this puzzling question. In reality, it expressed both the "radical" and the "conservative" attitudes according to Troeltsch. On the one hand, there is the love communism of the Jerusalem Church of Acts 2:4,5 in which can be seen the beginnings of a revolutionary principle of complete community. On the other hand, there is the rather uncritical acceptance of the system of Roman society by the Pauline churches. In one of his outstanding statements, Troeltsch has summed up the two initial attitudes of Christianity with the following words:

> In reality Christianity seems to influence social life in two ways: Either, on the one hand, it develops an idealistic anarchism and the communism of love, which combines radical indifference or hostility towards the rest of the social order with the effort to actualize this ideal of love in a small group; or, on the other hand, it develops along social-conservative lines into an attitude of submission to God and to His Will, so far as the world is concerned, combined with a strong independence of an organized community which manages its own affairs, which, as its range of influence increases, finds that it cannot ignore secular institutions, but that it must do its utmost to utilize them for its own purposes. The first ideal is the source of ever-renewed radical social plans...while the second ideal produces the conservative principles of patience and suffering within the world, whose ordinances are permitted by God, whose possibilities Christians use for their own ends, and whose continuance they endure, because inwardly they are unaffected by them.[9]

D. *Significance of Paul.* The first steps in the direction of the acceptance of the permanent structures of the world were made under the influence of Paul. Paul shared the basic Christian antagonism for the world. His unwillingness to employ the law courts (I Cor. 6) and his personal religious bias against marriage and all unnecessary distractions, as well as his instructions to "come out...and to be separate from them" (II Cor. 6:17), make him no genuine friend of the world. Nevertheless Paul represents a transition in the life of the early church from the love absolutism of Christ and the early Jerusalem community and rural Judean agrarian simplicities to the complexities of the permanent structures of society under the conditions of the Roman Empire.[10] This is the beginning of a policy of "compromise" which was calculated to meet the requirements of the "Israel of God" which was no longer to be considered a culturally detached circle of itinerant disciples but a permanent fellowship entrenched within the natural and social orders. This adjustment by Paul followed what Troeltsch called the "conservative tendency."[11] By the principles of conservatism Paul gained a foothold within Roman society for the church. The church, though by no means at peace with the world, nevertheless accepted the structures of society including marriage, economic activity and slavery as divinely ordered upon the assumption that the really important experience of "koinonia" was not prohibited by the world as it was organized. The church gradually relaxed its revolutionary tendencies and accepted one by one the permanent orders even as ordinances of God.[12]

The Anabaptists were confronted with the problem of natural community in terms not unlike that of the Early Church. As stated previously they interpreted Christianity as discipleship. This involved a return, as near as possible, to the conditions of primitive Christianity. This return included the concepts of literal obedience to the teachings of Christ, suffering, missionary mobility, "loose living" with regard to culture, intense brotherhood and an inclination to share life together in Christ. But the demands of the orders of creation which meant so much to the thinking of the Reformers could not be entirely avoided by Anabaptists. They too were involved in nature which meant that the pure essence of love needed to be related to social structure. For a while Anabaptists, like the Early Church, could express their religion in the purity of spiritual fellowship (Bible study groups) around the "present" Lord and with the radical unconcern of the unacculturated missionary. But eventually they had to live under settled conditions[13] and the question was, What form shall their corporate existence take?

II. The Anabaptist-Mennonite Answer

The Anabaptist-Mennonite answer to the problem of existence within natural community has been historically the "Mennonite community." The Mennonite community is the sociological expression of the Anabaptist faith. The term "Mennonite community" is a technical term. It carries specific ethical and sociological significance. It does not simply express the obvious fact that Mennonites have formed congregations and that the members of the congregation live in the same general location. If the expression were used in this way it could be applied to any denominational group. The "Mennonite community" is a term which stands for a "people" who are tied together by a common faith and a common life, a people who are separated from other groups and from society at large by their peculiar practices. The Mennonite community is a community within other communities such as the village, the province or the nation. Mennonites have always been conscious of the larger natural groupings. To these they devote themselves with greater or less devotion. But their supreme devotion, their most intense sense of belonging and their highest commitments are directed to the community of faith. It is the community of faith which provides a genuine social context, a moral pattern, economic security, marriage, and opportunities and responsibilities for sharing in the spirit of brotherhood. Many of the elements of community which are generally supplied by the secular community are supplied by the community of faith. The extent to which the Mennonite community is independent and self-sustaining is the extent to which it may truly be called a "Mennonite community."

A. *The Mennonite Community -- A Religious Community.* The Mennonite community is essentially a religious community.[14] It is a community dedicated to Christ and supposedly ordered by the law of love.[15] The place which religion occupies is central. Sociologists who study the Mennonite community frequently find that the standard community pattern does not fit the Mennonite situation.[16] This is because of the religious influence of the church plays a far more determinate role in the formation of social attitudes and patterns than may be generally expected. The influence of the church is not limited to "spiritual" affairs in contradistinction to the social or material affairs of life. The church is so much a part of the community that:

> In common usage the terms 'Mennonite Community' and 'Mennonite church (congregation) are used interchangeably almost to the point of being synonymous.... When applied to Mennonites...the term 'community' is basically a religious concept with certain sociological implications. The economic, the social, and the political aspects of the Mennonite community are all subordinate to the religious.[17]

B. *The Theoretical Possibility of Unambiguous Social Structures.* This means that despite the unavoidable anticultural tendencies of discipleship (which incidentally never became a matter of critical reflection), Mennonites have accepted many aspects of culture in their own community building. Theoretically they have accepted culture *per se* and recognize no intrinsic conflict between Christ and culture. That is to say, although Mennonites recognize a conflict between Christ and the "world" by which they mean the evil institutions of the world, they do not see any necessary conflict between Christ and the facts of life imposed by natural corporate existence as such.[18] The Mennonite strategy of separation which has led a cultural historian such as H. Richard Niebuhr to place the Mennonites within the category of "Christ Against Culture" is certainly valid if by culture he means the general stream of worldly life which is obviously sinful. Mennonites are against culture in so far as they are against the "world." Mennonites have never recognized a tension between the command of Christ and the principles of natural social existence. They are opposed to the general stream of history but they still hold to the possibility of an unambiguous social order which will include all the natural elements of life. Mennonites have declared confidently that "all" of life must be "Christianized" and by "Christianized" they mean that all can be brought into perfect harmony with the will of Christ. Hence the words of Harold S. Bender:

> Have we not historically, and in our highest thought, always held
> that to be 'Christian' means to follow Christ in *all* our ways including
> what the world calls 'secular' and that the 'church' is a brotherhood
> of love in which all the members minister to each other in all their
> needs *both* temporal and spiritual? And what more is a Christian
> community than a fellowship of disciples of Christ sharing a common
> faith, and under a common Lord helping one another achieve the
> fullness of abundant life which the Saviour came to bring?...
> ...I...hope...(we may) eliminate from our minds the dangerously
> unscriptural and un-Mennonite duality by which we so often draw a
> line between sacred and secular, between church and community.[19]

What this really means is that the Mennonite as community builder confidently asserts the possibility of "unambiguous" social structures. At this point
not a trace of tension between Christ and culture is evident. The disciple is no
longer the "missioner" "cut loose from the world, from wife, from father, and
mother and sister...and from all men".[20] He is now settled down within the
family, the occupation, the home, the neighborhood, and, in a sense remotely,
yet effectively, within the nation. Now the task has shifted to the Christianization of all relationships and the dedication of the structures of natural existence
to common life in the brotherhood.

C. *The Mennonite Community and Calvin's "Holy Community."* Does this
mean that the community building phase of discipleship really amounts to the
adoption of a Calvinistic conception of the Holy Community? Does this mean
that Mennonites in their settled communities are really trying to do what Calvin carried out with the greatest of intensity, law, organization and vision? Is
the Mennonite community really a sectarian counterpart to Geneva? On the
surface this appears to be the case. For example, both profess to Christianize
"all things." Furthermore both Mennonites and Calvinists emphasize the Biblical basis for community and both know nothing of compromise. Neither of
them sees any essential conflict between Christ and the cultural process *per se.*
Calvinism even sees no conflict between Christianity and politics.[21]

In spite of certain parallels between the conception of the Mennonite
community and Calvin's Holy Community, there are fundamental differences.
The first has to do with the range of cultural control. Although both Calvin
and the Anabaptists profess to bring the "entire" community under the discipline of the transforming power of the New Covenant, only Calvin thought in
truly inclusive terms.[22] Calvin alone attempted to bring a *total* culture under
the Lordship of Christ. His conception of totality proceeded from the *political*
framework of this thought. For Calvin the political boundary established the
boundary of cultural transformation. Absolutely everyone and everything
within the political unit was to be governed according to God's laws. Therefore, since the political unit was the most inclusive social unit, the close tie
between the church and the state gave the program of the church the same
universal range of responsibility. For, although the political and the ecclesiasti-

cal were clearly separated in Calvin's mind and although in his administration of Geneva the duties of both were clearly separated,[23] they were mutually dependent and coextensive in operation. Calvin's approach to Christian culture was one of theocratic universality.

D. *A Restricted Community.* The Mennonite community, in contrast to Calvin's Holy Community, is not universal in the same sense. In reality, the Mennonite community is a partial approach to the total problem of a Christian culture. There are certain areas of social existence which the Mennonite community does not attempt to comprehend and which are important aspects of the total problem. Admittedly the range of culture control depends upon which type of Mennonite community one has in mind.[24] However, it is apparent that when Mennonite scholars such as Harold S. Bender, Guy F. Hershberger, and J. Winfield Fretz speak of bringing "all of life" under the rule of the Kingdom of God, they do not have in mind the same frame of reference as Calvin and his successors.[25] By "all of life" they mean all aspects of life as traditionally included in Mennonite life, but Mennonite life is clearly culturally restricted. It is bound to a limited view of culture. It includes activities which are called economic, familial, artistic and educational. However, it is limited by the fact that the political dimension is completely absent. No attempt is made to consolidate the processes of cultural transformation through political action; no effort is made to achieve social justice through a systematic control of the overall structures of life. The conceptual reference is always individualistic and partial. It is individualistic is no far as cultural phenomena are generally understood by the simple process of adding individual activities of Mennonites without due regard to the unique problems of social organization in which the whole is clearly different from the sum of the parts. It is partial since it does not reckon the political realm as an effective determinate of its social life.

E. *An Agrarian Community.* Furthermore, the Mennonite community is a partial approach to the problem of Christian culture since it has been limited to agrarianism. Next to New Testament literalism or discipleship as the ideological starting point, agrarianism has been the most determinate factor of the life of Mennonite communities. There are no urban Mennonite communities in existence. It is true that there are some Mennonite urban congregations but these bear no resemblance to the Mennonite community as a type. These have been swallowed up in the forces of world culture and therefore retain virtually none of the essential characteristics of the Mennonite community.[26] The Mennonite community has been historically a rural community. This has been true ever since the 16th century in spite of the fact that Anabaptism arose in the city. Modern scholarship has revealed the strange fact that Anabaptism could hardly have arisen among the rural peasantry and yet it has been able to perpetuate itself only in agrarianism.[27] It has been shown that as soon as Mennonites settle in the city they lose their Mennonite principles.[28] Hence in the mind of a number of scholars, Mennonitism is tied to agrarianism as the best support for the "Mennonite way of life."[29]

The attachment of Mennonitism to rural life and economy has a number of roots. Historically it can be shown that Anabaptists adopted farming primarily as a result of persecution in the cities. The early Anabaptists were not farmers in the first instance. The recent exhaustive study by Paul Peachey entitled *Die Soziale Herkunft der Täufer in der Reformationzeit* in which he examined the calling (*Beruf*) of more than a thousand Swiss Anabaptists whose names were obtained largely from court records indicates that Anabaptism had a broad social base.[30] It conclusively proves that Anabaptism in its initial phases cannot be associated with a particular class. However, before the movement was ten years old most of the leaders had been destroyed and this meant that the leadership fell to less educated men and the *Täufer* sought to preserve themselves and their ideals in the mountains and small valleys of Switzerland and South Germany. To the present day Mennonitism has never recovered the physical and psychological loss of this early tragedy. Agrarianism has been a refuge to the broken will of Anabaptism. Mennonitism has never reentered the city nor attempted to control the main structures of society. Farming has been accepted as the ideal life because it has provided a living with the least amount of conflict with the social order.

There are probably deeper reasons, however, why Mennonites have held to the agrarian way of life. These are internal and not historical. They are religious and ethical and not accidental. They issue from the nature of Anabaptism as a radical interpretation of Christianity.

For example, Mennonites have always exalted simplicity. Simplicity has characterized their theology, their ethics and their social relations. Complexity has been consciously averted on all levels. By happy coincidence agrarianism has seemed to support simplicity, especially in the social realm. The social value of agrarianism is that it most unambiguously supports primary relationships and intimate personal interaction while it promotes at the same time independence from the complicated, abstract, legal structures of bureaucratic industrial society and the reliance upon the artificialities of civilization.

The preference of Christianity for simple social conditions has been acknowledged by a number of modern theologians. The ethics of Troeltsch,[31] Reinhold Niebuhr[32] and Emil Brunner[33] concede that the ethic of Jesus as love prefers simple social conditions. Bureaucracy, impersonality and complexity make pure love only an occasional possibility. Only within extremely simple conditions of personal relationships can love become the "ordering" principle. This is not to say that these theologians believe with the Mennonites that life can and must be kept within the conditions of simplicity. Nevertheless, it is generally accepted that when the simplicity of the primary relationships are subjected to the conditions of complexity, these relationships tend to become "political" in nature. Love is qualified by justice, personality is replaced by impersonality and freedom is hampered by organizational inhibitions. Troeltsch makes the statement that "simple conditions (are) favorable to Christianity" and he goes on to show why with the following:

> Christianity has a distinct leaning...towards little groups and corporations which are closely bound together in personal relationships,

in which the formal, legal and economic tendency of a dehumanized and abstract organization of the common life has not yet forced purely personal relationships and decisions into the sphere of isolated instances.[34]

The Mennonite community is really an extension of the ethic of the family into the ecclesiastical fellowship. Apologists for this approach to the problems of Christian ethics frequently use the family as a model for the entire community.[35] This is the meaning of brotherhood. The intimacies, affections and mutual responsibilities of the family which elude complex social structures of the world are prized beyond all other values and are thought to comply with Christ's real intention for His followers.

Furthermore Mennonitism has held to agrarianism because it has fostered social uniformity. From the very beginning Mennonites have resisted class distinctions within the Brotherhood. Differences in social and economic rank have been deplored as violations of Christian "koinonia." Even though most Mennonite groups have refused to carry the principle of uniformity to its absolute expression in love communism, Mennonites have associated true fellowship in Christ with social and economic equality, at least within reasonable limits. They have held that spiritual brotherhood cannot be separated from its material or social implications.[36]

Accordingly Mennonites have looked to man's position of relative equality before the land as a natural support to spiritual uniformity. Especially under conditions of pre-scientific agriculture, the uniform resistance as well as response of the soil and the general fortuity of climate were accepted by Mennonites as a natural basis for social equality. They have been suspicious of the city because of the inequalities which it has historically fostered. It is true, of course, that there have been periods in history when the very reverse was true. It has been pointed out that the rise of the mediaeval city was a protest against the inequalities of the feudal system.[37] Troeltsch even goes so far as to say in this connection that the city parallels to a great extent the demands of Christian ethics.[38] However, Mennonitism came into history with the breakdown of the feudal system and the beginnings of capitalism and industrialism. Feudalism as a system was so far gone that it imposed no serious class inequalities within the brotherhood though the capitalistic spirit was recognized immediately as a dangerous potential for the church. Not only did farming offer a general economic uniformity but it assured a uniformity of cultural interests. Mennonites have always had the feeling the Christian fellowship is broken by too wide a range of cultural affections. Christian unity is more likely to obtain where there is common participation in a uniform task. When all are farmers, together with those who are engaged in farm-related small industries, the basis is laid for a uniform Christian culture corresponding to the uniformity of the Gospel.

Another advantage of the rural situation for the Mennonites has been its social independence. Much romantic literature has been written regarding the freedom of rural life and of primitivism. The protest against the binding artificialities of urbanism is a common theme of naturalists, poets and historians. To the Anabaptists and Mennonites, however, escape from the city is far more serious than romantic and aesthetic preferences. *The rural community is to the Mennonite tradition an ethical alternative to the social process of the city.* From the very beginning of Anabaptist history, there emerged a clash between Anabaptist ethics of love and the partisan struggles of commercial and political groups. The student of social ethics is likely to detect elements of competitive struggle in the rural life as well as in urban life. However, it is quite evident that until the modern period the rural area has been considerably less caught up in competitive struggle than the city. One of the first areas of conflict between the Anabaptists and the structure of urban society was the guild.[39] To the Anabaptist the guild involved a partisan commitment, an oath to support the partial advantages of a particular social or economic block. It involved the organization of power for personal advantage. It involved participation in the dynamics of power politics and power economics. To make a living and to engage constructively in the community necessitated the compromise of group interest. This Anabaptism could not tolerate and so the only alternative was to remain in the "open places" of the world where a way of life could be organized along independent lines. In agrarianism, competition and class interest are greatly diminished. The city is the great center of economic and political struggles where the forces of egoism converge. Hence Mennonitism may be characterized by a continuous search for rural sanctuary where economic struggle, partisan involvement and the balancing of egos can be replaced by lines of mutuality and cooperation. To the Mennonites the city was not a community since it appeared impossible to apply the principles of "true community" upon structures which presuppose other principles.

Another reason why the Mennonites have held to agrarianism is simply social inertia. Ever since the persecution of the 16th and 17th centuries, Mennonites both in Europe (with the exception of Mennonites in Holland) and in America have been socially retarded. Mennonite psychology clearly combines a doctrine of separation from the world with a broken spirit, a combination which has encouraged a retreat into rural communities. Until recent years Mennonites have desired only to be left alone. They have taken pride in their communities and they have been good neighbors. Their farming has attracted agricultural experts and their reputation of honesty and uprightness needs no elaboration here. And yet the great problems of the nation and the world, the problems of justice in economic and social relations have been untouched by Mennonites until recent years because of an introverted feeling of social insecurity. None of the Mennonite communities exhibit the conceptual virility and the transforming power of Calvin's Geneva. The Mennonite community is probably less a conscious "strategy" than John C. Bennett seems to imply in his *Christian Ethics and Social Policy.*[40] Certainly there are elements of conscious deliberation in the forming of Mennonite communities, especially among the Hutterites. However, much of Mennonite life has been the weary search for a place to live in peace. Mennonites have suffered so much persecution that their policy has often been simply the negative search for refuge. Consequently when freedom is finally found, very few moral and spiritual resources are left for social reconstruction beyond the immediate requirements of life.

III. Types of Mennonite Communities

It has been stated that the Mennonite community is the answer of the Anabaptist-Mennonite tradition to the problem of natural community. The Mennonite community is an attempt to achieve a new order, based upon the principles of Christ in separation from the world. Historically this community has been agrarian. This has been due to the fact that (1) persecution drove the Anabaptists to the rural parts of Europe and (2) because of the essential conflict between Mennonite principles and urbanism.

It would be wrong, however, to think of the Mennonite community as a fixed and uniform type. A number of community types have developed during Mennonite history. These present a variety of sociological principles. Differences in community organization have unfortunately become the basis for considerable tension between Mennonite groups. The terms "conservative" and "liberal" are used to designate the degree of separation from the world and the degree of inward cohesion which these communities embody. The ideal of the conservative communities is that of a self-sustaining, independent religious community in which all of the essential decisions of the individual are subject to the discipline of the group.

Historically there have been three types of communities among the Mennonites. They are: (1) the absolute (full) community of Hutterianism; (2) the theocratic (closed) community of the Russian Mennonites; and (3) the partial (open) community of the Old Mennonites.

A. *The Hutterian Pattern of "Full Community."* The Hutterites,[41] named after Jacob Hutter, d. 1536, have taken the idea of community to its logical extreme. Completely rejecting the world, not only with respect to war, but also with respect to litigation, the oath, the guild and concern for the total social order, the Hutterites have set up independent societies in which private ownership, the independence of the family, private inheritance and vocational individualism have all been submitted to communal organization. The Hutterites have formed virtually complete, self-sustaining social units (Bruderhof) in which the love principle takes the form of complete community. It is an order in which an attitude of self-surrender (Gelassenheit) is communalized and extended to all areas of life. All those differences which tend to keep people apart in world society are completely abolished.

Hutterianism, the Austrian branch of the Anabaptist movement, had a precarious and somewhat uncertain beginning in the early period of Anabaptist history. The movement began under the rather loose direction of George Blaurock in the Tyrol until his martyrdom in 1529.[42] The radicalism of Hutterianism grew out of the dispute between the "Stabler" (staff-bearers) and the "Schwertler" (sword bearers) under the leadership of Balthasar Hubmaier.[43] The "Stabler" represented a completely nonresistant approach to life. Severe persecution forced the Anabaptists of Tyrol to move to Austria where thousands of Anabaptists from Switzerland, S. Germany and Bavaria likewise sought refuge. As the "Stabler" were fleeing into Austria an emergency lack of food and other provisions compelled them to share their possessions.[44] This was not intended at the time to express the ideology of love communism nor to duplicate the practice of the Jerusalem church. However, the Anabaptists in Austria practiced various forms of brotherhood sharing even though this was not carried to the extreme of "full" community until 1531. The organization of the Austrian Anabaptists into communistic colonies came with the able leadership of Jacob Hutter.[45] Hutter formulated the principles of absolute community which have remained for over four hundred years. He is described in words of highest praise in the *Chronik*. He was executed by Innsbruck in 1536 and his wife met a similar fate two years later at Schöneck.

The story of the Hutterites is another story of heroic suffering. On one occasion, a certain group of Hutterites were fleeing from Moravia by foot under the leadership of Hutter and were "driven into the field like a herd of sheep.... They lay down on the wide heath under the open sky with many wretched widows and children, sick and infants."[46] Finally Hutter wrote to the governor Kuna von Kunstadt these moving words:

> Now we are camping on the heath, without disadvantage to any man. We do not want to wrong or harm any human being, not even our worst enemy. Our walk in life is to live in truth and righteousness of God, in peace and unity. We do not hesitate to give an account of our conduct to anyone.... If all the world were like us there would be no war and no injustice. We can go nowhere; may God in heaven show us where we shall go. We cannot be prohibited from the earth, for the earth is the heavenly Father's; may he do with us what He will.[47]

However, when persecution was relaxed in Moravia and Slovakia around 1565, the Hutterites flourished in every way for a period of about forty years. This was called the "Golden Period."[48] During this time Hutterianism considered itself a "city set upon a hill." It had a strong sense of destiny, a missionary zeal, a vocational drive and a literary interest. The Hutterian colonies became "colonies of heaven" whose craftmanship and expertise in medicine, agriculture and mill work led that part of the world.[49] Hutterites worked both within the colony and without. They were famous for their surgeons and they practiced the segregation of the sick before the germ was discovered. The colonies exhibited matchless organization. Everyone was disciplined and ordered. The Hutterites describe their own communal operations in these words:

> Just as in a clock each wheel drives another and each part is necessary to move another, so that it serves its purpose; or as in a colony of bees in the common hive one part prepares the honey, another the wax, another furnishes water, and another does some-

thing else so that the precious sweet honey may finally be produced, and that in an amount not just sufficient for their own needs but enough that man may also be supplied; so was it among them.[50]

The unique feature of Hutterianism is the abolition of the institution of property. The community of goods has two roots. The first root is the Christian command of love which they interpreted to mean that they should "prove the spiritual also in things temporal."[51] *Every aspect of life including property must be made as free as the Spirit.* To offer Christ to the brother while withholding one's material goods from him with legal titles was regarded as a violation of the communion of the saints. They saw the incongruity between common participation in the Lord's supper and private use of goods. The Hutterites said, "Our Christian faith says, a holy Christian church and a communion (Gemeinschaft) of saints; whoever now recognizes the communion (Gemeinschaft) of saints with the mouth but does not maintain Community (Gemeinschaft), he is false."[52] The Hutterites went so far as to say that where there is no community of goods there is no true church. The poverty of Jesus, the Jerusalem communal experiment, the Rich Young Ruler, Christ's exaltation of the poor widow who gave all that she had in true *Gelassenheit*, Paul's admonition to the church at Corinth concerning the ministering to the saints in Jerusalem as well as copious references to the Old Testament prophets were supposed to have pointed to the perfect order of community of goods.[53]

The communistic practices of the Hutterites should not be evaluated from the standpoint of economic theory. Community of goods was simply a religious application of "koinonia." It has nothing to do with the development of socialist economic ideology. The Hutterites simply wished to make love an ordering principle. What they tried to do was to translate the "anarchy of love" (Troeltsch) into ordered love without destroying its essence. They wished to establish the dream of utopians, namely, a *system* of human relations without coercion. They wanted social harmony without law and without force, i.e., a fellowship in which order resulted from love alone. They desired a society of perfect mutuality in the spirit of Christ. This they felt lay within the possibilities of God's grace for man if man would only submit to his brother, the most important step of which is the surrender of his goods along with the hope of personal accumulation in the future and the hope of transmitting wealth to his children. They contended that only when this is done can men speak of the communion of the saints. Then only can Christ's followers pray that the Kingdom may come on earth as it is in heaven. For "in heaven there is no ownership; hence there are found content, true peace, and all blessedness. If any one there took upon himself to call anything his own, he would straightway be thrust out into hell, and there would become a devil. Where one will have self-will, there is all manner of misery and wretchedness. So is it also here on earth."[54]

The keeping back of one's property from common use was regarded as failure to understand the meaning of brotherhood and they called this *Geiz*, i.e., avarice or greed. The only way to overcome this, they thought, was by

inner self-conquest. They realized that the surrender of one's goods is the surrender of one's self "for where one's treasure is there in his heart also." They
acknowledged the close connection between property and the real person.
Therefore until one surrenders his goods he has not surrendered his self. The
called it the "narrow path" and although the *Chronik* does not overlook the
temporal advantages of the system of communal living, Hutterian literature
acknowledges that the initial giving up to the brother in community of goods is
difficult. "Communal living would not be hard, if there were not such self-
regard."[55]

Not only is community of goods rooted in Christ's commandment of love,
but it also corresponds to the condition prior to the fall.[56] This is the second
main root. Peter Ridemann maintained that property is a curse as a result of
the fall of Adam. In the original state (Urstand) all things were in common.
In this condition there was no war, no power, no human law, no violence and
no property. But when man sinned, then there came into his vocabulary the
words "mine" and "thine." Along with these words came wars, violence, toil,
deceit and separation between men. Therefore property clearly belongs to the
world. It is in heathendom. All things should be free like the air, rain, snow
and water. "Temporal goods, which God in the same proportion and measure
hath given for common use, should not and may not be made one's own. This
cannot be in accordance with divine and Christian right, for owning and ownership is against the nature and character of His creation. Whosoever encloseth
and maketh his own what is and should be free, acteth against Him who hath
made and created it free, and that is sin."[57]

The conviction that ownership is against the nature and character of His
creation is clearly a reference to the Absolute Law of Nature. This theme,
which is rare in Anabaptist literature as a whole, frequently appears in the writings of Peter Ridemann. Hutterite communities were intended to restore the
lost paradise. The way to return to the original estate is to renounce "created
things" and cleave to Christ. The form of renunciation is abolition of property.
"He who will have the one must let the other go." In communal consumption
things do not displace Christ, but in individual consumption the substitution of
the thing for Christ is inevitable. In common use things sustain life without
corrupting the heart. The return to paradisiacal equality was begun by the
Jerusalem church and continued by small groups and shall be consummated by
the church which has renounced everything.

The Hutterite interpretation of *Gemeinschaft* was a source of irritation
between the various groups of Anabaptists. Most Anabaptists refused to
believe that Christ intended "complete community." Conrad Grebel rejected
Christian communism.[58] The stress on *Gemeinschaft* is found everywhere in
Anabaptism but this was usually interpreted to imply the sharing of surplus
and, of course, sharing everything in case of emergency. In principle Anabaptists believed that all the property of the membership belongs to the Brotherhood. However, Hutterianism goes beyond common practice by removing
individual *control* of goods at every point. In Hutterianism, sharing is a part of
the social organization. Sharing requires no individual decision. It is an

integral part of the system.

When one compares Hutterianism with the attempts of mediaeval monasticism to embody the perfect law of love through the renunciation of property, one can find a general similarity. Hutterianism, however, introduces a fundamental difference. It has included the family. To say that Hutterianism is monasticism with the addition of the family is a valid, general observation. In this sense Hutterianism is unique in the history of "ethical Christianity." It seeks to carry through the rigorous demands of Christ as did the monastics, but it attempts to take the family along. It must be acknowledged, however, that within the communal order many prerogatives of the family were denied and so it is not correct to say that Hutterianism absorbed the family with all of its usual freedom and individualism. The authority of the parent for the child was definitely qualified by the community rule.[59] Parental possessiveness and control was limited by the brotherhood. The family was included but greatly subordinated. The essential unit of organization was the body of Christ and not the natural family. The school, the nursery and the craft under the domination of group and under the immediate supervision of the *Diener des Wortes* and the *Diener des Notdurft* probably mitigated the strongest natural desire to "possess" one's own children.

The significance of the Hutterites for our study is that they carried the essential ideas of Anabaptism to their logical conclusion. Anabaptism stands for separation from the world, a new society representing the pure ethic of love, for brotherhood and for the superiority of the Kingdom to the family. Hutterianism is the most consistent from of Anabaptism. It is the Mennonite community in its most unadulterated form. In Hutterianism, Anabaptism is completely true to its own principles. Here everything, including property, submits to the "Kingdom." In the Hutterite colony, love is not an occasional possibility. It is "structuralized." It is not an infrequent exception to the egoism of worldly structures. *It is an alternative structure.* According to the Hutterite idea, everything submits to the "fellowship" of the saints including property and all the powers of individualism and self-determination which go along with it. Hutterianism is Anabaptism in its absolute form.

B. *The "Closed" Community.* The second type of Mennonite community in the history of the church is the theocratic (closed) community. This form of community is a Mennonite anomaly. It is a supreme example of the tendency noted by such scholars as Joachin Wach, Liston Pope and Roland Bainton for the sect to become a "church."[60] This form of community begins with Anabaptist sectarian characteristics such as a basic attitude of separation from the world, absolute nonresistance, a brotherhood church, loose "charismatic" organization and emphasis upon the cross. It keeps itself completely removed from the larger society. But as it attempts to perpetuate itself in its closed communities and as it tries to retain its principles and consolidate its gains, it becomes institutionalized. It relies upon political forces and restraints, it relaxes its discipline, its membership becomes "ethnic" and its baptismal policies become, for all practical purposes, those of a *Volkskirche.* Eventually the total community, including civil government, comes under the domination of the church as the "Shepherd," as the protector of values, as the agent and the symbol of the total culture.

According to the interpretation of such scholars as the Catholic sociologist E. K. Francis and Robert S. Kreider, this is the experience of the Russian Mennonite colonies from their beginning at the end of the eighteenth century to the time of the Russian revolution.[61] This is significant for our study since it is one of the very few occasions in Mennonite history when the Mennonite church unwittingly accepted total social responsibility, albeit within its own protected boundaries as a little "state within a sate." This chapter of Mennonite history exhibits many of the forces and objectives of "Christian civilization" of the great "inclusive" churches of history.

The Mennonites moved to Russia in response to the invitation of Czarina Catherine II and in accordance with her manifesto of July 22, 1763 which offered special advantages to foreign settlers.[62] They were offered the privilege of a colonial type of socio-economic and ecclesiastical autonomy. They were offered responsibility for civil administration of their colonies and religious freedom. They were guaranteed perpetual freedom from military service. Their only limitation was denial of the right to evangelize among the Russian citizenry. According to Robert S. Kreider, "Here was opened a unique opportunity in the history of Mennonitism to apply Mennonite principles to the whole range of life's activities."[63]

The Mennonites who responded to this call were Prussian Mennonites whose church life had suffered by its conflict with the Prussian state. Among the Prussian Mennonites the spiritual fervor of Anabaptism had already diminished. The brotherhood ideal had been considerably dissipated. Nevertheless the residual spirit of ethical religion was strong enough to prompt hundreds of families to pull up stakes and trek to South Russia along the Molotschna and Chortitza rivers. Here they were at complete freedom to realize their ideal of the perfect Christian order without the interference of the world. In this case, conflict with the larger society was no hindrance to the attainment of the ideal.

This is, of course, not a perfect experiment in Anabaptist idealism for two reasons. In the first place the movement lacked strong leadership and its spiritual life was far below the original Anabaptist level. Secondly, the system of privileges offered by Russia conflicted with the original Anabaptist vision of a purely voluntary church. Membership in the colony was determined by blood rather than faith. In order to receive the colonial privileges one had to be a Mennonite by natural birth. Hence, from the beginning, it was more of a "natural" community than a "founded" community.

The church pattern among the Russian colonies was originally along lines of the Prussian Mennonite congregations. Each congregation was independently controlled. The ministry was three-fold, the elder, several ministers and a deacon. The worship and the churches were simple. Although the love communism of the Austrian Anabaptists was far from their thoughts, they engaged in the kind of mutual aid which is likely to be practiced under conditions of primitive colonization, especially when religious feeling and ethnic ties are combined. One crucial factor in their church life was that everyone became a church member. Joining the church became the automatic result of membership in the colony. All institutions within the colony tended to take on a religious character. The ministers were increasingly called upon the regulate "civil" affairs such as the schools. "The necessity of frequent consultations of the church officers led to the establishment in 1851 of a new institution, the *Kirchenkonvent*, where all controversial questions concerning church affairs and orders were decided. This Kirchenkonvent was resented by many for its alleged possession of monarchical powers."[64]

The political life of the colony was internal. In 1801 the Russian Imperial instruction granted the Mennonites local self-government. The local government consisted of the village assembly composed of one representative from each farm and the village office composed of a *Schultz* (mayor) and two *Beisitzers* (assistants). The village assembly met at least once a week. The duties of the assembly consisted of the collection of all revenues and taxes, levying minor fines, keeping records and transmitting orders and instructions from the government. The *Schultz* was the "pivotal figure in the scheme of local government."[65] He was responsible for the maintenance of law and order and for settlement of disputes. He could prohibit the sale of liquor to colonists who were addicted to drunkenness and luxury. He was responsible for enforcement of church attendance and participation in holy communion. Failure to attend to religious duties was punishable by fine. His powers also extended over the agricultural program as well as commerce and industry. He exercised the right to enforce work at sunrise and to regulate farm production by official rotation of crops. His powers were virtually dictatorial.[66]

The political authority of the entire colony was the district assembly headed by the *Ober-Schultz*. This political body was directly responsible to the district office of the Russian Advisory Commission at Odessa.[67] Powers of corporal punishment were given to the Ober-Schultz. However most of the social, economic and political affairs were handled by the local assemblies.[68]

Frequently religious affairs were decided by the civil body. The union of the civil and religious life was sometimes achieved by illegal collaboration between the leaders of the religious and civil realism. This frequently led to protests by those who remembered that the principle for which Anabaptism became a separate religious movement in the Zwinglian reform was the complete independence of the religious realm from civil control.

One of the great problems of the colonies was the unequal distribution of surplus land. By 1860 the Molotschna Colony had a landless proletariat. The landless sought help from the preachers but with little response since the ministers usually were among the wealthier land owners. Added to economic unrest, certain "pietistic" religious attitudes among the "poor" contributed to the unhealthy state of affairs. The district head eventually tried to crush the uprising by force. Finally in 1866 a reform movement was innovated by an *Imperial* Rescript.

In his study of "The Mennonite Church in Its Russian Environment," Robert Kreider points out that the Russian Mennonites experienced two religious crisis which brought to light the essential conflict between the Mennonite profession of nonresistance and separation of church and state on the one hand and the realities of force inherent in the closed colony on the other.[69] The first had to do with the *Kleine Gemeinde*. This consisted of a few followers of Claas Reimer. This group was disturbed because of the close association of the church and police power. This was by no means the first protest of its kind. In 1855 a Mennonite elder by the name of Heinrich Wiens was banished because he refused to give a beating to a member of the church.[70] The *Kleine Gemeinde* brought before the conscience of the church and the "state" the remembrance of Anabaptist principles of the avoidance of the office of the magistracy and police. For a while the *Kleine Gemeinde* was threatened with banishment to Siberia. However in 1843 it was granted the status of a Mennonite church.

According to the *Kleine Gemeinde*, the awful effects of the inherent compromise of the "state-church" system had descended upon the Mennonites. One involvement led to another until the church as the protector of the entire life of the colony was chocked with secularism, carelessness and institutionalism. The tie of the church and the civil authorities led to laxity in discipline. Since the church was identified with the total community, and since there was really no world to receive the excommunicated, the church simply absorbed the evil in the manner of the great state churches against which the Anabaptists had dissented.

The second crisis in the life of the colony was that of the *Brüder Gemeinde*.[71] This was a movement influenced by German pietistic warmth but which called also for the original Anabaptist pattern of "charismatic" leadership, scriptural discipline and non-participation in political affairs. The result was a new congregation called *Mennoniten Brüdergemeinde*. This congregation was immediately reported to the Mennonite political authorities. These officials threatened the seceders with punishment and attempted to enforce the law against secret societies. Kreider comments, "there is startling parallelism between these attacks on the new group and the condescending attacks of the Reformers on the Anabaptists. Five Mennonite elders submitted a statement to the provincial government condemning the new group as sectarians, *Schwärmer*, destroyers of unity, disorganizers of the social order, Biblicists...and the *coup de grace*--perfectionists."[72]

It would be unfair to dwell only upon the negative side of Mennonite colonial life. From the standpoint of community development, agricultural progress, hospitals, schools and small industry, the Russian Mennonite colonies became the pride of the Czars. They brought to Russia the virtues of honesty and industry and certain superior elements of German culture. From the standpoint of the advancement of material culture, the Mennonites contributed considerably to Russia.[73]

From the standpoint of the vision of the Anabaptists, however, the Mennonite Russian experiment was a failure. It was a failure in so far as it depended largely upon cultural supports and ethnic lines of continuity instead of pure spirituality. Employing from the very beginning the principles of the

Volskirche with its inclusive membership, with its lack of discipline and its disregard for the Great Commission, membership in the church became as automatic as membership in the colony. The Christian community moved progressively in the direction of a natural community.

E. K. Francis of Notre Dame University declares that the Mennonites in Russia moved from a religious group into an ethnic group in less than three generations.[74] As personal commitment was replaced by group decision and as suffering discipleship was replaced by collective securities, the quality of personal religion declined. Paul Peachey, commenting on the experience of the Russian experiment, concludes, "Where maximum community security is achieved,...Mennonite society quickly becomes ethnic."[75]

On the basis of the Russian experience in constructing a total Mennonite culture, it would appear that the real question is whether Anabaptism in its socio-religious applications can ever accept responsibility for all of life, even its own life, especially in the political realm. As stated previously, Anabaptism is emphatically opposed to the world order. For this reason, Anabaptists have suffered the fate of the prophets. They have been martyred or driven into the wilderness. Here they have chosen to build communities--especially since they have families. This means, of course, that they have had to face some of the facts of cultural life. They have had to construct some kind of social order of their own. *Then comes the crucial question as to: 1) how inclusive the order is to become and; 2) how it shall be perpetuated.* At this point the Hutterites and the Russian communities adopted different policies. The Hutterites accepted responsibility for all aspects of their corporate existence *except* the political. They insisted that whatever police duties were necessary would be handled by the outside. Furthermore, they insisted upon internal discipline through the ban to assure that the perpetuation of the life of the community would be on the basis of spiritual experience rather than blood inheritance. The Hutterites insisted also that there must be a world. This world must be near at hand to receive the erring children. Under this arrangement nearly all of life has been brought under the influence of Christian culture, but not absolutely all. Hence they have remained a sect.

The Russian Mennonites, on the other hand, accepted, for practical purposes, *all* of culture according to the inclusive policies of the *Volkskirche*. Under this arrangement, *all* elements of culture were to be brought together in a common Christian ethos. It was assumed that, since they were separated from the influences of the world, they could create their own all-inclusive culture without the failures associated with Christendom. Furthermore this line of thought corresponded to an authentic and elemental aspect of the Gospel, i.e., its universal aspect. Does not the logic of Christianity as a universal religion suggest not only the possibility but the duty to penetrate *all* the structures of life with the Christian spirit, to bring *everyone* and *everything* into captivity for Christ (Col. 1:16-20, Eph. 1:10)? Should not the family, the farm, the business, social life, recreation, art, "secular" literature and civil order be brought under the dominion of the spiritual realm? Should not this new order include all persons and all classes? Furthermore would a policy of the Christianization of the totality of life not finally result in the creation of an environment which would make Christianity result from a "natural" and even unconscious inclination rather than a crisis decision?

The theocratic policy of the Russian Mennonites which, in view of the weakness of human nature, eventually resulted in the inclusion of both saints and sinners in the church and which relied upon institutional and cultural methods of perpetuation in the absence of spiritual life and discipline, seems to indicate that Anabaptism cannot maintain itself within a total culture of its own making. It must provide only part of the cultural life of its people. It may not attempt to tie together its spiritual gains too securely by cultural bonds and especially it must never attempt to maintain itself by political means. Anabaptism needs to be near a world culture so that the world can provide those services which it cannot supply for itself and so that it may be provided with a receptacle for sinners and dissenters lest the whole lump be corrupted. Anabaptism, it would appear, cannot "go it along." It needs the world to deal with the problem of sin--not simply the sin of the world but the sin of its own children. It can neither accept responsibility for the world nor for its own society as a completely independent order.[76] E. K. Francis has summed up the Mennonite dilemma in this way:

> The Russian period of Mennonite history thus brings clearly to the fore the dilemma and utopian character of a sect. It must either suffer pagans and sinners to run the world, thereby preserving the purity of its ideals without putting them to the test, or it must, like Dostoyevski's Grand Inquisitor, accommodate itself to the stark realities of life in this world, thereby losing its original character. In the period between 1790 and 1870 the Mennonite sectarians in Russia had become a people whose conspicuous secular successes were bought at the price of institutionalization of religion and secularization of the inner life of the group.[77]

C. *The "Open" Community of American Mennonites.* The third type of Mennonite community organization is the "open" community. This is characteristic of the (Old) Mennonite Church in its American environment and therefore it lies close to the problem of this thesis. The term "open" stands for the fact that the Mennonite community in this instance does not attempt to constitute a solid population block, nor a totally independent unit. Its separatism is limited by the fact that it is a community which mingles, to a certain extent at least, with other groups within a pluralistic democratic society. The open community is a community with next door non-Mennonite neighbors. It does not attempt to control a given geographical territory. Its independence from the larger social order is limited to certain distinct areas of life. It is true that in certain small sections, such as the Kishacoquillas Valley in Pennsylvania, Mennonites and their Amish cousins are in a majority. The population of Lancaster County, Pennsylvania, is also strongly Mennonite. However, no attempt is made in these communities to control the countryside or to introduce totally different structural forms. The open community is a community of people who by reason of a common faith and a sense of brotherhood and common background share a concern for each other. They exercise certain kinds of mutual aid and support a more or less common culture. This common culture, however, does not result in a completely independent order as in the case of the Hutterite community of the closed colony. It is neither communistic nor theocratic. It accepts the general sociological and political organization of society as its framework of life even though it treats with reserve or with complete abstention certain dimensions of the social and political order. This is to say that the open community accepts the institutions of property, legal rights (though it is opposed to litigation), business and trade, public education and public welfare. Mennonite participation in these areas of public life has been retarded because of attitudes of social inferiority, agrarianism and lack of education, but they are by no means completely closed to them.

The beginning of the open community pattern is due to accident as much as design. The open community is essentially the result of the policy of colonial Pennsylvania which opened its communities to all religious groups.[78] From the beginning there were strong pluralistic tendencies in Pennsylvania which eventually spread to other colonies. Except for the short lived, unwitting "Germantown Experiment,"[79] Mennonites never tried to control a given geographical area either culturally or politically. They have always assumed that they should live among the other people and although Mennonites of the open community type have been considerably removed from the main stream of culture, they have participated in the culture in many ways. They have had many contacts with the world. The differences between the Mennonite community and the larger community is often more a matter of patterns of dress, language, ethnic backgrounds and minor cultural idiosyncrasies than fundamental differences of social organization. It may be said of the open community that it is by no means a threat to the total social structure like that of the Hutterites since it is inclined to take within itself the general features of society.

The significance of the Mennonite community in its American environment has been recognized by American Mennonites as a unique sociological phenomenon only within the last twenty-five years. Before that time the Mennonite community was maintained simply by the forces of traditionalism and family ties with no attempt to understand its community life as an objective phenomenon. Mennonites were aware of being a "peculiar people." They were conscious of their strange dress, language and other regulations but they were quite unaware of the sociological laws which held them together. This lack of awareness arose partly from the fact that sociology of religion is itself a fairly recent science. Social analysis of religious groups was born of the labors of Max Weber and Ernst Troeltsch during the earlier part of the twentieth century. Furthermore it was only by the middle of the 1930's that the Mennonite church had produced scholars of her own who were qualified to survey Mennonite history, sociology and ethics objectively and scientifically.

The question arises as to why Mennonite scholars have become interested in the study of the Mennonite community. *The reason for interest in the Mennonite community is the conviction that the propagation of the Mennonite faith and way of life is closely tied to the maintenance of the Mennonite community.* One gathers from the writings of J. Winfield Fretz and Guy F. Hershberger the implication that if the Mennonite community vanishes, Mennonitism as a unique form of Christianity is likely to vanish with it.[80] Hence the writings of these scholars attempt to show the Christian advantage of their rural communities, their *small* businesses, their traditional folkways and their historical heritage. They state that Mennonitism as an interpretation of Christianity includes a rural philosophy of life.[81] They emphasize the advantage of rural life for the cultivation of loving primary relationships. The many attractive pictures of successful farming in the *Mennonite Community* mix pure religious sentiments with elements of prosperity and contentment. Various *simple* vocations (usually farm related) are described as openings for discipleship. It may be confidently stated that the past twenty years have seen a "back to the farm" emphasis which gained momentum shortly after World War II as young men returned to their homes.

The real significance of the emphasis upon the Mennonite community can be understood only when it is seen against the backdrop of the great social developments in the modern world and their meaning for the church. During the past one hundred years, life in the Western World has undergone a social revolution. With the industrial revolution, modern technology and the rise of the modern city, the church has found itself in a "new situation." The new situation is a world which is no longer congenial to the spirit and values of Christ. It has led to great concentrations of power, to an impersonal social ethos, to a system of abstract law, to the artificialities of urbanism and to sensate materialism. It was Max Weber and his colleague Ernst Troeltsch who first sensed the meaning of the industrial revolution for Christianity. It was Weber and Troeltsch who defined the "social problem." The guiding theme of Weber's political sociology was, "How can the individual maintain his independence in the presence of the total bureaucratization of life?"[82] Modern theologians such as William Temple, Paul Tillich and Reinhold Niebuhr, together with the generation of Niebuhr's students, have added their own individual interpretation of the problem. It may be said that the fundamental problem of social ethics during the last forty years has been the working out of a constructive relation between the Gospel message and the realities of the modern industrial culture.

The peculiar approach to the problems of the world for which the Mennonite community stands is one of parallelism. Instead of meeting the problems in the context of the world where they appear, Mennonites retreat into agrarian enclaves and attempt to create conditions which are so ideal that the problems do not appear. No attempt is made to change the main stream of history by calling for reforms or taking a public stand on the side of justice. Mennonites make general statements about justice and fair play in social affairs but they seldom take sides on specific social issues. To the contrary, the approach of the Mennonites is to avoid direct encounter with social problems by creating ideal communities for their own people which may incidentally witness to the world about the possibility of a better way. In a world of industrial conflict between huge industrial organizations and organized labor, the Mennonites attempt to set up their own *small* factories on a brotherhood labor-management basis. If an economic depression sends millions to the government for aid, Mennonites seek ways of taking care of their own through the church. If it is impossible for young farmers to get bank loans, Mennonites organize their own brotherhood financial institutions. If there are racial tensions in our land, Mennonites seek to transcend racial tensions in their own ranks. The conception of the ideal community as an alternative to the world is contained in Guy F. Hershberger's phrase "islands of sanity." Hershberger has done more to promote the idea of the Mennonite community than any other man.

Undoubtedly, the one major social problem which has done more to encourage the Mennonite community than any other is industrial conflict. In his book, *War, Peace and Nonresistance* (1944), Hershberger points out that Mennonites have always attempted to apply nonresistance to all of life. Historically, this principle has been applied to the areas of international conflict, litigation and political responsibility. However, one of the difficult problems of the Mennonite in his modern environment is his relation to competing industrial interests. This is a recent problem.[83] Involved in it is an attitude toward the general structure of modern industrial society.

The Mennonite Church felt compelled to take an official action in 1941 regarding its attitude toward industrial conflict. The problem became acute since some Mennonites were working in factories and joining unions.[84] The church was not ready to condemn unionism as such, since the history of industrial relations clearly showed the necessity of collective bargaining and effective sanctions in order for labor to receive justice. Mennonites nevertheless saw in industrial conflict the violation of the principles of the cross. Therefore the "Committee on Industrial Relations" recommended a general approach which was adopted by the Mennonite Church in 1941 as follows:

> While our present labors with industrial organizations are necessary and worth while, it would be better if the social and economic situations of the Mennonite Church were such as to make them unnecessary. So long as the brethren work in factories where industrial unionism threatens the principles of the church, the church must do what it can to protect its members and its principles. But a more worth-while task would be for the church to get nearer the roots of its problem and do what it can to provide a social and economic situation where its members would not be troubled with unionism at all. If this could be done, the Mennonite testimony to the world would be greatly strengthened. A few nonunion workers in a factory can and do give a testimony, but a Mennonite community, co-operatively directing its entire economic and social life in such a way as to exemplify the economic and social ethics of the New

Testament, would be a stronger and a better testimony.... Your committee believes that if the Mennonite and Christian way in economic relations is to prevail among our people the church will need to examine more closely the roots of its problem and take steps to develop a forward-looking program of community building, so challenging as to keep the thought and the energies of all the members focus upon it. Your committee believes that the church does not yet realize as it should the possibilities for fostering the Mennonite, and we believe the Christian, way of life through such means as effective organization for mutual aid, hospitalization, medical care, the co-operative purchasing of land to assist young farmers in need of help, and the co-operative operation of community industries where New Testament business and social ethics and means of security prevail.[85]

Although Mennonites have never spelled out clearly just what kind of business principles are in line with New Testament ethics, Hershberger gives us something of a description of what may be involved. The ideal Mennonite community will be basically agricultural, but will meet the modern necessity for industrial production by Mennonite factories in which conflict will be settled in an atmosphere of brotherly love. These factories should be small so as to encourage personal relations. Hershberger quotes Reinhold Niebuhr to the effect that "all social co-operation on a larger scale than the most intimate social group, requires methods that are out of harmony with a New Testament ethic."[86] Hershberger is thinking of a factory which will be necessarily small, where people know each other intimately "like members of a single family." For him the major problem is how to operate a factory on the basis of personal intimacy.

Hershberger is certain that this can be done and so he called the church in his numerous writings to set up systematically the means of developing Mennonite industries where industrial conflict would not arise. His major appeal in 1944 for a planned community was a courageous attempt to put Mennonite principles into operation in the modern world. Hershberger wrote:

Among the Mennonites of America today there are a number of industrial employers. These Mennonite employers of labor have an excellent opportunity, and a responsibility, to give clear witness to the nonresistant faith. Sociologists, and experts in the United States Department of Agriculture, today are citing Mennonite agricultural communities as models of agricultural stability and community solidarity. These writers recognize that there is something about the Mennonite faith and the Mennonite way of life which helps to make these agricultural communities what they are. If this view is correct, then it would seem that the Mennonite way of life should have something to contribute in the field of industry as well. It should, for example, keep Mennonite factories from growing so large that they become impersonal, soulless corporations.... Mennonite employers dare not delay the introduction of progressive measures for the improvement of working and living conditions, and for the development of wholesome employer-employee relationships....[87]

Specifically, Hershberger called for such modern labor policies as the yearly wage, security against personal layoffs and profit sharing. All this should be conducted in the spirit of the nonresistant faith which means that the employer seeks the highest welfare of his employees for the employees' sake, while at the same time employees seek the welfare of their employer for the employer's sake.[88] Of course this is to take place in the rural community since "no environment is more favorable for the perpetuation of the nonresistant faith than is the rural community; and for this reason the Mennonite churches will do well to keep themselves established in such communities, with a high percentage of their members directly engaged in agriculture."[89]

Hershberger has in mind a planned community. Plans would include a church-sponsored counseling service, credit bureaus which charge a low rate of interest and a mutual aid organization to provide aid in times of sickness and death. Brethren with money should loan to those who have none instead of investing in stocks and bonds on the open market where it might be used to support industrial conflict. Young people who attend college should give their lives to the Mennonite community. This ideal community needs Mennonite doctors, nurses and teachers. Mennonite hospitals should be erected which serve the entire community on a co-operative basis.

But the most important of all, this ideal community must be permeated with the spirit of Christ. The nonresistant way of life must direct its every work and motive. The spirit of Christian brotherhood must govern all of its relationships. In such a community there should be no opportunity for the seeds of industrial conflict even to take root. And in such a community, so conceived and so dedicated and so managed, there ought to be happiness, contentment, and security, such as will prevent any appreciable drift of the Mennonite population to the larger urban centers of industrial conflict.[90]

In addition to the impulse to community building supplied by modern industrial conflict with associated problems of urbanism, was the impulse supplied by the experience of Mennonite conscientious objectors during World War II. During the war thousands of Mennonite youth were closely associated in "projects of national importance" under the direction of Civilian Public Service. The experience of standing together for their convictions in the face of unpopular public sentiment gave many Mennonite youth a strong sense of loyalty to their historic background. Reading materials about the Mennonite faith, study classes and discussions added to the morale of many young Mennonites. The question which faced nearly all these youth was their future location and job--a need which the government met for the soldiers of the armed forces by the G.I. Bill of Rights. To meet the needs of Mennonite youth returning from alternative service, considerable thinking was done regarding their place in the founding of ideal Mennonite communities. The result was in part the publication of a *Mennonite Community Source Book* (1946).[91] This book is a collection of references to books and articles dealing with all important phases of community life such as devotional exercises, religious readings, agricultural methods, home economics, mental health, pacifism, family, music, recreation and education. The emphasis was upon the combination of piety and the "good life." The assumption was that all phases of life are to be Christianized and all are to be brought together under the conception of the Mennonite community.

The interest of C.P.S. men in the Mennonite community idea was manifested in the vision and the work which went into the publication of the *Mennonite Community* monthly magazine (first issue January, 1947). Former C.P.S. men, including H. Ralph Hernley, Atlee Beechy, John E. Lehmann, Olen L. Britch and Grant M. Stoltzfus, the editor, were involved in this emphasis. The publication was the result of a vision. Paul Erb described the *Mennonite Community* magazine as the initial dream of S. F. Coffman of Vineland, Ontario. The dream was "formulated" by G. F. Hershberger and a number of C.P.S. men. It was finally "realized" through the Mennonite Community Association which was organized June 3, 1946.[92]

At this stage of development, the idea of the *Mennonite Community* clearly shows a romantic tendency. Although it would be wrong to say that the philosophy of the Mennonite community is the identification of Christianity with the rural way of life, the truth is not far from it. It brings Christianity and "soilism" in close proximity. This is understandable in view of the fact that "Christianity has a distinct leaning towards comparatively simple conditions of living.[93] However, the impression one gets in reading the *Mennonite Community* is not one of pure simplicity--at least not simplicity in terms of poverty and discipleship in the sense of the stage of the "circle of disciples." These disciples are "settled" on farms, they are prosperous in small businesses, they are securely entrenched in time honored traditions and they are versed in the arts of cooking.[94] In other words the *Mennonite Community* has a tendency to bring together the contradictory elements of radical discipleship with the conservative elements of natural securities, property, social stabilities and "simple" contentment.

Not only is the idea of the Mennonite community as it appears in the magazine by the same name romantic, but it also runs the danger of identifying the Kingdom of God with a particular cultural expression. This danger is, of course, inherent in the Mennonite conception of the relation of the Church to the Kingdom of God. For Mennonites the relation is undialectical. The Church and the Kingdom of God must be one. The Kingdom of God must be realized on earth and the church is the agent for its realization. This understanding explains the striving for purity, discipline, separation from the world and the Christianization of all of culture within the church. Harald S. Bender says, "The Mennonite believes rather that the kingdom of God can be and should be set up within the fellowship of the Church here and now, and lived out to its fullest meaning. The world may be full of devils...but the life within the Christian brotherhood community is satisfyingly full of victory, peace, love and joy."[95] Thus the strategy and the energies which have gone into the Mennonite community are nothing less than an attempt to establish the Kingdom of God on earth. The danger of identifying the Kingdom of God with the particular cultural form which seems most reasonable at the time is a constant danger facing any religious body which attempts nothing less than to bring in the Kingdom.

IV. Conclusion

Historically, Mennonites have lived in more or less isolated agrarian communities. This isolated existence was impressed upon the Mennonites (Anabaptists) by persecution. They were forcibly rejected by civilization. Gradually, however, the broken spirit of Mennonitism and the conflict between their nonresistant way of life and the fundamental structure of urban life resulted not in a grudging acceptance of agrarianism but in the exaltation of it as the most favorable circumstance for the realization of Christian principles. Three types of community organization resulted. The most rigorous and consistent type is the Hutterite communistic colony of "full" community and love. The most isolated and introverted is the closed colony type of the Russian settlements which resulted in a *Volkskirche*.

The open community of American Mennonitism lies closest to the world. In order to protect the Mennonite community from disintegration before the forces of modern industrialism, certain outstanding leaders of the church have attempted to reinforce the Mennonite community in the minds of the church by the application of modern scientific principles of the "small" community. The result is Mennonite "islands of sanity," ideal communities where the unwholesome forces of the modern technological world can be "solved" under conditions of primary relationships of love. However, the exaltation of the Mennonite community has resulted in a combination of Christian principles and rural romanticism. This combination runs the danger of identifying the Kingdom of God with a peculiar sociological expression. *In any event, the Mennonite community makes no attempt to solve the problems of society in the context of the world where they originate and where they must eventually be handled.*

Endnotes

1 Joachim Wach, *Sociology of Religion* (Chicago: The University of Chicago Press, 1944), Ch. V.

2 Wach regards the following religions as "founded religions": Christianity, Buddhism, Jainism, Zoroastrianism, Mohammedanism, Manichaeism, Confucianism, and Taoism.

3 Ibid., p. 134.

4 Cited by *ibid.*, p. 135.

5 *Ibid.*, p. 137.

6 *Op. cit.*, p. 138.

7 Max Weber delcares that the severance of tribal and family bonds and the establishment of the superiority of religious over natural community is the greatest achievement of "ethical" religions. "Die grosse Leistung der ethischen Religionen, vor allem der ethischen und asketis-chen Sekten des Protestantismus, war die Durrchbrechung des Sippenbandes, die Konstituierung der Ueberlegenheit der Glaubens--und ethischen Lebensführungsgemeinschaft gegenüber der Blutsgemeinschaft, in starkem Masse selbst gegenüber der Familie." *Gesammelte Aufsätze zur Religionssoziologie*, I (Tübingen: J.C.B. Mohr, 1920), p. 523.

8 Cf. Ray C. Petry, *Francis of Assisi* (Durham, North Carolina: Duke U. Press, 1941), p. 37.

9 Troeltsch, *STCC*, I. p. 82

10 *Ibid.*, p. 81.

11 *Ibid.*, p. 81f.

12 A highly documented account of the social attitudes of the Early Church is C. J. Cadoux, *The Early Church and the World* (Edinburgh: T. and T. Clark, 1925).

13 Mennonite history is largely a history of Mennonite communities. The only major exception to the rule is the very early stage of Anabaptism before the movement congealed into fixed forms.

14 The interaction of religion and culture within the Mennonite community is discussed by Paul Erb, "The Religious Basis of the Mennonite Community," *MQR*, XIX (April, 1945), pp. 79-85. Cf. also G. F. Hershberger, "Appreciating the Mennonite Community," *The Mennonite Community*, I (Jan. 1947). Hershberger says, "Mennonites have always made God and the church central in the life of their communities." p. 7. Ernst Correll, a student of Max Weber, declares that "as a cultural group in history, the economic significance of the Mennonites is a distinct by-product of their religio-sociological existence." "The Sociological and Economic Significance of the Mennonites as a Cultural Group in History," *MQR*, XVI (July, 1942), p. 162.

15 J. Winfield Fretz speaks of the religious foundation of the Mennonite community as follows: "The Anabaptists wished to reproduce a community embodying the religious beliefs and social practices of the primitive Christian community in Jerusalem.... This concept of the church was not an economic or a political theory, it was a spiritual vision.... Because of this spiritual conception of the church, the Anabaptists and their descendants the Mennonites, have often been referred to as 'communities of the spirit.'" "Mennonites and Their Economic Problems," *MQR*, XIV (Oct., 1940), pp. 201-202.

16 Cf. Guy F. Hershberger, "Appreciating the Mennonite Community," p. 7. Also Walter M. Kollmorgen, *Culture of a Contemporary Rural Community*, Rural Life Studies: 4, U.S. Dept. of Agriculture, Sept., 1942.

17 J. Winfield Fretz, "Community," *The Mennonite Encyclopedia*, eds. Harold S. Bender

and C. Henry Smith, I (Scottdale, Pa.: 1955), p. 656.

18 Paul Mininger emphasizes the unambiguous character of culture by making the distinction between conflict "with" culture and conflict "in" culture. Drawing heavily upon the doctrine of the goodness of creation and interpreting cultural activity as creativity through the arts and the sciences, he says that "culture, as such, is not in conflict with Christian discipleship." Mininger recognizes that there are many demonic forces in culture against which the Christian must contend. He does not state, however, how it is possible to take a responsible position within the culture of the world without really being "of" it. In other words, Mininger does not consider the problem of the essential conflict between the perfect love of Christ and the "organizational" ambiguities of social structure. His presentation does not recognize the conflict between love and justice, personal self-giving and corporate responsibility, or, to put the problem in the terms of Reinhold Niebuhr, the conflict between "moral man and immoral society." Mininger's presentation is typical of the attitudes of Mennonites toward culture in the modern period. "Culture for Service," *MQR*, XXIX (Jan., 1955), pp. 3-15.

19 "The Mennonite Conception of the Church and Its Relation to Community Building," *MQR*, XIX (April, 1945), p. 90.

20 Cited by Littel, *op. cit.*, p. 99.

21 "Nothing stands out so characteristically in Calvin's ethic as the absence of any sense of the need to justify and balance the radical ethic of love of the Sermon on the Mount over against the claims of the social ethic of the practical life of politics and of Society." Troeltsch, *STCC*, II, p. 599.

22 *Ibid.* p. 596. For the role of the covenant with the Christian community according to the Mennonite interpretation see Guy F. Hershberger, *War, Peace and Nonresistance.* Ch. II.

23 Cf. Georgia Harkness, *John Calvin* (New York: Henry Holt & Co., 1931), p. 22).

24 Cf. p. 137ff.

25 Cf. Harold S. Bender, "The Mennonite Conception of the Church," *MQR*, XIX, (April, 1945); John C. Wenger, *Separated Unto God* (Scottdale, Pa.: 1951), Chs. I-III; Ernst Correll, "Sociological and Economic Significance of the Mennonites as a Cultural Group in History," *MQR*, XVI (July, 1942); Melvin Gingerich, *Mennonites of Iowa* (Iowa City, Ia.: The State Historical Society of Iowa, 1939), Ch. XIV; C. Krahn, "Mennonite Community Life in Russia," *MQR*, XVI (July, 1942); J. Winfield Fretz, "Mennonites and Their Economic Problems," *MQR*, XIV (Oct., 1940); Guy F. Hershberger, *War, Peace and Nonresistance*, Ch. X; Hersh., "Islands of Sanity," *Gospel Herald*, XLV (March 25, 1952), p. 293.

26 Guy F. Hershberger expresses extreme concern over the tendency toward urbanization in our culture and the adverse effect this may have on the principles of the Mennonite community. Some of the things he fears are the spirit of materialism, secularism, social conformity. He defines the church (Mennonite community) as a large family where God is the father and where the children think of each other as brothers and sisters. Hershberger laments the passing of rural community as a crisis in world culture. He agrees with P. A. Sorokin that the world can be saved only by "replacing the present compulsory and contractual relationships with purer and more godly familistic relationships." P. A. Sorokin, *The Crisis of Our Age* (New York: E. P. Dutton and Co., 1941), p. 320.

27 The urban setting of early Anabaptism follows from the fact that it arose in the Zwinglian-Calvinist context of the Reformation within such centers as Zürich and Geneva. Conrad Grebel's father was a member of the commercial class which was opposed by the feudal aristocracy and many of the Anabaptists belonged to the class of artisans which was on the rise to

power in Swiss and South German cities such as Strasbourg and Augsburg. These participated in the commercial spirit which was destined to shape the modern world. Speaking of the significance of South German and Swiss cities out of which Anabaptism emerged, Paul Peachey says: "Here the Reformation emerged clearly, so far as its social dimensions were concerned, as a product of the medieval city now flowering into the modern mercantilistic and republican nation-state. It was the religious genius of the Genevan republic that was destined to shape the religious and political character of modern society, as Max Weber has so dramatically shown, rather than the conservatism of Wittenberg." "Early Anabaptists and Urbanism," *Conference on Mennonite Educational and Cultural Problems* (Chicago: Mennonite and Affiliated Colleges, 1955), p. 77. Peachey says that Anabaptism as a dynamic protest against society makes it impossible to "escape the conclusion that Anabaptism would hardly have arisen in a purely peasant setting." *Ibid.*, p. 78.

28 Cf. J. Winfield Fretz, *A Study of Mennonite Religious Institutions*, in Chicago, Univ. of Chicago (library), June, 1940, Abstract. This study indicates that a majority of Mennonites who settle in Chicago do not retain their membership with the Mennonite church. See also Fretz, "Reflections at the End of a Century," *Mennonite Life* (July, 1947). A careful study of the processes of secularization is Karl H. Boehr, *The Secularization Among the Mennonites*, B. D. Thesis, Univ. of Chicago, 1942.

29 This is the point of view of two journals on Mennonite culture first published shortly after World War II, namely *The Mennonite Community* and *Mennonite Life*. As an attempt to set the heritage of rural Mennonitism in its best light and to combat the breakdown of the Mennonite community before the powerful forces of urbanism and secularism, they contain articles of considerable value on the basis of sociological and historical research. They include articles by non-Mennonites who, for example, praise the Amish of Lancaster County, Pa. for the most stable rural communities in America. Walter Killmorgen, *op. cit.* O. E. Baker of the U. S. Dept. of Agriculture expresses his conviction that "our modern urban culture is ephemeral, and that the Christian rural culture, as exemplified by the Mennonite church, is lasting." "The Effects of Urbanization on American Life and on the Church," *MQR*, XIX (April, 1945), p. 119. In a leading article in the first issue of *The Mennonite Community*, Guy F. Hershberger presents the "call" to "the new and better Mennonite community of tomorrow...with an improved agriculture, based on the sound Mennonite traditions of the past, and taking advantage of the best findings of scientific research...." "Appreciating the Mennonite Community," *op. cit.*, p. 7. J. Winfield Fretz says in the first issue of *Mennonite Life* that the future of society must have its hope in the rural community. Others point out that the Mennonite church has unwittingly accepted certain institutional patterns and educational responsibilities which destroy the foundations of agrarianism. E.g., O.E. Baker reports that around the year 1942 he questioned forty Mennonite college students, thirty-eight of which came from farm homes, regarding their future occupation. Only two reported an intention to return to the farm, much to his dismay. *op. cit.*, p. 117.

30 Peachey explains that sudden shift of the Anabaptists from urban to rural as follows: "Die Tatsache, dass das Täufertum nicht in ersten Linie eine Sozialbewegung war, ist vor allem daraus ersichtlich, dass die täuferische Idee zunächst bei Geistlichen, bei Akademikern und bei Bürgern Fuss fasste, d.h. auf sozial vielschichtigem Boden, und dass die Bewegung schliesslich alle Schichten der Gesellschaft berührte. Eine teifgehende Anderung in ihre Sozialstruktur erfuhr die Bewegung aber dadurch, dass für sie nach 1527 sehr rasch sämtliche nichtäuerlichen Bevölkerungskreise verschlossen waren. Die Rückwirkung war z. T. eine allmähliche Erstarrung, die allerdings erst später akut wurde, weil in den bäuerlichen und kleinhandwerklichen Kreisen die Fähigkeiten nicht ausrechten, um auf dem Grund der geistigen Einsichten, aus denen die

Bewegung entstanden war, schöpferisch weiter zu bauen. Trotz allem wussten die Baueren und kleinern Handwerke sich mit erstaunlicher Zähigkeit und oft mit tiefgehender Eisicht zu behaupten. So wurden sie letzten Endes doch die Erben und Bewahrer der täuferischen Idee." (Karlsruhe: H. Schneider, 1954), p. 95.

31 *STCC*, I, p. 86ff.

32 Niebuhr's whole system of ethics rests upon the conflict between Jesus' ethic of pure love which prefers simple social relationships and the complexities of the social and political order. This is the central thrust of his *Interpretation of Christian Ethics* (1935) and his *Moral Man and Immoral Society* (1932). In fairness to Niebuhr it should be conceded, however, that he does not see even primitivism as a way of fulfilling the absolute demands of Christ though they may be more closely approximated within a simple situation. Niebuhr sees all of life in violation of the "unprudential rigorism" of Jesus' ethic. Cf. *An Interpretation of Christian Ethics*, p. 41f.

33 Brunner has made the conflict between the Christian ethics of *agape* which apply in primary relations and the civil ethics of justice which apply to economic and political relations even more absolute than does Reinhold Niebuhr. Brunner claims that love knows nothing of systems. *Justice and the Social Order*, Ch. XV.

34 *STCC*, I, p. 86.

35 Hershberger, *War, Peace and Nonresistance* (Rev. Ed., 1953), p. 248.

36 A sixteenth century writer described the Anabaptist brotherhood as follows: "They broke bread with one another as a sign of oneness and love, helped one another truly with precept, lending, borrowing, giving, taught that all things should be in common and called each other, 'Brother.'" Cited by R. J. Smithson, *The Anabaptists* (London: James Clarke, 1935), p. 115.

37 Christopher Dawson, *Religion and the Rise of Western Culture* (New York: Sheed and Ward, 1950), Ch. IX.

38 Troeltsch, *STCC*, I, p. 255.

39 *Schleitheim Confession*, Art. IV and VII.

40 John C. Bennett, *Christian Ethics and Social Policy* (New York: Charles Scribner's Sons, 1946), pp. 41ff.

41 The main primary sources of the Hutterite movement are: *Die äteste Chronik der Hutterischen Brüder* (1577), *op. cit.* This is the Hutterite's own voluminous account of their history. Peter Ridemann, *Confession of Faith* (1565), trans. K. E. Hasenberge, is the most instructive theological statement of the Hutterites (Suffolk: Hodder and Stoughton, Ltd., 1950). Peter Walpot, *The Great Article Book*, Art. III, trans. K. E. Hasenberge, is presented as *A Notable Hutterite Document* (Shrapshire, England: Plough Publishing House, 1957). A valuable secondary source is John Horsch, *The Hutterian Brethren 1528-1931* (Goshen, Ind.: Menn. Hist. Soc., 1931). See also Franz Heimann, *Die Lehre von der Kirche und Gemeinschaft in der huterischen Täufergemeinde*, Doctoral Dissertation, U. of Vienna, 1927. Copy in Mennonite Historical Library, Goshen College, Goshen, Indiana.

42 J. Loserth, "Jakob Hutter," *The Mennonite Encyclopedia*, II, pp. 851-854.

43 *Ibid.*

44 The Hutterite *Chronicle* reports this event in these words: "Zu der Zeit haben dise Männer ein mantel vor dem Volck nider gebrait/vnd yederman hat sein vermögen dargelegt mit willigem gemüt Vngezwungen zu vnderhaltung der Notdurfftigen/nach der leer der Propheten vnd Apostelen." *Chronik*, p. 87.

45 Horsch, *The Hutterian Brethren*, p. 8ff.

46 Cited by Loserth, *op. cit.,* p.852.

47 Cited by *ibid.,* p. 24

48 The "golden" period, when Hutterianism was able to carry out its own principles, came during the reign of the tolerant Emperor Maximilian II (1564-76) and continued until about 1592. Cf. Robert Friedmann, "Economic Aspects of Early Hutterite Life," *MQR,* XXX (Oct., 1956), p. 259. At the time of their height the total baptized membership of the Austrian Hutterite colony is estimated at 50,000.

49 Horsch, *The Hutterian Brethren,* pp. 21ff.

50 *Chronik,* cited by *ibid.,* p. 24.

51 Cf. Franz Heimann, "The Hutterite Doctrines of Church and Common Life," *MQR,* XXVI (April, 1952), p. 156.

52 "The Five Articles" (1547) cited by Littell, *op. cit.,* p. 84.

53 Cf. Peter Walpot, *op. cit.,* Article Three.

54 *Ibid.,* No. 147, p. 45.

55 An early Hutterite saying quoted by Horsch, *the Hutterian Brethren,* p. 74.

56 Heimann, "The Hutterite Doctrines of Church and Common Life," *op. cit.*

57 Peter Walpot, *op. cit.,* No. 143. p. 42.

58 Bender, *Conrad Grebel,* p. 205.

59 Horsch, *The Hutterian Brethren,* pp. 34ff.

60 Cf. Wach, *Church, Denomination and Sect* (Evanston, Illinois: Seabury-Western Theological Seminary, 1946); Liston Pope, *Millhands and Preachers* (New Haven: Yale U. Press, 1942); Roland A. Bainton, "The Sectarian Theory of the Chruch," *Christendom,* XI (Summer, 1946), 382-387.

61 Cf. E. K. Francis, *In Search of Utopia* (Altona, Manitoba: D. W. Friesen and Sons, LTD., 1955); Francis, "The Russian Mennonites: From Religious to Ethnic Group," *The Ammerican Journal of Sociology,* LIV (Sept., 1948), pp. 101-107; also Robert S. Kreider, "The Anabaptist Conception of the Church in the Russian Mennonite Environment," *MQR,* XXV (Jan., 1951), pp. 17-33.

62 Horsch, *Mennonites in Europe,* p. 271.

63 *Op. cit.,* p. 21.

64 *Ibid.,* p. 24.

65 David G. Rempel, *The Mennonite Colonies in New Russia,* Doctoral Dissertation, Stanford University, 1933, p. 89.

66 *Ibid.*

67 Kreider, *op. cit.*

68 Rempel, *op. cit.,* p. 93.

69 *Op. cit.,* p. 26.

70 Horsch, *Mennonites in Europe,* p. 276.

71 Kreider, *op. cit.,* p. 27.

72 *Ibid.,* p. 29.

73 Cf. Cornelius Krahn, "Some Social Attitudes of the Mennonites of Russia," *MQR,* IX (Oct., 1935), pp. 165-177.

74 "The Russian Mennonites: From Religious to Ethnic Group," p. 105.

75 "Early Anabaptists and Urbanism," pp. 76f.

76 Many of the problems of the Russian Mennonites have appeared also in Mennonite colonial settlements in Paraguay.

77 *In Search of Utopia*, p. 27.

78 Cf. Smith, *The Story of the Mennonites*, pp. 536ff.

79 The "Germantown Experiment" is the attempt of the Mennonites to accept responsibility for the civil adminstration of Germantown between 1691 and 1707. See Ch. VI.

80 Hershberger says: "It is probably no accident that the rural Mennonites of Russia and America succeeded in preserving their nonresistant way of life long after the urban Mennonites of Holland and North Germany had lost theirs." "Maintaining the Mennonite Rural Community," *MQR*, XIV (Oct., 1940), p. 220. Fretz points out that urbanization not only leads to secularization but the disorganization of the Christian home and family, "Mennonites and their Economic Problems," p. 213.

81 Melvin Gingerich says: "The Mennonites have generally been farmers. In those places where they have preserved a distincitive Christian testimony for generations, they have been people of a rural philosophy.... With this background, does it not follow that the Mennonites should try very definitely to preserve their way of life, a way that according to the views of our leading rural sociologists can help save our society and civilization from destruction?" "Rural Life Problems and the Mennonites," *MQR*, XVI (July, 1942), p. 171.

82 J. P. Moyer, *Max Weber and German Politics* (London: Faber and Faber, Ltd., 1943), p. 12.

83 Cf. *War, Peace and Nonresistance*, 1st. ed., p. 268.

84 The report of the Committee on Industrial Relations to the General Conference referred to a survey made by D. A. Yoder according to which 300 members of the congregations of his Bishop oversight were working in factories and about one-third of these were unionized.

85 The complete statement may be found in Hershberger, *War, Peace and Nonresistance*, 1st ed., Appendix 6, pp. 378ff.

86 "Maintaining the Mennonite Rural Community," p. 218. Hershberger is referring to the thesis of Niebuhr's volume, *Moral Man and Immoral Society.*

87 *War, Peace and Nonresistance*, 1st ed., pp. 289-290.

88 *Ibid.*, p. 290.

89 *Ibid.*, p. 291.

90 *Ibid.*, pp. 292f.

91 *Mennonite Community Sourcebook*, Esko Loewen, Ed. (Akron, Pa.: C.P.S. see Menn. Central Comm., 1946).

92 Paul Erb, "A Vision and Its Realization," *The Mennonite Community*, I (Jan., 1947), pp. 8ff.

93 Troeltsch, *STCC*, I, p. 86.

94 Cf. Mary Emma Showalter, *Mennonite Community Cookbook*, (Philadelphia: Winston, 1950).

95 Harold S. Bender, "The Mennonite Conception of the Church," *op. cit.*, p. 100.

CHAPTER 6
MENNONITE SOCIAL SERVICE

In the previous chapter it was shown that the traditional Anabaptist-Mennonite response to the world has been one of separation through retreat to ideal agrarian communities. Sometimes these communities have reflected no more social planning than can be expected of refugees. At other times they have reflected deliberate planning. It would be misleading, however, to leave the impression that all of Mennonite social and ethical thought and energies have gone into strategies of withdrawal. Especially since World War I, the American Mennonites have had an increasingly exciting encounter with the world in various forms of social outreach. The purpose of this chapter is to analyze Mennonite social outreach both from the standpoint of its positive acceptance of certain forms of responsibility and from the standpoint of its rejection of other forms. Only when both the positive and the negative attitudes are held together can we understand the Mennonite contribution to the problems of society.

The author has deliberately chosen to characterize the Mennonite social approach by the term "service" rather than "action." This choice is made in view of the Mennonite position that the church's main responsibility to the world is expressed by direct and personal acts of Christian love in the spirit of the Good Samaritan, within the context of the church. It stands over against the approach, commonly called "social action" which, in addition, attempts to influence society through the moulding of public opinion. The former assumes a general withdrawal from responsibility for the comprehensive structures of society with an emphasis upon personal charity. The latter assumes an attitude of *full* responsibility for society. Although social action does not deny the necessity of church sponsored programs of charity, it contributes to society mainly through the processes of democratic life.[1]

I. The Rejection of Political Responsibility

From the standpoint of the ideal of full social responsibility, which is assumed by the democratic way of life and which is frequently accepted in theory by the major denominations as consonant with Christian duty, the Mennonite approach to the social order is "apolitical." The Mennonite approach seeks to avoid political involvement. Mennonites seek to alleviate the problems of suffering, injustice and tyranny by purely nonpolitical means. At best,

Mennonites may work in government social programs and assist in government-operated institutions such as hospitals, experimental projects and even as "guinea pigs" in government sponsored medical programs. Nevertheless, such endeavors, important as they are, are not political in nature since they do not seek to influence the policies of the nation. In this sense, Mennonites may be "in" the stream of public life without being "of" it. The entire political dimension of life lies beyond the sphere of direct concern.

To say, however, that Mennonites have been completely removed from political responsibility is at least a slight exaggeration since there have been some instances in Mennonite history to the contrary. Although no exhaustive statement of the Mennonite encounter with politics is possible here, it is necessary to point to certain instances in Mennonite history, especially in recent years, which throw light upon Mennonite attitudes. This will serve as a background to our understanding of Mennonite social service which, according to the analysis of the author, is considered by Mennonites as an alternative to political action.

As previously stated, the early Anabaptists were rigidly opposed to any kind of political involvement. The Schleitheim Confession could have rejected the political realm with no greater force and determination. Interpreting politics as power politics, the whole political realm was dismissed. It was rejected on the basis of its clash with Christian ethics and because of the relation of the church to government in the New Testament. When we examine, however, the position of Menno Simons, we find it slightly ambiguous since he clearly implies that his Anabaptist followers should not consider politics as a Christian calling and yet he addresses magistrates as Christians and advises them to rule in a Christian way--in strange contradiction to the original Swiss Anabaptist way of thinking.[2] Menno Simon's lack of conceptual precision, however, is shared to a slight degree at least by American Mennonites. For although Mennonites have as a body rejected politics, there has always been a slight dissatisfaction with this attitude by those who desire a more positive response to the total needs of the world.

The ambiguity of the American Mennonite attitude toward the state is illustrated by the so-called "Germantown Experiment" in colonial Pennsylvania. The Germantown Experiment is the short-lived attempt of the earliest Mennonite settlers to operate the affairs of a village. In 1691, Germantown was incorporated under the laws of the province. The form of government was a closed corporation. The members of the corporation were granted the exclusive rights of franchise, of legislation and admission of new members. The first corporation members were Mennonites and Mennonite-Quakers. C. Henry Smith sums up the experience of these Mennonites with the art of politics as follows: "So long as village ordinances and local litigation concerned themselves only with stray pigs and line fences there was little difficulty in securing Mennonite officials, but with the building of a jail and the introduction of stocks and whipping posts, they lost their desire for office."[3] In 1701 a complaint was lodged with Penn to the effect that it was virtually impossible to find men who would serve in the General Court. Hence in 1707 the village lost its charter. Smith remarks: "We have here the unparalleled instance of a corporation losing its charter because no one could be found who was willing to hold office."[4]

The Germantown Experiment brought together a number of elemental facts and forces which tended to pull in opposite directions and continued as a source of tension among Mennonites. First, there was the strong conviction for nonresistance. This was part of the Anabaptist-Mennonite birthright and it could not easily be discarded. Furthermore, during the colonial period, Mennonite nonresistance took on the added note of hope for a new nation on the continent of North America which would be dedicated to love and peace. Secondly, there was the elemental fact of political life which even Mennonites when left to themselves could not completely escape. For, where people live together within a system entailing property and a common life, civil administration is *natural* and therefore necessary. The Germantown Experiment represents the inevitable course of events in the direction of political association which, in this case, was able to come into Mennonite life and experience almost unawares because of unusual conditions. These conditions are the extreme simplicity of a colonial village and the predominantly Mennonite population.

However, even such restrained enthusiasm for politics was soon dispelled by the general trend of American history. As long as politics in Pennsylvania remained in Quaker hands, the traditional Anabaptist dualism which placed politics outside the Kingdom of God was for practical purposes qualified. But as soon as Quaker influence declined before the pressure of non-pacifist elements, a pressure which led eventually to the relinquishment of political control to non-pacifist groups,[5] Mennonites sensed that the vision of a warless continent might not become a reality. Hence as early as the first half of the 18th century, fears of religious persecution were revived in the Mennonite heart. They appreciated religious freedom but they were fearful that, with the contest between the Quakers and the more aggressive Scotch-Irish and with the growing sense of nationalism in relation to British sovereignty, war would result with the consequent loss of religious freedom, at least in so far as military exemption was concerned. This apprehension was expressed in a notable letter by Jacob Gottschalk to a congregation in Amsterdam.[6] A concrete expression of this fear was the publication of the *Martyr's Mirror*, appearing as early as 1748. This was intended to reinforce the spiritual heritage of martyrdom, and it indicated the general path which the Mennonites would take as the nation moved in the direction of an independent power among the nations of the world. The following quotation from Gottschalk's letter brings this out very clearly:

> Our further concern is, Dearly Beloved, inasmuch as we cannot know what the future has in store, and since the flames of war are evidently rising higher, that to the nonresistant Christians tribulation and persecution may come to their house, and for this reason it will be needful to fortify against such visitation in patience and

obedience, and to prepare for firmness and perseverance in faith. It has been the consensus of opinion of this congregation that it were well if we could have the *Bloody Martyrs' Mirror* by Tielman Jans van Braght translated into the German language, and especially, since in this country in our congregations many young people have grown up and our number much increased, so that coming generations may have the testimony of true witness to the truth, who have walked in the way of truth, and given their life for it. Much as this has been desired for several years, the wish is yet not fulfilled.[7]

With the coming of the Revolutionary War the attitude of the Mennonites was fixed. Although there was no disposition to take part in the dispute between the colonies and Britain, they did display certain sympathies for the British arising from a sense of appreciation for the religious liberty which the British flag had guaranteed and arising also from their promised allegiance to the King. To revolt against the King seemed to them to constitute a breach of promise. At any rate, the Revolutionary War and the problems of conscription and taxation connected with it galvanized a "we" and "they" dichotomy respecting American Mennonites and the state--an attitude which is implicit in Mennonite theology and which comes to the fore with each national emergency.

The political attitudes of American Mennonites may be gauged by their participation, or lack of it, in three functions of American democratic life. They are (1) the franchise, (2) office-holding and (3) prophetic witness to the state. The extent of political responsibility which Mennonites accept may be determined by their participation in each of these functions.

A. *Mennonites and the Franchise*. With respect to voting, Mennonites represent no consistent pattern. The early settlers in Pennsylvania voted, as a rule. In fact, their vote was an important factor in the early days of the Pennsylvania settlement.[8] Furthermore, as Mennonites pushed westward into Western Pennsylvania, they retained a sense of local responsibility for school administration and road building. Hence, they continued to vote on local issues and for men who were not too far removed from the elemental requirements of life amid agrarian simplicity. We have no records which show exactly how many Mennonites have voted at any period of American history. Nevertheless, it is safe to say that Mennonites voted "without hesitation" during the colonial period and voting was retained as a rather common practice.

In recent years, however, especially since World War I, there has been a general Mennonite withdrawal from the polls, although the extent of withdrawal is hard to determine. One Mennonite sociologist says: "It appears that today (1956) there is less voting and less office holding than there was in 1900."[9] The shift in practice is illustrated by the conference rulings of the Franconia Mennonite Conference of Pennsylvania. The Franconia Conference stated in 1901 that "Brethren may quietly vote at the polls but shall not 'electioneer' nor attend mass meetings."[10] In 1933 the discipline was revised to state, "It is advisable to abstain from voting."[11] A similar decrease in voting by Mennonites in Iowa is noted by Melvin Gingerich.[12] To the author's knowledge, no conference district makes voting a test of membership but it is safe to say that Mennonites are frequently encouraged not to vote and that the conviction against voting has been growing in recent years. In the October 31, 1950 issue of the *Gospel Herald*, the official Mennonite organ, an article appeared by Harvey W. Bauman entitled, "Pray--Vote: Which?"[13] Bauman argues that the sovereignty of God makes voting useless. Moreover, it is dangerous because the Christian is likely to be prejudiced by his Christian principles into voting for the candidate who exhibits the most statesmanlike and sincere qualities, whereas God's eternal purposes may be carried out best by "an unrighteous and vile person." Bauman continues: "Does it not seem reasonable to conclude that a Christian before the mercy seat of this omnipotent sovereign will wield a more dynamic and lasting influence in his community than does the citizen at the polls."[14] Bauman does not carry his logic to its conclusion by making voting and prayer an absolute either-or. However, the intention of the article is clearly to discourage voting in state and federal election.

One of the arguments frequently used against voting is its possible implication for conscientious objection to war. John L. Stauffer wrote in the April 21, 1953 issue of the *Gospel Herald*[15] that "Bible believers in non-resistance cannot consistently exercise the franchise and refuse participation in military service. The two go together and belong to the 'earth dwellers' and not to those holding heavenly citizenship and living as 'pilgrims and strangers' in this world." The argument that voting implies support for the policies of the office holder is frequently found among Mennonites. However, there is one case on record to the exact opposite. In an article in the October 3, 1912 issue of the *Gospel Herald*, I. G. Musser relates an incident which occurred during the time of the Civil War. A preacher, Amos Herr, and a layman of the Pequea District of Lancaster County called upon Governor Andrew G. Curtain, who was governor of Pennsylvania. The purpose of the meeting was to obtain exemption from military service for Mennonites. Musser reports that "the governor listened and when they had finished he said, 'Well, what do you do for us? Do you vote?' They said, 'Yes.' Then he said, 'We will do something for you.' When Curtain was through one of his men said, 'How can you do that? If all were like them, what would you do then?' The governor, said, 'That would be easy to decide. There would be no war.'"[16]

The connection between the franchise and military exemption has not been so much a matter of theoretical reasoning as the general feeling at times of war that the farther one can remain from the entire political order, the more likely his conscientious objection will appear consistent. To enter into political affairs at any point appears to detract from the complete religious orientation which seems most consonant with the absolutist view. The fact that, since 1917, the United States has been involved in two world wars, the Korean struggle and a continuous state of "cold war" has had the effect of discouraging Mennonites from the polls.

B. *Mennonites and Office-holding.* With respect to direct participation in politics, the Mennonite attitude is more firmly negative than with respect to voting. In the history of the (Old) Mennonite Church in America, there is no instance of a member in good standing who occupied a major political office. Even if one were to generalize on the basis of the entire Mennonite church with its more "liberal" branches included, one could agree with the statement of Guy F. Hershberger as follows: "While many Mennonites vote in public elections, many abstain, and some Mennonite groups either forbid such participation or strongly advise against it. So far as we are aware no Mennonite group urges very active participation in the political field, especially not in holding public office. Usually even those who favor voting hesitate to hold public office."[17] Cases can be cited of Mennonites who entered the political realm, particularly as diplomats, but they were invariably "lost to the church."[18] Normally office holding is not an occasion for church discipline since active interest in politics is usually accompanied by a transfer of membership to another denomination.

The theoretical problems of political involvement have never been made a matter of thorough scholarship among the Mennonites. Having been generally withdrawn from politics, Mennonite scholars have never been drawn deeply into the problems of political theory. *For this reason the question as to how far a Mennonite can enter politics has never been a matter of critical study.* Mennonites have not penetrated beyond the obvious fact that nonresistance clashes with certain fundamental aspects of the activities of the state and that the state is alien to the church. Nevertheless some attention has been given to the question in Hershberger's *War, Peace and Nonresistance.* Hershberger says:

> The question is sometimes raised whether a nonresistant Christian can serve in an administrative or legislative capacity, such as that of president, prime minister, or mayor or councilman of a city. The answer should not be very difficult, however, when it is remembered that the president is commander in chief of the army and navy, and that the city police are under the direction of the mayor. Congressmen and members of the parliaments have the responsibility of declaring war and appropriating funds for military purposes...and all types of legislative bodies fix penalties for violation of the law. As a rule Mennonites who have held important state positions have not been active in the promotion of the church's peace testimony and frequently they have not been nonresistant at all.[19]

Hershberger cites several examples of Mennonites of branches other than the (Old) Mennonite branch who have found their way into state legislatures. He acknowledges that these have been exceptions to the rule even for groups other than the (Old) Mennonites. With respect to the problem of the appropriation of funds for the military, Hershberger is of the opinion that:

> Theoretically it would be possible for a nonresistant Christian to serve as a congressman or a national legislator without compromis-

ing on the war question. He could refrain from casting his vote for military appropriations or military measures of any kind. He could even vote against them. There may be some states in certain periods of history where such a nonresistant national legislator could continue for years without encountering embarrassing involvements on the war issue. The same might be true of city mayors in certain countries at certain times. It is doubtful, however, whether this would be possible in a powerful country like the United States in the twentieth century.[20]

In practice Mennonites have occasionally held minor political responsibilities such as membership on public school boards, road commissioners and public utilities offices.[21] Such offices have been accepted without a feeling of compromise. Objections arise, however, when office holding becomes a matter of competitive *seeking* for office and when the office entails the exercise of power in the context of impersonal relationships. The reason why some Mennonites, while being generally opposed to participation in politics, have served nevertheless with good conscience on village boards of education and in similar minor public service capacities is that, in most cases, these offices can hardly be said to be political in the real sense. Politics in reality is the formulation and administration of laws in a complex social ethos. Politics is the art of balancing diverse interests, of relating men to each other as classes and groups, of obtaining *justice* for contending parties, of relating people to neighbors whom they do not know. That the word politics comes from *polis*, the Greek word for city, is suggestive. Politics properly belongs to the city where simple solutions based upon common understandings which have been cultivated in personal face-to-face relationships are no longer possible and where the abstract rules of law and justice have replaced a simple and uniform mode of life. Mennonites have been able to serve the public as long as the office is *offered* as a neighborly act of confidence for the solution to problems which presuppose a more or less uniform point of view and where contacts are personal. But when the public constituency becomes highly individualistic and pluralistic, when it represents a number of points of view and when the problems of office involve the relation of contending parties and points of view, Mennonites, who have no interest in abstract justice and especially in the "dividing" of public assets between contending egos, generally retire from the scene.[22] This may explain why Mennonites have been disappearing in recent years from the boards of education in many communities, as the schools are consolidated.[23] As long as the little red school can be regarded as a project of neighbors with a common point of view, public representation of the board of education is really not political in nature. But as the public school increasingly represents the diverse interests of an impersonally conceived pluralistic society, its administration becomes political in nature.

This, of course, is another instance of the Mennonite dilemma. The logic would seem to lead to complete retirement from public life as the small community adopts the features of bureaucratic civilization. It would appear that

the general trend of culture in the direction of the city may sharpen the
dilemma inherent in Anabaptism, i.e., it may require Mennonites to find new
and more cunning modes of withdrawal from public life than hitherto attained
or it may require them to submit to the stream of bureaucratic culture with the
consequent loss of at least certain elements of the Anabaptist vision.

One of the conspicuous absences of political criticism by American Mennonites is that of corruption. In contrast to Menno Simons, whose *Pathetic
Supplication to all Magistrates*[24] abounds with warnings to princes to fulfill their
responsibilities with justice and truth, and to lay aside the abuses so frequently
associated with power, American Mennonites have seldom accused public officials of corruption. This may be due to the fact that Mennonites have formed
their ideas of the political office more from their understanding of Paul's
respect for authority as represented by Romans 13 than from intimate knowledge of the operations of the state. At any rate it is not from high places but
the contradiction between the operations of power and the principles of pure
love as represented by Christ's oft repeated admonitions.

C. *Mennonites and Prophetic Witness to the State.* In addition to attitudes
regarding the franchise and actual participation in politics, the Mennonite
sense of responsibility to the political order may be gauged by their attempts to
witness to the state. To what extent has the Mennonite church felt compelled
to speak to government and to influence legislation? In making the distinction
between social service and social action at the beginning of this chapter, it was
acknowledged that the Mennonites exercise so little influence upon the state
that their social outreach cannot properly be called social action in the
accepted sense of the term. However, upon *rare* occasions, American Mennonites have attempted to influence political conditions. By noting especially
the interaction between the Mennonite church and government, particularly in
recent years, it is possible to gather the main tendencies of their witness,
limited as it is.

Most notable in the history of American Mennonites is the petition of
1688 against slavery which was drawn up by Mennonites and Mennonite-
Quakers for presentation at a Quaker Monthly meeting in Philadelphia. This
is the first public protest against slavery on record in America.[25] Strictly
speaking, this was not an attempt to influence the institution through political
channels. Their action was directed mainly to Quakers in their religious capacity rather than in their political capacity. Nevertheless, slavery was conceived
as a public problem. The protest declares that "those who hold slaves are no
better than Turks for we have heard that ye most part of such Negers are
brought hither against their will and consent, and that many of them are
stolen."[26] Actually the political consequence of this petition was negligible,
possibly for the reason that the Mennonites made no effort to follow it with
anything which would resemble an antislavery movement.[27]

*The Mennonite church has attempted to influence government on only one
issue and this issue is closely related to its own interests. This is the issue of
peace and war.* Official bodies of the church have in recent years spoken to
governments about the necessity of peace. The most active and significant body

representing the denomination is the Peace Problems Committee of the General Conference which was organized in 1917 to deal with emergency problems arising in connection with World War I. In so far as the American Mennonite church has attempted to influence public opinion, it has been almost entirely through this committee. In 1919 it was made a continuing committee of the General Conference.[28] In 1921 the committee statement of the Mennonite peace position which was sent to President Wilson. In addition, a petition for peace was circulated among the churches to which 20,000 attached their signatures.[29] In 1925 the work of the committee seemed to be past since there was no threat of war. However, the committee recommended to the General Conference of that year that "the subject of peace, as upheld by the church, should be kept before the people, the public, and government officials."[30] In 1927 the Peace Problems Committee became somewhat more aggressive. This was the time when pacifism was growing into popularity among the larger denominations and consequently Mennonites threw in their lot with the general movement for peace. Hence in 1927 the Committee adopted a three point program of "aggressive peace work." The first point concerned witness to the Mennonite church; the third point concerned witness to other Christians regarding the peace position; the second point concerned witness to the government and was stated as follows: "To represent the church and her position on this doctrine before any departments of our state, provincial and national governments which have to do with legislation or the enforcement of legislation affecting our status as Nonresistant citizens and to encourage officials whenever possible in a wider application of the policy of good will rather than that of force or war."[31] The committee reported that "on point two very little has been accomplished."[32] Nevertheless in comparison to both previous and subsequent performance, 1927 seems to have been the most adventurous year of the Mennonite church into the world of international politics. According to the report, "Letters have been written to government officials in connection with the Welsh Bill before the last Congress which aimed to take the compulsory feature out of military training in our public schools and colleges. Other letters were forwarded at the time when the international situations as regards Nicaragua, Mexico and China seemed acute and to encourage our President in his program of naval reduction.... We owe it to the 'powers that be' to let them know our position on this question."[33]

The report of the committee in 1929 also showed signs of activity. It recommended to the General Conference a message of appreciation to President Herbert Hoover, "a real friend and advocate," for his efforts for peace.[34] In 1931 the committee reported that there had been some correspondence with government officials in connection with the 1930 London Naval Conference. Also it stated that the committee was currently "laying before government officials our prayers, wishes, and hopes regarding the 1932 Geneva Disarmament Conference."[35] In 1933 the committee sponsored a page in the *Gospel Herald* for the purpose of keeping the church informed of world events as they bore upon world peace.

In 1937 a major revision of the Mennonite peace position was accepted by

General Conference meeting in Turner, Oregon.[36] This reflects the growing apprehension of war. It expressed appreciation to our government for its endeavor to keep out of war. It went further, however, by calling definitely for a national policy of "neutrality and nonparticipation in disputes between other nations."[37] However, one district conference (Virginia) objected to the part of the statement which involved government policy. The Virginia Conference said, "we favor making appeals to the government in regard to our constitutional privileges for religious liberty and freedom of conscience and commend making contact with government officials to explain to our position on nonresistance but we do not favor giving advice to the government in any way."[38]

In the years immediately before America's entry into the war, the Peace Problems Committee turned its attentions more closely to the problem of working out an arrangement with the government for conscientious objectors in the event of war, rather than to the problems of international peace. Mennonite representatives, together with Quaker and Brethren representatives, called upon President Franklin D. Roosevelt in 1937 and 1940. The purpose of these visits was to explain the peace positions of the historic peace churches. In 1940 concrete proposals were made to the President for alternative service in the event of conscription. Such proposals were taken before the House Committee on Military Affairs in July 1940.[39] When being questioned about the larger issues of war and peace by the House Committee, the Mennonite representative implied that he was not interested in opposing the Burke-Wadsworth Bill. He was simply interested in the provision for conscientious objectors.[40]

During the war, the church turned its energies into the administration of the Civilian Public Service Camps. This provided numerous contacts with government officials. However, very little attention was given to political affairs from the point of view of the policies of government. By this time the international situation had become so involved that Mennonites were hesitant to speak of the immediate problems of international relations. Their characteristic struggle for existence as a unique, nonconforming group dominated their approach to the war problem. During this time, the Mennonite Central Committee, as the administrative agent of Mennonite Civilian Service Camps, entered into numerous relations with Selective Service, often through the National Service Board for Religious Objectors, but almost entirely for purely practical purposes of administration.[41]

After the war, the first major political issue faced by the Mennonites was Universal Military Training. On a number of occasions, Mennonites testified before congressional committees warning against the dangers of militarism. Plans for continued recognition of the C.O. position were mixed with warnings that U.M.T. may lead to militarism as a way of life. Among the most significant witnesses was that of Harold S. Bender representing the Mennonite Central Committee in March, 1955 before the House Committee on Armed Services.[42] *This is one of the few occasions in American Mennonite history when a Mennonite witnessed before the state about a problem which extended beyond Mennonite interest.* In this instance, Bender witnessed for the best interests of the nation and of the world. Bender said:

> I am not here to suggest that Mennonites know better than the members of Congress how to provide for the necessary defense of this nation, nor would I minimize the danger of the safety and security of all of us today, for we follow with deep concern the evidence of heightened international tension with its explosive possibilities.
>
> We do plead with you, however, that, whatever the pressure of this moment, you do not take even the first small step toward any type of that Universal Military Training which the people of this nation, and its elected Congress, have always rejected and never approved.[43]

Bender stated further that U.M.T. would lead to a military way of life and this would mean the abandonment of our American democracy. He called for a shift of emphasis from the "purely military approach to security to an approach which will employ all the various and effective methods of aid to needy and underdeveloped areas of the world such as relief, use of surplus foods, technical assistance, Point Four programs, peaceful diplomacy, peace leadership."[44] He called for more "positive" action which is "truly Christian." In closing Bender said, "I have not come to plead any particular privileges for those whose Christian conscience does not permit them to participate in war and military training in any form.... I have only come to plead with you, that for the best interest of our nation and through our nation, of the world, you do not recommend HR 2967 for passage."[45]

Another development of significance is the note of confession of failure contained in the report of the Peace Problems Committee in 1955.[46] Two weaknesses of the church were mentioned. The first is a false sense of innocence in connection with international conflict. The second is a tendency to overlook large areas of human experience as outside Mennonite responsibility. *It is, of course, too early to say fully what these confessions signify. However, these statements seem to indicate a growing awareness of involvement and guilt, a sense of social and moral solidarity and participation in the corporate acts of the nation. This is a new emphasis.* The report repeats the basic Mennonite conviction that "God works through the dedicated Christian community to achieve His purpose.... At the same time, the inability to perform certain political and military tasks does not free us from all responsibility."[47]

Furthermore, a series of articles by Paul Peachey in the *Gospel Herald* entitled, "Love, Justice and Peace" brought before the Mennonite people in 1956 an unprecedented analysis of the meaning and relation of love and justice.[48] This analysis incorporated the main insights of modern scholarship and lifted the discussion of the ethical problem of the Mennonites to a new high. Probably for the first time in the history of Mennonite scholarship, the problem of love and justice was treated in a manner conversant with modern thought. Taking a position which reflects the point of view of Emil Brunner, Peachey showed that the problem of love and justice is broader then the problem of church and state. The antagonism between love and justice even applies to the internal operations of the Mennonite church since it has become involved in organization and impersonal structures.

The troubled conscience of the Mennonite church was also revealed in a study conference sponsored by the Peace Problems Committee on September 21-22, at Laurelville, Pa. This conference examined the theme of "Nonresistance and Political Responsibility." It is, of course, too early to estimate the significance of the conference. *Nevertheless, the fact that such a conference was held indicates that the feeling and language of responsibility is creeping into the thinking of the leaders of the church.* It is noteworthy that the word "responsibility" which has been adopted by the World Council of Churches as a catalytic agent for its social thought was adopted for the conference. By inference as well as by explicit statement, political responsibility was upheld as a good thing, providing it could be kept within the limits allowed by the Mennonite peace position. By inference the traditional policy of radical separation was criticized. That a policy of separation tends to violate the outgoing character of Christian love was acknowledged. Therefore the question upon which the conference hinged was: How can Mennonites become involved with the world on the various levels of local civic affairs and in a policy of witness to government on the basis of the principles of love and nonresistance, without "losing out" as a church? The question was asked, "Do we need isolation? Are we strong enough to stand up to opposition...?"[49] Furthermore it was acknowledged that the Mennonite church is not clear about its message to the state today. These questions were mixed with disquieting expressions to the effect that the Mennonite position may have serious implications in principle for civilization. One leader of the conference said: "Actually we are blamed for the disintegration and the crisis of our modern life much in the way Christians in the fifth century were blamed for the disintegration of the Roman Empire."[50] The reports of the various committees almost invariably called for "more study" on the theological foundations of the relation of the Christian to the state. With respect to participation in local civic affairs, one committee recommended that the matter be brought to the attention of the General Council of General Conference. This committee pointed out that help on the question of the criteria for participation is needed. "We need a statement well grounded in theology, growing out of our time and situation which will give guidance to the conscience of our brotherhood."[51]

The somewhat uncertain state of mind of the Mennonite church regarding political involvement is also reflected in a key editorial by Paul Erb in a 1954 issue of the *Gospel Herald* entitled "Political Neutrality."[52] The editorial raises the question of how far the Christian should take part in politics. This editorial states that "there is much to be said for complete political absention." The following reasons are given: (1) Jesus took a neutral attitude toward political matters. He refused to be an agitator despite the abuses of the Roman system. "His methods of teaching and working were nonpolitical." His total orientation was the Kingdom of God. "The Son of Man was politically neutral because He had a spiritual calling and dynamic which kept Him above all partisanship." (2) The Early Church refused to descend to party or national loyalties. They refused to be influenced by political aspirations. (3) Politics is a diversion from the true business of the Christian, namely "working for spiritual renewal."[53] The true Christian is dominated by his concern for the church and spiritual things. Erb suggests that although the Christian should not lose all "interest in political affairs, he must keep this interest to a minimum." Then he goes on to say that if the Christian does participate in politics, he must do it on "high principle." He deplores the fact that Mennonites who vote are so predominantly Republican and that they have a tendency to vote Republican simply because of party membership. "Any voting Christian will have to be an independent, giving his support to the just cause and the Christian attitude."[54] What he finally calls for is a perspective which "puts political and social partisanship far below us."[55]

Confusion arises, however, from the fact that some of the arguments used in the editorial, especially those based upon Christ's complete "apoliticism," should lead logically to the rejection of all political involvement. However, Erb lets the door open for "non-partisan" politics if kept to a minimum. The weakness in this argument lies in the fact that nowhere in this editorial or in the Mennonite tradition in general is theological basis given for even *minor* involvement and for even *minor* political activity.

Mennonites have a theological basis for separation, but none for the minor extent of political participation which they seem ready to allow in practice. Therefore, so far as Mennonites become involved in society, this involvement must be explained simply as an accident or as an accommodation to culture. There is no place in the Mennonite ethic and doctrine of the church for a positive approach to involvement even though involvement is kept to a minimum.

Erb properly described the general attitude of Mennonites toward politics by the term "neutrality."[56] Both as individuals and as a denomination, Mennonites refuse to "take sides" except in extremely rare occasions. They may become interested in such local affairs as an option on the sale of liquor or in similar "moral issues." However, they have shown little or no interest in the weighty matters of justice and truth which have been fought out during the past four hundred years in western civilization. Sometimes their neutrality has been simply one of political default. At other times, it is a matter of policy or agreement with political authorities.

Except for the early years of Anabaptism before their expulsion from Zürich and Geneva, Mennonites have made no significant contribution to the political history of Western civilization. Three great revolutionary movements in the history of the West have found the Mennonites completely uninvolved.

First is the rise of the democratic state. Despite the fact that modern democracy stands for some of the spiritual and human values for which the Anabaptists died, the lineal descendants of the Anabaptists as a group have had virtually no part in their political realization.[57] These are introduced, oddly, by the descendants of their persecutors under the secular auspices of the

French Revolution and under the religious auspices of the Puritans in New England.

A second great revolution in western society with which Mennonites have had nothing to do is the emancipation of the laboring class. Mennonites literally "contracted out" of this revolution in the economic life of Europe and America by deliberately refusing to participate in the clash of economic interests between labor and management.[58] This attitude, though possibly related to the fact that Mennonites have traditionally had no natural interest in either party of the struggle, due to their agricultural situation, has been based upon a conscience against "struggle" as such.

The third great revolution with which Mennonites have had virtually nothing to do is the emancipation of the Negro race. As stated previously, Mennonites have not been completely indifferent to slavery.[59] However, they have never attempted to influence public opinion nor have they supported legislation on civil rights or attempted in any way to bring pressure to bear through public agencies. It is true that the Committee on Social and Economic Relations has sponsored conferences and produced literature about Christian race relations.[60] An attempt has been made to face the problem as a denomination. The church has instructed its own people regarding right attitudes toward other races in light of the New Testament. *However, no attempt has been made to face the problems of racial prejudice on the broader basis of social and political policy.* The Mennonites have not sought the equality of the races by influencing public attitudes and/or in any way exerting social and political pressure. Mennonites do not hesitate to speak in general principles about the evils of racism, but when it comes to the stubborn and often mixed programs of action, they remain totally aloof.

Their complete removal from active participation in the great struggles for liberty and justice in the world does not mean that they have had no appreciation for these great achievements. Nor does it mean that they have been unaffected by them. Large segments of Mennonite history consist of the search for sanctuary in countries which offer liberty and justice.[61] Mennonites have been a pilgrim people trekking from country to country and sailing from continent to continent to find a political climate congenial to their peculiar way of life. They have been called a people endlessly moving, "Ewig Wanderung." Often they have been the first to suffer the pains of tyranny because of their moral sensitivity to war and political involvement. But the answer of the Mennonites to tyranny has almost always been a simple one--to "flee." *Interpreting the instruction of the Lord to the disciples that, "when they persecute you in this city, flee into the next"* (Matt. 10:23), *as a strategy for His children throughout all the ages, Mennonites almost instantly respond to unwholesome social conditions by fleeing to another country.* Hence they have been scattered all over the world in search of freedom and have sometimes entered into formal agreements with foreign countries according to which they are granted certain unequal privileges in exchange for their recognized contribution to the economic and natural development of the land.[62]

D. *The Basis for Nonparticipation.* Why do the Mennonites refuse to express their love of justice in concrete action? They do not become involved in the intricate problems of justice primarily because of their reticence to adopt the means by which justice is achieved in the social and political realms. Justice is accomplished to a large extent through the struggle of contending parties. Even though the conflict between groups is legal and even though the entire system of government and social change recognizes contest as a legitimate basis for change, the system, however, falls below the highest Christian ideals of unity and peace, not to speak of the cross. In the last analysis, Mennonites hesitate to enter the realm of justice because of the nature of social change. They are fundamentally opposed to *contending* by pitting one ego or one group against another ego and another group. To gain an advantage at the cost of another against his will is to go against the Mennonite conscience. *Hershberger interprets the Christian ethic to mean that no Christian may do anything which would "deny to mature and responsible individuals the use of their God given right to choose between different lines of action--or even between good and evil."*[63] Even such nonviolent tactics as those used by Gandhi are rejected as unworthy of the gospel because they are intended to compel the enemy to comply against his will."[64] Hershberger points out that the ethic of Christ is one of absolute nonresistance according to which "if a man compels you to go a mile, go with him two miles, but he never gives Christians the right to compel others."[65] Thus it makes no difference how urgent the need for justice is or how far one's motivation may be lifted above personal ambition or gain, he may not use *compulsion* in any form to gain an objective. *The problem is not one of violence or corruption but of the right to overpower the will of another.*

The reluctance of Mennonites to participate in social and political contest is illustrated by their relation to industrial conflict. While recognizing that the labor movement has been necessary as a means of obtaining justice for the worker, Mennonites have sensed that the organization of labor is essentially an attempt to obtain justice through a struggle for power, "whereas Biblical nonresistance enjoins submission even in injustice rather than to engage in conflict."[66] According to the official position of the church" these two principles directly oppose each other.... They are mutually exclusive."[67]

Therefore in order to avoid participation in the conflict while at the same time remaining on the job, an official" basis of understanding "has been arranged between the Committee on Economics and Social Relations of the Mennonite church and several of the major unions according to which Mennonites may remain at work if they agree to pay an equivalent to union dues into the welfare fund of the union and if they agree to "maintain an attitude of sincere neutrality."[68] Neutrality in this case means that, in case of a strike, the Mennonite "will side neither with the employer by remaining at work, nor participate in the strike."[69] The intention of this "agreement of understanding" is clearly to avoid having anything to do with the conflict of interests which enter into industrial relations in deference to the pure love nonresistance. As a polity it is one of contractual neutrality in a manner which is illustrative of the general policy of Mennonites toward the power structures of society. It is an agreement to do nothing and say nothing which will in any way forward the advantage of one party over another. It is an attempt to transcend the entire system of industrial organization of America and Europe in so far as organized labor with the power to strike or to use other means of forceful equity is an integral factor. To the student of social ethics, many questions regarding the actuality and the validity of this position of "neutrality" may be asked. Most pressing is the question whether a position of neutrality is possible so far as the actual lines of power relations are concerned? By not taking part in a strike or in the negotiations leading up to the strike, may not the Mennonite actually be taking sides, depending, of course, upon the immediate situation? Obviously the side which is being favored depends upon how many Mennonites are working in the industrial plant in question. At any rate, it may be questioned whether the neutrality is one of actuality or one of paper. Another question concerns the propriety of an agreement which in effect silences the prophetic voice. Is the right to work in a "closed shop" the adequate compensation for the right to speak to the practical problems arising out of one of the greatest revolutions in western history?

The "basis of understanding with the labor movement is typical of a general unwritten and more or less unconscious agreement between Mennonites and worldly powers according to which Mennonites will do little or nothing to disturb the equilibrium of social and political forces providing they are given the privileges of living a quiet and godly life in isolation. Ever since the fateful days when the Anabaptists were thrust out of the main centers of population in 1527 and shortly thereafter, Mennonites have given up any serious attempt to change the course of history. *Rather, their energies have gone into the unique problems of the preservation of the sect.* The strategy of preservation has been one of the upholding of the principles of justice, freedom and truth in their own communities and witnessing to these in "general terms." However, they have studiously avoided "taking sides" on the immediate problems of social and political affairs lest they become involved in the ambiguities of power struggle and lest they incur the wrath of those in responsibility. In recent years, various governments of the world have offered Mennonites special "colonial" privileges. These have been granted with the understanding that Mennonites will receive military exemption and with the general assumption that they will remain a quiet minority so far as the total problems of political responsibility are concerned.[70] Hence Mennonites have sometimes cultivated psychological, sociological and political attitudes in line with the peculiar set of laws which go into the preservation of a small minority frequently referred to as *Die Stille im Lande*. Only with rare exception do Mennonites speak or act on social issues of the larger community unless their own religious interests are concerned. The exceptions have been noted earlier in this chapter.

II. An Alternative Approach to the Problems of Society

Notwithstanding the areas of withdrawal which are implicit in the ethical position of the Mennonite church, one of the objectives of the modern Mennonite church is to be socially relevant.[71] This desire is a fairly recent and growing one. Its roots are both internal and external. The sense of responsibility for the world results *internally* from a spiritual awakening which occurred toward the close of the nineteenth century under the ministry of the evangelist John S. Coffman. As a result of his ministry, the Mennonite church was lifted from almost one hundred and fifty years of spiritual decline and social irrelevance. As a result of the "Great Awakening" of the church, the present program of missions, higher education, publication and social service was instigated.[72] *This spiritual revival brought the world into the perspective of the Mennonites.* The sense of responsibility has arisen *externally* from the unavoidable needs of a world in an almost continuous state of emergency. Since 1917 the world has experienced two global wars, a Great Depression, the Korean conflict and an arms race in a context of international tension. *The "needs of the world" have become a fundamental point of reference for the Mennonites, especially during the past twenty years, in whatever way these needs may be defined and met.*

The new life from within and the challenge from without has, however, intensified the Mennonite dilemma of how to be in the world without being of it. How can Mennonites as ethical absolutists enter into the problems of the world which lives on a relative moral plane? *The answer has been an alternative approach to the problems of society in the form of world relief, rehabilitation and social service under the auspices of the church and closely integrated to its missionary program.* This alternative approach is in line with the fundamental strategy of the Mennonites in so far as it rejects the position of ultimate responsibility for the stream of history and yet seeks to express a position of responsibility by entering into the problems of the world at *crucial* if not *final* areas. This solution is in line with the forces of the world through cultural alternatives. Alternative social service applies the principles of withdrawal in the more dynamic setting of the main stream of culture and under conditions which are more intimately and directly related to the world crisis. Withdrawal is not so much geographical and cultural, in this instance, as vocational and ethical. Despite the fact of withdrawal implicit in alternative action, the program of alternative social outreach contains tremendous potential for the continuous development of contacts between the Mennonite church and the world. It has been the means by which hundreds of Mennonite youth have had foreign experience in projects of relief and rehabilitation. It has brought departments of the church into vital relations with national and international agencies dealing with world rehabilitation. It has stimulated among Mennonites an unusually keen awareness of the conditions of the underdeveloped countries of the world. It has brought the church into a position of continuous response to world conditions. *Thus the relation of the Mennonite church to the world is more complex than simple withdrawal. It is no longer pure isolation. It is one of withdrawal from certain areas for the sake of dynamic penetration in others.*

A. *Significance of the Problem of War.* The issue which is most responsible for the alternative approach to society and which has stimulated the development of what is virtually an "alternative" philosophy of life, is of course, that of war. The beginning of the alternative way of thinking and acting goes back to American Revolutionary times and may be traced to the attitude of the Continental Congress in dealing with those who refused to join the voluntary militia. When sentiment against the Mennonites and other conscientious objectors approached mob violence, the Continental Congress assured objectors that their religious convictions would be respected. They recommended that they "contribute liberally in this time of universal calamity, to the relief of their distressed brethren in the several colonies, and do all other services to their oppressed country which they can, consistently with their religious principles."[73] Melvin Gingerich suggests that "this may be the first instance in history of a national government recommending that its citizens whose consciences forbid participation in war perform alternative service in lieu of military service."[74] The response of the Mennonites was contained in a letter to the Continental Congress in 1775 stating the view that they were willing at any time to relieve the suffering or distressed: "It being our principle to feed the hungry and to give the thirsty drink, we have dedicated ourselves to serve all men in everything that can be helpful to the preservation of men's lives...."[75] *Basically this has been the position of the Mennonite church throughout its American history.* It has attempted to find ways to express the love and care through means which are unmixed by the passions of nationalism and hatred. It is true that, from the time of the Revolutionary War to World War I, the Mennonite church did very little except attend to its own affairs. During the Civil War, Mennonites reluctantly took advantage of a law which permitted the conscientious objector to hire a substitute or to pay a commutation free of $300 to $500.[76] This unsatisfactory arrangement reflected a lack of forethought and policy both on the part of the church and the government with respect to the problem of the conscientious objector.

It is not within the interest of this writing to trace the historical circumstances attending the development of alternative service as a national policy in dealing with conscientious objectors in the two great world wars. Suffice to say that some conscientious objectors were permitted to do alternative service during World War I in Europe under the Friends Service Committee. The handling of the C.O.'s, however, was unsatisfactory both from the standpoint of the government and the church during World War I. Therefore, by the time of World War II, the government had given considerable thought to the problem and had consulted with the Historic Peace Churches (Mennonite, Quaker and Brethren) whose views were expressed in "The Plan of Unified Action in the case the United States is Involved in War" (1935).[77] The result was the formulation of the Selective Training and Service Act of September 16, 1940, which provided for alternative service in projects of "national importance." Hence, during World War II, 4,600 Mennonite young men served in Civilian Public Service camps. About 60 camps and other CPS units were operated under Mennonite direction. Unfortunately draftees were not allowed to do relief work in foreign countries. The Mennonite church, including all its branches, contributed over $3,000,000 to the operation of CPS camps through the Mennonite Central Committee.[78] The total contribution of Mennonites to

CPS was about $21.45 per member.[79]

In 1951 a new alternative service program was inaugurated which gave the conscientious objectors greater freedom to select their areas of service including foreign assignments. Working in state hospitals as technicians, orderlies and nurses, on Indian reservations as teachers and counselors, in South America as road builders in the jungles, in Europe as relief workers and rehabilitation officers, in Africa as soil reclamation workers, in Asia as medical personnel and material aid distributors, Mennonite draftees have been serving humanity in lieu of military service.[80] The spirit of service may be judged by the fact that 85 percent of the men volunteered before their period of induction when the present alternative program was begun. It is the opinion of Melvin Gingerich that "The western world is slowly accepting the principle of alternative service as a legitimate expression of religious conviction."[81]

B. *Voluntary Service--An Integral Aspect of Mennonite Life.* The most significant aspect of the alternative service program of the Mennonite church, however, is not that which deals directly with military draft. Service in response to the draft may result in a significant contribution to society as numerous expressions by government officials and others have indicated. *The most significant result of the war experience for the Mennonite church, however, has been the conception of voluntary service as an integral aspect of Mennonite life.*[82] Just as missions have been accepted by modern Christianity as an essential part of the total program of the church since the beginning of the nineteenth century, so voluntary social service by laymen under the direction of the church has in recent years come to be accepted by Mennonites as an essential part of the total witness of the church. Church-sponsored corps of workers are presently occupying positions of responsibility in public mental hospitals, in state agricultural experiment stations, in scientific laboratories, in welfare institutions, community rehabilitation projects, in disaster areas, in foreign relief and rehabilitation projects of all kinds.[83]

The possibility of relief and service units as a permanent aspect of Mennonite life was considered first in 1942 by the Peace Problems Committee in response to a proposal by the Virginia Peace and Industrial Relations Committee. A report of a special study committee was submitted to the Peace Problems Committee in 1943. This report envisaged service units consisting of auto mechanics, carpenters, foresters, social workers, dietitians, and cooks.[84] There should also be "nurses, doctors, business men and those trained in teaching and evangelistic efforts."[85] The principles of their operation would depend largely upon the need of the area served--whether on an emergency basis or on a long term rehabilitation basis. "We see the possibility of such service being rendered in times of emergency arising from epidemics, floods, forest fires, and immigration. A service unit of a more permanent type could be set up for relief work in foreign lands such as China, Greece, and other sections of Asia and Europe with a view to establish a definite missionary program along with the relief which we would hope to have continued after the war conditions have been relieved.... The service unit should consider one of its major duties the conducting of religious services in the community where they labor and to build up a permanent congregation of Christian people."[86] With respect to financing the project, those who serve are expected to contribute their time, clothing and personal equipment. The cost of unit training, unit equipment, and of maintenance and travel is to be borne by the church.

This vision has become increasingly realized through the operations of the Mennonite Relief Committee of the (Old) Mennonite Church and through the Mennonite Central Committee representing all the Mennonite branches. In 1955 Harold S. Bender reported to the Committee on Armed Services of the House of Representatives that the Mennonites have sent nearly 2,000 men and women to foreign service appointments in 26 countries on a voluntary basis since 1945. Bender stated: "They are still in 18 countries including South Vietnam in Indo-China as our most recent entry."[87] In the statement of program and planning for 1957 of the Mennonite Central Committee, relief and rehabilitation programs, most of which have been going on for a number of years, were outlined for Europe, Middle East, Asia (Indian, Southeast, North Pacific), and Lower South America.[88] In addition, over 100 men were expected to be employed as PAX workers (foreign voluntary workers who accept personal responsibility for major financial expenses such as transportation to foreign countries). MCC services include also the administration of three mental hospitals and other mental health services. It includes also the administration of a Boy's Farm and assorted services. In 1956, 500 relief and service workers received appointments for one year or longer under the Mennonite Central Committee. Furthermore the Mennonite Relief Committee appointed 150 voluntary service workers. Nearly 700 men were in service in 1956 in lieu of military service.[89]

Another alternative service of the church is in the form of regional disaster units.[90] The first one was organized shortly after World War II in Kansas. These units have been organized for the purpose of assisting in the repair of damage resulting from flood, hurricane or any kind of major event resulting in destruction to life or property. Sometimes referred to as "Mennonite Minute Men," volunteers are sent from the congregations to scenes of disaster where they assist the Red Cross, Civil Defense and local public authorities in building houses, repairing roads and other services. These services usually involve industrial workers for a short period of a week or more so that men ordinarily engaged in business, farming, or professional work may coordinate such work with their ordinary callings.

C. *The Guiding Principles of Voluntary Service.* What are the unique social and ethical principles implied by voluntary service programs of the Mennonite church in relation to the problem of social responsibility?

In the first place, voluntary service is intended to express agape love in its purity and in its simplicity in accordance with the synoptic ideal. This involves the recreation of the New Testament *situation* which love presupposes, namely, one of personal, face-to-face relations.

It is frequently pointed out that the situation which the love commandment and the Sermon on the Mount assumes is simple.[91] It is the relationship of one individual to another. No attempt is made to show how love may constitute the relationship between groups. The parable of the Good Samaritan is typical of a situation in which one man cares for another man who is in need. Likewise, the commandments to love the enemy, to go the second mile, to turn the other cheek, to give to him who asks and to exceed the demand for a coat by giving a cloak as well, invariably take no countenance of the social context. Only two persons are involved. Paul likewise reflected the simple situation when he advised the Romans that "if thine enemy hunger feed him; if he thirst, give him to drink" (Romans 12:20). Love is understood in the New Testament primarily, if not entirely, as a personal relationship between individuals.

At the same time, it is frequently pointed out that *agape* is qualified as soon as a third party is introduced into the situation. The more persons and groups added and the more points of view represented, the more difficult it is to express love in the form of pure *agape*. Inevitably the complications of number and variety require group defenses, preferential loyalties, deference to prior obligations, prudential schemes and the rational division of goods. These exemplify principles of abstract justice rather than "heedless" *agape* love.

Alternative service is intended to serve society under conditions in which pure love is a possibility. With the Good Samaritan as a model, Mennonites have gone to numerous countries seeking the individual neighbor in his need. This method of social outreach involves the close *identification* of the Christian with the recipient. He weeps with those who weep and rejoices with those who rejoice (Romans 12:15). What is sacrificed in numbers is supposedly gained in true spiritual communication. In the act of giving a gift or in the ministry of healing, the love of God is reflected in a way which is not possible in social programs calculated to meet the general needs of the masses. As a part of his relief training, the Mennonite relief worker is reminded that his duties go beyond mere distribution of goods or the proper manipulation of social tools.[92] He is to enter into the total situation of the individual as a child of God. This follows the conviction that a person is not loved until he is *known* and he cannot be known unless the communication is personal. This is sometimes called "the way of love" or the "way of the Cross" by Guy F. Hershberger[93]-- admittedly a rather loose term but implying nevertheless that love in the New Testament is more than a vague sentiment that may express itself in any way depending upon the situation. Love suggests a "way" of dealing with people, the very essence of which is to give one's self in direct relationship.

It is of no small interest that, in view of the emphasis upon *agape, justice* is virtually absent from Mennonite thinking. The literature dealing with Mennonite social outreach invariably sees the problem of the world as one which can be settled only by *agape*. The program of the Mennonite church is calculated to meet this fundamental need. Guy F. Hershberger devotes only a few lines to justice in his *War, Peace and Nonresistance*.[94] The object of Mennonite relief is seldom, if ever, stated in terms of a contribution to the just rights of the underprivileged and to the victims of tyranny. The object of Mennonite relief is not to create a situation of social justice through the ordinary legal channels of civil righteousness. The task of social outreach is not that of helping the neighbor by the larger processes of social change. The total philosophy is stated in terms of the expression of love by direct self-giving. It is by no accident that the official voluntary service periodical of the Mennonite church is entitled *AGAPE*.[95] The term justice lies virtually outside the Mennonite vocabulary.

Parenthetically, it may be said that the lack of emphasis on justice may be due to several reasons. In the first place, Mennonite social thought is based entirely upon the New Testament and especially on the synoptics where the norm is love and where justice is subordinate to love. Love has a warm evangelical feeling, an affinity for brotherhood and sacrificial connotation which justice does not have. Justice is associated more naturally with the Old Testament, to which the Mennonites have paid little regard, and with the Greek philosophical tradition, to which Mennonites have paid no attention. Secondly, Mennonites have been so far removed from the comprehensive problem of society during their four hundred years of history that they have never been forced to face the problems of justice. Hence they have no vocabulary with which to define even the simple daily interactions which the theologians can readily see as instances of civil righteousness. Almost invariably Mennonites speak of justice, for want of a theological or philosophical vocabulary, as "doing the right thing." By this they mean giving just measurement or dealing fairly.

The alternative service program of the Mennonite church is designed to reinstate the simple synoptic situation in which love can flow with the least hindrance from intermediate factors of organization and bureaucracy. The voluntary service program must be seen as over against the work of "social action" which tries to meet the needs of the neighbor through the indirect processes of law. In the latter case, the neighbor is conceived as a class. The neighbor is not helped directly but through changes in the general social and political situation. For example, Mennonites do nothing to influence civil rights legislation though they have community projects in the Southern states which are calculated to meet the problem of integration at the grass roots level.[96] Here Mennonites conduct Sunday schools and operate medical clinics in which Christian love is clearly intended to bring the races together on the basis of Christian brotherhood.

It is true that Mennonite social outreach cannot always proceed on quite the extremely simple basis of the New Testament picture since much of the work is carried out within governmental agencies and within vast institutional programs. For example, hundreds of Mennonites have worked as orderlies and technicians and sometimes as administrators of government or community-sponsored hospitals where they have fit into the general policies of the hospital. On close examination, their duties may appear to reflect the principles of justice more than love. Nevertheless, they have assumed responsibilities under such circumstances and have attempted to utilize the numerous personal relations afforded the orderly and the nurse to express an *added* quality of care and sympathy. Admittedly, because of the political character of organization and the tension between bureaucracy and pure love, not many Mennonites will be found in the *top* policy-making positions of public institutions or government programs. Top administration gives the impression of political ambiguity. Hence Mennonites prefer generally to work under the administration of *others* utilizing their position as a place where *agape* may be expressed. For example, Mennonites have worked closely with the Point IV program in foreign countries by supplying technicians and experienced relief workers. Sometimes they even work under government direction. However, it is rather hard to conceive of a Mennonite becoming involved in the responsible policy-making echelons of the government having to do with foreign aid. *As a matter of principle, Mennonites congregate where agape may be expressed least ambiguously, i.e., where relations are most simple, most direct and least political.* For this reason Mennonite relief workers are ordinarily found at the "grass roots" level.

In the second place, the Mennonite alternative service is service under the auspices and supervision of the church. It is *ecclesiastical* social work in the sense that it is administered by men and women who are appointed by the church and represent the church as a missionary represents a congregation or a denomination. It is the church in action. If the difference between secular and religious work may be measured by the degree of Christ-consciousness which accompanies it, Mennonite social service is by profession religious. Everything is done "in the name of Christ"and for his church.[97] This ideal was stated in the previously mentioned report of the Study Committee of the Peace Problems Committee in 1942 as follows: "These units should be made up of Mennonite people who can by word and by life give a consistent testimony to our Mennonite faith and practices. These Mennonite service units should in the main be designed to provide an avenue of expansion for Christian testimony through our youth.... All that is done in the way of material help and in meeting the temporal needs of the community must be done in the name of Jesus."[98] This means that a deliberate attempt is made to make a Christian impact with social service all along the way by placing Christian men and women at the points where contact is made with those who benefit by the program.

The significance of this kind of social approach is realized most clearly when it is compared with "social action." Social action seeks mainly to express Christian concern by a prophetic message. This message is intended to influence the general public, including Christian people, and to culminate in social and political change. Christian action is appropriately called Christian in so far as it is initiated by Christian people who feel responsible for the larger problems of society. *However, since the action which is called for is necessarily carried out by secular social groups or the state, it is difficult for the action to carry with it a clear Christian testimony.* Usually such action is regarded solely as the work of the secular state. It is seldom associated in the mind of the public with the church, especially in view of the separation of the church and the state. For example, even though a foreign aid program of the American government may be instigated by Christian social action, it runs a very real danger of complete secularization by the time it takes tangible form. Seldom is the action of any government of the modern world interpreted as Christian action. To be sure, those who engage in Christian social action are not necessarily dismayed by this fact since justice is generally regarded as an end in itself. However, the danger of secularization which always accompanies social action has led the Mennonite church to devote its major energies to a direct approach in which the fullness of the Gospel may be expressed in personal encounter.

This is not to say that Mennonites see no place *whatsoever* for social action. Harold S. Bender, in his testimony before the Committee on Armed Services of the House of Representatives, combines in an *unusual way* for a Mennonite both the approach of social action and alternative service, with accent, of course, on the latter. He calls for a shift of emphasis "from the purely military approach to security to an approach which will employ all the various and effective methods of aid to needy and underdeveloped areas of the world such as relief, use of surplus foods, technical assistance, Point Four programs, peaceful diplomacy, peace leadership."[99] Bender continues, "Let us have much more positive action which is truly Christian and which will build that good will and cooperation and moral value which is the basis of true world community and enduring peace."[100] Bender does not stop here, however. He reflects the emphasis of the Mennonite church by promising that "in such a program of world wide service and peaceful construction, we as churches with our church service agencies and our small resources of men and money not only will cooperate but have cooperated.... Our experience in this effort teaches us of the real and great value of this approach. What some of us Christian groups are trying to do in a small way could be greatly multiplied both by voluntary church action and by a national governmental program on a large scale."[101]

In the third place, Mennonite alternative service is a program of lay Christianity. To speak of Mennonite social outreach as ecclesiastically centered (see above) does not mean that it is carried out by the clergy or necessarily under clerical direction. This work is mainly that of young people under the direction of experienced lay workers.[102] The appeal of voluntary service is that *every* member of the church should be confronted with the needs of the world and should give serious consideration to a period of service for the church and the world according to his talents and circumstances. Robert Kreider, a leader of the European relief program in 1947 said at the Elspeet conference: "I...think of the Mennonites as a lay church where the rank and file pour out their time in the service of the kingdom.... We should be prepared to give several years of our life to the service of the church."[103] Although this ideal is far from achieved, it would appear that the Mennonite church is moving in this direction. The compulsion to serve the suffering which is endemic to Mennonitism from the days of Menno Simons has become "the continuing compulsion"[104] and a mounting compulsion in response to a world in which crisis has become continuous. Furthermore, thousands of Mennonite young people who have returned to their communities within the last fifteen years after periods of domestic or foreign service bring to a traditionally withdrawn and isolated laity a vision of the world seen from the standpoint of its suffering and its need.

The result is that Mennonite people are becoming a people of motion. *Die Stille* are now moving so rapidly that they may before many years represent before the world a quite different picture than the traditional one of a quiet and conservative, introverted people which is tied to the land. The creation of their own travel service with branch offices in Beirut, Lebanon and Montevideo, Uruguay in addition to those already existing in several European cities indicate that Mennonites are becoming a mobile people.[105] The people who are "eternally moving" away from persecution may become a people who, within the conditions of tolerance, are devoted to the work of peace and the alleviation of suffering in the world.

In the fourth place, the Mennonite alternative service program intensifies the principle of voluntary giving in relation to society. The term"voluntary service" describes the financial and organizational circumstances of the work. Those who accept service appointments ordinarily receive maintenance (food, housing, medical bills) plus an allowance of $10 per month during the first year and $20 per month during the second year.[106] In the event of children, suitable allowances are made. This means that only minor accommodation is made for future security. Obviously the basic motivation is not the accumulation of wealth or the drive to settle down in life. The orientation is simply one of service--service to Christ and humanity. This attitude may be seen as a radical reversal of the dominant strivings of humanity to accumulate wealth and guarantee security. Over against the ambitions of wealth and power which underlie the very structure of society and which lie close to the basic spiritual problem of humanity, voluntary service attempts to introduce an entirely different principle rooted in the Gospel.

The consequence of the voluntary principle for a denomination and ultimately for the Christian church and the world is revolutionary, depending, of course, upon the extent to which it is actually put into concrete practice. One can hardly imagine what could happen to the world and to the church if Protestantism as a whole were to devote its laity and its financial wealth, in proportion to its size, to a global program of personal service. One can only wonder what this expression of "responsibility" for the world could accomplish. This is the challenge of the Mennonite church to Protestantism which was implied by Harold S. Bender's testimony before the Committee on Armed Services when he said, "Our experience in this effort teaches us of the real and great value of this approach. What some of us Christian groups are trying to do in a small way could be greatly multiplied by...voluntary church action."[107]

Voluntary service means ultimately the introduction of the sacrificial principle into social structure. It is a kind of "functional" asceticism which is implicit in the command to "seek first the Kingdom of God." Voluntary service is the denial, albeit partial and temporary, of certain natural desires and inclinations for the sake of the Kingdom. It is true that voluntary service is not open to all Christians. Some must devote themselves to the world's work under conditions of competitive gain and struggle, while others contribute to society on a nonprofit basis. *However, the practice of sacrificial voluntary service by young people, even if for a brief period of one to three years, may help to bring*

*to the consciousness of the Protestant church as a whole an emphasis which has
been virtually lost through the Reformation and subsequently through the
secularization of Christianity.*

*In the fifth place, alternative service, as an approach to the needs of society,
is an extension of the redemptive community.*[108] This follows the conviction that
social disorder is ultimately reducible to spiritual disorder (Eph. 6:12) and
spiritual disorder cannot be corrected genuinely except by the full impact of the
community of Christ. Therefore, Mennonite voluntary service expects its social
effectiveness to take the form of actual conversions in the context of Christian
community. The ultimate goal is a Christian *koinonia* which will express
socially the implications of the Gospel and in this way become the salt of the
earth and the conscience of society.[109] *This means that the voluntary service
and the missionary work of the church proceed on the basis of common motiva-
tions and common goals.* This approach seeks to avoid the dangers of the
secularization of the social process.

The emphasis is therefore upon redemption rather than reform. Many
reform movements, necessary as they are, lead to disillusionment,[110] fail to
express their Christian origins and frequently give the impression that
Christianity implies mere cleanup in morals and mere social reconstruction.
The Mennonite approach calls for the building up of communities of Christ
which are dedicated to the full dimensions of life within the Kingdom. This
approach assumes that the church's greatest social effectiveness is
accomplished when the social program is tied closely to the normal work of the
church. This does not mean that evangelism is a substitute for social concern.
It means that evangelism and social concern are combined in an effort
designed to create a "new" society fully conscious of what it means to be the
"people of God" living in the context of the world.

The redemptive approach assumes also that peace and justice can be
achieved in this world only when men are *reconciled* to one another in Christ.
Mennonite alternative service ideally is a ministry of reconciliation. The
material aspects of relief, rehabilitation and service in their multiple forms are
intended to reflect a desire to be reconciled inspite of national or racial
enmities. It is intended to express in a small and feeble way the love of God
"who through Christ reconciled us to himself and gave us the ministry of reconciliation" (II Cor. 18). In this way "the church becomes the redemptive and
creative minority through whom mankind is healed."[111]

This redemptive approach does not deny the necessity of enlightened
political programs intended to reform society and create just and peaceful conditions between nations. Rather, it emphasizes the utter importance of the
"proper" work of the church, i.e., the ministry of reconciliation as the major
concern of the church and, in the final analysis, the only permanent basis for
peace and justice. According to the Mennonite view, this approach is "relevant" to the social problems of the world, depending, of course, upon the quality of spirit which accompanies it and the number of people who become
occupied in it.

Endnotes

[1] The term "Christian Action" has come into general use since the publication of the *Monthly Newsletter of Christian Action* by the National Council of Churches of Christ and through the organization of a fellowship by that name in 1951. The latter organization published a quarterly called *Christianity and Society* until the Summer of 1956 with Reinhold Niebuhr as editor. Membership in the fellowship was 1200 in 1954. From the beginning, the purpose of Christian Action has been to correct the "Protestant aversion to politics." "Protestant church members often feel that politics is a dirty business. They remove themselves from the political arena, leaving daily decisions about bread, about freedom, and about the faith that should motivate the rulers and the ruled in this world to 'worldly' men who do not mind soiling their hands with compromises and 'unsavory' power struggles." Cited by Robert T. Handy, "Christian Action in Perspective, *Christianity and Society*, vol. 21 (1956), p. 13.

[2] Cf. "A Pathetic Supplication to all Magistrates, 1552," *Complete Works*, pp. 523-531. *The Story of the Mennonites*, p. 541.

[3] *The Story of the Mennonites*, p. 541.

[4] *Ibid.* For a more detailed account of the Pennsylvania Experiment, see C. Henry Smith, *The Mennonite Immigration to Pennsylvania* (Norristown, Penna.: Norristown Press, 1929), Ch. IV.

[5] Cf. Guy F. Hershberger, *Non-resistance and the State--The Pennsylvania Experiment in Politics* (Scottdale, Penna.: Mennonite Publishing House, 1936), pp. 1ff.

[6] *Mennonite Yearbook and Almanac* (Goshen College Library, Goshen, Indiana, 1910), p. 25.

[7] *Ibid.*, p. 26.

[8] Harold S. Bender, "Church and State in Mennonite History," *MQR*, XIII (April, 1939), p. 92. Cf. also G. P. Mode, "Mennonites and Quakers in Politics," *Source Book and Bibliographical Guide for American Church History* (Menasha, Wisc.: Collegiate Press, 1921), pp. 172f.

[9] Paul Peachey, "Mennonites in Local Civic Life," p. 16. Unpublished papers prepared for the Conference on Nonresistance and Political Responsibility, Laurelville, Penna., Sept. 21-22, 1956, Peace Problems Committee, Mennonite Historical Library, Goshen, Indiana.

[10] John C. Wenger, *History of the Mennonites of the Franconia Conference* (Telford, Penna.: Franconia Menn. Hist. Soc., 1937), p.55.

[11] "Constitution and Discipline of the Franconia Mennonite Church," *Ibid.*, p. 433.

[12] Melvin Gingerich, *The Mennonites of Iowa*, p. 160.

[13] XLIII, p. 1071.

[14] *Ibid.*

[15] LXVI, pp. 369, 379, 381.

[16] V, p. 429.

[17] "Present Trends and Activities Among Mennoniites in Their Approach to the State," Unpublished manuscript, Mennonite Historical Library, Goshen, Indiana, p. 1.

[18] Interview with Guy F. Hershberger.

[19] Revised ed., pp. 160-161.

[20] *Ibid.*, p. 162.

[21] It is not uncommon to find Mennonites working for the government as civil servants with no awareness of compromise. Weber noted the distinctions between the *Fachbeamte* and *politis-*

che Beamte and the ethical distinctions accompanying both. The latter formulates policy and gives commands whereas the former obeys. The true civil servant must be nonpolitical. Mayer, *op. cit.*, p. 87.

[22] The tendency to avoid the problems of justice as they effect external affairs was one of the chief points of criticism laid against their Anabaptist forefathers by the Reformers. Cf. *Melanchthons Werke*, I, *Reformatorische Schriften*, ed. Robert Stupperich (Gütersloh: C. Bertelsmann, 1951), pp. 306f.

[23] Peachey, "Mennonites in Local Civil Life," p. 17. Also Note 9, p. 186.

[24] *Complete Writings*, pp.525-531.

[25] C. Henry Smith, *The Story of the Mennonites*, p. 540.

[26] *Ibid.*

[27] The failure of the conscience of the Mennonites to become effective in the social and political realm is a basic problem of the Anabaptist Mennonite tradition. Because of their sensitivity, Anabaptists and Mennonites have pioneered on significant points such as religious freedom and separation of church and state. However, they have seldom been able to get a following. In this respect Roland Bainton compares the Anabaptists to the Norsemen who reached America first but with no sequel. Bainton says: "From the days of Constantine to the Anabaptists these principles (the voluntary church, the separation of church and state, and religious liberty) to us so cardinal, had been in abeyance. They were not, however, transmitted to us by the Anabaptists, but rather by the Puritan revolution and the French Revolution." "The Anabaptist Contribution to History," *The Recovery of the Anabaptist Vision*, ed. Guy F. Hershberger, p. 317.

[28] Guy F. Hershberger, *The Mennonite Church in the Second World War* (Scottdale, Penna.: Mennonite Publishing House, 1951), p. 1.

[29] *Report of the Twelfth Mennonite General Conference, 1921*, Mennonite Hist. Libr., Goshen, Indiana, p. 8.

[30] *Report of the Fourteenth Menn. Gen. Conf., 1925*, Menn. Hist. Libr., Goshen, Indiana, p. 9.

[31] *Report of the Fifteenth Menn. Gen. Conf., 1927*, Menn. Hist. Libr., Goshen, Indiana, p. 13.

[32] *Ibid.*

[33] *Ibid.*

[34] *Report of the Sixteenth Menn. Gen. Conf., 1929*, Menn. Hist. Libr., Goshen, Indiana, p. 22.

[35] *Report of the Seventeenth Menn. Gen. Conf., 1931*, Menn. Hist. Libr., Goshen, Indiana, p. 23.

[36] *Report of the Twentieth Menn. Gen. Conf., 1937*, Menn. Hist. Libr., Goshen, Indiana, pp. 123-126.

[37] *Ibid.*, p. 126.

[38] *Minutes of the Virginia Mennonite Conference*, 2nd ed. (Scottdale, Penna.: Va. Menn. Conf., 1950), p. 226.

[39] Guy F. Hershberger, *The Mennonite Church in the Second World War*, p. 14.

[40] Edgar Metzler, "Mennonite Witness to the State: Attitudes and Actions, World War I-1956," p. 51. Unpublished papers prepared for the Conference on Nonresistance and Political Responsibility, 1956, Peace Problems Committee, Menn. Hist. Libr., Goshen, Indiana.

[41] *Ibid.*

[42] For the complete text of Bender's statement, see National Reserve Plan: Hearings Before Subcommittee No. 1 of the Committee on Armed Services House of Representatives Eighty-fourth Congress (Washington: U.S. Printing Office, 1955), pp. 1957-1963.

[43] *Ibid.*, p. 1958.

[44] *Ibid.*, p. 1959.

[45] *Ibid.*, p. 1960.

[46] *Twenty-ninth Mennonite General Conference, Hesston, Kansas, Aug. 23-26, 1955* (Scottdale, Penna.: Menn. Publishing House, 1955), pp. 75-80.

[47] *Ibid.*, p. 79.

[48] Paul Peachey, "Love, Justice and Peace," *Gospel Herald*, XLIX, pp. 177, 189, 273, 278, 369, 465, 477, 680f.

[49] Non-Resistance and Local Civil Affairs," Report of Group A, Unpublished papers for Laurelville Conf., p.20, Menn. Hist. Libr., Goshen, Ind.

[50] Irvin B. Horst, "Some Principles and Limitations Guiding the Christian Witness to the State," *ibid.*, p. 48.

[51] Report of Group A, Laurelville Conference, p. 20.

[52] XLVIII, p. 291.

[53] *Ibid.*

[54] *Ibid.*

[55] *Ibid.*

[56] *Ibid.*

[57] Cf. Bainton, "The Anabaptist Contribution to History," *The Recovery of the Anabaptist Vision*, p. 317.

[58] Cf. Ivan R. Lind, *The Labor Union Movement in the Light of Non-resistance as Held by the Mennonite Church*, 1941, Unpublished thesis, Mennonite Historical Library, Goshen, Indiana.

[59] Reference to the first public petition against slavery in 1688.

[60] Cf. *Christian Race Relations: Proceedings on Christian Community Relations* (Scottdale, Penna.: Committee on Economic and Social Relations, 1955). Also "The Way of Christian Love in Race Relations," Official position of Gen. Conf. adopted 1955, Menn. Hist. Libr., Goshen, Ind.

[61] For a history of Mennonite migrations resulting from World War I and especially for the "Introduction" by Harold S. Bender in which he summarizes Mennonite migrations over four hundred years, see Sanford Yoder, *For Conscience Sake* (Scottdale, Penna: Herald Press, 1945). See also J. Winfield Fretz, *Pilgrims in Paraguay* (Scottdale, Penna.: Herald Press, 1953) for a detailed historical and sociological anlaysis of the Mennonite colony in Paraguay.

[62] Cf. J. Winfield Fretz, *Mennonites in Paraguay*.

[63] "The Disciple of Christ and the State," *Report of the MCC Peace Section Study Conference, Winona Lake, 1950*, Menn. Hist. Libr., Goshen, Ind. p. 54.

[64] Hershberger, *War, Peace and Nonresistance*, rev. ed., p. 192.

[65] *Ibid.*

[66] Cf. "Industrial Relations: a statement adopted by the General Conference of the Brethren in Christ Church and by the Menn. Gen. Conf. in 1941, *Twenty-second Menn. Gen. Conf.*, Menn. Hist. Libr., Goshen, Ind., p. 50.

[67] *Ibid.*

[68] Official "Basis of Understanding." Copy available at Menn. Hist. Libr., Goshen, Ind.

[69] *Ibid.*

[70] Cf. Fretz, *Mennonites in Paraguay*, Ch. III.

[71] Cf. John D. Unruh, *In the Name of Christ: A History of the Mennonite Central Committee* (Scottdale, Penna.: Herald Press, 1952), pp. 294ff.

[72] John C. Wenger, *Glimpses of Mennonite History*, pp. 188ff.

[73] Quoted by Melvin Gingerich, "Discipleship Expressed in Alternative Service," *The Recovery of the Anabaptist Vision*, p. 263.

[74] *Ibid.*

[75] Pa. Archives, Eight Series, 8:7349. Copy of a contemporary document containing the petition is in the Menn. Hist. Lib., Goshen, Ind.

[76] Gingerich, "Discipleship Expressed in Alternative Service," *op. cit.*, pp. 263-264.

[77] Guy F. Hershberger, *The Mennonite Church in the Second World War*, p. 9.

[78] Gingerich, "Discipleship Expressed in Alternative Service," *op. cit.*, p. 266.

[79] A complete history of Mennonite cooperation with the Civilian Public Service program may be found in Melvin Gingerich, *Service for Peace* (Akron, Penna.: Mennonite Central Committee, 1949).

[80] Cf. *Handbook of the Mennonite Central Committee, 1954* (Scottdale, Penna.: Mennonite Publishing House), pp. 12ff.

[81] Gingerich, "Discipleship Expressed in Alternative Service," *op. cit.*, p. 271.

[82] Unruh, *op. cit.*, p. 256.

[83] Cf. William T. Snyder, *The Program and Planning for 1957*, Unpublished report to Mennonite Central Committee, Akron, Penna.

[84] See Hershberger, *The Mennonite Church in the Second World War*, p. 220.

[85] *Ibid.*

[86] *Ibid.*, p. 221.

[87] See note 42, p. 187.

[88] See note 83, p. 189.

[89] Boyd Nelson, "How Shall They Hear?" *Gospel Herald*, XLIX (Oct. 16, 1956), p. 985.

[90] Cf. *Activity Summary Number II*, Mennonite Disaster Service, Akron, Penna.

[91] Cf. Paul Ramsey, *Basic Christian Ethics*, pp. 157ff.

[92] Cf. "Standards for Relief Workers." *Handbook of the Mennonite Central Committee*, pp. 29f, Mennonite Central Committee, Akron, Penna.

[93] Guy F. Hershberger, *The Way of the Cross in Human Relations*, 1956, Ch. I, Unpublished manuscript, Goshen, Indiana.

[94] Hershberger's position is summed up by the following: "The New Testament way is to aim at love, not at justice. In aiming at justice the result is frequently a selfish struggle for power, position and wealth. In aiming at love, however, the result is often justice as well as love. But even if this result does not follow, the Christian must continue to love anyway, for according to the teaching of Christ His disciples should be willing to suffer injustice rather than to forsake the way of love." Rev. ed., p. 53. In the appendix Hershberger gathers together a number of Scriptural references which uphold the ideal of "doing, not demanding justice."

[95] Published by the Mennonite Board of Missions and Charities, Elkhart, Indiana.

[96] E.g., the Mennonite Community projects at Gulfport, Miss. Hershberger, *The Mennonite Church in the Second World War*, pp. 227-228.

[97] Unruh, *op. cit.*, p. 296.

[98] Cited by Hershberger, *The Mennonite Church in the Second World War*, p. 39.

[99] See note 42, p. 187.

[100] *Ibid.*

[101] *Ibid.*

[102] *Voluntary Service 1957*, pamphlet prepared by the Mennonite Board of Missions and Charities, Elkhart, Ind., see p. 12.

[103] Cited by Hershberger, *The Mennonite Church in the Second World War*, p. 230.

[104] Unruh, *op. cit.*, pp. 356ff.

[105] William T. Snyder, *op. cit.*

[106] *Voluntary Service 1957*, p. 14.

[107] See note 42, p. 187.

[108] Cf. Paul Peachey, *The Relevance of the Peace Witness of the Prophetic Christian Community*, 1953, Unpublished manuscript, Mennonite CentralCommittee,Akron, Penna.

[109] Paul L. Lehmann emphasizes the importance of the *koinonia* for social ethics in a way which undoubtedly seeks to prevent, in a manner not unlike the Mennonites, the loss of concrete Christian reality in the social realm. Lehmann declares that Christian ethics are *koinonia* ethics. "The *koinonia* is a fellowship of working together for the Gospel. And the *koinonia* is a fellowship of organic integration and growth of its several parts, whose vitality and integrity are derived from the Head, and in which men learn the meaning and purpose of life, learn, too, what their responsibilities in life are." "The Foundation and Pattern of Christian Behavior," *Christian Faith and Social Action*, pp. 103-104.

[110] Albert T. Rasmussen, *Christian Social Ethics*, p. 126.

[111] Paul Peachey, *The Relevance of the Peace Witness of the Prophetic Christian Community*.

CHAPTER 7
THE CHALLENGE OF THE RESPONSIBLE SOCIETY

Since the sixteenth century the Mennonite church and the major churches of Christendom have held fundamentally different positions regarding the relation of the church to society. As previously stated, the problem of the relation of the church to the world resulted in a life and death struggle between the Anabaptists and the major parties of the Reformation. Subsequently, virtually all discussion between the Anabaptist-Mennonite tradition and the larger Protestant bodies has ceased. As a retiring sect, the Mennonites have chosen to concentrate their energies on survival rather than influence. Furthermore, the separation of church and state, the free church and the rise of democracy have softened the differences and have created an ethos in which pluralistic social policies are not only possible but seemingly desirable. Nevertheless, study of the social policies of the Christian churches reveals that the lines of demarcation between the larger Protestant churches of the Reformation and the Anabaptists extend into the modern period. The conceptual framework and the direction of the social thought of the major denominations today differ fundamentally from the thought and outlook of the Mennonites.

The difference of social orientation is apparent to anyone who compares Mennonite assumptions with the assumptions of representative theologians of the modern period such as Reinhold Niebuhr, John C. Bennett, Karl Barth, Emil Brunner and William Temple. However, the contrast may be seen in broader perspective if a comparison is made between the Mennonite position and the position of the churches as represented by the ecumenical movement. That this can be done is significant in itself. It underscores the fact that despite all the differences of social policy and social experience among the churches which comprise the ecumenical movement, these churches have certain common fundamental convictions regarding the relation of the church to society which place them in a different category from the Mennonites.

The major point of difference concerns the attitude of responsibility toward the social order. Stated most categorically, the social policy of the major denominations today assumes responsibility. It is assumed by the ecumenical church that the world, including the organizations and structures governing its social, economic and political life, lies within the church's sphere of concern and influence.[1] The problems of the world are the problems of the church. The church is understood to be a part of the world system and it must therefore assume responsibility for the world. It must find ways of translating the Gospel into forms which are "relevant" for the life of the world. Both as an ecclesiastical body and as the totality of individual Christians, the church must exert its influence for the sake of world order, justice and peace.[2] The Mennonite church, on the other hand, refuses to accept responsibility for the social order. Because of its emphasis upon the pure church, its perfectionistic ethic and its primitivistic Biblicism, it has spent the major part of its energies perfecting ways of separation. In contrast to the ecumenical church, the Mennonite church regards the world as alien to itself and therefore outside the sphere of responsible action except by the indirect and largely unconscious and unplanned influence of personal morality and evangelistic influence.

This chapter is intended to explore the idea of the Responsible Society, the normative idea of the ecumenical movement for social problems, and to state in what way this conception challenges the traditional Mennonite view in the light of the modern world. It is not an exaggeration to say that the idea of the Responsible Society has caught the imagination of the Christian world. It has become the basis for discussion on the Christian ordering of human society since the First Assembly of the World Council of Churches at Amsterdam in 1948. Although the conception of the Responsible Society needs clearer articulation and more critical examination from the standpoint of its theological and ethical foundations than has been possible in the brief number of years since it was proposed, it has already been compared to such over-arching ideas as Augustine's "City of God," the "Holy Community" of the Puritans and the "Kingdom of God on Earth" of the Social Gospel Movement.[3] Although the idea of the Responsible Society needs to be further developed before it can be said to constitute an ethical philosophy in its own right, it is sufficiently definite to point in the general direction of a Christian philosophy of social relations in the modern world. In recent years it has become the rallying point around which the churches have been working out their own approach to particular problems. Consequently it has been grasped by The National Council of Churches of Christ (New York) as the basis for nation-wide study conferences on problems dealing with economic life, politics and international relations. In 1949 the Department of Church and Economic Life of the National Council of Churches sponsored a study of the relationship between religion and economics in which the concept of responsibility was assumed throughout. Six significant volumes were published, of which the study by Howard R. Bowen entitled *The Social Responsibilities of the Businessman* makes explicit the meaning of social responsibility in the complexities of modern business life.[4] Furthermore, a larger number of popular books intended to spell out the practical meaning of the "Responsible Society" for the average layman have been appearing in recent years, among which are John C. Bennett, *The Christian as Citizen*,[5] William Muehl, *Politics for Christians*,[6] Edgar M. Carlson, *The Church and the Public Conscience*,[7] Albert T. Rasmussen, *Christian Social Ethics*[8] and J. Richard Span, ed., *The Church and Social Responsibility*.[9]

I. The Meaning of the Responsible Society

What is the meaning of the Responsible Society? The Responsible Society was formulated at a meeting of the Preparatory Commission a year before Amsterdam. A participant read the following sentence from a manuscript under discussion: "The solution of the problem of power in the totalitarian state is to concentrate economic and political power in the same hands." This person asked: "What is *our* solution?" The answer was the idea of the Responsible Society--referred to subsequently as "a symbol of the social arrangement maintaining in dynamic equilibrium freedom and order, liberty and justice while barring the road to tyranny and anarchy."[10] This idea thereupon became the subject of a major document prepared by J. H. Oldham[11] for Amsterdam and it resulted in the *working conception* of Section III of the Assembly on "The Church and the Disorder of Society."[12] The idea of the Responsible Society remained the basis for discussion between Amsterdam and the Second Assembly in Evanston in 1954. Some of the ambiguities of the idea were clarified during the intervening year.

The technical definition of the Responsible Society is "one where freedom is the freedom of men who acknowledge responsibility to justice and public order, and where those who hold political authority or economic power are responsible for its exercise to God and the people whose welfare is affected by it."[13] At this stage of its development, the Responsible Society is not an alternative social or political system. It is not a social blueprint. *It is a criterion by which all social orders are judged.* A responsible social order is one in which Christians are called to live responsibly to God and to the neighbor in *all* areas of life.[14] The World Council of Churches does not claim that the Responsible Society exists today in its final form. *It is a norm and a goal for all Christian social action.* It stands for a society in which responsibility moves in three directions--the responsibility of the community as a whole to God, the responsibility of the citizen for justice and public order and the responsibility of those who exercise power to the people who are affected by it.[15]

A. *The Relation of the Responsible Society to Democracy.* It may be observed that the idea of the Responsible Society closely resembles the idea of democracy. John C. Bennett, whose name is closely associated with the idea, acknowledges this affinity but he explains that the word "democracy" was not used by the Assembly in 1948 because of its frequent use as a slogan by totalitarian governments. Therefore the Responsible Society was used instead of democracy as a "constructive alternative to totalitarianism."[16] "Democracy" would not have served this purpose since totalitarian countries frequently referred to themselves as democracies.

Does this mean that the World Council of Churches identifies Christianity with democracy even though for reasons of clarity the term democracy is not used? This is not the case. The WCC repeatedly stated its refusal to identify Christianity with democracy or any other social ideology. *Nevertheless, it is clear that what Section III was calling for can be realized with greater facility within a democracy than within any other known system.* The relation between Christianity and democracy may be close. Karl Barth, for example, sees a relation between Christianity and the "intentions of democracy." Barth says:

It must be admitted that the word and the concept "democracy" ("rule of the people") is powerless to describe even approximately the kind of State which, in the Christian view, most nearly corresponds to the divine ordinance. This is no reason, however, why it should be overlooked or denied that Christian choices and purposes in politics tend on the whole towards the form of the State, which, if it is not actually realized in the so-called "democracies," is at any rate more or less honestly intended and desired.[17]

In another connection Barth says:

It is true that a man may go to hell in a democracy, and achieve salvation under a mobocracy or a dictatorship. But it is not true that a Christian can endorse, desire or seek after a mobocracy or a dictatorship as readily as a democracy.[18]

The Responsible Society and democracy has this in common--both imply constitutional protection for the rights of minorities to organize and to seek to influence society, and both support, in fact demand, broad public consent in government. The Responsible Society assumes that the entire population will have a "concern" for public affairs and that effective channels will be kept open for the expression of that concern. Section III of the Evanston Assembly states these objectives as follows:

(1) Every person should be protected against arbitrary arrest or other interference with elementary human rights. (2) Every person shall have the right to express his religious, moral, and political convictions. This is especially important for those who belong to minorities. (3) Channels of political action must be developed by which the people can without recourse to violence change their governments. (4) Forms of association within society which have their own foundations and principles should be respected and not controlled in their inner life, by the state. Churches, families, and universities are dissimilar examples of this nonpolitical type of association.[19]

B. *The Relation of the Responsible Society to Totalitarianism.* The idea of the Responsible Society can be understood only against the backdrop of modern totalitarianism. Totalitarianism was a dominant concern of the Amsterdam Assembly at a time when the struggle between the free nations and Communism was taking the form of "cold war." C. L. Patijn referred to the totalitarian state as an "entirely new phenomena."[20] The Report of Section III of Amsterdam recommends the following attitude of Christians toward totalitarianism:

The Church should seek to resist the extension of any system, that not only includes oppressive elements but fails to provide any means by which the victims of oppression may criticize or act to correct it. It is a part of the mission of the Church to raise its voice of protest wherever men are the victims of terror, wherever they are denied such fundamental human rights as the right to be secure against arbitrary arrest, and wherever governments use torture and cruel punishments to intimidate consciences of men.[21]

Totalitarianism was rejected by the ecumenical community because it violated freedom and justice.

The conception of the Responsible Society is really an attempt to define freedom and justice in the face of modern totalitarianism. Amsterdam's definition of freedom climaxed an extensive ecumenical effort to define freedom in terms of the contemporary situations.

In 1925, at Stockholm, freedom meant "the free and full development of the human personality."[22] At the Geneva Conference of 1932, the churches emphasized economic freedom. In 1933, at Rengsdorf, the ecumenical church articulated a theology of freedom by declaring that "the Church is not bound absolutely to any particular social order, and has freedom to judge any social order on its merits."[23] Oxford, in 1937, emphasized freedom from the autocracy of capitalism, the creation of a new sense of personal worth of workers and the ideal of freedom as the full development of personality. Since the war, however, freedom has come to be associated mainly with the struggle against the power of totalitarianism whether fascist, communist or religious. The Evanston Assembly confirmed the stand of the First Assembly with respect to the conflict between Christianity and totalitarianism.

II. The Scope of the Responsible Society in the Light of the Modern Problems

One significant aspect of the Responsible Society is its scope. If one asks what set of social conditions the idea is intended to meet, the answer must be given in terms of the total social situation. *It is an overall conception intended to speak to the social problem of the modern world in its totality.* Obviously this conception does not have detailed answers to *individual problems*--especially matters of economic and social policy which must necessarily be worked out by the technically qualified on the basis of the peculiar needs of the situation. It does, however, address itself to the *major* problems of modern social life with a view to the encouragement of an *attitude* of social responsibility from which specific answers may be found.

Besides the problem of totalitarianism, what are some of the major problems of modern society to which the idea of the Responsible Society speaks?

A. *The Problem of Technical Civilization.* Foremost in the minds of Section III of the Amsterdam Assembly was technological civilization and the problem of technics for the realization of personal and spiritual values. J. H. Oldham, in his preparatory paper for the conference, stated that "science and technics...have brought about a new form of social existence, which is manifested in the free as well as in the totalitarian societies."[24] *Since men have learned not only to invent but also the technique of invention, the whole structure of existence is undergoing a huge change and reorganization constituting one of the great turning points in history.*[25] This change is due to the industrial revolution and to the preoccupation of men with material existence. Tied up with this change is the loss of personal values, the surrender of individuality, the substitution of mechanistic for organic ways of thought, the loss of natural community, the monotony and meaninglessness of work and the subordination of ends to means. *This constitutes a crisis in culture.* Jacques Ellul is even more emphatic than Oldham and other contributing members of Section III. In his essay on "The Situation in Europe," he insists that the development of technics and the primacy of production have changed the position of man in relation to culture. "Today man is subordinated to *things* and the coming society is a society made for these things and not for man.... The primacy of the *thing* is the highest note of triumph of technics and production. Man must subordinate himself to the necessity of things, or be considered as a thing himself--a fact easily accepted by modern science and utilized by modern politics."[26] Ellul goes on to say that it is possible for a society to be totalitarian in the absence of a totalitarian doctrine. Even French and English democracies tend toward totalitarianism as they subordinate the individual to the mass on the basis of a common subservience to technics and as the state increasingly assumes responsibility for unifying life. Ellul claims that "the difference between countries of Europe is no longer a difference in kind but a difference of degree; they are all moving in the same direction, but are at different stages."[27]

The problem is really deeper than technics, however. Oldham speaks of a "crisis of man" by which he means that the development of civilization in the direction of technology is prefaced by a deep change of spiritual and intellectual outlook. Technology is symptomatic of a shifting world view. *Technology is the attempt of man to create his own destiny since he has lost faith in Providence.* "Men are now beginning to discover in their own experience the implications of the assertion that God is dead. They are coming to see what it means to inhabit a universe which cannot be conceived as in any sense the expression of an intelligent creator's will."[28] The preoccupation with technics is an attempt to lay hold of powers by which man insures himself against an indifferent neutral universe. Therefore Oldham asks, "Given the conditions of a technical society, what are the political and economic arrangements which Christians ought to favor for the preservation of the human values involved in the Christian conception of man and what action (if any) can and ought the church to take to further such arrangements?"[29]

Oldham suggests, in the first place, the encouragement of social consciousness through numerous human associations "smaller than the state" in which men may have direct personal associations. This is what he calls "the practice of communal living."[30] In these associations--cultural, religious, recreational, philanthropic and civic--men and women may find opportunity for mutual sharing and spiritual support. These will provide cultural rootage and protection against one's remaining a mere unit in a sandheap of separate atoms. This experience in responsible living in the context of the immediate community will prepare modern man to combat the conformist tendencies of technological culture and equip him for the political task. Having participated in small groups too tough to be digested by the state, he will then use the political office responsibly, i.e., with direct reference to rights and freedoms of the individual and diverse groups in society.

B. *The Problem of Work.* Another way in which the idea of Responsible Society is intended to meet the problem of technics in the social realm is by the development of a theology of work.[31] The impersonal and meaningless character of work in the modern factory must be replaced by a devotional attitude signified by the statement *laborare est orare.* Oldham says, "We must either translate 'laborare est orare' into modern English and mold our civilization upon it, or else acknowledge as pretentious survivals every remaining bastion of the Christian culture."[32] In the Responsible Society, work is accomplished with an attitude of responsibility to God and to society. It is valued not simply from the standpoint of production but from the standpoint of service rendered in support of the ultimate purposes of the common life. In the Responsible Society work is accepted as a source of joy, creativity and pride. It is a means by which men express their social regard.

C. *Justice and Freedom and the Centralization of Power.* Furthermore, the Responsible Society stands for social justice. It has already been stated that the Responsible Society insists upon freedom. However, freedom is a social value only if it is disciplined by responsible attitudes. True freedom implies responsibility for the just rights of others.[33] The Responsible Society is a just society. Justice, however, is not conceived arbitrarily as the mechanical division of goods and privileges but as a concern for the total situation. Justice is a dynamic concept which embraces all sound goals, all operations of power in industry and the general needs of men. *The feel for justice and the sense of social responsibility are one.* They may be used interchangeably as long as justice is used in the dynamic sense of regard for the needs and privileges of others. Justice is simply the ability to see one's self and one's interest in the total social context with a view to the general welfare.

The emphasis upon justice within the Responsible Society becomes all the more necessary during the modern period. The vast extensions of power made possible by the breakdown of cultural and intellectual restraints and by the increased mechanization of life aggravate the problem of justice. "It may be regarded as axiomatic that the less a community is held together by cohesive forces of life, the more it must be held together by power," declares Reinhold Niebuhr.[34] This has placed society in the dilemma of deploring the centralization of economic and social power while finding it necessary to create greater constellations of power in order to curb those which already exist.

The Responsible Society meets the problem of power in its modern form by subjecting power to responsibility, i.e., by regarding the exercise of power as a trust from God and from the citizenry for the sake of the general good.

Certainly this sense of responsibility does not provide immediate solutions to practical problems of a socio-economic or political nature. However, it provides the basic frame of mind which, when placed alongside the inevitable technical aspects of social and political life, may lead to "proximate solutions." Ultimately the sense of responsibility as a frame of mind is grounded in love. Love enables one to discover injustices and the sense of responsibility leads to the unselfish exercise of corrective and creative power.

III. Modes of Social Influence

One of the most pressing problems facing the World Council of Churches is the method by which the church should seek to influence the social and political life of the world. This represents a shift in emphasis from *whether* the church is responsible for the world to *how* this responsibility may be exercised. The question of *how* the church may seek to influence society was a concern of Evanston. It is frequently acknowledged that the church remains relatively ineffective in the area of social action.[35] Much discussion on social questions is bogged down as soon as the question of a practical program is raised. The fact supports the criticism that discussion of the Responsible Society frequently indulges in ideological vagaries. It is in danger of becoming merely a "slogan" or a "caption" for a remote ideal which has not been brought face to face with the facts of the world as it is. Edward Duff has commented upon this phase of the work of the ecumenical community with these words:

> The World Council of Churches has frequently asserted that the Church has a role to play in the right ordering of society, a responsibility to fulfill in changing economic life. Both Assemblies (Amsterdam and Evanston) described some modes of exercising an influence in the political and social sphere. Neither Assembly, however, defined in any detail the nature of this function.[36]

The problem of the mode of influence is crucial not simply for the obvious reason that discussion and growing convictions are of little value unless they are translated into effective action, but also because the real issues of social policy are manifested only when the practical aspects of social communication are raised. To spread abroad in the world the social implications of the Gospel, to transform the world in its collective life, to make Christ relevant to the power structures of the world, to bring into being a social order which will reflect Christ in a secular world involve deep theoretical problems which become most keenly apparent when the practical task of influence is considered.

Much of the ambiguity concerning practical influence grows out of uncertainty regarding the agent. It is of crucial importance whether a given task is expected of one or another manifestation of the total life of the church. The church appears as: 1) the denominations or national groups joined collectively in the World Council of Churches or National Councils, 2) as individual denominations or national groups; 3) as individual congregations in the community; 4) as unofficial interdenominational social action groups or; 5) as the total individual membership of the church in the common life at home, at work and at play. Many ecumenical summonses to responsibility fail to articulate which of these manifestations of the church is intended as the bearer of practical responsibility. It is clear that all of these entities have a role to play in the promotion of the Responsible Society, though some are more perfectly adapted to certain kinds of action than others.

A. *Public Pronouncements.* One of the methods by which the church exerts influence is church *pronouncements.* This is a way by which the church molds opinion through its larger entities such as the ecumenical community, the denominations and social action groups. In reality the public pronouncement serves the dual purpose of consolidating Christian opinion and shaping the public conscience.[37] It is difficult to evaluate the public pronouncement as a method of social influence. Factors such as the concreteness of the pronouncement, the acuteness of the social issue under consideration and the intensity of the historical situation determine the result of the pronouncement.[38]

A number of problems attend the public pronouncement. One major problem is the extent to which pronouncements should offer *concrete* guidance to the complex issues of modern economic and political life. To what extent should the church take a stand on specific problems of justice? To what extent should the church suggest practical alternatives to the field of labor and management, domestic politics and international relations? This has been a major problem of discussion since the Oxford Conference.[39] It raises the question of what constitutes a social ethic and how far the various units of the church may put it into practice. Discussion of the problem usually centers around two dangers. On the one hand, specific commitments regarding immediate social and political problems afford the danger of error due to a lack of technical knowledge and a failure to appreciate all the relevant factors which make up the social problem in its complexity. Frequently the labor leader, the business man and the politician are unimpressed by the sincere but naive advice of theologians and church leaders who fail to recognize fully the distance between Christian principles and the realities of the modern situation. Specific instruction also sometimes leaves the impression that certain ideologies and existing political systems are identified with the will of God in contradistinction to the "Protestant Principle" of subjecting all social systems and human ideologies, including the Church's own, to the criticism of the transcendent ideal of God.[40] On the other hand, shying away from commitment about specific problems frequently leads to pronouncements in the form of "harmless" generalities which may be accepted by many but seldom understood and seldom turned into concrete forms of influence. The more general the statement, the more likely it is to secure agreement. However, it may result in agreement that is really noncommittal.[41]

The problem of the church's technical incompetence in worldly affairs has been described as the "heart of the question" of social influence by C. L. Patijn in a document prepared for the Amsterdam Assembly. Patijn said, "Our deepest perplexity is that the problems of society are for the most part of such a technical character that there is little or no apparent relation between many decisions to be taken and the driving ethical principles of the Christian faith."[42] Patijn pointed out further that the decisions of the Oxford Conference, though good in themselves, have not always been helpful to men in positions of responsibility. The difficulties are not removed as soon as pronouncements about international relations, human rights, trade and industry are established. They begin with their application.[43] Seeing the social problem in relation to the entire situation is the most difficult aspect of social criticism for those not directly engaged in social and political responsibilties.

To meet the danger of incompetent and irresponsible pronouncements on specific social problems on the one hand and vague generalizations on the other hand, the Oxford Conference devised the "middle axiom."[44] John C. Bennett has described middle axioms as those goals for society which are more specific than universal Christian principles and less specific than concrete institutions and programs of action.[45] They are attempts to define the direction and the spirit of constructive social change without stating precisely what intermediate socio-political efforts should be employed and what concrete form security demands. Middle axioms are necessary in view of the constant social change characteristic of the modern period. It is no longer possible to advocate a definite social program except for the more or less immediate situation, since changes in social climate invalidate long term commitment. The middle axiom attempts to keep before the statesman, the businessman and the labor leader a clear understanding of the direction toward which social institutions should move while letting the technicians work with the problem of the means to be employed in light of the actual situation. This protects the church from alignment with political parties, economic programs and ideologies.

An illustration of the failure to take into consideration the actual facts of the social situation is the attitude toward capitalism expressed in the Report of Section III at Amsterdam. In the Report of Section III communism and *laissez-faire* capitalism are jointly denounced with the following words: "The Christian Churches should reject the ideologies of both communism and *laissez-faire* capitalism, and should seek to draw men away from the false assumption that these extremes are the only alternatives."[46] Between the Amsterdam and Evanston Assemblies, however, there occurred a significant reassessment of capitalism. This reassessment resulted in the recognition that classical *laissez-faire* capitalism is virtually non-existent among Western nations.[47] The conception of capitalism which has formed the background for the ideological debate of this century is no longer relevant since *laissez-faire* capitalism has been largely replaced. It has been replaced by a mixed economy which has retained many of the features of the older capitalism such as private enterprise, private ownership, and capitalistic techniques of production and distribution but which at the same time has introduced many controlling elements designed to curb monopoly. Beside the traditional deterrents to the concentration of economic power such as state control and the force of competition, numerous "countervailing powers"[48] have emerged in recent years. Examples are the labor movement, the farm bureau and the powerful distributing agencies such as chain stores and discount houses. These have tended to reduce the egoistic excesses of manufacturers and curb their freedom to the extent that *laissez-faire* capitalism is a term which belongs virtually to the past. Furthermore, the general tendency in Europe and America is in the direction of the "welfare state" as a result of which social power has been more equitably distributed. Various social security programs, government labor mediation boards and public health requirements have had the general effect of broadening the business goals beyond the sole criteria of production and profits. According to V.A. Demant, "This twentieth century of ours is witnessing on a widespread scale the disappearance of the economic autonomy of the capitalist era."[49] Today one may notice a "great reversal of all the tendencies which made for the independence of economic activity from the total demands of society and from ethics."[50]

The Report of Section III, which by implication viewed communism and *laissez-faire* capitalism as equally existent and equally menacing, lacked adequate recognition of the actual facts of history. It is an instance of the general tendency, especially dominant during the nineteenth century and the earlier part of the twentieth century, to approach social programs ideologically rather than analytically. It is easier to make ecclesiastical pronouncements by comparing ideologies than by the comparison of facts. Unless the church is able to move back and forth across the lines separating ideology from social actuality, even the built-in safeguards of "middle axioms" are of little avail.

B. *Social Action Programs*. Another method by which the church may seek to influence society is through *social action* programs. This method assumes the right and the duty of the church to relate itself *directly* to social problems by taking sides on specific issues and by attempting to influence at close range those who exercise social power. Social action programs are conducted with greater facility by separate denominations and local congregations or regional congregational associations than by the World Council of Churches. The vastness of the social and political field and the multiplicity of points of view within the World Council forbid social action programs on the ecumenical level except in a limited number of areas.[51] The World Council of Churches has, of course, assisted refugees on a vast scale since World War II; it has helped coordinate the world relief and rehabilitation programs of the churches; it has stimulated denominational groups to accept responsibility for the alleviation of suffering as a result of the war. In addition, its Commission on Churches in International Affairs has been represented at the United Nations in order to inform the churches of significant trends in international relations. The World Council of Churches has also encouraged professional groups--doctors, lawyers, journalists, labor leaders and business men--to gather together for discussion of means by which Christian principles may be applied in their professions. Nevertheless, the ecumenical movement cannot be said to foster a full and responsible social action program.

One of the most direct forms of social action is the Christian political party. Christian political parties have been organized especially among European Catholics. The argument for the Christian political party is that in this way Christian principles and concrete organizations of power are brought into immediate relation. Those who advocate Christian political parties are usually critical of the haphazard way by which the church ordinarily attempts to influence social decisions. The Christian political party supposedly stands for a united effort to control portions of social life on the basis of a well-conceived, concrete social and political program.

The attitude of the Ecumenical Assembly at Amsterdam regarding the formation of Christian political parties was, however, negative. The Report of Section III contains the categorical statement that "the Church as such should not be identified with any political party, and it must not act as though it were itself a political party."[52] One reason given in support of this attitude is that Christian political parties can easily lead to the confusion of Christianity with the "inherent compromises of politics." Furthermore, the identification of Christians with a single party may tend to isolate certain Christians from others and cut them off from opportunities to leaven other parties and groups. Also, the natural rivalry between political parties may lead to rivalry against Christianity itself. At Amsterdam it was acknowledged, however, that under special circumstances Christian social influence may express itself through the formation of political movements in order to achieve specific objectives. This concession was accompanied by the warning, however, that Christians should not claim that this is the only possible expression of Christian concern in the situation.[53]

The question of how social action programs should be organized, who should sponsor them, and to whom they should be directly responsible has not been clarified by the ecumenical movement. Repeatedly the statement is made that Christians should express their political and economic convictions but the matter of organized channels for this expression is left unanswered. The idea of the Responsible Society is indefinite on this point. In the meantime, the National Council of Churches of Christ (New York) has a Department of Church and Economic Life stemming from the Federal Council's Conference on the Church and Economic Life, which was held in Pittsburgh in 1947. Separate denominations have organized or expanded departments for social action in recent years. A number of independent groups such as The Fellowship of Reconciliation, The Fellowship of Southern Churchmen and Christian Action keep interest in social questions alive.[54]

C. *Responsibility of the Christian as an Individual.* The method, however, upon which the ecumenical assemblies placed their greatest emphasis is the indirect influence of the church through the individual Christian as he goes about his normal responsibilities as a Christian. Ultimately the most effective witness to social institutions is the witness of men and women in the home, the school, business and public office, as they relate their work to the principles of Christianity and as they form a conscience for the public order as a whole. According to the Amsterdam Report:

The social influence of the Church must come primarily from its
influence upon its members through constant teaching and preaching of Christian truth in ways that illuminate the historical conditions
in which men live and the problems which they face. The Church
can be most effective in society as it inspires its members to ask in a
new way what their Christian responsibility is whenever they vote or
discharge their duties of public office, whenever they influence public opinion, whenever they make decisions as employers or as
workers or in any other vocation to which they may be called.[55]

What seems most necessary is the development of a common ethos, common
convictions concerning the destiny of man and his relation to society. This
means "political preaching," an expression used by Karl Barth to describe
preaching which attempts to relate the revelation of God to the work of God in
"secular" history.

One of the major tasks of the World Council of Churches has been to
make Christians conscious of their social responsibility as Christian citizens.
The average Christian sees little or no connection between Christianity and
politics.[56] The reasons for political and social reserve are many. Politics has
traditionally carried with it a connotation of "worldliness" or selfishness, corruption and evil. Pietism in Europe and Fundamentalism in America have
emphasized individual salvation and personal morality with the naive assumption that social change results automatically from individual conversion.[57]
Sometimes the theory of the separation of the church and the state has been
construed to mean that religion has nothing to do with politics. Protestants
frequently regard politics as "dirty." George A. Graham says that the
American attitude toward politics is one of "mingled pride and shame" with its
"indiscriminate honoring of the long dead and its dishonoring of the living in
the field of public affairs."[58] Some fear the inherent moral compromise of
politics.[59] Others, especially in the European context, have been influenced by
the Lutheran dichotomy of the "two realms" in a way which finally results in a
strange combination of disregard for political institutions and almost fatalistic
obedience to government.[60]

In America many of these attitudes were partially overcome by the Social
Gospel movement pioneered by Walter Rauschenbusch.[61] In recent years the
Social Gospel movement has been severely criticized but the significance of the
Social Gospel movement is by no means nullified by its errors. It is frequently
blamed for its optimistic estimate of human possibilities, its failure to
understand the essential difference between personal and corporate morality,
for its misunderstanding of the teachings of Jesus concerning the Kingdom of
God and its confusion of the "way of the cross" with the ways of bourgeois
society.[62] Nevertheless, the development of Christian social attitudes toward
greater participation could not have reached its present attainment if it had not
been for the contribution of the Social Gospel movement in America. Contemporary social thought in America, especially the thought initiated by Reinhold Niebuhr, would have been impossible apart from the central concern

inherited from the Social Gospel, namely the concern for a dynamic relation between the church and society as a whole.[63] Nevertheless, any realistic understanding of the situation among the churches must come to grips with the fact that the churches continually struggle with the temptation to neglect social responsibility.

IV. The Limitations of the Idea of the Responsible Society

We have noted that the ecumenical fellowship has yet to consider in systematic fashion the methods of social influence open to the church. It has acknowledged its weakness in this area. In recent years, the leaders of Protestantism have been imbued with the conviction that the church should be more active in social affairs. However, the ways of social influence have not been studied from a scientific point of view except by a few individual scholars working on an independent basis. The question arises, however, whether ambiguity in this area does not stem from deeper uncertainties having to do with the social philosophy of the ecumenical church.

The question arises whether the ecumenical movement has a social philosophy. It has accepted with enthusiasm the idea of the Responsible Society. We have noted that the idea of the Responsible Society has become the framework for the social thought of the ecumenical movement since 1948 and that much of the thinking of the individual churches on social questions is dominated by the idea of responsibility. The main question of social ethics has become, what does it mean to be "responsible?" But is the idea of the Responsible Society equivalent to a social philosophy or is it simply a caption? Does it suggest anything more definite as a pattern of Christian society than what can be expected from a general diffusion of sentiments of social concern? *Does it go beyond the negative reaction to totalitarianism, laissez-faire capitalism, racial discrimination, the dehumanization of industrial civilization to a positive statement of what society ought to be?* Certainly the ecumenical movement has extolled justice and freedom and to a limited extent it has judged contemporary society by these principles. But does the ecumenical movement represent a concrete and comprehensive social ideal which answers the questions expected from a coherent social philosophy?

Before this question can be answered, another more basic question must be considered. What are the marks of a mature and complete social philosophy by which the adequacy of the Responsible Society may be judged? The first mark of a Christian social philosophy is clarity regarding its sources. Are they theological or philosophical or both? Does the social philosophy rest upon a strictly Biblical ethic? If so, how is the Bible employed? Is the Bible regarded primarily as a source of "inspiration" or as a deposit of commands and principles? On the other hand, if the social philosophy is said to rest upon extra-Biblical sources, what is the nature of the "coalition"[64] and what are those sources? Obviously this brings up the problem of the place of "natural law" or the "orders of creation." Furthermore, questions need to be asked about the nature of justice, i.e., whether justice is conceived dynamically or in formal terms. What is the relation of the social order to the Kingdom of God and to the meaning of history? To what extent does the Christian ethic attempt to save civilization? What is the relation of the church to the state? What should be the attitude of Christianity to war? How are the non-Christian peoples to be related to the social ideal?

An adequate social philosophy must answer these and many other fundamental questions. However, it is clear that the idea of the Responsible Society is far too nebulous to answer them. The impression one gets in examining the most widely disseminated documents of the World Council of Churches is that the idea of the Responsible Society needs to be reinforced with clearer theological foundations and technical understandings of modern society before it can constitute an independent Christian social philosophy. Furthermore, the obvious question arises as to whether the ecumenical movement is capable of a definite social philosophy in view of the differences of theological and ethical outlook of the churches and the prevalence of the point of view that Protestantism rejects in principle any social philosophy which attempts to state in a final and concrete way what Christian society is.

Underlying the question of the possibility and the necessity of a concrete social ethic by the ecumenical community remains the fact that great differences regarding the nature of Christian ethics exist within the ecumenical community. These differences turn most fundamentally upon the question of whether the Christian ethic is *determinate* or *indeterminate*. By a determinate ethic we mean an ethic which is oriented toward certain fixed principles or permanent laws of social behavior, an ethic which recognizes a hierarchy of values, which seeks to take the initiative from the ebb and flow of events by bringing society under the domination of a great comprehensive ideal. In other words, a determinate ethic is "an ethic of ends." By an indeterminate ethic we mean a dynamic ethic of "spiritual inspiration," that is to say, an ethic which attempts to bring into immediate relation the ever changing situation and the will of God. In this case ethical decision is made not on the basis of deductions from static principles or legal formulas but from an immediate understanding of the will of God as inspired by God's word and His spirit. Already in 1937, J. H. Oldham stated the problem in preparation for the Oxford Conference. He stated that the "urgent" decision before the churches is the decision between "an ethic of inspiration" and an "ethic of ends."[65] Oldham preferred an ethic of inspiration for the reason that "the fundamental and characteristic thing in Christian action is not obedience to fixed norms or to a moral code, but living response to a Person."[66] His contention was that the knowledge of God's will is never obtained through a doctrine, that knowledge of God is obtained only through personal encounter with God as a "living person." Accordingly, ethics is distinguished from morality with the latter's roots in a static conception of God and man. Hence "the primary concern of the Christian ethic is not with ends, purposes or programs, but with faith and obedience.... Christians are called to share in his (God's) creative work, but this does not mean that they have a plan or program, clear in its outlines, for the realization of which they must work."[67]

One of the main developments of ethical thought in recent years is the search for an alternative to a determinate ethic of fixed principles. The reasons given for the rejection of fixed principles vary. Sometimes they take the form of a protest against the pretense of sinful human reason to construct an ethic suitable to God.[68] The ethic of ends inevitably means "natural law" and "natural law" opens the gate to speculative reason. Reliance upon natural law is held to be possible only at the expense of "Biblical insights." The close connection between the "natural law" theories of the Stoics of antiquity and modern secular theories is construed by some people to mean that the association of natural law with Christian theology for over a thousand years during the Middle Ages was a fateful concession to paganism.[69] Ethics based upon "Biblical insights" alone are frequently held to be consonant with the nature of Christianity as a revealed religion and with the operations of the Holy Spirit.

Others seek a nondeterminate ethic because of the impossibility of reconciling moral principles to the exigencies of life within the conditions of modern society. The ethic of Dietrich Bonhoeffer immediately comes to mind. According to Bonhoeffer the very thought of a "system of ethics" seems "superfluous" in the light of modern conditions. He declares that the "wise man is aware of the limited receptiveness of reality for principles; for he knows that reality is not built upon principles but that it rests upon the living and creating God.... Principles are only tools in God's hand to be thrown away as unserviceable."[70] Bonhoeffer regards the incarnation as an instance of the divine wisdom which chose the form of a man rather than a universally valid principle, program or law.[71] Furthermore he feels that the approach to ethics through systems results in a needless dualism between Christ and the world, a dualism which was begun with the Middle Ages and was continued by "pseudo-protestant" thought following the Reformation.[72]

Another modern theologian who rejects laws and principles as the starting point for Christian ethics is Paul Lehmann. Lehmann holds that the "saving activity" of God is the basis for ethics.[73] He quotes Emil Brunner approvingly as follows: "In the Christian view that alone is 'good' which is free from all caprice, which takes place in unconditional obedience.... But this obedience is rendered not to a law or a principle which can be known beforehand, but only to the free, sovereign will of God.... Man only knows how he himself ought to love by allowing himself to be drawn by faith into this activity of God."[74] But he is critical of Brunner for looking to the "law in the three-fold sense" for the ordering of the Christian life. Lehmann describes his own ethic as a "contextual ethic." This is an ethic which "regards the concrete complex of the actual situation out of which the ethical problem arises as itself ethically significant."[75] What Lehmann means to say is that if one is to indulge in ethics of law the only logical source of law is the body of Christ's teachings but these are not so easily accessible and they cannot be applied in the world because of the stubborn diversity and complexity of the actual situation. Therefore normative ethics is impossible.

Reinhold Niebuhr is another outstanding advocate of an ethic without law and principles. He declares that "Christian legalism, as every other advocacy of inflexible rules for shifting historical situations, is embarrassed today."[76] But Niebuhr is troubled by the haunting dangers of moral relativism and declares that there must be some way of resolving the debate between the legalists and the relativists "which will refute the legalists when they make too sweeping claims for fixed standards of conduct and which will, at the same time, avoid the abyss of nihilism on the edge of relativism."[77] Niebuhr holds that the "law of love" is the antidote for both legalism and lawlessness since it transcends law without leading to excesses. The problem of relating love, which he prefers to call a "law," to the relativities of the human situation is the basic problem of Niebuhr's ethics. By making love indeterminate however, i.e., by stating that love is ultimately a motive rather than a "way," he seeks to resolve this problem so that he can hold both to love and society.

On the other hand, Emil Brunner, whose significance to ecumenical thinking on social questions has been considerable, makes a place for laws, principles and norms in Christian ethics based upon the "orders of creation."[78] This, of course, recalls the frame of reference of Reformation ethics, particularly in Lutheranism. The orders of creation tend to structuralize ethics. According to Brunner, the "*Ordnungen*" present the world as it is. They define the sphere of action and set the limits and the possibilities of ethical action. On the basis of the *Ordungen*, the essential principles and the laws of such social phenomena as the state, the family and the economic order may be known,[79] even if room is made for temporal and local adaptations. "They form the skeleton of the life of civilized historical humanity."[80] This means that goals for the social life of humanity may be stated with considerable concreteness. The validity of this approach is defended by Brunner in the face of the usual attacks against "natural law." By interpreting natural law through the eyes of faith, i.e., by assigning a single source to the realms of creation and redemption, he seeks to avoid the error of "autonomous ethics" of the natural law tradition beginning with the Stoics.[81] Furthermore, by insisting upon the primacy of the ethics of Revelation with its source in Christ and the Holy Spirit, the qualitative uniqueness of the ethics of Revelation is preserved. This is an underlying emphasis of Brunner's *Justice and the Social Order* with its sharp distinction between love and justice. At any rate, Brunner's ethics, and one may also include the ethics generally emanating from the Anglo-Catholic tradition as well, bring to ecumenical discussion definitions of justice, civil righteousness, and equality which advance the cause of clarity and precision in the search for a concrete conception of the society which the Christian churches may work toward.

Not only has the ecumenical movement come short of a clear conception of the *foundations* and the *pattern* of ethical conduct from which alone the outlines of a Christian society may be set down, it has also failed to agree upon a Christian eschatology, apart from which a genuine social vision is impossible. That eschatology is supremely relevant for Christian social ethics is a conviction which had struck the Christian mind only in recent years. Thirty years ago it was assumed that ethics had gone *beyond* eschatology.[82] Christians had become interested in the social realm precisely because they had ceased to

expect the Kingdom of God. That such a view was indicative of the secularization of the world and the church is incontrovertible. Today, however,
theologians are saying that every system of ethics implies an eschatological
view and, implicitly or explicitly, the eschatological idea is the key to the ethical
system. According to Visser 't Hooft, we can say to each other, "Tell me what
your eschatology is and I will tell you what your attitude is in relation to
Church, state and society."[83] If ethics is to be Christian it must reflect a view of
history. Christian ethics cannot be derived from metaphysics. This is the same
as to say that whatever values Christian ethics may derive from ancient and
modern philosophical systems, these values must not be accepted by negating
the significance of history implied by the incarnation and the "eschaton." To
Christian ethics the first question is not one of "being"[84] but of Christ, and
Christ cannot be known except in the context of his historical manifestation
which, of course, is to be understood in terms of the Kingdom of God and the
Second Coming.[85] It is Christian eschatology which states most distinctly the
unique attitude of Christianity toward the social process, toward human progress, toward cultural formations, property and wealth. Ultimately the whole
historical process is judged by the Christian view of the "last things." When the
subject of eschatology is raised, all other systems are judged with respect to
their ultimate meaning. Furthermore such questions as the relation of the
church and the state and the general question of the relation of Christianity
and culture and the cultural implications of the church and the world cannot be
avoided if eschatology is taken seriously. Therefore Visser 't Hooft says,
"From the first beginnings of the modern ecumenical discussion at Stockholm
until our own days this (eschatology) is the underlying theme to which we are
forced back again and again. And let no one say that he has no place for
eschatology, for there is no Christian faith which does not imply a conscious or
unconscious conviction about the ultimate events and their relation to our present life and action."[86]

In view of the importance of eschatology for social ethics, it is to be
expected that unity of social thought must be accompanied by unity of
eschatological hope. For this reason the Second Assembly of the WCC meeting at Evanston assumes crucial importance. At this assembly the theme was
eschatological in nature--"Christ the Hope of the World." Since few Christian
doctrines present greater problems and few topics expose the diversity of
opinion among the churches so obviously, it took courage to adopt "the
Christian hope" as the theme of the Assembly.

Evanston attempted to synthesize the main eschatological claims of the
Gospel: 1) "Christ came;" 2) "Christ has come;" and 3) "Christ will come."[87]
The effort to synthesize these claims is an effort to avoid the excesses which
follow an emphasis upon anyone. Those who emphasize the fact that Christ
came have a tendency to interpret Christianity as remote from the life of the
world. Those who emphasize the fact that Christ has come have a tendency to
associate Christ too closely with existing social structures and thus overlook the
Gospel as a judgment on all human organizations. Those who emphasize only
the future coming of Christ are likely to fall into anarchism or some kind of

social irresponsibility. Despite the efforts of Evanston to synthesize the various elements of eschatology into a common view, "the resolution of differences remained inconclusive."[88] According to James Hasting Nichols, the most important division was between "humanistic" and "Biblical" ways of hoping.[89] Conceding that "humanism" as a coherent philosophy involving belief in the independence and perfectibility of man is inevitably hostile to the Christian faith, it was recognized at the same time that many, while not humanists as such, nevertheless tend to hope in terms of progress through human systems such as democracy, science and social programs. The Word of God is meant to "transform" existing institutions into Christian patterns.[90] The hope of others rested more clearly upon the work of God less closely associated with the world. This view was represented by Edmund Schlink. Although he professed concern for civil righteousness, he argued strongly against hope which is centered in the good fortunes of the world.

> If in our thinking about this subject we place the emphasis on the preservation of this threatened world, then we shall miss the point of our Assembly theme completely. If we expect Christ to insure this world so that men may continue undisturbed their pursuit of liberty, may carry on their business, and seek an improvement in their standard of living, then Christ is not the hope of the world, but rather the end of all the world's hopes.... We have only to tell the world who its Lord really is. It is not up to us to save men.[91]

These differences make it clear that the ecumenical church is by no means settled regarding the eschatological question and for that reason its ethical position is uncertain at crucial points.

We may be forced to conclude that many crucial differences regarding the foundation and pattern of Christian social ethics exist within the World Council of Churches. Therefore it follows that the idea of the Responsible Society cannot be regarded at this stage of its development as a systematic and comprehensive social theory. As long as the idea of the Responsible Society cannot be said to stand for a more or less uniform set of convictions regarding the nature of Christian ethics, the relation of the Bible to Christian conduct, the relation of the church to the state and the meaning of eschatology for social ethics, it can indicate at best the general direction and the spirit of social thought.

V. Basic Theological Convictions

It is misleading to dwell upon the differences of theological ideas among the churches comprising the ecumenical movement unless due consideration is given to at least two fundamental convictions which may be considered root ideas of the conception of the Responsible Society. They are: 1) the Christian conception of man; and 2) the Lordship of Christ. Both of these have been prominent theological subjects in recent years. Interest in them has been aroused by events in the modern world and by the rediscovery of Biblical faith and doctrine.

A. *The Christian Conception of Man.* In the Report of Section III at the Amsterdam Assembly, the idea of the Responsible Society was prefaced by a statement regarding the Christian conception of man. "Man is created and called to be a free being, responsible to God and his neighbor. Any tendencies in State and society depriving man of the possibility of acting responsibly are a denial of God's intention for man and His work of salvation."[92] This statement attempts to define the inviolable nature and responsibility of man as a being created by God and for God and the neighbor. Therefore, the basic problem facing Section III of the Amsterdam Assembly was: How is it possible to promote the freedom, the responsibility and the personal dignity of man as described in the Bible in view of the confusion and the complexity of the modern world? Or, how is it possible to create the conditions of true community in which the true nature of man can be fostered in a world characterized by materialism, industrial power,[93] technics, urban culture, mass communication, impersonality and bureaucracy? This is not to say that the ecumenical community sought conditions in support of a typical humanistic understanding of man. It was seeking rather to understand on the one hand what God intends man to be and on the other hand to understand how modern institutions which have replaced organic and traditional forms of society can be altered to support man's nature and responsibility. The answer to Amsterdam and Evanston is the Responsible Society. The Responsible Society is a society in which man is no longer a means for political and economic ends. "Man is not made for production, but production for man."[94] Nor is man made for the state. Man is made for God and he can serve God only by the free and creative use of his potentialities in true community. This is precisely the meaning of the Responsible Society.

B. *The Lordship of Christ.* Since the earlier pages of this chapter were devoted largely to the problem of man and modern civilization, it is unnecessary to enlarge on the relevance of the doctrine of man for the Responsible Society. We turn, therefore, to the meaning of the Lordship of Christ for the Responsible Society. The rediscovery of the Biblical doctrine of the Lordship (Kingship) of Christ is one of the notable theological developments of recent years. Forced by the rise of totalitarianism to decide who possesses final authority in the world, the church, especially the Confessing Church of Germany, evoked the conception of the Kingship of Christ traditionally associated with Calvin. During the 1930's and during the Second World War, when man's ultimate devotion was demanded by human authorities, the church with the aid of its theologians turned to the New Testament with the result that a clear grasp of the position and authority of Christ in relation to all human powers was achieved. The conviction that "Christ is Lord," recalling the confession of the early church (*Kyrios Christos*), resulted in the revitalization of segments of the church and the kindling of enthusiasm for the great Christological passages of the New Testament. Emphasis upon the Lordship of Christ gave impetus to the Christological view of the universe, of human authority and of destiny.

It is impossible even to summarize here the meaning of the Kingship of Christ for theology in general or to interpret the Biblical doctrine. This has been done admirably by W.A. Visser 't Hooft in *The Kingship of Christ*[95] and by Oscar Cullmann in numerous writings, but especially in *Christ and Time*.[96] Suffice to say that the idea of the Kingship of Christ means that Christ is ruler over all human authorities and institutions (Matt. 28:18) and therefore nothing is "autonomous" in the world. "In him all things were created, in heaven and on earth, visible and invisible, whether thrones or dominions or principalities or authorities--all things were created through him and for him" (Col. 1:16). Christ's purpose in coming was "to reconcile to himself all things, whether on earth or in heaven, making peace by the blood of the cross" (Col. 1:20). Therefore it follows that the Christian must somehow be interested in and assume responsibility for the world. Christ is, to be sure, uniquely related to the church which is his body. However, His Lordship extends beyond the church to include *all things* in heaven and in earth. This becomes the theological basis for political responsibility. Politics, economics, technology are not autonomous spheres, nor are they somehow subsumed under God's providential rule apart from Christ while Christ rules the Church. When Christ ascended to be with the Father, he assumed authority over all things including the social and political realms. Even a rebellious world and the evil powers are defeated in principle by the victorious Christ.[97]

The Responsible Society was therefore conceived at Amsterdam and at Evanston as the social implication of Christ's Lordship over the entire world. The world was visualized in its entirety as Christ's world. According to the Report of Section III at Evanston:

> Christian Social Responsibility is grounded in the mighty acts of God, who is revealed in Jesus Christ our Lord. He has created the world, and all time is embraced within His eternal purpose. He moves and acts within history as the ever living God. The center of world history is the earthly life, the cross and the resurrection of Jesus Christ.... In him God entered history decisively, to judge and forgive. In Him are revealed the present plight of man, and the end toward which the world is moving.... The call to social righteousness is sustained by the sure hope that the victory is with God, who in Christ has vanquished the powers of evil and in His own day will make this victory fully manifest in Christ.[98]

Thereupon the Report continues with the declaration that "From Christ men receive the direction for their service, the obligation to share heartily in the world's work and daily tasks, and the responsibility to seek a better social and political life."[99]

The significance of these remarks is apparent if it is remembered that the positive relation of Christ to social and political realms has not always been emphasized by Christian social thought. This emphasis runs counter to a side of Luther's dualistic teaching which at least placed a question mark upon the "secular" realm for the Christian and which tended to drive a wedge between vital Christianity and social and political affairs. It also runs counter in even a more remarkable way to the sectarian tendency to exclude Christ altogether from all those social and political structures which lie outside the immediate control of the church.

It is the evocation of the Calvinistic emphasis upon the Christological foundation of the state which lies behind a great deal of the present emphasis upon the relation of Christ's rule to social and political reality. According to Wilhelm Niesel, Calvin believed that God does not govern human affairs immediately. God directs affairs through Christ the King. Human authorities are Christ's representatives. Niesel explains Calvin's position as follows:

> This mode of the divine government of the world is grounded in the fact that God exercises His sovereign power only mediately. He has exalted Jesus Christ as the eternal king and now reigns with His help. Christ is, as it were, the vice-regent of God and all earthly rule is like "a symbol of the Kingly authority of our Lord Jesus Christ." Thus, when Calvin teaches that civil government was instituted of God, he is not thinking of an ill-defined supernatural foundation of human rules but of the one Lord Jesus Christ. The kingdoms of this world are grounded in Him and maintained by Him.[100]

VI. The Responsible Society and the Mennonite Church

When the Responsible Society as a Christian social philosophy is placed beside the Mennonite social philosophy, the question arises as to whether they are not so fundamentally different in outlook that they can have little to do with one another. It may appear that their differences are so basic that if each were carried to their logical conclusion they would totally exclude one another. It is the writer's conviction that the differences are theoretically deep. Nevertheless, as one examines the daily activities of Christians (Mennonites and Non-Mennonites), the practical differences are not as great as they would seem to be on the theoretical level. This is particularly true in light of developments within the Mennonite church during the past 10 years.

We must, however, indicate briefly some of the basic differences between the approach of the Responsible Society and the approach of the Mennonites.

A. *The Framework of Social Ethics.* The most fundamental difference between the ethical approach of the ecumenical community and the Mennonites has to do with the framework of Christian ethics. For the churches associated with the ecumenical community, i.e., those churches which subscribe in a general way to the ideal of the Responsible Society, the frame of reference is the *world*. The problems of the ecumenical church are the great problems of modern society considered as a whole. Those social forces and political developments which have a way of engulfing the entire world are the problems faced by the ecumenical church. These, of course, include the problems of labor and management, race relations, colonialism, political developments and international peace. The problems of the ecumenical church are the problems of Detroit, Washington and Moscow. They are not problems peculiar to Christians conceived as a separated people. Rather, they are the problems of Christians who think of themselves as being involved in the major stream of society. The attempt is therefore made to bring Christian influence to bear upon those social institutions which have largely fallen into the hands of secular powers but which nevertheless can be directed toward just ends. It is therefore no accident that the Responsible Society was discussed at Evanston "in World Perspective."

The framework of Mennonite social ethics, is, by comparison, severely restricted. It is restricted denominationally to the Mennonite church and sociologically to the Mennonite community. The social problems considered by Mennonites have been those which have emerged in the Mennonite community. Of course, these problems cannot be completely divorced from the problems of the world. But the Mennonites have addressed themselves to world problems only as they have become immediate problems to the Mennonites. Therefore their social witness has been limited to the confines of the Mennonite community. In the field of economics, for example, the problems of modern industrial life were completely overlooked as they first appeared in Detroit and the cities of New England. Only when industrialism began to invade the fringes of Mennonite community life did Mennonites face the problem. Furthermore, Mennonites have never attempted to help solve the problems of industrial life from the standpoint of the world at large. Mennonite social ethics represent an attempt to carve out a unique pattern of social conduct within the semi-autonomous community under conditions which are quite distinct from the problems as they appear in society at large.

In reality these fundamentally different approaches to social problems have their roots in the attitudes toward society which developed in the Middle Ages and continued during the Reformation. The Responsible Society is the logical extension of the *corpus christianum* ideal under the conditions of modern secularism and pluralism. This is not to say that the architects of the Responsible Society are deliberately trying to duplicate the system of the Middle Ages so far as its formal characteristics are concerned. They are not, for example, reinstating the formal relations of the church to the empire of the Middle Ages nor are they reverting to ancient attitudes regarding religious liberty and ecclesiastical control over secular institutions. However, it is undeniable that the ideal of the *corpus christianum*, i.e., a world culture in which Christ is acknowledged as Lord, lies behind the idea of the Responsible Society.[101] Undoubtedly if such an ideal were achieved today it would take a far different form than it did in the days of the Middle Ages or the Reformation. Historical developments such as industrialism, democracy, religious freedom, individualism, technology and various pluralisms would make the difference. Nevertheless, the Responsible Society corresponds to the *corpus christianum* in so far as it represents the ideal of total society under the domination of the Christian ethos.

The Mennonite ideal, on the other hand, is the ideal of the separated few who despair of making the world Christian as a whole. Emphasis is placed on the church as a disciplined minority. The church faces the problems of the world only insofar as the few are involved and within the context of the few. This means that Mennonites cannot accept the Responsible Society as a comprehensive ideal without denying their own presuppositions. There are many forms of activity, considered apart from the comprehensive ideal, which correspond to the best interests of the Responsible Society. Such virtues as honesty in business, just relations with employees, enlightened policies of soil conversation, private charity and church welfare programs all work to the best interests of the Responsible Society. However, Mennonites have traditionally regarded these as meritorious in themselves and only secondarily as public virtues. In this respect Mennonite social thought follows the sectarian pattern.

B. *The Social Implications of the Lordship of Christ.* The universal Lordship of Christ which has been presented as one of the leading theological doctrines underlying the idea of the Responsible Society has never been emphasized by the Mennonites. It cannot be said that the Mennonites deny the universal range of Christ's authority. However, they have never worked through the implications of this doctrine for social ethics. The reason for this is that Mennonites generally limit the Lordship of Christ to the Church. Christ is conceived entirely in terms of the Redeemer and his Lordship extends only over those who have accepted Him. Insofar as Deity is related to the world as Creator and Sustainer, this is the work of God.[102] For all practical purposes the work of "God the Creator" and "Christ the Redeemer" are separated. To relate Christ to the realm of preservation and judgment has not as yet become a matter of serious theological enterprise among the Mennonites. This means that they have not as yet worked through the implications of the Logos Christology and the implications of the great Christological passages of Ephesians and Colossians in which Christ is declared to be Lord over "all things." Certainly the theoretical implications of the universal Lordship of Christ have not been thought through finally by any theological tradition. Furthermore, the problems of both a practical and a theoretical nature are numerous and vexing, particularly in view of modern secularism. Nevertheless, this is an area of theological study which must engage Mennnoite thought lest the uniqueness of the relation of Christ to his Body, the Church, excludes the broader implications of Christ's rule.

VII. Conclusion

We have noted that the Responsible Society is the comprehensive controlling idea of the World Council of Churches and that this idea has been accepted in a general way by most Protestant denominations in recent years. It is a young idea and it has not yet been developed into a complete system of social thought. Partly because of the divergent systems represented within the ecumenical church and partly because of the inherent difficulty in constructing complete ethical systems apropos to modern dynamic, pluralistic society, it may never become more than a motif. Nevertheless, this is an important motif since it challenges the churches to prophetic speech and remedial action. In view of the fact that the idea of responsibility is clothed with many ambiguities in so far as a final theory of Christian society and the specifics of social action are concerned, it is most significant when understood simply as a call for Christians to exercise a concern for social institutions commensurate to the vast changes in social organization within the modern period. This is the challenge which comes to the Mennonites as well, in view of their changing social position, even though their perfectionistic tendencies may not permit them to accept complete responsibility for the world.

Endnotes

[1] To state that the major religious groups represented by the ecumenical community agree on social responsibility as an essential task of the church is not to be unmindful of the apathy and indifference of many of the churches about social questions. The actual interest of the church in social affairs is frequently far behind the exhortations of theologians. Not all the churches regard social responsibility with equal enthusiasm and not all are in agreement regarding the practical meaning of responsibility. Furthermore the bewildering complexity of social and cultural backgrounds of the churches make any united policy and program of social action exceedingly difficult. Nevertheless it can be safely said that the ecumenical community has expressed a growing conviction in recent years, especially since the Oxford Conference in 1937, that the church should attempt to understand and influence the social life of the world. In the Report of Section III of the Evanston Assembly of 1954, Christian social responsibility was largely taken for granted and therefore less time and space was devoted to a justification of that concern than at Amsterdam in 1948. *Reports from the Second Assembly of the World Council of Churches* (SCM Press, 1954), p. 42. Edward Duff, commenting on the social policy of the World Council of Churches at Evanston says, "The duty of Christians to seek what Amsterdam called 'new, creative solutions' to contemporary economic and political problems, to work for the construction of the Responsible Society, was not contested by a sizable segment." *The Social Thought of the World Council of Churches* (New York: Assoc. Press, 1956), p. 165. The renewed interest in social problems since World War II seems paradoxical in light of the general decline of influence by the Christian church in western society. Hence Paul Albrecht comments: "To many realistic people it may seem paradoxical that the churches of the World Council should launch a new inquiry on Christian action in Society at a time when the likelihood of any effective action appears so uncertain.... The great complexity of economic and social life today, the comprehensive character of the problems which confront men and which frequently seem beyond human control, and the strength of the forces of evil make the possibility of significant improvements in community life seem slighter than ever before. In addition, the atmosphere of ill-will, suspicion and hatred which pervades the whole world has resulted in a feeling of despair about social change, especially in the West." *Ecumenical Review*, II (Winter, 1950), p. 141.

[2] An ecumenical survey prepared under the auspices of the WCC for the conference at Evanston points out that the three great conferences dealing with social questions, Stockholm (1925), Oxford (1938), and Section III of the First Assembly of the WCC, Amsterdam (1948), "have all emphasized two fundamental points regarding the Christian attitude toward society: (1) Christians must work for social justice, and (2) no particular political or economic system can be identified with the will of God or equated with the Kingdom of God." *The Responsible Society in a World Perspective* (New York: Harper and Brothers, 1954), p.1.

[3] Walter G. Muelder, *The Idea of the Responsible Society* (Boston: Boston Univ. Press, 1955), p. 3.

[4] Howard Bowen, *The Social Responsibilities of the Business Man* (New York: Harper and Brothers, 1953).

[5] (New York: Assoc. Press, 1955).

[6] (New York: Assoc. Press, 1955).

[7] (Philadelphia: Muhlenberg Press, 1956).

[8] *Op. cit.*

[9] (New York: Abingdon-Cokesbury Press, 1953).

[10] Edward Duff, S.J., *op. cit.*, p. 191.

[11] J. H. Oldham, "A Responsible Society," *Man's Disorder and God's Design*, III, pp. 120-154.

[12] *Ibid.*, pp. 189-197.

[13] *Ibid.*, p. 192.

[14] "Report of Section III," *Evanston Speaks* (London: SCM Press, 1954), p. 48.

[15] "Report of Section III," *MDGD*, III, p. 192.

[16] "The Church Between East and West," *Christian Faith and Social Action*, p. 78. Terms such as "the Free Society," "Civitas Humana," the "Good Society" (Lippman) and the "Open Society" (Popper) represent approximately the same idea as the "Responsible Society."

[17] Karl Barth, *Against the System* (London: SCM Press, 1954), p. 44. Barth, despite his tendency to place Christianity in the realm of the transcendent, says also: "When I consider the deepest and most central content of the New Testament exhortation, I shall say that we are justified, from the point of view of exegesis, in regarding the 'democratic conception of the state' as a justifiable expression of the thought of the New Testament." *Church and State*, trans. by G. Roland Howe (London: SCM Press, 1939), p. 80. One recalls also the memorable epigram of R. Niebuhr: "Man's capacity for justice makes democracy possible; but man's inclination to injustice makes democracy necessary." *The Children of Darkness and the Children of Light* (New York: Charles Scribner's Sons, 1944), p. xi.

[18] Karl Barth, *Church and State*, p. 90.

[19] "Report of Section III," *Evanston Speaks*, p. 51.

[20] C. L. Patijn, "The Strategy of the Church," *MDGD*, III, p. 163.

[21] "Report of Section III," *MDGD*, III, p. 194.

[22] "Message of the Universal Christian Conference on Life and Work," (Stockholm, 1925), para. 6. Cited by Muelder, *op. cit.*, p. 14.

[23] "Conclusions," Ecumenical Study Conference on the Church and the Problem of Social Order (Rengsdorf, 1933), para. 5. Cited by Muelder, *ibid.*, p. 15.

[24] J. H. Oldham, "The Respnsible Society, *op. cit.*, p. 137.

[25] J. H. Oldham, "Technics and Civilization," *MDGD*, III, p. 29.

[26] Jacques Ellul, "The Situation in Europe," *MDGD*, III, p. 56. Brunner attributes the sickness of contemporary anxiety to "the reduction of the human person to a cog in the social machine, and the disintegration of organic community life." Emil Brunner, "And Now," *MDGD*, III, p. 176.

[27] Ellul, *op. cit.*, pp. 58f.

[28] *Ibid.*, p. 123.

[29] Cited by Duff, *op. cit.*, p. 185.

[30] *Ibid.*, pp. 126ff.

[31] *Ibid.*, pp. 130ff.

[32] *Ibid.*, p. 131.

[33] Cf. S. Paul Schilling, "The Christian Basis of Rights, Freedoms, and Responsibilties," *The Church and Society Responsibility*, pp. 12ff.

[34] *The Children of Darkness and the Children of Light* (New York: Charles Scribner's Sons, 1947), p. 114.

[35] The World Council Study Booklet, *Christian Action in Society*, contains summary acknowledgment of the weakness of the program of social action of the churches: "All discussion

of the church's action must begin with the admission that the church has been relatively ineffective in the sphere of social action. It has allowed secular groups and agencies to take the initiative and these rather than the church have, in the modern period, 'given form to life.'" (New York: World Council of Churches, 1949), p. 12.

[36] Edward Duff, *op. cit.*, pp. 222-223.

[37] J. H. Oldham, *The Church and its Function in Society* (New York: Willett, Clark and Co., 1937), p. 207. Admittedly an ecclesiastical pronouncement must not simply be intended to convince the church. To be honest it must represent a core of solid opinion.

[38] An outstanding example of an effective denominational pronouncement coming at a strategic time in American history is the vigorous statement prepared by John A. Mackay, the Moderator of the General Assembly of the Presbyterian Church (U.S.A.) and adopted by the General Council of that church entitled, *A Letter to Presbyterians Concerning the Present Situation in our Country and in the World*, October 321, 1953, issued by the Office of General Assembly, Philadelphia.

[39] Cf. J. H. Oldham, *The Church and its Function in Society*, p. 193.

[40] "Protestantism has a principle that stands beyond all its realizations. It is the critical and dynamic source of all Protestant realizations, but it is not identical with any of them.... It transcends them as it transcends any cultural form." Paul Tillich, *The Protestant Era*, trans. James Luther Adams (Chicago: Univ. of Chicago Press, 1948), p. 163. John Dillenberger and Claude Welch have expressed Protestantism's critical attitude toward all historical forms with these words: "Though it (Protestantism) is always expressed in cultural forms and influences culture, it cannot be bound to any one form--not even to western civilization as a whole." *Protestant Christianity* (New York: Charles Scribner's Sons, 1954), pp. 324f.

[41] R. H. Tawney insisted in a paper prepared for Oxford that Christianity should ask the question whether it has anything distinctive to say about how men ought to act toward their fellows. If it has, then, Tawney says, the Church ought "whatever the cost, to state fearlessly and in unmistakable terms what precisely they conceive that distinctive contribution to be. If they do not, then let them cease reiterating secondhand platitudes, which disgust sincere men and bring Christianity into contempt." Quoted by Oldham, *The Church and its Function in Society*, p. 197.

[42] Patijn, *op. cit.*, p. 159.

[43] *Ibid.*, p. 160.

[44] *The Church and its Function in Society*, p. 194.

[45] Bennett, *Christian Ethics and Social Policy*, p. 77.

[46] *The First Assembly of the World Council of Churches*, ed. by Visser 't Hooft (New York: Harper and Brothers, 1949), p. 80.

[47] *Evanston Speaks*, pp. 43f.

[48] Cf. John K. Galbraith, *American Capitalism--The Concept of Countervailing Power* (Cambridge, Mass.: Riverside Press, 1952).

[49] V. A. Demant, *Religion and the Decline of Capitalism* (New York: Charles Scribner's Sons, 1952), p. 27.

[50] *Ibid.*, p. 20.

[51] Cf. Edward Duff, *op. cit.*, pp. 229-232.

[52] *MDGD*, III, p. 196.

[53] The possibilities of direct service to international politics through work with the United Nations were considered favorably at the Evanston Assembly.

[54] *The Responsible Society in World Perspective*, pp. 22-23. The study by Albert T. Rasmus-

sen, *Christian Social Ethics*, is unique among the literature of its field since it describes methods of social action with the practical emphasis of a volume in Christian education. Rasmussen suggests possible community projects for the local congregation. He lists six great imperatives for building a church of influence. They are: 1) sensitize; 2) organize; 3) investigate; 4) discuss; 5) decide; 6) act, pp. 186-198.

[55] *Op. cit.*, p. 196. An emphasis upon the importance of small groups is found in the Evanston Report. It maintains that the family is most frequently neglected as an important element in the Responsible Society.

[56] Cf. William Muehl, *op. cit.*, Ch. I.

[57] J. H. Oldham has referred to "a pietistic as well as a liberal *laissez-faire*. However pious the intention, it is a denial of God's reign in the world, of the Lordship of Christ over History." "A Responsible Society," *MDGD*, III, p. 138.

[58] George A. Graham, *Morality in American Politics* (New York: Random House, 1952), p. 5.

[59] Cf. Edward LeRoy Long, Jr., *op. cit.*, pp. 8-10.

[60] Reinhold Niebuhr has frequently criticized the general tendency in Lutheranism to prefer order to justice. John C. Bennett, *Christian Realism* (New York: Charles Scribner's Sons, 1942), p. 93.

[61] John A. Hutchison speaks of the rediscovery of the social nature of the Christian faith as the "enduring achievement of the Social Gospel." "Two Decades of Social Christianity," *Christian Faith and Social Action*, p. 35.

[62] Roger L. Shinn, "The Christian Gospel and History," *Christian Faith and Social Action*, p. 35.

[63] Cf. John C. Bennett, "Reinhold Niebuhr's Social Ethics," *Reinhold Niebuhr*, ed. by Charles W. Kegley and Robert W. Betall, p. 64.

[64] The term "coalition ethics" has been introduced by Paul Ramsey in *Basic Christian Ethics*, p. 344.

[65] J. H. Oldham, *The Church and Its Function in Society*, pp. 218ff.

[66] *Ibid.*, pp. 219-220.

[67] *Ibid.*, p. 21.

[68] Hendrick Kraemer takes the position that "Christian living on the individual plane and on the social plane in the light of the dealing and will of God whose ways and thoughts are always higher than ours, cannever be stablized in any historical or theoretical system, the splendid theocratic laws of the Old Testament included. There may be systems of philosophical ethics: there can never be a system of Christian ethics, at least if it is true to its nature. That would mean to forget and deny that God is an active God whose love, holiness and justice transcend all possible standards. All legalism and moralism stand condemned under the judgment of the ever-dynamic and ever-new dimension of God's activity." Cited by Duff, *op. cit.*, p. 103.

[69] A famous essay on the historical relation of Christianity and natural law is Ernst Troeltsch, "The Ideas of Natural Law and Humanity in World Politics," published in a single volume entitled *Otto Gierke, Natural Law and the Theory of Society*, trans by Ernest Barker (Cambridge; Cambridge Univ. Press, 1950).

[70] Dietrich Bonhoeffer, *Ethics*, p. 7f.

[71] *Ibid.*, p. 22.

[72] *Ibid.*, pp. 62ff.

[73] Paul L. Lehmann, "The Foundation and Pattern of Christian Behavior," *op. cit.*, p. 99.

[74] *Ibid.*, pp. 99-100.

[75] *Ibid.*, p. 105.

[76] Reinhold Niebuhr, *Faith and History*, p. 172.

[77] *Ibid.*, p. 173.

[78] Cf. *The Divine Imperative*, Chapters XXI-XXIV.

[79] *Ibid.*, pp. 220-221.

[80] *Ibid.*, p. 221.

[81] *Ibid.*, Ch. XII.

[82] Cf. Heinz Dietrich Wendland, "The Relevance of Ethics," *Ecumenical Review*, V (July, 1953), 4, p. 364.

[83] W. A. Visser 't Hooft, *The Kingship of Christ* (New York: Harper and Brothers 1948), p. 83.

[84] An attempt to understand the meaning of ethical terms familiar to the Christian's vocabulary by ontological analysis is Paul Tillich's *Love, Power and Justice*. Tillich says, "Ontology asks the question of being, i.e., of something that is present to everybody at every moment," p. 23. Without denying the value of the ontological approach to philosophical ethics, it must be insisted that ontology must be subordinate to history for purposes of Christian doctrine and ethics.

[85] John Bright, *The Kingdom of God*, pp. 244ff. See also Amos N. Wilder, *Eschatology and Ethics in the Teaching of Jesus*, rev. ed. (New York: Harper and Brothers, 1950), p. 13f.

[86] *The Kingship of Christ*, p. 83.

[87] Cf. Duff, pp. 140ff.

[88] James Hastings Nichols, *Evanston--An Interpretation* (New York: Harper and Brothers, 1954), p. 88.

[89] *Ibid.*

[90] This is the position of Robert Calhoun who delivered an address at the opening of the meeting of the Assembly. Calhoun, by no means a "humanist," reflected, nevertheless, the relevance of the Christian message for the world. He repeats the American tendency to hope for the Kingdom to come to earth. The Gospel's "most characteristic prayer is 'thy kingdom come, thy will be done on earth.' Its characteristic hope looks for the...manifestations of God's sovereignty and the power of His promises in human history." H. G. G. Kerklots, *Looking at Evanston* (London: SCM Press, 1954), pp. 28-29.

[91] *Ibid.*, p. 31.

[92] Report of Section III, *MDGD*, III, p. 192.

[93] Duff says: "At bottom, the subject preoccupying Amsterdam's thinking on cultural, political and ecumenical affairs was the consequences of modern industrialism." *Op. cit.*, p. 172.

[94] Report of Section III, *MDGD*, III, p. 192.

[95] *Op. cit.*

[96] *Op. cit.*, pp. 144ff.

[97] Cullmann, *Christ and Time*, p. 198.

[98] *Evanston Speaks*, p. 47.

[99] *Ibid.*, p. 48.

[100] Wilhelm Niesel, *The Theology of Calvin*, trans. by Harold Knight (Philadelphia: Westminster Press, 1956), p. 231.

[101] One of the fundamental observations of Troeltsch is that the ideal of the Christian unity of civilization which was inherited by Protestantism from the Middle Ages remains the Protestant ideal in the modern period even though conditions have so drastically changed. He

says, "this ideal is still retained as a natural fundamental theory which only needs to be placed on a new basis." *STCC*, I, p. 202.

[102] An exception to the rule is found in the "Waldeck Catechism" of 1778. To the question, "By whom did God create all things?" the answer is, "He created all things by Jesus Christ, by whom also he made the worlds." (Eph. 3:9; Heb. 1:2).

CONCLUSION

The writer has attempted to set forth the problem of social responsibility from the Mennonite perspective. This has involved not only an analysis of contemporary social policy of the Mennonites but also a study of the most significant theological ideas upon which Mennonite social policy rests--especially the idea of discipleship and the idea of the church.

In conclusion, the writer wishes to underscore the fundamental conflict in which Mennonites are involved. It is the conflict between a professed ethical absolutism in the form of nonresistance, the "way of the cross," the simple life and the relativities of the social order. Traditionally Mennonites have assumed that this conflict could be resolved by retreat into the simplicities of semi-independent agrarian communities. In recent years, however, (especially within the past fifteen years), cultural isolation has become impossible. The industrial and technical revolutions have been invading Mennonite communities at an alarming rate. As a result, the community life of Mennonites has changed drastically. The simplicity, the independence, the mutuality of Mennonite life have been replaced to a considerable extent by the complexity, the bureaucracy, the interdependence, the "other-directedness" and the power struggle of society. Undoubtedly an objective analysis of traditional Mennonite life would indicate that relations within the Mennonite community have never been totally separated from the evils of world culture. However, it is reasonable to say that the social and economic revolutions of modern times, which have turned the basically agrarian economy into a highly organized industrial and technical society, are challenging Mennonite ethics in much the same way that the thought of Ernst Troeltsch and Reinhold Niebuhr was challenged earlier in this country. The question which Troeltsch and Niebuhr asked was: How can Christ's absolute ethic of love become relevant to the structure of modern life. Ernst Troeltsch asked this question in the face of the Marxian interpretation of social dynamics and Niebuhr asked this question in the context of economic conflict in Detroit in the 1920's. Both came to the conclusion that the love ethic of Christ cannot be applied directly to the affairs of society. This is not to deny the relevance of the Gospel for the economic and political realms. It does mean, however, that the Gospel ethic cannot be applied as an operative principle. The result has been a revolution in ethics comparable to the revolution in society.

In the light of this development (assuming that Mennonites will not pull out of the modern social ethos),[1] the question arises whether they will be forced to reconsider their traditional social policy. It is the writer's conviction that the present crisis in Mennonite life will require a revision of the present Mennonite approach to society. This is not to suggest that Mennonites should consider "selling out" to world culture because of the intrinsic difficulties of embodying the ethic of Christ in the power arena. Rather it is to suggest that Mennonites must seek their traditional goals of brotherhood, peace and mutuality under the conditions of compromise. Mennonites must realize that they are a part of the world-system and that they share the guilt and responsibility for corporate evil and that their attempts to be obedient to Christ and "be" the true church must take into consideration the "ambiguities" of their actual situation. This realistic approach will prevent perfectionistic illusions and despair.

Specifically, a place must be made in Mennonite ethics for power. Traditionally the Mennonite position has assumed that Christians can live without the exercise of power--that is, power in the form of compulsion and force. It may be agreed that, given the ideal combination of saintliness and simplicity, a small Christian society can live with a minimum amount of power. But certainly business organizations, educational institutions and even highly organized mutual aid societies cannot operate by the pure principles of the "love feast." All institutions are to a certain degree political in character even though the service motive and personal piety can mitigate the political principle. For this reason Mennonites must re-examine the validity of nonresistance as a comprehensive norm for all Christian relations. It is the view of the writer that if nonresistance were actually practiced as an absolute principle, it would literally take Christians out of this world. A practical alternative would be nonviolent resistance as an approximation of the absolute ideal, which affords at the same time an opportunity to participate in the "ambiguous" struggles for justice in society.

Furthermore, the Mennonite ethic must be reconsidered from the standpoint of its complete neglect of justice as a Christian goal. As stated earlier, justice has virtually no place in the Mennonite vocabulary. This has led to confusion as well as social apathy. If has left Mennonites without a word to describe the vast majority of their dealings with each other since justice is the basic norm of economic life. The most unfortunate result of the neglect of justice is, however, the tendency to shy away from the social problems of the world where justice, rather than pure love, characterizes both the method and the goal of social action. It is true that the Mennonite emphasis on love has had the advantage of going straight to the heart of the Christian ethic. However, it is a fact of social existence that love must take the form of justice if it is to be effective.

But before the practical decision can be made regarding the extent of Mennonite participation in society, certain prior decisions must be made on the level of hermeneutics. Today Mennonite Biblical hermeneutics are in an uncertain state. To thoughtful Mennonites it is no longer clear, for example, just how literally Jesus' commands are to be kept. It is uncertain which of Jesus' commands are "binding" and whether the relation of the church to society in the New Testament is normative for all later periods. It is uncertain whether the ethic of Jesus and the ethic of Paul are basically the same and to what extent the Old Testament may be used as a guide for Christian conduct. Problems of interpretation such as these could be greatly extended. Suffice to say, that the problem of social responsibility as it is faced by the Mennonite church is baffling not only because of the universally admitted practical difficulty of knowing how to influence society but also because Mennonites (like many other groups) are not certain of their presuppositions. Until Mennonites produce a system of ethics which will have wrestled both with the essentials of Christianity on the one hand and the realities of modern life on the other hand, no final solution to the problem of social responsibility will be possible.

Despite these uncertainties, it is the conviction of the writer that some of the peculiar practices and theological emphases of Mennonites should be continued and actually extended. Emphasis upon non-conformity to the world should be emphasized, especially in view of the current tendency toward mass conformity. The tendency of the universal church to identify itself uncritically with the prevailing culture must be counter-balanced by the sectarian emphasis upon obedience to Christ. Over against the growing institutional character of church life, Mennonites may witness to the place of Christian brotherhood in the life of the church. In the area of social service, the unique personal ministry of Mennonites to human suffering in the form of voluntary relief and rehabilitation service should be multiplied. The most difficult area of Mennonite life, the area of peace education, also opens before the Mennonites an overwhelming responsibility, especially in view of the atomic crisis. It must be assumed that greater interest in social and political affairs should not displace those attitudes and practices which were authentically Christian and which lie most closely to the internal life of the Church of Christ.

In view of modern, dynamic, social pluralism, the time is probably past for comprehensive and final social policies. At best, Mennonites can formulate a general policy for the future which will be kept flexible at many points for the guidance of the Holy Spirit.

Endnote

1 To assume that Mennonites will remain in their present position of involvement is to discount as a live possibility what is frequently considered the most strategic solution to the Mennonite problem, i.e., the communistic colony in the manner of the Hutterites or the Society of Brothers. From the standpoint of the radical principles of the Anabaptist-Mennonite tradition, it would appear that these principles can be expressed with less conflict in communism than in any other social form. In Christian communism the very "structure" of social relations is designed to make pure love a social possibility. It is the view of the writer that the communistic Christian community would be the answer to the Mennonite problem if the criteria for judgment were limited to the internal principles of Anabaptism. A small number of Mennonites have joined Hutterite colonies in recent years. There has been, however, no large scale acceptance of Christian communism.

BIBLIOGRAPHY

A. *Primary Sources*

Aquinas, Thomas, *Summa Theologica*, III, Institute of Mediaeval Studies of
    Ottawa, 4 vols., Ottawa: College Dominicain d' Ottawa, 1941.
Ausbund, Lancaster, Penna.: Lancaster Press, Inc., 1941.
Calvin, John, *Institutes of the Christian Religion*, John Allen, translator; Vol. II,
    Philadelphia: Presbyterian Board of Christian Education, 1936.
Chronik der Hutterischen Bruder, Die älteste, A. J. F. Zieglschmid, editor;
    Ithica, New York: Cayuga Press, Inc., 1943.
Complete Works of Menno Simons, The, Elkhart, Indiana: John F. Funk and
    Brother, 1871.
Complete Writings of Menno Simons, The, Leonard Verduin, translator; John
    C. Wenger, editor; Scottdale, Penna.: Herald Press, 1956.
Egli, Emil, *Aktensamlung zur Geschichte der Züricher Reformation 1519-1533*,
    Zürich, 1878.
Kierkegaard, Soren, *Attack Upon "Christendom,"* Walter Lowrie, translator;
    Princeton, New Jersey: Princeton University Press, 1946.
Letter to the Continental Congress in 1775, Pennsylvania State Archives, Eight
    Series, 8:7349. Copy in Mennonite Historical Library, Goshen,
    Indiana.
Luther, Martin, *Works, Weimarer Ausgabe*, Kirchenpostille, 1922.
_____, "Secular Authority," *Works*, Philadelphia Edition.
Melanchthons Werke, I, Reformatorische Schriften, Robert Stupperich, editor;
    Güterisch: C. Bertelsmann, 1951.
Mode, G. P., *Sourcebook and Bibliographical Guide for American Church His-
    tory*, Menasha, Wisconsin: Collegiate Press, 1921.
*Quellen und Forschungen Zur Geschichte der oberdeutschen Taufgesinnten im
    16, Jahrhundert*, J. Loserth, editor; Wien und Leipzig: Carl Fromm,
    1929.
Plato, *The Republic*, Benjamin Jowett, translator; New York: Willey Book
    Co., 1901.
Ridemann, Peter, *Confession of Faith* (1565), K. E. Hasenberg, translator;
    Suffolk: Hodder and Stoughton, Ltd., 1950.
_____, *Rechenschaft unserer Religion, Lehre und Glaubens*, Berne: Hut-
    terischen Brüder Gemeine, 1902.
_____, *Rechenschaft unserer Religion, Lehr und Glaubens, von den Brüdern*,

so man die Hutterischen nennt, ausgongen . . .1565, Ashton Keynes, Wilts, England: Cottswold-Bruderhof, 1938.

Thomas a Kempis, *The Imitation of Christ*, Aloysius Croft and Harry F. Bolton, translators; Book I, Milwaukee: Bruce Publishing Company, 1940.

Van Braght, Thieleman J., *Martyr's Mirror*, Joseph H. Sohm, translator; Scottdale, Penna.: Mennonite Publishing House, 1950.

Walpot, Peter, *A Notable Hutterite Document*, Shrapshire, England: Plough Publishing House, 1957.

B. *Official Documents of the Mennonite Church*

Activity Summary Number II, Akron, Penna.: Mennonite Disaster Service, 1956.

"Basis of Understanding," Copy available at Mennonite Historical Library, Goshen, Indiana, 1941.

Christian Race Relations; Proceedings on Christian Community Relations, Scottdale, Penna.: Committee on Economic and Social Relations, 1955.

Directory of Mennonite Employers, Unpublished document of the Mennonite Research Foundation, Goshen, Indiana, March, 1956.

"Disciple of Christ and the State, The," *Report of the Mennonite Central Committee Peace Section Study Conference, Winona Lake, 1950*, Mennonite Historical Library, Goshen, Indiana, 1950.

Minutes of the Virginia Mennonite Conference, 2nd edition, Scottdale, Penna.: Virginia Mennonite Conference, 1950.

Report of the Twelfth General Conference, Mennonite Historical Library, Goshen, Indiana, 1921.

Report of the Fourteenth Mennonite General Conference, Mennonite Historical Library, Goshen, Indiana, 1925.

Report of the Fifteenth Mennonite General Conference, Mennonite Historical Library, Goshen, Indiana, 1927.

Report of the Sixteenth Mennonite General Conference, Mennonite Historical Library, Goshen, Indiana, 1929.

Report of the Seventeenth Mennonite General Conference, Mennonite Historical Library, Goshen, Indiana, 1931.

Report of the Twentieth Mennonite General Conference, Mennonite Historical Library, Goshen, Indiana, 1937.

Snyder, William T., *The Program and Planning for 1957*, Akron, Penna.: Menonite Central Committee, 1957.

Twenty-ninth Mennonite General Conference, Hesston, Kansas, August 23-26, 1955, Scottdale, Penna.: Mennonite Publishing House, 1955.

"Way of Christian Love in Race Relations, The," Adopted by General Conference. Mennonite Historical Library, Goshen, Indiana, 1955.

C. *Secondary Sources*

Anderson, Bernhard W., *Understanding the Old Testament*, Englewood Cliffs, New Jersey, 1957.

Bainton, Roland H., *Here I Stand*, New York: Abingdon-Cokesbury Press, 1950.

_____, *The Travail of Religious Liberty*, Philadelphia: Westminster Press, 1951.

Barth, Karl, *Against the Stream*, London: SCM Press, 1954.

_____, *Church and State*, G. Roland Howe, translator; London: SCM Press, 1939.

Bates, Searle M., *Religious Liberty, an Inquiry*, New York: International Missionary Council, 1945.

Beach, Waldo and Niebuhr, H. Richard, *Christian Ethics*, New York: Ronald Press, 1955.

Bender, Harold S., *Conrad Grebel*, Goshen College, Goshen, Indiana: Mennonite Historical Society, 1950.

Bennett, John C., *The Christian as Citizen*, New York: Associated Press, 1955.

_____, *Christian Ethics and Social Policy*, New York: Charles Scribner's Sons, 1946.

_____, *Christian Realism*, New York: Charles Scribner's Sons, 1942.

Bernstein, Eduard, *Sozialismus und Demokratie in der grossen englischen Revolution*, Stuttgart: J. H. W. Dietz, 1922.

Blanke, Fritz, *Brüder in Christo, Die Geschichte der ältesten Taufergemeinde*, Zürich: Zwingli-Verlag, 1955.

Boehr, Karl H., *The Secularization Among the Mennonites*, B.D. Thesis, University of Chicago, 1942.

Bohatec, Joseph, *Calvins Lehre von Staat und Kirche*, Breslau: M.H. Marcus, 1937.

Bonhoeffer, Dietrich, *The Cost of Discipleship*, R. H. Fuller, translator; New York: Macmillan Company, 1949.

_____, *Ethics*, Eberhard Bethge, editor, H. H. Smith, translator; London: SCM Press, 1955.

Bowen, Howard, *The Social Responsibilities of the Business Man*, New York: Harper and Brothers, 1953.

Bright, John, *The Kingdom of God*, New York: Abingdon Press, 1953.

Brunner, Emil, *The Divine Imperative*, Olive Wyon, translator; Philadelphia: Westminster Press, 1947.

_____, *Justice and the Social Order*, New York: Harper and Brothers, 1945.

Cadoux, C. J., *The Early Church and the World*, Edinburgh: T. and T. Clark, 1925.

Carlson, Edgar M., *The Church and the Public Conscience*, Philadelphia: Muhlenberg Press, 1956.

Carlyle, R. W., and A. J., *A History of Mediaeval Political Theory*, vol. II, 3rd edition, London: William Blackwood and Sons, Ltd., 1936.

Channing, William Ellery, *Discourses On War*, Boston: Gin and Company, 1903.

Childs, Marquis, and Cater, Douglas, *Ethics in a Business Society*, New York: Harper and Brothers, 1954.

Christian Action in Society, World Council Study Booklet, New York: World Council of Churches, 1949.

Cochrane, Charles Norris, *Christianity and Classical Culture*, New York: Oxford University Press, 1944.

Commager, Henry Steel, *The American Mind*, New Haven: Yale University Press, 1950.

Cullmann, Oscar, *Christ and Time*, Floyd V. Filson, translator; Philadelphia: Westminster Press, 1950.

_____, *The State in the New Testament*, New York: Charles Scribner's Sons, 1956.

Dawson, Christopher, *Religion and the Rise of Western Culture*, New York: Sheed and Ward, 1950.

Demant, V. A., *Religion and the Decline of Capitalism*, New York: Charles Scribner's Sons, 1952.

Die Geschichte--Bücher der Wiedertäufer in Osterreich-Ungarn, Josef Beck, editor; Wein: Carl Gerald's Sohn, 1883.

Dillistone, F. W., *The Structure of the Divine Society*, Philadelphia: Westminster Press, 1951.

Duff, Edward, *The Social Thought of the World Council of Churches*, New York: Associated Press, 1956.

Farner, Alfred, *Die Lehre von Kirche und Staat bei Zwingli*, Tubingen: J.C.B. Mohr, 1930.

Ferré, Nels F. S., *Christianity and Society*, New York: Harper and Brothers, 1950.

First Assembly of the World Council of Churches, The, Visser 't Hooft, editor; New York: Harper and Brothers, 1949.

Forrell, George Wolfgang, *Faith Active in Love*, New York: American Press, 1954.

Francis, E. K., *In Search of Utopia*, Altona, Manitoba: D. W. Friesen and Sons, Ltd., 1955.

Fretz, J. Winfield, *Pilgrims in Paraguay*, Scottdale, Penna.: Herald Press, 1953.

_____, *A Study of Mennonite Religious Institutions*, Abstract, Chicago: University of Chicago Library, June, 1940.

Friedmann, Robert, *Mennonite Piety Through the Centuries*, Goshen, Indiana: Mennonite Historical Society, 1949.

Fromm, Erich, *The Sane Society*, New York: Rinehart and Company, 1955.

Galbraith, John K., *American Capitalism--The Concept of Countervailing Power*, Cambridge, Massachusetts: Riverside Press, 1952.

Gierke, Otto, *Genossenschaftsrecht*, 4 vols., Berlin: Weidmannsche Buchhandlung, 1868-1913.

_____, *Political Theories of the Middle Age*, F. W. Maitland, translator; Cambridge: Cambridge University Press, 1900.

Gingerich, Melvin, *Mennonites in Iowa*, Iowa City, Iowa: State Historical Society of Iowa, 1939.

_____, *Service for Peace*, Akron, Penna.: Mennonite Central Committee,

1949.

Glaubenszeugnisse oberdeutscher Taufgesinnten, Lydia Müller, editor; Leipzig: M. Heinsuis Nachf., 1938.

Graham, George A., *Morality in American Politics*, New York: Random House, 1952.

Handbook of the Mennonite Central Committee, 1954, Scottdale, Penna.: Mennonite Publishing House, 1954.

Harkness, Georgia, *John Calvin*, New York: Henry Holt and Company, 1931.

Heering, G. J., *The Fall of Christianity*, J. W. Thompson, translator; London: George Allen and Unwin, Ltd., 1938.

Heimann, Franz, *Die Lehre von der Kirche und Gemeinschaft in der hutterischen Täufergemeinde*, Doctoral Dissertation, University of Vienna, 1927.

Heinecken, Martin J., *The Moment Before God*, Philadelphia: Muhlenberg Press, 1956.

Henry, Carl F. H., *The Uneasy Conscience of Modern Fundamentalism*, Grand Rapids, Michigan: William B. Eerdmans Publishing Company, 1947.

Herklots, H. G. G., *Looking at Evanston*, London: SCM Press, 1954.

Hershberger, Guy F., *The Mennonite Church in the Second World War*, Scottdale, Penna.: Mennonite Publishing House, 1951.

_____, *Non-resistance and the State--The Pennsylvania Experiment in Politics*, Scottdale, Penna.: Mennonite Publishing House, 1936.

_____, *War, Peace and Nonresistance*, Scottdale, Penna.: Herald Press, 1944.

_____, *The Way of the Cross in Human Relations*, Unpublished Manuscript, Goshen, Indiana, 1956.

Hillerbrand, Hans J., *Die Politische Ethik des oberdeutschen Täufertums...des 16. Jahrhunderts*, Erlangen, Unpublished Doctoral Dissertation, 1957.

Hofmann, Hans, *The Theology of Reinhold Niebuhr*, Louise Pettibone Smith, translator; New York: Charles Scribner's Sons, 1956.

Holl, Karl, *Gesammelte Aufsätze zur Kirchengeschichte*, Tubingen: J. C. B. Mohr, 1923.

Hordern, William, *Christianity, Communism and History*, New York: Abingdon Press, 1954.

Horsch, John, *The Hutterian Brethren, 1528-1931*, Goshen, Indiana: Mennonite Historical Society, 1931.

_____, *Mennonites in Europe*, Scottdale, Penna.: Mennonite Publishing House, 1950.

Hudson, Winthrop C., *The Great Tradition of the American Churches*, New York: Harper and Brothers, 1953.

Hutchison, John A., editor, *Christian Faith and Social Action*, New York: Charles Scribner's Sons, 1953.

Jenny, Beatrice, *Das Schleitheimer Täuferbekenntnis 1927*, Thaynagen: Karl Augustin, 1951.

Kautsky, Karl, *Die Vorlaufer des neueren Sozialismus*, Stuttgart: J. H. H. Dietz, 1895.

Kierkegaard, Soren, *Concluding Unscientific Postscript*, David F. Swenson and Walter Lowrie, translators; Princeton, New Jersey: Princeton University Press, 1941.

Kiwiet, Jan J., *Hans Denk and His Teaching*, Unpublished B.D. Thesis, Ruschlikon-Zürich: Baptist Theological Seminary, February, 1954.

_____, *Pilgram Marpeck*, Doctoral Dissertation, Zürich, April, 1955.

Klausner, Joseph, *Jesus of Nazareth*, London: George Allen and Unwin, Ltd., 1925.

Kollmorgen, Walter M., *Culture of a Contemporary Rural Community*, Rural Life Studies: 4, U.S. Department of Agriculture, September, 1942.

Kroner, Richard, *Culture and Faith*, Chicago: University of Chicago Press, 1951.

Kühn, Johannes, *Toleranz und Offenbarung*, Leipzig: F. Meiner, 1923.

Lind, Ivan R., *The Labor Union Movement in the Light of Nonresistance as Held by the Mennonite Church*, Unpublished thesis, Mennonite Historical Library, Goshen, Indiana, 1941.

Littell, Franklin H., *The Anabaptist View of the Church*, New York: American Society of Church History, 1952.

Long, Edward LeRoy, *Conscience and Compromise*, Philadelphia: Westminster Press, 1954.

Mayer, J. P., *Max Weber and German Politics*, London: Faber and Faber, 1943.

Mennonite Community Sourcebook, Esko Loewen, editor; Akron, Penna.: Civilian Public Service, Mennonite Central Committee, 1946.

Mennonite Encyclopedia, The, Harold S. Bender and C. Henry Smith, editors; 3 vols., Scottdale, Penna.: Mennonite Publishing House, 1955.

Mennonite Yearbook and Almanac, Goshen College Library, Goshen, Indiana, 1910.

Muehl, William, *Politics for Christians*, New York: Associated Press, 1955.

Muelder, Walter G., *The Idea of the Responsible Society*, Boston: Boston University Press, 1955.

Müller, Lydia, editor; *Glaubenszeugnisse oberdeutscher Taufgesinnten*, Leipzig: M. Heinsuis Nachf., 1938.

Muralt, Leonhard von, *Konrad Grebel als Student in Paris*, Zürich, 1936.

Neff, Christian, *Die Taufgesinnten-Gemeinden*, Karlsruhe: Heinrich Schneider, 1931.

Newbigin, Lesslie, *The Household of Faith*, New York: Friendship Press, 1953.

Nichols, James Hastings, *Evanston--An Interpretation*, New York: Harper and Brothers, 1954.

Niebuhr, Reinhold, *Faith and History*, New York: Charles Scribner's Sons, 1951.

_____, *An Interpretation of Christian Ethics*, New York: Harper and Brothers, 1935.

_____, *Moral Man and Immoral Society*, New York: Charles Scribner's Sons, 1932.

_____, *The Children of Darkness and the Children of Light*, New York: Charles Scribner's Sons, 1944.

_____, *The Nature and Destiny of Man*, vol. II, London: Nisbet and Company, 1943.

_____, *Reflections on the End of an Era*, New York: Charles Scribner's Sons, 1934.

Niebuhr, H. Richard, *Christ and Culture*, New York: Harper and Brothers, 1951.

_____, *The Kingdom of God in America*, Chicago: Willett, Clark and Company, 1937.

_____, *The Social Sources of Denominationalism*, New York: H. Holt and Company, 1929.

Niesel, Wilhelm, *The Theology of Calvin*, Harold Knight, translator; Philadelphia: Westminster Press, 1956.

Nygren, Anders, *Agape and Eros*, Philip S. Watson, translator; London: SPCK, 1953.

Oldham, J. H. *The Church and its Function in Society*, New York: Willett, Clark and Company, 1937.

Parsons, Talcott, *The Structure of Social Action: A Study in Social Theory with Special Reference to Recent European Writers*, New York: McGraw-Hill Book Company, 1937.

Peachey, Paul, *Die soziale Herkunft der Schweitzer Täufer in der Reformationszeit*, Karlsruhe: Heinrich Schneider, 1954.

Petry, Ray C., *Francis of Assisi*, Durham, North Carolina: Duke University Press, 1941.

Pope, Liston, *Millhands and Preachers*, New Haven: Yale University Press, 1942.

Prenter, Regin, *Spiritus Creator*, John M. Jensen, translator; Philadelphia: Muhlenberg Press, 1953.

Ramsey, Paul, *Basic Christian Ethics*, New York: Charles Scribner's Sons, 1951.

Rasmussen, Albert T., *Christian Social Ethics*, Englewood Cliffs, New Jersey, 1956.

Rauschenbusch, Walter, *Christianity and the Social Crisis*, New York: Macmillan Company, 1912.

_____, *Christianizing the Social Order*, New York: Macmillan Company, 1917.

Recovery of the Anabaptist Vision, The, Guy F. Hershberger, editor; Scottdale, Penna.: Herald Press, 1957.

Rempel, David G., *The Mennonite Colonies in New Russia*, Doctoral Dissertation, Stanford University, 1933.

Responsible Society in a World Perspective, The, New York: Harper and Brothers, 1954.

Richardson, Alan, *The Biblical Doctrine of Work*, London: SCM Press, 1952.

Rieker, Karl, *Rechtliche Stellung der evangelischen Kirche Deutschland in ihrer geschtliche Entwicklung bis zur Gegenwart*, Leipzig: Hirshgeld, 1893.

Riesman, David, *The Lonely Crowd*, New Haven: Yale University Press, 1950.

Rowe, H. K., *History of Religion in United States*, New York: Macmillan Company, 1924.

Showalter, Mary Emma, *Mennonite Community Cookbook*, Philadelphia: Winston, 1950.

Smith, C. Henry, *The Mennonite Immigration to Pennsylvania*, Norristown, Penna.: Norristown Press, 1929.

_____, *The Story of the Mennonites*, Berne, Indiana: Mennonite Book Concern, 1941.

Smithson, R. J., *The Anabaptists*, London: James Clarke, 1935.

Sohm, Rudolph, *Kirchenrecht*, vols. I and II, Leipzig: Duncker & Humbolt, 1892.

Sorokin, P.A., *The Crisis of Our Age*, New York: E. P. Dutton and Company, 1941.

Spann, Richard, editor; *The Church and Social Responsibility*, New York: Abingdon-Cokesbury Press, 1953.

Tillich, Paul, *Love, Power and Justice*, London: Oxford University Press, 1954.

_____, *The Protestant Era*, James Luther Adams, translator; Chicago: University of Chicago Press, 1948.

Tocqueville, Alexis de, *Democracy in America*, New York: Knopf, 1945.

Tolstoy, Leo, *My Confession, My Religion*, Mary K. Tolstoy, translator; New York: T. Y. Crowell and Company, 1899.

_____, *The Kingdom of God is Within You*, Leo Wiener, translator; Boston: Dona Estes and Company, 1905.

_____, *The Law of Love and the Law of Violence*, Mary K. Tolstoy, translator; New York: Rudolph Field, 1948.

Toynbee, Arnold J., *A Study of History*, vol. V, 5th edition, London: Oxford University Press, 1951.

Troeltsch, Ernst, *Soziallehren der christlichen Kirchen und Gruppen*, I, Tübingen: J. C. B. Mohr, 1919.

_____, *The Social Teachings of the Christian Churches*, 2 vols., Olive Wyon, translator; 3rd edition, London: George Allen and Unwin, Ltd., 1931.

Unruh, John D., *In the Name of Christ: A History of the Mennonite Central Committee*, Scottdale, Penna.: Herald Press, 1952.

Van Kirk, W. W., *Religion Renounces War*, Chicago: Willett, Clark and Company, 1934.

Visser 't Hooft, W.A., *Memorandum on the Ethical Reality and Functions of the Church*, Mimeographed, Geneva: Study Department of the World Council of Churches, 1940.

_____, *The Kingship of Christ*, New York: Harper and Brothers, 1948.

Wach, Joachim, *Church, Denomination and Sect*, Evanston, Illinois: Seabury-Western Theological Seminary, 1946.

_____, *Sociology of Religion*, Chicago: University of Chicago Press, 1944.

Welch, Claude, *Protestant Christianity*, New York: Charles Scribner's Sons,

1954.

Wenger, John C., *The Doctrines of the Mennonites*, Scottdale, Penna.: Mennonite Publishing House, 1950.

———, *Introduction to Theology*, Scottdale, Penna.: Herald Press, 1954.

———, *Glimpses of Mennonite History and Doctrine*, Scottdale, Penna.: Herald Press, 1947.

———, *History of the Mennonites of the Franconia Conference*, Telford, Penna.: Franconia Mennonite Historical Society, 1937.

Whitehead, Alfred North, *Adventures of Ideas*, New York: Macmillan Company, 1933.

Wilder, Amos N., *Eschatology and Christian Ethics*, New York: Harper and Brothers, 1950.

———, *Eschatology and Ethics in the Teaching of Jesus*, rev. edition, New York: Harper and Brothers, 1950.

Williams, George H., and Mergal, Angel M., *Spiritual and Anabaptist Writers*, Philadlephia: Westminster Press, 1957.

Wright, G. Ernest, *The Biblical Doctrine of Man in Society*, London: SCM Press, Ltd., 1954.

Yoder, Sanford, *For Conscience Sake*, Scottdale, Penna.: Herald Press, 1945.

D. *Official Government Documents*

Bender, Harold S., National Reserve Plan: Hearings Before Subcommittee No.1 of the Committee on Armed Services, House of Representatives Eighty-fourth Congress, Washington: U. S. Printing Office, 1955.

E. *Articles and Essays*

Agee, James, *Partisan Review*, (February, 1950), pp. 108-109.

Albrecht, Paul, "Christian Action in Society," *Ecumencial Review*, II, (Winter, 1950), pp. 141-151.

Bainton, Roland, A. "The Anabaptist Contribution to History," *The Recovery of the Anabaptist Vision*, Guy F. Hershberger, editor; Scottdale, Penna.: Herald Press, 1957.

———, "Ernst Troeltsch--Thirty Years Later," *Theology Today*, Hugh T. Kerr, Jr., Editor ; VIII (April, 1951), pp. 70-96.

———, "The Sectarian Theory of the Church" *Christendom*, XI (Summer, 1946), pp. 382-387.

———, "The Struggle for Religious Liberty," *Church History*, X (1941), pp. 95-124.

Baker, O.E., "The Effects of Urbanization on American Life and on the Church," *Mennonite Quarterly Review*, XIX (April, 1945), pp. 117-142.

Barth, Karl, "The Christian Community in the Midst of Political Change," *Against the Stream*, London: SCM Press, Ltd., 1954, pp. 53-124.

Bauman, Harvey W., "Pray--Vote: Which?" *Gospel Herald*, XLII (October1, 1951), p. 1071.

Bender, Harold S., "The Anabaptists and Religious Liberty of the 16th Century," *Archiv für Reformationsgeschichte*, Jahrg. 44 (1953), pp. 32-51.

————, "The Anabaptist Theology of Discipleship," *Mennonite Quarterly Review*, XXIV (January, 1950), pp. 25-32.

————, "Anabaptist Vision," *Church History*, VIII (March, 1944), pp. 3-24.

————, "Church and State in Mennonite History," *Mennonite Quarterly Review*, XIII (April, 1939), pp. 83-103.

————, "The Mennonite Conception of the Church," *Mennonite Quarterly Review*, XIX (April, 1945), pp. 90-100.

————, "Pacifism of the Sixteenth Century Anabaptists," *Church History*, XXIV (June, 1955), pp. 119-131.

Bennett, John C., "Reinhold Niebuhr's Social Ethics," *Reinhold Niebuhr*, Charles W. Kegley and Robert W. Bretall, editors; Macmillan Company, 1956, pp. 46-77.

Bossert, Gustave, "Michael Sattler's Trial and Martyrdom in 1527," *Mennonite Quarterly Review*, XXV (January, 1951), pp. 201-180.

Brunner, Emil, "And Now," *Man's Disorder and God's Design*, III, New York: Harper and Brothers, n.d., pp. 176-180.

Correll, Ernst, "The Sociological and Economic Significance of the Mennonites as a Cultural Group in History," *Mennonite Quarterly Review*, XVI (July, 1942), pp. 161-166.

————, "Harold S. Bender and Anabaptist Research," *The Recovery of the Anabaptist Vision*, Guy F. Hershberger, editor; Scottdale, Penna.: Herald Press, 1957, pp. 13-28.

Eby, Kermit, "Education for Sectarians," *Gospel Messenger*, Vol. 104 (April 23, 1955), pp. 6-9.

Ellul, Jacques, "The Situation in Europe," *Man's Disorder and God's Design*, III, New York: Harper and Brothers, n.d., pp. 50-60.

Erb, Paul, "The Religious Basis of the Mennonite Community," *Mennonite Quarterly Review*, XIX (April, 1945), pp. 79-85.

————, "A Vision and Its Realization," *The Mennonite Community*, I (January, 1947), pp. 8-10.

Francis, E. K., "The Russian Mennonites: From Religious to Ethnic Group," *The American Journal of Sociology*, LIV (September, 1948), pp. 101-107.

Fretz, J. Winfield, "Community," *The Mennonite Encyclopedia*, Harold S. Bender and C. Henry Smith, editors: I, Scottdale, Penna.: 1955, pp. 656-658.

————, "Mennonites and Their Economic Problems," *Mennonite Quarterly Review*, XIV (October, 1940), pp. 195-214.

————, "Reflections at the End of a Century," *Mennonite Life* (July, 1947), pp. 33-34.

Friedmann, Robert, "Anabaptism and Protestantism," *Mennonite Quarterly Review*, XXIV (January, 1950), pp. 12-24.

————, "Concerning the True Soldier of Christ," *Mennonite Quarterly*

Review, V (April, 1944), pp. 87-99.

_____, "Economic Aspects of Early Hutterite Life," *Mennonite Quarterly Review*, XXX (October, 1956), pp. 259-266.

_____, "The Epistles of the Hutterian Brethren," *Mennonite Quarterly Review*, XX (July, 1946), pp. 147-177.

_____, "Conception of an Anabaptist," *Church History*, IX (1940), pp. 341-365.

Gingerich, Melvin, "Discipleship Expressed in Alternative Service," *The Recovery of the Anabaptist Vision*, Guy F. Hershberger, editor; Scottdale, Penna.: Herald Press, 1957.

_____, "Rural Life Problems and the Mennonites," *Mennonite Quarterly Review*, XVI (July, 1942), pp. 167-173.

Handy, Robert T., "Christian Action in Perspective," *Christianity and Society*, Vol 21 (1956), pp. 10-14.

Heimann, Franz, "The Hutterite Doctrines of Church and Common Life," *Mennonite Quarterly Review*, XXVI (April, 1952), pp. 142-160.

Heinecken, Martin, J., "Kierkegaard as a Christian," *The Journal of Religion*, XXVII (January, 1957), pp. 20-30.

Hershberger, Guy F., "Appreciating the Mennonite Community," *The Mennonite Community*, I (January, 1947), pp. 6-7.

_____, "Maintaining the Mennonite Rural Community," *Mennonite Quarterly Review*, XIV (October, 1940), pp. 214-223.

_____, "Nonresistance: Its Foundation and Outreach," *Mennonite Quarterly Review*, XXIV (April, 1950), pp. 156-162.

_____, "Present Trends and Activities Among Mennonites in Their Approach to the State," Unpublished manuscript, Mennonite Historical Library, Goshen, Indiana, pp. 1-8.

_____, "Islands of Sanity," *Gospel Herald*, XLV (March 25, 1952), p. 293.

Horst, Irvin B., "Some Principles and Limitations Guiding the Christian Witness to the State," Report of Group C, Unpublished papers of Laurelville Conference, September 21-22, 1956, Peace Problems Committee, pp. 44-48.

Hutchison, John A., "Two Decades of Social Christianity," *Christian Faith and Social Action*, John A. Hutchison, editor; New York: Charles Scribner's Sons, 1953, pp. 1-22.

"Industrial Relations: A Statement adopted by the General Conference of the Brethren in Christ and by the Mennonite General Conference in 1941," *Twenty-second Mennonite General Conference*, Mennonite Historical Library, Goshen, Indiana, 1941, pp. 46-47.

Johnson, Benton, "A Critical Appraisal of the Church-Sect Typology," *American Sociological Review*, XX (February, 1957), pp. 88-92.

Kaufman, Gordon D., "Some Theological Emphases of the Early Swiss Anabaptists," *Mennonite Quarterly Review*, XXV (April, 1951), pp. 75-99.

Krahn, C., "Mennonite Community Life in Russia," *Mennonite Quarterly Review*, XVI (July, 1942), pp. 174-177.

_____, "Some Social Attitudes of the Mennonites in Russia," *Mennonite Quarterly Review*, IX (October 1935), pp. 165-177.

Kreider, Robert S., "The Anabaptist Conception of the Church in the Russian Mennonite Environment," *Mennonite Quarterly Review*, XXV (January, 1951), pp. 17-33.

_____, "Anabaptism and Humanism," *Mennonite Quarterly Review*, XXV (January, 1951), pp. 123-141.

Lehmann, Paul L., "The Foundation and Pattern of Christian Behavior," *Christian Faith and Social Action*, John A. Hutchison, editor; New York: Charles Scribner's Sons, 1953, pp. 93-116.

Loserth, J., "Jakob Hutter," *The Mennonite Encyclopedia*, II, Scottdale, Penna.: Mennonite Publishing House, pp. 851-854.

Mackay, John A., *A Letter to Presbyterians Concerning its Present Situation in our Country and in the World*, Office of General Assembly, Philadelphia, October 21, 1953, pp. 2-8.

Metzler, Edgar, "Mennonite Witness to the State: Attitudes and Actions, World War I--1956," Unpublished papers preparing for Laurelville Conference on Nonresistance and Political Responsibility, Peace Problems Committee, Mennonite Historical Library, Goshen, Ind. 1956.

Miller, Alexander, "Towards a Doctrine of Vocation," *Christian Faith and Social Action*, John A. Hutchison, editor; New York: Charles Scribner's Sons, 1953, pp. 117-136.

Miller, William, "A Theologically Biased View of Protestant Politics," *Religion in Life*, XXI (Winter, 1952), pp. 52-64.

Mininger, Paul, "Culture for Service," *Mennonite Quarterly Review*, XXIX (January, 1955), pp. 3-15.

Nelson, Boyd, "How Shall They Hear?" *Gospel Herald*, XLIX (October 16, 1956), pp. 985-986.

Niebuhr, Reinhold, Transvaluation of Values," *Beyond Tragedy*, London: Nisbet and Company, 1938, pp. 197-213.

_____, "Why the Christian Church is Not Pacifist," *Christianity and Power Politics*, New York: Charles Scribner's Sons, 1940, pp. 1-32.

"Non-resistance and Local Civil Affairs," Report of Group A, Unpublished papers of Laurelville Conference, Peace Problems Committee, September 21-22, 1956, pp. 19-20.

Oldham, J. H., "A Responsible Society," *Man's Disorder and God's Design*, Vol. III, New York: Harper and Brothers, n.d., pp. 120-154.

_____, "Technics and Civilization," *Man's Disorder and God's Design*, Vol. III, New York: Harper and Brothers, n.d., pp. 29-49.

Patijn, D. L., "The Strategy of the Church," *Man's Disorder and God's Design*, New York: Harper and Brothers, n.d., pp. 155-175.

Peachey, Paul, "Early Anabaptists and Urbanism," Proceedings of the Tenth Conference on Mennonite and Cultural Problems, Chicago, 1955, pp. 75-83.

_____, "Love, Justice and Peace," *Gospel Herald*, XLIX (1956), pp. 177,

189, 273, 287, 369, 477, 680.

_____, "Mennonites in Local Civic Life," Unpublished papers for Conference on Nonresistance and Political Responsibility, Laurelville, Pennsylvania, September 21-22, 1956, Peace Problems Committee, Mennonite Historical Library, Goshen, Indiana, 1956.

_____, *The Relevance of the Peace Witness of the Prophetic Christian Community*, Unpublished manuscript, Mennonite Central Committee, Akron, Penna., 1953, pp. 1-5.

_____, "Toward an Understanding of the Decline of the West," *Concern*, I (1954), Scottdale, Penna.: Herald Press, pp. 8-43.

_____, "The Modern Recovery of the Anabaptist Vision," *The Recovery of the Anabaptist Vision*, Guy F. Hershberger, editor; Scottdale, Penna.: Herald Press, 1957, pp. 327-340.

Rauschenbusch, Walter, "The Zürich Anabaptists and Thomas Muntzer," *American Journal of Theology* (1905), pp. 91-106.

"Report of Section III," *Evanston Speaks*, London: SCM Press, 1954.

"Report of Section III," *Man's Disorder and God's Design*, III, New York: Harper Brothers, n.d., pp. 189-197.

Schilling, S. Paul, "The Christian Bases of Rights, Freedoms and Responsibilities," *The Church and Social Responsibility*, J. Richard Spann, editor; New York: Abingdon-Cokesbury Press, 1953, pp. 11-24.

Schlesinger, Arthur, Jr., "Reinhold Niebuhr's Role in American Political Thought and Life," *Reinhold Niebuhr, His Social and Political Thought*, Charles W. Kegley and Robert W. Bretall, editors; New York: Macmillan Company, 1956, pp. 126-150.

Smucker, Don E., "The Theological Basis for Christian Pacifism," *Mennonite Quarterly Review*, XXVII (July, 1953), pp. 163-186.

Shinn, Roger L., "The Christian Gospel and History," *Christian Faith and Social Action*, John A. Hutchison, editor; New York: Charles Scribner's Sons, 1953, pp. 23-36.

Stauffer, Ethelbert, "Täufertum und Martyrertheologie," *Zeitschrift für Kirchengeschichte*, LII (1933), pp. 545-598.

Swartzendruber, A. Orley, "The Piety and Theology of the Anabaptist Martyrs in van Braght's *Martyr's Mirror*," *Mennonite Quarterly Review*, XXVIII (January, 1954), pp. 5-26.

Troeltsch, Ernst, "The Idea of Natural Law and Humanity in World Politics," *Otto Gierke, Natural Law and the Theory of Society*, Ernest Barker, translator; Cambridge: Cambridge University Press, 1950.

_____, *Protestantism and Progress*, W. Montgomery, translator; London: G.P. Putnam's Sons, 1912.

Two Kinds of Obedience. An Anabaptist Tract on Christian Freedom, John C. Wenger, translator and editor; *Mennonite Quarterly Review*, XXI (January, 1947), pp. 18-22.

Voluntary Service, 1957, Pamphlet prepared by the Mennonite Board of Missions and Charities, Elkhart, Indiana, 1957.

Waltner, Erland, "The Church in the Bible," *Proceedings of the Study Conference on the Believer's Church*, Newton, Kansas: General Conference Mennonite Church, 1955, pp. 55-72.

Weber, Max, "Die protestantische Ethik und der Geist des Kapitalismus," *Gesammelte Aufsätze zur Religionsoziologie*, Vol. I, Tübingen: J.C.E. Mohr, 1920, pp. 17-206.

_____, "Politik als Beruf," *Gesammelte Politische Schriften*, Munchen, Drei Masken Verlag, 1921.

Wenger, John C., "Life and Work of Pilgram Marpeck," *Mennonite Quarterly Review*, XII (July, 1938), pp. 137-166.

_____, "The Theology of Pilgram Marpeck," *Mennonite Quarterly Review*, XII (October, 1938), pp. 205-256.

Wendland, Heinz Dietrich, "The Relevance of Eschatology for Social Ethics," *Ecumenical Review*, V (July, 1953), pp. 364-368.

Yoder, John Howard, "The Anabaptist Dissent," *Concern*, I, Scottdale, Penna.: Herald Press, 1954, pp. 45-68.

Zuck, Lowell, H., "Anabaptism: Abortive Counter--Revolt Within the Reformation," *Church History*, XXVI (September, 1957), pp. 211-226.

Lawrence B.   April 21, 1989

Out of China experience. WWII — (Pastor?
a church in a rural N.Y. area. Eventually went
to go to China — Reflecting on suffering of the
Chinese, etc.
- First, a "good Amal- Mennonite", classical
views -
- Now, trying to deal with justice, ambivalence regard
power (never discussed), trying to use force.
- rather "mercy", "infinite love", "nonresistance"

(Guy Hershberger, H.S. Bender, a few MQR articles
on real "Menno. Theology".)

- Compromising began, but how to justify it?

- Princeton, c̄ P. Lehmann, others. The dilemma
ones had seen dealt with for centuries Since August?
Even Anabaptists had a realistic view. They
saw difference between love and justice, but
their solution was to separate from the world
- (Schleitheim seen an attempt to set a papers
structural principle).

- { BUT ... Mennonites would participate more and
  { more and would identify with / feel responsible
  { possible for the world ... Concern for
the world, trying to contribute to a+ just world -
R & R. Niebuhr were fruitful for social
analysis in Theol. perspective -

- From non-resistance to non-violence, a major
  shift (witness, implicit + allowed)

- a ptocentric view
- Responsibility + then prophecy, including policy decisions

How should we interpret Jesus? (Today more of a mystery, his ethics?)

L B = I can't get rid of the perfection of the law

Agape & justice must be kept in dialectical tension
- shalom is a good synthesizing concept

Grace (should be given a higher place, like in classical Reformation). They shouldn't be reduced to ethics. Not an adequate view of Grace in Anabaptist sources. Grace makes discipleship possible (Reinhold N. - "Beyond Tragedy", Grace frees one to be a disciple).